THE PARTHIAN AND EARLY SASANIAN EMPIRES: ADAPTATION AND EXPANSION

THE PARTHIAN AND EARLY SASANIAN EMPIRES: ADAPTATION AND EXPANSION

PROCEEDINGS OF A CONFERENCE HELD IN VIENNA, 14–16 JUNE 2012

Edited by

VESTA SARKHOSH CURTIS, ELIZABETH J. PENDLETON, MICHAEL ALRAM AND TOURAJ DARYAEE

BIPS

Published by the British Institute of Persian Studies (BIPS)
Archaeological Monographs Series

OXBOW | books
Oxford & Philadelphia

First published in the United Kingdom in 2016. Reprinted in 2017 as a paperback by
OXBOW BOOKS
The Old Music Hall, 106-108 Cowley Road, Oxford, OX4 1JE

and in the United States by
OXBOW BOOKS
1950 Lawrence Road, Havertown, PA 19083

Paperback edition: ISBN 978-1-78570-962-3
Digital Edition: ISBN 978-1-78570-208-2 (epub)

A CIP record for this book is available from the British Library

Library of Congress Cataloging-in-Publication Data

Names: Curtis, Vesta Sarkhosh, editor. | Pendleton, Elizabeth J., editor. | Alram, Michael, editor. | Daryaee, Touraj, 1967- editor.
Title: The Parthian and early Sasanian empires : adaptation and expansion : proceedings of a conference held in Vienna, 14–16 June 2012 / edited by Vesta Sarkhosh Curtis, Elizabeth J. Pendleton, Michael Alram and Touraj Daryaee.
Description: Oxford : Oxbow Books, 2016. | Series: Archaeological monographs series | Includes bibliographical references.
Identifiers: LCCN 2016017931 (print) | LCCN 2016021369 (ebook) | ISBN 9781785702075 (hardback) | ISBN 9781785702082 (eBook) | ISBN 9781785702082 (epub) | ISBN 9781785702099 (mobi) | ISBN 9781785702105 (pdf)
Subjects: LCSH: Arsacid dynasty, 247 B.C.-224 A.D.–Congresses. | Parthians–Congresses. | Sassanids–Congresses. | Iran–History–To 640–Congresses. | Iran–History–640-1256–Congresses. | Iran--Antiquities–Congresses. | Coins, Parthian–Congresses. | Coins, Sassanid–Congresses.
Classification: LCC DS285 .P375 2016 (print) | LCC DS285 (ebook) | DDC 935/.064–dc23
LC record available at https://lccn.loc.gov/2016017931

For a complete list of Oxbow titles, please contact:

UNITED KINGDOM
Oxbow Books
Telephone (01865) 241249
Email: oxbow@oxbowbooks.com
www.oxbowbooks.com

UNITED STATES OF AMERICA
Oxbow Books
Telephone (800) 791-9354, Fax (610) 853-9146
Email: queries@casemateacademic.com
www.casemateacademic.com/oxbow

Oxbow Books is part of the Casemate Group

Front cover: Rock carving at Naqsh-e Rostam, Iran: Ardashir I (left) tramples the defeated Parthian king Artabanus IV and receives his symbol of kingship from Ohrmazd, the Wise Lord, © G. Herrmann; Sasanian silver coin, showing bust of Ardashir I (AD 224–240) and the Zoroastrian fire, © Trustees of the British Museum.

Contents

Introduction

In 2011 it was decided to hold an international conference at the British Museum on the Partho-Sasanian periods in connection with the *Sylloge Nummorum Parthicorum* (SNP) project.This international project, directed by Dr Michael Alram and Dr Vesta Sarkhosh Curtis, has as its aim the publication of a series of volumes dealing with the coinage from the beginning of the Parthian period in the third century BC to its ending with the advent of the Sasanians in the early third century AD. The project is principally numismatic in nature but also deals with the history, religion and art of the Parthian period. Coin holdings from the American Numismatic Society, the Berlin Coin Cabinet, the Bibliothèque nationale in Paris, the British Museum, the Coin Cabinet of the Kunsthistorisches Museum in Vienna, and the National Museum of Iran in Tehran will be published by representatives of these institutions, who are working in close cooperation with Chris Hopkins, the database manager of www.parthia.com. He has custom-built a web-based database for this project, www.sylloge.org, so that project members can all access the most up-to-date data simultaneously. In addition to coins from the participating institutions, the collection of the late David Sellwood will be included. Where necessary to present a complete picture of the Parthian monetary system, coins from auction catalogues are also incorporated. In 2012, not long after the conference, the first volume of the SNP was published by the Austrian Academy of Sciences.Written by Fabrizio Sinisi, this first book to appear is chronologically the seventh in the series and covers the period from Vologases I to Pacorus II. This will be followed by the coins of Mithradates II (Volume 2) and Phraates IV to Orodes III (Volume 5) in 2017–18.

Although much of the primary information about the Parthian period comes from coins, it is essential to widen the spectrum and to include scholars from different disciplines working on the Parthian and early Sasanian periods. This conference was planned specifically to provide a platform to scholars from a broad range of disciplines.

By the end of the 2011, however, political relations between the UK and Iran had deteriorated and the British Embassy in Tehran had closed. It became clear that London would not be able to host Iranian scholars at such a symposium. During a period of despair, Neil MacGregor, the Director of the British Museum, came up with an ingenious suggestion that allowed the conference to go ahead. He identified that the obstacle lay in the location, not the conference itself, and suggested finding a different venue. After discussions between the project's co-directors in London and Vienna, Vesta Sarkhosh Curtis and Michael Alram, the Kunsthistorisches Museum and the Austrian Academy of Sciences wholeheartedly agreed to host the event instead. The conference was swiftly switched to Vienna, invitations sent out and visas arranged. All this would not have been possible without the quick and efficient response of the Austrian partners at very short notice. This offers a perfect example of international cooperation whereby colleagues could help each other to provide a forum for scholarly discussions at a politically sensitive time.

The conference opened at the Kunsthistorisches Museum on 14 June 2012 and was held over two and a half days. Neil MacGregor flew in especially from London to be at the opening and gave a speech in which he emphasised the importance of international cooperation and dialogue between institutions separated by political boundaries. His enthusiasm and support were much appreciated by the organisers and participating scholars, especially the Iranian colleagues who otherwise would not have been included in this symposium.

After a brief introduction by the joint directors of the *Sylloge Nummorum Parthicorum* project, the conference was launched with a series of papers covering various aspects of the Partho-Sasanian empires. Although the SNP project focuses solely on the Parthian period, the existence of the well-established and highly acclaimed *Sylloge Nummorum Sasanidarum*, headed by Michael Alram and Rika Gyselen, prompted the organisers to extend the remit of this Vienna conference to include papers on Sasanian themes. In addition, a further impetus to encompass the Sasanians came from the successfully completed *Sylloge of Sasanian Coins in the National Museum of Iran* by Vesta Sarkhosh Curtis, M. Elahé Askari and Elizabeth J. Pendleton. Despite a change of ruling dynasty, the two empires were closely connected and cannot be regarded as totally separate entities. The continuation of Parthian influence particularly into the early Sasanian period cannot be disputed. Indeed, it is hoped that the continuity between the Parthian and Sasanian empires will be the subject of a second conference in the future.

In the last decade or so, more interest has been noticeable in the Arsacid Parthians and their material culture but this period is still underestimated.Various reasons account for this, including the relatively few excavated archaeological sites dating to the Parthian period in Iran and western scholars' lack of knowledge of recent excavations and their results that are usually published in Persian. Although an attempt has been made by several scholars in the west to place this important Iranian dynasty in its proper cultural context, the traditional Greco-Roman influenced approach is still prevalent, even in the twenty-first century.

The present volume presents fourteen papers covering various aspects of Parthian and early Sasanian history, material culture, linguistics and religion:

JÉRÔME GASLAIN discusses aspects of the political and military history of the early Arsacids. Contrary to traditional interpretations, based principally on classical sources, he dismisses the notion that Arsaces I and the Parni were nomadic invaders with no knowledge of the Seleucid political system. He argues that "from early on, the Arsacids surely occupied an important place in the political game of the satrapies", which is contrary to the image presented by ancient sources such as Justin, Polybius and Strabo, a view followed by a number of modern scholars. Gaslain suggests that the early Arsacids were skillful rulers both domestically and in their foreign policy. They were a force to be reckoned with by both the Seleucids in the west and the Bactrians in the east.

RAHIM SHAYEGAN examines Arsacid royal ideology within the context of other kingdoms of the Hellenistic period, including Mithridates VI of Pontus and the kings of Commagene. He focuses on the presentation of their ancestry and argues that the Arsacids under Mithradates II adopted the title King of Kings through Babylonian traditions rather than as a conscious revival of the Achaemenid past. This type of conscious manipulation of ancestry comes into play during the reign of Artabanus II, when Tacitus reports that the Arsacid king justified his territorial claims over Armenia by referring to both the Achaemenids and Alexander. Shayegan then draws a parallel between this passage and similar claims by Mithridates VI of Pontus, as reported in Justin's *Epitome*. He goes on to examine genealogical constructs in Commagene and concludes that here the inspiration came perhaps from the Arsacids.

MAREK JAN OLBRYCHT looks at the rivalry amongst the Arsacid ruling dynasty in the first century BC, in particular the conflict between the Sinatrucids and the descendants of Mithradates II. This resulted in a dichotomy amongst the elite, with the aristocratic clans supporting one or other of the factions. He goes on to examine potential links between the Indo-Parthians and the Sinatrucids in the first to second centuries AD. He also re-examines the relationship between the coins of the later Gondopharids under Farn-Sāsān and those of Ardashir I and prefers the theory that Ardashir imitated coins of Farn-Sāsān rather than vice versa, as has been generally accepted. He concludes that Ardashir may have been an Arsacid prince who came to power with the support of the Sūrēn and Kārin clans. Both he and his successor, Shapur I, presented a different view of their ancestry by downplaying the role of Sāsān.

TOURAJ DARYAEE gives an overview of the use and meaning of elephants from the Achaemenid period to Islamic times. He draws on a variety of sources, including the *Karnamag* of Ardashir and the *Shahnameh* and classical authors such as Ammianus Marcellinus and Tacitus, as well as less familiar Armenian accounts. In addition, he examines representations of elephants in Parthian, Sasanian and Roman art, as well as on coins. He describes differing military tactics of using elephants both as "tanks" and also as a centre of operations. He sees elephants both as a weapon of terror and as a symbol of kingship in the ancient Iranian world.

MEHRDAD GHODRAT-DIZAJI discusses the physical location of the province of Parthia from Achaemenid to Sasanian times. In the Achaemenid period there is a striking similarity between Herodotus's location of the Parthian satrapy in the north-east and the list of north-eastern provinces given by Darius at Bisitun. The Arsacid province of Parthia seems to have occupied a similar location as in the Achaemenid period. It is generally believed that Parthia occupied the same territory in the Sasanian period as it had in Parthian and Achaemenid times. Dizaji, however, cites evidence to suggest that from the late Parthian period, the province of Parthia shifted to the central plateau, bordering Pārs and Khuzistān. Over time, it expanded still further to the west.

ANDREA GARIBOLDI looks at the question of historical awareness of the Sasanians in Roman sources, particularly Ammianus Marcellinus and Julian. He addresses the vital question of whether the Romans were aware of the change from the Parthian to Sasanian dynasty. Ammianus does not refer to the dynastic change in Persia and uses the terms *Persae* and *Parthi* for the Sasanians. According to Julian, the Sasanians did not wish to be identified with the Parthians and therefore presented themselves as Persians. Gariboldi discusses to what extent this is purely a Roman rhetorical device or whether the Sasanians were truly aware of the Persian past. He concludes that ancestry is an important aspect of Iranian historiography.

ANTONIO PANAINO discusses the Sasanians and their impact on the development of Zoroastrianism, in particular in western Iran. Here he uses evidence from ritual and theological Mazdean texts, established during and after the Sasanians came to power. While this tradition in the west is rich, we have little information about the eastern Zoroastrian liturgy, where local traditions were strong. This gap in data for the east is partly filled by archaeological evidence. Panaino examines Kirdēr's inscriptions to illuminate his position at the Sasanian court and within society at large, and comes to the conclusion that Kirdēr's "mission" may not have been fully shared by the Sasanian kings. Nevertheless, his influence on the Zoroastrian religion was crucial. He concludes by looking at Kirdēr's visions and how ritual had both theological and political ramifications.

RIKA GYSELEN takes as her subject the survival into the Sasanian period of Parthian, a Middle Iranian language of the north-east. She begins by making a clear distinction between Pahlavi/Pārsīg, or Middle Persian, a southern Middle Iranian language, and Parthian. She shows that Parthian survived as an official language employed by the early Sasanian kings until the end of the third century AD, after which no traces of it have been identified on royal monumental inscriptions. She then looks for evidence of the survival of Parthian into Sasanian times on non-royal objects, examining the silver plate of Krasnaya Polyana and four Sasanian seals, as well as the use of Parthian on Sasanian magic seals. She concludes that Parthian fell out of use as a "royal" language after the end of the third century and as a "common" language after the fourth/fifth century AD. In Parthian-speaking regions, Middle Persian replaced the Parthian language.

KHODADAD REZAKHANI deals with the epigraphic development from Aramaic to Pahlavi, as seen on the coinage of Persis. This particular group of coins, unlike other Hellenistic issues, does not use Greek for its inscriptions. He believes that Inscription Pahlavi is not purely a development from this script of Persis but that other influences can be detected. In addition to Inscription Pahlavi, there were other Pahlavi scripts including the Manichean script, derived from Aramaic, and Book Pahlavi, the most common Middle Persian script, the evidence for which dates mostly from the post-Sasanian period, as well as cursive Pahlavi. His examination of the Persis coinage suggests that under the last two kings of this dynasty significant changes can be traced in the letter forms. In order to account for these changes, he looks at the coin legends of Characene and Elymais, as well as Indo-Scythians in the east, and finally discusses briefly the possible origin of the Sasanian dynasty in Sakastan.

DARYOOSH AKBARZADEH focuses on two points as found in post-Sasanian sources: the confusion about the Parthian king Ardavan (Artabanus), who is described variously as both "the first" *(aqdam)* and "the last" (*afdom*). He discusses the beginnings of the Parthian dynasty and shows that Islamic sources agree that Ashk (Arsaces) ibn Ashk or Ashk ibn Dara was the founder of the Arsacid Parthian dynasty. He concludes that the discrepancy between "first" and "last" with reference to Ardavan is the result of scribal error. In his second note, he addresses the problem of the genealogy of the Parthians and focuses specifically on the relationship of the Parthians with Arash the archer.

ANTONIO INVERNIZZI discusses the reconstruction of the Round Hall at Nisa and rejects a Hellenistic antecedent for roofing the building as suggested by Pugachenkova. He searches instead for a Near Eastern model and rejects the theory that the inclination of the walls of the Round Hall was caused by an earthquake. He argues that the absence of other similar Parthian domes does not prove that they did not exist and that later Sasanian domes were technically so advanced that they could not have been a sudden invention. Invernizzi sees the origin of the domed Round Hall in the domed buildings of Chorasmia in the ninth to eighth centuries BC. It is in Central Asia that the domed structure was used for funerary purposes. This tradition continued under the early Arsacids when the Round Hall at Nisa was probably built to commemorate Mithradates I and his ancestors.

BARBARA KAIM examines in detail Iranian court life in Arsacid and the early Sasanian periods in view of the meagre and often biased written sources. She therefore focuses on an additional source of information, namely the architectural decoration of palaces. In her view, the only royal capital that provides information is Nisa and here she discusses the architecture and the theme of banquets and wine. She also includes in her study the iconography of early to mid-Arsacid coins and the change in iconography over time. Here she includes royal women and their role at court. In the current absence of residential buildings associated directly with Arsacid rulers, she moves to western Iran and the site of Qaleh-i Yazdigird, near Kirmanshah, with its rich figural and architectural stucco decorations. This was the seat of a Parthian noble. Both here and in her discussion of Bishapur in southern Iran, she touches on the question of Dionysian iconography and its role within a possible Zoroastrian context. She finally looks at Bishapur and its mosaic decoration and concludes that these were part of a royal palace.

PIERRE-YVES BOILLET aims at quantifying the monetary production in Parthian times at Ecbatana and Media and what impact the change from Seleucid to Parthian rule had on coin production. He examines the history of Media as presented in classical sources and points out that literary and archaeological evidence is limited. In the lack of these sources, coins provide important information and he bases his study on several thousand Parthian coins in major coin cabinets, as well as coins that feature in sales catalogues. Boillet performs various statistical analyses on this data set and shows that although there is nothing to indicate a change in the nature of trade from Seleucid to Parthian times, nevertheless the output of money seems to be reduced under the Arsacids. There is a decline in bronzes and a rise of minting drachms and the Seleucid tradition of minting tetradrachms at Ecbatana disappears completely. He raises the question of whether political instability and internal rivalries had an effect on coin production under certain kings.

In the final paper, NIKOLAUS SCHINDEL deals with the coinages of Paradan and Sind in the context of Kushan and Kushano-Sasanian coinage and addresses the question of whether Sasanian coins had direct influence on these eastern coins or not. He examines the depiction of ribbed ribbons on Kushan, Sasanian and Paradan coinage, which he believes argues against the commonly accepted date of 127 AD for the start date of the Kanishka era. His second subject is the coinage of Sind and its Sasanian prototypes. Here Schindel examines new material and comes to the conclusion that the Sind coinage was indirectly associated with Sasanian Iran. He suggests that the gold coins of Marw in the fourth and early fifth centuries AD were the possible inspiration behind the Sind coins, which were minted in gold rather than silver.

No conference can be organised without financial and human support, and the Vienna conference was no exception. Generous grants from the British Institute of Persian Studies at the British Academy, the Austrian Academy of Sciences, the British Museum and the Bahari Foundation, as well as the Royal Numismatic Society, made it possible to invite a wide range of scholars from the USA to Iran to gather together at the Kunsthistorisches Museum in Vienna for two and a half days to discuss various aspects of the Partho-Sasanian world. Just as important as financial help was the human support and encouragement from a number of quarters, including Neil MacGregor, Andrew Burnett, J.D. Hill, Philip Attwood and Mark Bates of the British Museum, and Ali Ansari, Mariam Emamy and the Research Board of the British Institute of Persian Studies (BIPS).

The Editors
London
April 2016

HISTORICAL

1

Some Aspects of Political History: Early Arsacid Kings and the Seleucids

Jérôme Gaslain
AURORHE*

The beginnings of the Arsacid dynasty remain mysterious in many ways. It is difficult to determine accurately the process of the creation of the kingdom. The period that most challenges us is the third century BC, which does not provide information reliable enough to draw a detailed picture of the Arsacid world of that time. It is unfortunate, for example, that we are still unable to ascertain firmly the dates of the reigns of the first sovereigns,[1] to establish which territories were actually under their control, or to understand the intricacies of their domestic politics.[2]

Some events can, however, be used to establish landmarks in the first decades of the Arsacid dynasty in the context of the Upper Satrapies, when the transition between Seleucid power and Arsacid authority took place.

In this paper, far from considering the Arsacid kings as nomads arriving by chance to seize power in Parthia, we propose to evaluate, as much as possible, the knowledge of the Seleucid government that they could have had. One cannot indeed see them as ignorant of the political stakes in the region. In search of proof, we will focus on the first two Arsacid reigns, those of Arsaces I (238–210 BC) and his son Arsaces II (210–190 BC). This will give us the opportunity to show that the Parthians had a political consciousness from their very entry into history.[3]

Arsaces I and Seleucid satrapian power

The image of Arsaces is that he was a nomad who managed to seize power in Parthia with some companions in arms, after the murder of the satrap Andragoras, himself emancipated from Seleucid power in 247 BC.[4] This version of events comes from the Greco-Latin texts, which, though often contradictory,[5] all agree that Arsaces was an enigmatic character who took advantage of the weakness of the Seleucid government in the Upper Satrapies to establish his own authority. Without going into any detail, let us make a simple remark. Overthrowing a satrap who himself had been able to defect from Seleucid power could not have been an easy matter. It goes without saying that the warlord Arsaces was more than a *simple thief*, and saying, as Justin claimed (41, 4, 7), that he overthrew the satrap by "surprise" is pure historical fantasy. In other words, Arsaces could not have just been the enigmatic nomad at the time of the death of Andragoras (238 BC).

We know that even before his emancipation in 247 BC, Andragoras held an important position in the Seleucid administration at the time of Antiochus I.[6] His authority was therefore well established and Arsaces could not ignore this situation when he *attacked* Parthia. Andragoras was not merely a rebellious satrap without military[7] and economic resources. It therefore appears that Arsaces had real means to eliminate a satrap, who must himself have been fully aware of the dangers in and around Parthia.

*

Following Strabo (*Geography*) and Justin (Epitome of the *Philippic Histories* of Pompeius Trogus),[8] the Parni, a part of the Dahae confederacy (Scythians), came from the Aral Sea region. They had migrated to the south, maybe early in the third century BC, and then were repelled by Bactrian forces (Strabo, 11, 9, 2–3).[9] That is why they went to the west.[10]

* AURORHE: Archéologie Urbaine de l'Orient Hellénisé, UMR 8546–9 (CNRS-ENS), 45, rue d'Ulm, 75005 Paris.
I want to thank warmly M. Alram and V.S. Curtis, and all the members of the Sylloge Nummorum Parthicorum group, for their support.

It is difficult to reconstruct the exact movement of these nomads, the exact reasons for this movement, the true place and role of Arsaces in relation to these nomads[11] and how he finally arrived in Parthia and seized power.[12] For example, some scholars have supposed that Arsaces was a mercenary. This is an attractive hypothesis.[13] Even if we have no actual evidence supporting it, it seems not impossible to see Arsaces as a member of the local "élite" of Parthia, with a real knowledge of the military and political spheres of the Seleucid satrapy. With early Parthian history, we must be very careful to remember that we can consider these assertions only as a hypothesis. Nevertheless, the role of Arsaces before 238 BC must not be understated, as we shall see.

What is important for us is that the Parni were well aware of the territories and knew the populations and political situation of the region. Following the texts, it seems that the migration of the Parni was progressive, rather than a single stride resulting in the conquest of Parthia proper.[14] From 282/1 to 238 BC, the Parni had exerted a real influence around the Parthian area.[15] Arsaces, as a member of this confederacy, seems therefore far from being the instigator of an accidental invasion. The presence of these nomads did not, however, profoundly disrupt the structure of the Upper Satrapies before the conquest of Media by the Arsacids (148/7 BC),[16] but this position provided the Parthians with the means profitably to control the trade routes, and so the taxes, which connected Media to the cities of Margiana, Bactria and beyond.

The simultaneous Greco-Bactrian and Parthian "secessions" in the middle of the third century BC were in fact a response to the failure of Seleucid power combined with the will of the new leaders, Diodotus and Andragoras, to create new protective authorities for the region.[17] This was not only a question of personal ambition, but also a necessary action to reassure the Greek and Iranian populations about these new leaders. When Arsaces seized power in 238 BC,[18] this requirement still remained and he could devote no less effort to satisfy it. From a political point of view, Arsaces had a double mission: he needed to be recognised within his own kingdom as the new authority and, for this to happen, he had to confirm his presence at the head of Parthia in the eyes of the Bactrian leader especially and, afterwards, in the eyes of Seleucid central power. To achieve these goals, Arsaces needed to call upon every possible tool at his disposal, not only military,[19] but also political and diplomatic.

When Justin indicates that Arsaces raised a large army in fear of Diodotus I, it proves not only that the threat was real for the Parthians but it also shows that, from early on, the Arsacids surely occupied an important place in the political game of the satrapies. That is why, when Strabo writes that Arsaces was Bactrian (11, 9, 3), we agree that it could signify that he had been in the Seleucid territories for a long time.[20] Justin (41, 4, 9) continues his comment by indicating that Arsaces finally became an ally of the second Bactrian ruler. This treaty of alliance – of which we know no details – at least proves that contacts between Arsacid and Bactrian leaders had probably been established for a long time. Thus negotiation formed part of the early Arsacids' political practices and this established fact was not unknown to the Seleucids. At the time of the emancipation of Andragoras and Diodotus, it seems difficult to believe that on one hand both parties were unaware of the other's actions; equally on the other hand both must have known the position of the Parni, as a buffer between Bactrian and Parthian territories. Consequently, when our sources state that a treaty of alliance was concluded between Arsaces I and Diodotus II, it seems to be merely a renewal of the practice introduced between Parthia and Bactria some years before, out of diplomatic necessity. This treaty of alliance must not be considered as an exceptional operation.

*

That said, although it is difficult to doubt that the Parthians were nomads who invaded the territory of Parthia, this does not mean that Arsaces was part of a sudden invasion. He maybe could have taken advantage of his favourable position to lead rather a *revolution*, which inevitably implied an invasion of the territory of Parthia-Hyrcania, as our sources emphasise. The fact that Arsaces was able to raise thereafter a large army (Justin 41, 4, 8) could confirm the importance of his military capacities.

A decade elapsed between the time Andragoras took power in 247 BC from the Seleucids and the time when Arsaces seized control from Andragoras (238 BC). Justin informs us that Parthians had already rebelled against the Seleucid government at the time of the First Punic War in the mid-third century BC (41, 4, 3–4). In a recent publication, historians have tried to involve Arsaces in these first revolts which they date back to 247 BC, which would explain why the Arsacid calendar was dependent on that year. In the same vein, they maintain that Arsaces emerged victorious from a battle against Seleucus II, then viceroy of the Upper Satrapies, and suppose that Arsaces would have been crowned king in 247 BC as a celebration of this victory.[21]

We are more than sceptical with regard to this vision of history.[22] First, this supposed battle appears nowhere in the sources, as Justin simply tells us that the Parthians "rebelled", adding that this defection "remained unpunished" (Justin, 41, 4, 3–4). Moreover, we should not forget that the inhabitants of Parthia are *not* interchangeable with Arsaces's Parthians, and it is very difficult to grasp who the Parthians were for Justin in this passage of "his" *Historiae Philippicae*. Besides, if Arsaces had won a victory against the Seleucid armies, for which, we should remember, we have no evidence, either direct or indirect, then this would mean that there was on the political scene of Parthia a winner who not only did not exploit his victory but even allowed Andragoras to take power and then to emancipate his territory. If this scenario were correct, Arsaces must have allowed a decade to pass before eliminating the satrap, and yet no source mentions this failure to follow through. This version seems therefore difficult to accept.[23]

So, let us remain cautious as to the progress of events. The year 247 BC may correspond to the seizure of power by Andragoras, who subsequently escaped from Seleucid power, maybe in 245.[24] Thus 247 BC might have been important enough to result in the creation of a calendar which is called "Parthian" rather than "Arsacid", and which the Parthians took as the starting point of their territory's independence.

Arsaces I, Arsaces II and the Seleucid military campaigns

The military campaigns of Seleucus II (228 BC) and Antiochus III (209 BC) in the Upper Satrapies aimed at restoring Seleucid authority in those regions and bringing back a semblance of order that had been lost for some years. During these two expeditions, the Seleucid armies faced the forces of the Arsacid sovereigns, Arsaces I and Arsaces II. In the light of the literary sources, it would be difficult to form a definitive opinion of the outcome of these confrontations:

- Strabo (11, 8, 8) comments that when faced with the Seleucid onslaught under Seleucus II, Arsaces I withdrew to the country of the *Apasiacae*. Justin (41, 4, 9), on the other hand, specifies that Arsaces "was victorious".
- As for Arsaces II, we learn that he fought with an "admirable courage" and that in the end he became "the ally" of Antiochus III. But according to Polybius (10, 28, 6 and 10, 29, 1), Arsaces II also "retreated with his army" and "abandoned his own territory" as the Seleucid army marched on Parthia.

Given the above conflicting accounts, how may we determine exactly what took place during the two Seleucid-Parthian encounters?

This question cannot be satisfactorily answered if we limit ourselves only to the military objectives of the two campaigns. We shall, therefore, attempt to throw a fresh light on some aspects of Parthian history by deviating slightly from the narrow vision, which suggests that the political awareness of the early Arsacids was somewhat limited. Considering the outcome of the two Seleucid military expeditions which the nascent Arsacid dynasty had to face, we believe that Arsaces I and his son Arsaces II were neither politically nor militarily inexperienced.

The flight of the two Arsacid sovereigns from their encounters with the Seleucids cannot be taken at face value as they are recounted in the literary sources. We shall, therefore, agree with Polybius (10, 29, 2) that Arsaces II, like his father Arsaces I, really had "another idea".

Arsaces I and Seleucus II

Around 228 BC, Seleucus tried to retake the Upper Satrapies.[25] If we follow the literary sources, we note that upon the arrival of the Seleucid troops, Arsaces I retreated to the territories of the Apasiacae. Following Strabo, it is thus necessary to maintain that the Seleucid king triumphed over his opponent. This is reflected in the coins struck to celebrate the Seleucid victory.[26] Despite the fact that Seleucus II had to abandon his Parthian expedition in order to return hastily and restore order in the western lands of his kingdom, the campaign in the east was thus deemed successful. This fact cannot be ignored, because if he had returned as a defeated ruler, Seleucus's authority would have been severely undermined.

Nevertheless, Justin writes that Arsaces I prevailed in this particular encounter and it is his version of the events that we must follow for several reasons. First, we are told that soon after Seleucus's march back to the west, Arsaces I returned and recaptured the land that he had lost to the Seleucid king. He thus extended his power, once again, up to the region of Hecatompylus, which had probably been under Parthian jurisdiction for some years.[27] Arsaces I then controlled Hyrcania, Comisene, Charene and Parthia itself. This view agrees with Polybius, who indicates that during the Anabasis of Antiochus III in 209 BC, Arsaces II was not surprised to witness the arrival of the Seleucid army, but he did not expect the Seleucid king to attack the territories beyond the Caspian Gates.[28]

The flight of Arsaces I cannot thus be considered as a defeat. Instead, it may be seen as a strategic withdrawal in the face of the powerful Seleucid army, probably well thought out and certainly tactically advantageous. It was not merely the return of Seleucus II to the west that rendered Arsaces victorious, but rather that this particular retreat made a great deal of sense, both in military and political terms. The Seleucid king had neither the means to pursue Arsaces beyond the southern shores of the Caspian Sea nor sufficient time to negotiate a peace treaty. In other words, Arsaces remained the master of the situation. He had since 238 BC controlled Parthia-Hyrcania and, following his accession to power – and even before as we have tried to demonstrate, gained a good knowledge of the political situation. He strove to be accepted by the populations of Parthia and seemingly gave priority to the affairs of his immediate neighbours too. Inspired by the Hellenistic traditions represented on the region's coinage (e.g. the legends in Greek and/or the diadem), Arsaces did not adopt the royal title on his coins[29] as the successor of Andragoras. Nevertheless, he distanced himself from purely Hellenistic traditions by using the so-called *bashlyk* and the enthroned archer holding the bow, a king of double language, leading to adaptation rather than upheaval.[30] Arsaces appears both as an experienced negotiator, if we consider his relationship with the Greco-Bactrians, and as a fine strategist with regard to the campaign of Seleucus II. The Seleucid king thus found himself confronting a leader with good political and military senses. When Antiochus III undertook his Anabasis, he did not set out from Ecbatana without careful planning, knowing that in order to march successfully as far as Bactria, he had to negotiate the roads through Parthian territories that were guarded by Arsaces II who was like his father, endowed with political awareness.

Arsaces II and Antiochus III

When Arsaces II ascended to the throne in 211 BC, the political situation was different from when Arsaces I revolted against the Seleucids. At this point, the Arsacids had controlled Parthia and Hyrcania for almost thirty years. They were thus perceived as the undisputed masters of the region with little to fear from their Bactrian neighbours. It is obvious that the Arsacids viewed the campaign of Antiochus III not so much as a logical attempt by the Seleucids to retake their lost satrapies, but more as an attack on a territory which had been theirs since, at least, 238 BC. This explains why, upon the arrival of the Seleucid army, the Parthian defenders destroyed the *qanats*[31] of Charene and Comisene, the most fertile region of Parthia. This was planned not only to slow down Antiochus's march, but also to be a testimony of resistance to a former occupying foreign force. In the eyes of the Parthians, the campaign of Seleucus II may have been justified, but the Anabasis of Antiochus III lacked legitimacy. Although they understood the reasons behind Antiochus's campaign, they took it as an infringement upon their authority, which had not been questioned since 228 BC. For Arsaces II, it was also a crucial moment to assert the power he had just inherited from his father, while for Antiochus III, it was an ideal opportunity to end the rising power of the Arsacid dynasty.

The abandonment of Hecatompylus by Arsaces II and its consequent fall were perceived even then as the sign of a Parthian defeat. Nevertheless, Justin speaks of peace and alliance between Antiochus III and Arsaces II (41, 5, 7) as well as between Arsaces I and Diodotus II. Unfortunately, as we have already mentioned, we know very little about these alliances and thus cannot offer any conclusion about their nature and content.[32] What seems certain, however, is that Arsaces II was not subjugated by Antiochus III any more than Arsaces I had been by Seleucus II. The flight of Arsaces II had been carefully planned to prevent his submission and this, we believe, is "the other idea" that Polybius implies. In order not to face the powerful Seleucid army and suffer a fatal defeat, Arsaces II retreated and by doing so was able to preserve his father's conquests. It is even possible that, in order to weaken the power of Euthydemus of Bactria, Arsaces II let the Seleucid army pass through the Parthian territories unopposed and march on Bactria. We can pose many questions on the treaty of alliance between Arsaces I and Diodotus II, to which we cannot offer any convincing answer. However, we believe that, by not facing the Seleucids, Arsaces II protected his territorial possessions both skilfully and pragmatically. This leads to a better understanding of the reasons behind the treaty of alliance between Arsaces II and Antiochus III.

*

In conclusion, it is important to recognise that the early Arsacids possessed a real awareness of their status, combined with an intimate knowledge of the Parthian territories and of the political situation of the region, even before they seized power. It is difficult to believe that Arsaces I and his son were only nomads lacking political finesse, as they are usually portrayed. The Seleucids, like the Greco-Bactrians, could not ignore this fact, and this is why we find the Arsacids from the very beginning as active players within the political context of the Upper Satrapies. The first two Arsacids played a crucial role in this. Arsaces I and his son were not only pragmatic kings[33] in their pursuit of foreign politics but also within the territories under their control.

Notes

1 Dąbrowa 2011, p. 249, n. 26.
2 Lerner 1999, p. 13–31.
3 Gaslain 2012, p. 255, n. 4.
4 Bivar 2005, p. 212–214.
5 Lerouge 2007, p. 175, p. 178. See also Muccioli 2007, p. 87–115.
6 Capdetrey 2007, p. 127.
7 Capdetrey 2007, p. 257, p. 357.
8 Magnelli 1993, p. 467–479. Lerouge-Cohen 2009, p. 361–392.
9 Coloru 2009, p. 169ff.
10 Will 2003, I, p. 303.
11 About nomadism and the Arsacids, Hauser 2005, p. 163–208 and Hauser 2006, p. 295–319.
12 Will 2003, I, p. 302–303, p. 307. Lerouge 2007, p. 176, n. 9.
13 Olbrycht 2003, p. 73.
14 Bernard 1994, p. 484. Houghton/Lorber 2002, p. 213.
15 Will 2003, I, p. 302. Houghton/Lorber 2002, p. 213.
16 About Arsacid Media, see Boillet 2009 and in this volume, see Boillet's paper.
17 Brodersen 1986, p. 378–381. Kalita 1999, p. 51–67. Luther 1999, p. 5–15. Luther 2006–2007, p. 39–55.
18 Wolski 1993, p. 66ff.
19 Olbrycht 2003, p. 75. Boyce 1994, p. 247.
20 Will 2003, I, p. 302.
21 Assar and Bagloo 2006, p. 25–35.
22 Gaslain 2009, p. 30, n. 27.
23 Will 2003, I, p. 281–282.
24 Will 2003, I, p. 302.
25 Will 2003, p. 308.
26 Houghton and Lorber 2002, I, p. 231, 233, 282.
27 Bernard 1994, p. 498ff.
28 Will 2003, p. 57.
29 See now Olbrycht 2013, p. 63–74 and Dąbrowa 2014, p. 304ff.

30 Curtis 2007, p. 8. Dąbrowa 2008, p. 26. See also Günther 2012, p. 53–66.
31 Polybius, X, 27.
32 Will 2003, II, p. 57.
33 On early Arsacid coinage, see the recent hypothesis in Koshelenko and Gaibov 2012, p. 24–33. On Arsacid coinage, see recently Ellerbrock 2013, p. 253–311 and Curtis 2012, p. 68–81.

References

Assar, G.F., and Bagloo, M.G. (2006). "An Early Parthian 'Victory' Coin", *Parthica* 8: p. 25–35.

Bernard, P. (1994). "L'Asie centrale et l'empire séleucide", *ΤΟΠΟΙ* 4: p. 473–511.

Bivar, A.D.H. (2005). "Andragoras: Independent Successor of the Seleucids in Parthia", in *Central Asia from the Achaemenids to the Timurids: Archaeology, History, Ethnology, Culture. Materials of an International Scientific Conference dedicated to the Centenary of Aleksandr Markovich Belenitsky*, 2–5 November 2004, Saint Petersburg: p. 212–214.

Boillet, P.-Y. (2009). Ecbatane et la Médie d'Alexandre aux Arsacides (c. 331 a.C–c. 224 p.C), Histoire monétaire et économique, Unpublished PhD thesis, Université Michel de Montaigne Bordeaux 3.

Boyce, M. (1994). "The sedentary Arsacids", *Iranica Antiqua* 29: p. 241–251.

Brodersen, K. (1986). "The Date of the Secession of Parthia from the Seleucid Kingdom", *Historia* 35: p. 378–381.

Capdetrey, L. (2007). *Le pouvoir séleucide. Territoire, administration, finances d'un royaume hellénistique (312–129 av. n. è.)*, Rennes.

Coloru, O. (2009). *Da Alessandro a Menandro: il regno greco di Battriana,* Studi ellenistici 21, Pisa and Rome.

Curtis, V.S. (2007). "The Iranian Revival in the Parthian Period", in V.S. Curtis, S. Stewart (eds), *The Age of the Parthians*, London: p. 7–25.

——— (2012). "Parthian coins: kingship and divine glory", in P. Wick, M. Zehnder (eds), *The Parthian Empire and its Religions: Studies in the Dynamics of Religious Diversity. Das Partherreich und seine Religionen: Studien zu Dynamiken religiöser Pluralität,* Pietas 5, Gutenberg: p. 68–81.

Dąbrowa, E. (2008). "The political propaganda of the first Arsacids and its targets (from Arsaces I to Mithradates II)", *Parthica* 10: p. 25–31.

——— (2011). "ΑΡΣΑΚΕΣ ΘΕΟΣ. Observations on the nature of the Parthian ruler-cult", in *Un impaziente desiderio di scorrere il mondo: studi in onore di Antonio Invernizzi per il suo settantesimo compleanno*, Florence: p. 247–253.

——— (2014). "Hellenistic Elements in Parthian Kingship: the Numismatic Portrait and Titulature", in R. Rollinger, K. Schnegg (eds), *Kuturkontakte in Antiken Welten: vom Denkmodell zum Fallbeispiel*, Leuven, Paris and Walpole, Ma: p. 301–312.

Ellerbrock, U. (2013). "Religiöse Ikonographie auf parthischen Münzen. Der Einfluss politisch-gesellschaftlicher Veränderungen auf das Bild der Göttin Tyche im Parthischen Reich", *Iranica Antiqua* 48: p. 253–311.

Gaslain, J. (2009). "A propos d'Arsace Ier", *Electrum* 15: p. 27–39.

——— (2012). "Quelques remarques sur la politique impériale des Parthes Arsacides et la prise d'Europos-Doura", in *Europos-Doura Varia* I: p. 255–266.

Günther, L.M. (2012). "Seleukidische Vorbilder der parthischen Münzikonographie", in P. Wick, M. Zehnder (eds), *The Parthian Empire and its Religions : Studies in the Dynamics of Religious Diversity. Das Partherreich und seine Religionen: Studien zu Dynamiken religiöser Pluralität,* Pietas 5, Gutenberg: p. 53–66.

Hauser, S. (2005). "Die ewigen Nomaden? Bemerkungen zu Herkunft, Militär, Staatsaufbau und nomadischen Traditionen der Arsakiden", in O. Schmitt, M. Sommer (eds), *Krieg, Gesellschaft, Institutionen: Beiträge zu einer vergleichenden Kriegsgeschichte*, Berlin: p. 163–208.

——— (2006). "Was There No Paid Standing Army? A Fresh Look on Military and Political Institutions in the Arsacid Empire", in M. Mode, J. Turbach (eds), *Arms and Armour as Indicators of Cultural Transfer. The Steppes and the Ancient World from Hellenistic Times to the Early Middle Ages*, Wiesbaden, Reichert: p. 295–319.

Houghton, A., and Lorber, C. (2002). *Seleucid Coins: A Comprehensive Catalogue, Seleucus I – Antiochus III*, vol. I–II, New York and Lancaster, PA.

Kalita, S. (1999). "The coins of Diodotus of Bactria and the problem of dating the Bactrian secession", *Notae Numismaticae* III–IV: p. 51–67.

Koshelenko, G.A., and Gaibov, V.A. (2012). "Parthian coinage in the reign of Arsaces II", *Journal of Historical, Philological and Cultural Studies* 4 (38): p. 24–33.

Lerner, J.D. (1999). *The Impact of Seleucid Decline on the Eastern Iranian Plateau. The Foundation of Arsacid Parthia and Graeco-Bactria*, Stuttgart.

Lerouge, C. (2007). *L'image des Parthes dans le monde gréco-romain. Du début du Ier siècle av. n. è. jusqu'à la fin du Haut-Empire romain*, Stuttgart.

Lerouge-Cohen, C. (2009). "Les livres 41–42 des *Histoires Philippiques* de Trogue Pompée résumées par Justin", *Iranica Antiqua* 44: p. 361–392.

Luther, A. (1999). "Überlegungen zur *defectio* der östlichen Satrapien vom Seleucidenreich", *Göttinger Forum für Altertumswissenschaft* 2: p. 5–15.

——— (2006–2007). "Zur Genealogie der frühen Partherkönige", *Iranistik, Deutschsprachige Zeitschrift für iranistische Studien. Festschrift für Erich Kettenhofen*, 5. Jahrgang, Heft 1 & 2: p. 39–55.

Magnelli, A. (1993). "Giustino (41. 1–6) e le origini del regno degli arsacidi", *Sileno* 19: p. 467–479.

Muccioli, F. (2007). "La rappresentazione dei Parti nelle fonti tra II e I secolo a.C. e la polemica di Livio contro i *levissimi ex Graecis*", in *Incontri tra culture nell'oriente ellenistico e romano, Ravenna 11–12 marzo 2005*, Milan: p. 87–115.

Olbrycht, M.J. (2003). "Parthia and Nomads of Central Asia", in *Orientwissenschaftliche Hefte. Mitteilungen des SFB "Differenz und Integration", 5: Militär und Staatlichkeit*, Halle and Saale: p. 69–109.

——— "The titulature of Arsaces I, King of Parthia", *Parthica* 15: p. 63–74.

Will, E. (2003[3]). *Histoire politique du monde hellénistique*, Paris.

Wolski, J. (1993). *L'empire des Arsacides*, Louvain.

2

The Arsacids and Commagene

M. Rahim Shayegan

University of California, Los Angeles

Introduction

The Commagenian kingdom, an Irano-Hellenistic polity bordering Cilicia and Cappadocia in northern Syria, which flourished in the first century before our Common Era, is much too complex a field of study to risk a treatment of its diverse religious, cultural and ideological manifestations within the confines of the present study.

We shall therefore limit ourselves to certain aspects of early Arsacid ideology, with which we may claim some familiarity, and its interactions with the Commagenian cult of ancestors. Although this term may ultimately prove inadequate, it will initially serve us well in this inquiry.

What connects both the early Arsacid and Commagenian ideologies is the incorporation of both Achaemenid and Macedonian/Seleucid ancestry in their genealogical constructions. On the face of it, this may not represent much of a novelty, as other Hellenistic kingdoms, be it Pontus under Mithridates Eupator, or be it Ariarathid Cappadocia, did so as well.[1]

Thus, this inquiry will attempt to determine whether the inclusion of Achaemenid and Seleucid προγόνοι is to be ascribed to a general pattern followed by the (post-) Hellenistic kingdoms, due to comparable dispositions; or was the result of serendipitous coincidences; or finally represented possible cases of emulation.

The Arsacids

But before proceeding further, a succinct depiction of the Arsacid political ideology may be in order. In a recent publication,[2] we argued that the imperial title of "King of Kings", the most distinctive Achaemenid attribute, which had fallen into desuetude in the wake of the Macedonian conquest and languished as a forlorn and futile vestige of the Achaemenid past during the Hellenistic period, had finally seen a comeback a few decades after the conquest of Mesopotamia by Arsacid forces in 141 BC.[3]

A few more decades had to pass before the imperial title was introduced by an Arsacid sovereign. It appears first, applied to the great Miθrdāt (Mithradates) II, on Babylonian documents in 111 BC.[4] Later it is attested on Arsacid coinage, and is also employed by other Hellenistic princes of Iranian descent.[5]

We have in the past argued that it was due to the Babylonian possession of its own literary past, namely, its uninterrupted cuneiform tradition, that the Achaemenid title of "King of Kings" may have been resurrected for the Arsacids. In other words, Babylonian scholars, drawing upon their own literary heritage, may have extracted for their new masters a title that had previously belonged to their former Persian overlords. This established a sense of imperial continuity that may have not otherwise existed without the Babylonian agency, and made the Arsacids the recipients rather than the actors in this complex operation of recovery.[6]

However, even the adoption of the former Achaemenid title is not indicative of a conscious political agenda and ideology among the early Arsacids. For this, we have to wait another century to find traces thereof in a letter addressed by the Arsacid king Artabān (Artabanus) II to the Roman emperor Tiberius.[7]

This letter, reported by Tacitus, discusses how Artabān (Artabanus) II, following the death of the Armenian king Artaxias in 35 AD, had placed his own son Aršak on the vacant throne of Armenia. It also mentions the Parthian king's further hostile intentions towards Rome. Indeed, Artabān II seems to have been voicing his claim to Syria and Cilicia, by virtue of his ancestral rights, that is, on account of the Parthian kings being heirs to both the

Achaemenid empire of Cyrus and the Macedonian empire of Alexander:

> Is [Artabanus] metu Germanici fidus Romanis, aequabilis in suos, mox superbiam in nos, saevitiam in populares sumpsit, fretus bellis, quae secunda adversum circumiectas nationes exercuerat, et senectutem Tiberii ut inermem despiciens avidusque Armeniae, cui defuncto rege Artaxia Arsacen liberorum suorum veterrimum inposuit, addita contumelia et missis, qui gazam a Vonone relictam in Syria Ciliciaque reposcerent; simul *veteres Persorum ac Macedonum terminos,* seque invasurum *possessa primum Cyro et post Alexandro* per vaniloquentiam ac minas iaciebat.[8]

> "He [Artabanus], in fear of Germanicus, was faithful to Romans and equitable to his own (subjects), but soon assumed (an attitude of) insolence towards us and of fierceness towards (his) people; relying on the wars he had carried out successfully against surrounding nations, disdaining the old age of Tiberius as defenseless, and coveting eagerly Armenia, he installed the eldest of his sons, Arsaces, (on the throne of Armenia) after the death of its king, Artaxias. He added insult to injury by sending emissaries to claim back the treasure left behind by Vonones in Syria and Cilicia. At the same time he threw vain talk and menaces with respect to *the old boundaries of the Persians and the Macedonians*, (saying) that he would seize *what was held first by Cyrus and afterwards by Alexander*."

What is striking about this double reference to the Arsacids' Achaemenid and Hellenistic forebears as a justification for claims over disputed territories against Rome is its similarity to another account. This is a well-known passage about the Pontic king Mithridates VI Eupator, written by the Augustan historian Pompeius Trogus, albeit transmitted in Justin's *Epitome*.

In this account, Justin relates a speech delivered by the Pontic leader to his people in arms on the eve of the first Mithridatic War against Rome in 89 BC. Here, in order to galvanize his constituencies, both Iranian and Hellenic, Mithridates evokes his *maiores*, his ancestors, deriving his house in paternal line from the Achaemenid kings, and in maternal line from Alexander, and the founder of the Seleucid kingdom, Seleucus:

> Se autem seu nobilitate illis conparetur clariorem illa conluvie convenarum esse qui paternos maiores suos a *Cyro Darioque conditoribus Persici regni* maternos a *magno Alexandro ac Nicatore Seleuco conditoribus imperii macedonici* referat.[9]

> "He [Mithridates] continued that if he was compared with them [the Romans] with respect to extraction, he was more illustrious than that collection of mixed people [the Romans], he, whose ancestors on his father's side were from *Cyrus and Darius, the founders of the Persian empire*, and on his mother's side, from *Alexander the Great and Seleucus Nikator, the founders of the Macedonian empire*."

The analogy between Justin's account of Mithridates Eupator and Tacitus's of Artabān (Artabanus) II are, in spite of their differences, sufficiently strong as to prompt the question of whether Tacitus may have been drawing on Pompeius Trogus's account, and, hence, whether the entire episode centred around the Arsacid king ought to qualify as a literary topos, void of historical content; or is there some substance behind these similarities (whether conscious or accidental) after all?

In order to determine the nature of these similarities, we have to draw upon yet another set of parallels and confuse our readers even further, before eventually shedding some light.

In the third and fourth centuries AD, in the context of more aggressive campaigns against Rome led by the Sasanian emperors Ardaxšīr (Ardashir) and Šābuhr (Shapur) I, and a century later by Šābuhr (Shapur) II, we encounter once more reports by contemporary Roman historians, among them Cassius Dio and Herodian, that explain Sasanian bellicosity in similar terms:[10]

> καὶ ἀπειλῶν ἀνακτήσεσθαι *πάντα* ὡς καὶ προσήκοντά οἱ ἐκ *προγόνων ὅσα ποτὲ οἱ πάλαι Πέρσαι* μέχρι τῆς Ἑλληνικῆς θαλάσσης *ἔσχον*.[11]

> "He (was) menacing to recover *all that the ancient Persians had once held* as far as the Greek Sea, on the grounds that all this belonged to him through *his ancestors*."

> ad usque Strymona flumen et Macedonicos fines tenuisse *maiores imperium meos,* antiquitates quoque vestrae testantur; haec me convenit flagitare ... splendore virtutumque insignium serie, *vetustis regibus* antistantem.[12]

> "That *my forefathers' empire* reached as far as the river Strymon and the boundaries of Macedonia even your own ancient records bear witness; these lands it is fitting that I should demand, since ... I surpass *the kings of old* in magnificence and array of conspicuous virtues."

In this context, it is noteworthy that Tacitus derives Artabān II's territorial claims from both the Achaemenid and Macedonian empires, whose founders, Cyrus and Alexander, are explicitly mentioned. In contrast, Dio and Ammianus refer solely to the Achaemenid empire, describing its confines as the Greek Sea (μέχρι τῆς Ἑλληνικῆς θαλάσσης) and the boundaries of Macedonia (*Macedonicos fines*). The reports of Dio and Ammianus also concur in hinting at the rulers of the past without any precision, respectively: the ancient Persians (οἱ πάλαι Πέρσαι), who are subsequently qualified as Ardaxšīr's (Ardashir's) forefathers (οἱ προγόνοι), and the ancestors (*maiores*) who are later identified as the kings of old (*vetusti reges*).

The fundamental difference between these accounts thus resides in the fact that in Tacitus's narrative the Arsacid

Artabān (Artabanus) II legitimises his claim over disputed Roman territories by associating himself with Alexander and the Macedonians, that is, the Seleucids, Alexander's heirs in Iran, as well as with Cyrus and the Achaemenids, the representatives of "Iranism" proper. In contrast, in the reports of Dio, Herodian, and Ammianus about Ardaxšīr (Ardashir) and Šābuhr (Shapur) II, the short-lived Macedonian and the following Seleucid empires are not mentioned. Thus, the absence of Alexander and his heirs in the accounts ascribed to the early Sasanians, and their presence within those pertaining to the Arsacids, may surprisingly be a means to validate the veracity of these assertions in spite of close parallels in structure and content among our classical texts.

Yet another piece of evidence could lend a helping hand to explain the dichotomy of the Hellenistic heritage in Arsacid and Sasanian Iran. Intriguingly, the divergence between the account of Tacitus and those of Dio/Herodian and Ammianus seems to mirror the contrast prevailing between Alexander as reflected in Middle Persian Zoroastrian writings, and Alexander in the Iranian national epic, the *Shahnameh*, that is, the dichotomy between Alexander's negative image in the Zoroastrian tradition as opposed to his favourable portrayal in the national epic.[13] Among the Middle Persian passages reporting on the calamities that befell Iran following the Macedonian conquest is a succinct and well-known passage reported by the *Bundahishn*:

> *pas andar xwadāyīh ī Dārāy ī Dārāyān *Aleksandar Kēsar az Hrōm dwārist ō Ērānšahr āmad Dārāy ī šāh ōzad hamāg dūdag ī xwadāyān mēnōg-mardān ud paydāgān ud Ērānšahr abesīhēnīd was marag ātaxš afsārd dēn ī māzdēsnān Zand stad ō Hrōm frēstād Abestāg sōxt Ērānšahr pad 90 kōdag-xwadāy baxt.*[14]

> "Thereafter, during the reign of Dārāy son of Dārāy, Alexander the Caesar moved from Rome (and) came to Iran. (He) killed King Dārāy, destroyed all the families of the lords, spiritual men, and illustrious people of Iran. He extinguished numerous fires, seized the *Zand* (Exegesis) of the Mazdean religion and sent it to Rome, burnt the Avesta, (and) divided Iran among 90 house-rulers."

In contrast, the *Shahnameh* reports how Alexander judiciously administered the Iranian lands by claiming the mytho-epic Kayanian heritage:

Nebeštand nāme be har kešvarī,
be har nāmdār o har mehtarī
Az Eskandar-e Fīlqōs-e bozorg,
ǰahāngīr o bā kēne-ǰōyān sotorg,
benazd-e bozorgān-e sālārfaš,
delīrān-e asp-afgan-e kēne-keš,
sōy-e mōbadān, nāme-yī hamčonēn
porr-afrōzeš o pōzeš o āfrīn
sar-e nāme az pādšāh-e keyān
sōy-e kārdārān-e Īrānīyān[15]

"They wrote letters to every province,
to all illustrious people and grandees,
from Alexander, son of Philip, the Great,
conqueror of the world, and stern with those seeking revenge,
to the magi also a letter (was written),
full of brilliancy, repentance, and praise,
the letter head (being): 'from the Kayanian king
to all the leaders of the Iranians.'"

Surely, Alexander's favourable reception in the *Shahnameh* may be accounted for by the great popularity of the Alexander Romance in Sasanian Iran. Nonetheless, for it to be incorporated into Iranian oral literature, we still have to assume that a quiescent predisposition towards the assimilation of the Alexander Romance existed prior to the emergence of the Romance and its circulation in Iran.[16]

This predisposition may have been due to the acceptance by the Arsacids of the double heritage of Alexander and the Seleucids, as well as that of Cyrus and the Achaemenids. The appropriation of Alexander and his subsequent association with the Achaemenids in Arsacid ideology could therefore be reflected not only in Tacitus's account, but also in the oral traditions captured by the *Shahnameh*. Indeed, it seems that we may have to presume two co-existing traditions: a positive oral tradition, which, as Tacitus's account bears witness, could have been an Arsacid creation, and a later hostile written tradition that probably had cast a *damnatio memoriae* on Alexander under the early Sasanians.[17] Thus, the presence of a positive Alexander image in the *Shahnameh*, which ultimately reflects his favourable image in the Arsacid period, in contrast to the hostile attitude of Zoroastrian writings in the Sasanian period, seems to mirror the difference between the account of Tacitus, in which the Arsacid Artabān (Artabanus) II legitimises his claim over disputed Roman territories by associating himself with both Alexander and Cyrus, and those of Dio/Herodian and Ammianus reporting on Ardaxšīr (Ardashir) and Šābuhr (Shapur) II, who exclusively mention their (Achaemenid) ancestors without any reference to the short-lived Macedonian and Seleucid empires.

Now, even if we were to presume that there was a kernel of truth in the report of Artabān's claim to the double heritage, we must still substantiate it by addressing how it came about.

The kingdoms of Pontus and Commagene

Prior to any *explicit* evidence for an Arsacid "Achaemenid revival," Mithridates VI Eupator was the first Iranian prince consciously to have emulated the Achaemenids, in parallel to his *imitatio Alexandri*, either as part of a political programme, which aimed at recovering parts of the Achaemenid dominions, or a mere propaganda tool destined to secure the allegiance of his Iranian subjects to his cause.[18]

If so, he may have provided the Arsacids with a source of inspiration, if not a model for direct emulation. As mentioned above, the Arsacids, by adopting the imperial title of "King of Kings" through Babylonian agency, stood in direct continuity with the great Achaemenids, although they may not yet have formulated the binary nature of their legitimacy.

There are certainly sundry indices that bear witness to Achaemenid reminiscences in ideological constructs of the Arsacid dynasty. Among the more striking are two reports attributed to Arrian's *Parthica* that were captured by Photios and Synkellos respectively. The first is a variation on the theme/legend of the Seven,[19] that is, the narratives of Dareios and the six noblemen who killed the magus Gaumāta, or the two usurper *magi*.[20] According to Photios's note: Ἀρσάκης καὶ Τιριδάτης ἤστην ἀδελφὼ Ἀρσακίδαι "Arsaces and Tiridates were two brothers", who were τοῦ υἱοῦ Ἀρσάκου τοῦ Φριαπίτου ἀπόγονοι "descendants of Arsaces, son of Phriapites". Photios adds: τὸν ὑπὸ Ἀντιόχου σατράπην αὐτῶν τῆς χώρας καταστάντα Φερεκλέα, ἐπεὶ τὸν ἕτερον τῶν ἀδελφῶν αἰσχρῶς ἐπείρασε βιασάμενος "these brothers killed the satrap of their land, Pherekles, who had been appointed by King Antiochos (called Theos), because of the shameful act attempted on one of the brethren." The brothers benefitted in this enterprise from the help of five accomplices (πέντε τὴν πρᾶξιν ἀνακοινωσάμενοι).[21]

Here, the eponymous founder Arsaces and his (fictive) brother Tiridates,[22] together with their five helpers, are being depicted as leaders of an insurrection against the Seleucid satrap (called here Pherekles) of an undetermined land (ἡ χώρα),[23] which eventually would lead to Arsacid dominion in Parthia proper.

The first step in this evolution is the creation of an implicit association with the Achaemenids through the legend of the Seven. Thereupon follows an explicit reference to Achaemenid descent, which again comes from Arrian's *Parthica*, but has been fortuitously preserved in Synkellos, and *caeteris paribus* could reflect the binary affiliation we have encountered above in Tacitus's report. Indeed, Synkellos mentions that the brothers Arsaces and Teridates [sic], who were, on the one hand, *Macedonian* satraps under Antiochos Kallinikos, and on the other hand, descendants of the *Achaemenid* king Artaxerxes (II),[24] eventually killed the commander (*eparchos*) of Persis, a certain Agathokles,[25] for the same reasons as described in Photios's narrative:

> Ἀρσάκης τις καὶ Τηριδάτης ἀδελφοὶ *τὸ γένος ἕλκοντες ἀπὸ τοῦ Περσῶν Ἀρταξέρξου ἐσατράπευον Βακτρίων* ἐπὶ Ἀγαθοκλέους Μακεδόνος ἐπάρχου τῆς Περσικῆς.[26]
>
> "Arsaces and Teridates, two brothers who *traced their lineage back to Artaxerxes, king of the Persians, ruled as satraps of the Bactrians* when Agathokles of Macedonia was governor (eparch) of Persis."

The theme of Arsaces, the eponym, being a Macedonian (or Seleucid) governor, rather than of Scythian descent, is not unique to Arrian's account (assuming Synkellos has faithfully transmitted its content). As others have judiciously indicated before,[27] this had already been reported by Strabo. While ascribing Scythian origins to Parthians, he nonetheless captured an alternative tradition, according to which Arsaces was originally a Bactrian or a Macedonian of Bactria:[28] ἀπὸ τούτων δ᾽ οὖν ἕλκειν φασὶ τὸ γένος τὸν Ἀρσάκην οἱ δὲ Βακτριανὸν λέγουσιν αὐτόν,[29] "on that account, then, some say he [Arsaces] derives his lineage [from the Scythians], and others say he was a Bactrian", who prompted Parthia to rebel.

It is therefore possible that we may possess in the excerpts ascribed to Arrian's *Parthica* an unequivocal reference to Achaemenid forebears in the context of genealogical and ideological constructs, and furthermore that the reference to the Macedonian/Bactrian origins of the eponymous Arsaces might in kernel represent the binary nature of Arsacid legitimacy as we have seen it fully developed in Tacitus's account (dating to the first century AD). The fact remains, however, that the *Parthica* belongs to the second century AD, and so the Achaemenid revival Arrian attributes to the earliest Arsacids may merely have been the result of his retrojecting well-established realities of his own time into earlier periods.

Another index of the early Arsacids' Achaemenid reception is the apparent use of the Middle Iranian term *kāren*, written in Aramaic script, on some of the early issues of Arsaces I.[30] The term evidently derives from Old Persian **kārā̆-na-*,[31] and is well attested in the *Nebenüberlieferung* as κάρανος, which is the title attributed to the supreme commander of Achaemenid forces in Asia Minor (mainly attested for Cyrus the Younger).[32]

More recently, following the publication of the Aramaic documents from Achaemenid Bactria published by Naveh and Shaked, a certain *wšt'sp krny* "Hystaspes *krny*" has been identified in a note announcing – during year 1 of an unidentified ruler – the dispatch of some forty sheep to an Iranian superior (*'l mr'y* "my lord") called *wdywr*, made possibly by (an agent by the name of) *kwpdt*.[33] It is not easy to gauge whose first regnal year it is, although Ochos, Artaxerxes IV Arsēs, Dareios III, Bessos or Alexander are all possible candidates.[34] What the role of Hystaspes *krny* in this transaction might have been is difficult to determine. He could have been either the administrative official under whose authority the agent *kwpdt* was delivering the sheep, or else the seller. We know of a certain Hystaspes among the high Persian nobility on the eve of the Macedonian conquest, for Curtius describes him as *propinquus hic Darei fuerat*.[35] Curtius further reports that his wife was the grandchild of Artaxerxes III Ochos,[36] and probably the daughter of Bisthanēs, son of Ochos.[37] Still following Curtius, this Hystaspes was commander of a large army

A B

Figures 2.1a and b: Obverse and reverse of drachm of Wahbarz, the kāren of Persis (After Klose & Müseler 2008, p. 27, fig. 17).

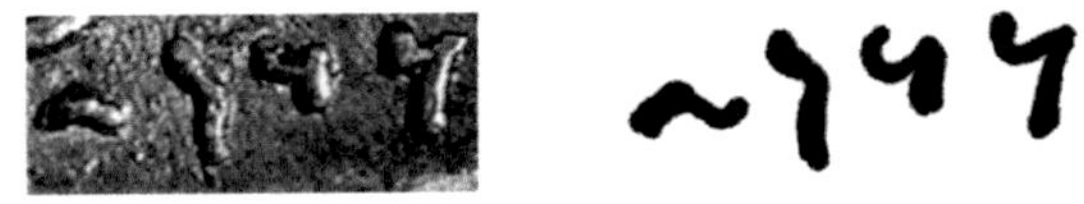

Figure 2.2: Photo and line drawing of right vertical legend <krny> on drachm (reverse) of Wahbarz, the kāren of Persis (Detail of photo from Klose and Müseler 2008, p. 27, fig. 17)

Figure 2.3: Photo and line drawing of left vertical legend <krny> on coin of Arsaces I (S 3.1–2; 4.1)

(*magni et ipse exercitus praetor*);[38] and had probably taken part in the battle at Gaugamela, for his wife fell into captivity only following Dareios III's death.[39] Hystaspes, whom Arrian calls "the Bactrian" (Ὑστάσπης ὁ Βάκτριος) was appointed by Alexander commander (*hēgemōn*) of the Iranian noblemen who were admitted to the *agēma* of the *hetaîroi*,[40] another sign of his high aristocratic lineage.[41]

If this Hystaspes is the same as *wšt'sp krny*, then he might have been in Bactria, as Arrian's note suggests, prior to his appointment as *hēgemōn* of the *agēma* by Alexander, and consequently could not have been in Bactria during the first regnal year of either Bessos or Alexander, which leaves Ochos, Artaxerxes IV Arsēs and Dareios III as the candidates. Hystaspes' family ties with Ochos could suggest placing him in Bactria during his reign.

As to the word *krny*, it could certainly be the same word as the κάρανος we know from Asia Minor,[42] or simply a family name, as Naveh and Shaked suggest.[43] It is true that the proposition that *krny* might reflect κάρανος resides primarily in our equating Hystaspes the Bactrian with *wšt'sp krny*, which is not unlikely but far from certain; and secondly, in assuming the function of *krny* was also attested in eastern Iran, for which this would be the only evidence. Again, the paucity of the material does not permit us to settle this one way or another.

In post-Achaemenid Iran, the title/name *kāren* is attested on the coinage of the local rulers of Persis, the *frataraka*.[44] On a Persid drachm – the authenticity of which has been contested[45] – which bears the name Wahbarz, the latter is depicted in Achaemenid dress finishing off a kneeling Greek foe (Fig. 2.1a/b).[46] The legend, which like those of other *frataraka* coins is split between three sides, distinguishes itself from other coins of Persis in that it introduces the title *kāren*. The legend, as suggested in our prior publication, reads: *Wahbarz wānēd/wānād ī kāren* "Wahbarz is/may be victorious, (he) who (is) the commander [*kāren*].[47] This victorious Wahbarz, the *kāren*, might have been identical with a certain Oborzos (Ὀβόρζος), known from Polyaenus,[48] and said to have been in charge of 3,000 Greek military settlers, the κατοίκοι, whom he executed on suspicion of rebellion.[49] The special issue of Wahbarz/Oborzos, exhibiting the term *kāren*, could thus have commemorated his killing of the Greek κατοίκοι.

Whereas there is little doubt that the *kāren* (<krny>) refers to the Old Persian **kārā̆-na-*, an impression that is supported by the iconography of Wahbarz's special issue, the same may not be assumed *ipso facto* for the coins of Arsaces I, where the same word appears to occur. The series with the presumed word *kāren* <krny> follows Arsaces I's first issues, which carry on the reverse the legend Ἀρσάκου αὐτοκράτορος in two vertical lines framing a seated archer.[50] The omission of αὐτοκράτωρ from the issues with <krny> has led some to believe that the presumed title *kāren* was a substitution for αὐτοκράτωρ.[51] Given the exalted position of the Achaemenid κάρανος, *kāren* would be an appropriate rendition of the Seleucid term αὐτοκράτωρ, as well as providing validation for the hypothesis that the early Arsacids had sought to establish ideological links with the Achaemenids.

Indeed, a comparison of the legends of the Persid (Fig. 2.2) and Arsacid (Fig. 2.3) issues on which <krny> occurs seems to suggest that we are dealing with the same word.

Nevertheless, their semantic range may not have been identical. The word αὐτοκράτωρ was translated into Parthian early on (even though a precise date may be elusive), for which an exact calque, namely, *xwatāw* < **x^{v}a-tāvaya-* "self-reliant", not otherwise attested in Old Iranian, was fabricated.[52] Although it is possible that the term αὐτοκράτωρ[53] might also have been rendered by the title *kāren*[54] – which basically signifies "leader of the people in arms/army" (*kāra-*) – the Arsacid creation of *xwatāw/wxatāw* to replicate the intrinsic meaning of αὐτοκράτωρ makes this assumption, at the very least, open to question, and forces us to ask whether *kāren* may indeed have been, in addition to the dynastic name Arsaces, a proper/family name.[55]

Thus, in the period preceding the letter of Artabān (Artabanus) II, we have an array of indices testifying to the Arsacid engagement with their Achaemenid past, but we still cannot read into them the same degree of historical/ideological consciousness as manifest in Artabān's letter, and which we first encountered in Trogus's account of Eupator's policies, whose *Vorbildwirkung* for the Arsacids still remain valid.

But, how about the kingdom of Commagene?

In the first century BC, Antiochos I, son of Mithradates Kallinikos and the Seleucid princess Laodike, ruled over the Iranian and Hellenistic kingdom of Commagene. It is Antiochos I who was mainly responsible for the establishment of an intriguing form of Greco-Iranian religious idiosyncrasy.[56] This featured an impressive pantheon that in its final shape boasted: Zeus-Oromasdes; Apollo-Mithra-Helios-Hermes; Artagnes [*Warθraγn*]-Herakles-Ares; and the goddess Commagene. Antiochos I promulgated its *nomos*[57] and established throughout Commagene a network of major cultic spaces (*hierothesia*) at Arsameia on the Euphrates, Arsameia on the Nymphaios and Nemrud Dağı, as well as more discreet *temenē*,[58] toward the celebration of the cult of the ancestors and/or the syncretized Irano-Hellenic divinities.

But of importance to us are the genealogical inscriptions, or fragments thereof, which were found on the site of the monumental terraces Antiochos I had built around a tumulus on the top of Nemrud Dağı, the highest mountain of the Antitaurus.[59]

At Nemrud Dağı, Antiochos I erected on the eastern and western terraces colossal statues of the three Greco-Persian divinities he had fashioned, along with the goddess Commagene and his deified Self, which completed this illustrious pantheon. He furthermore set up two distinct rows of stelae on each of the terraces, with each single row projecting an *Ahnengalerie* on the maternal, as well as the paternal side.[60] Each stele represented a standing ancestor, and bore on the back a Greek inscription providing the titulary of Antiochos I and his ancestor's name and genealogy.[61]

The maternal *Ahnenreihe* (comprising some 17 stelae), on account of Antiochos I's mother, the Seleucid princess Laodike, was taken all the way back to Alexander the Great, and the paternal row (a mere 15 stelae) to Dareios the Great. Antiochos I had forged a genealogy that would place as the dynastic founder of his house a certain Aroandas [I] (= Orontes), a Persian nobleman, who had probably served as satrap of Armenia and later Mysia under Artaxerxes II in the fourth century BC[62] – ancestor to another Aroandas [II], whom we know from the accounts of Alexander historians[63] – and who by virtue of being the husband of Rhodogune, daughter of Artaxerxes II, represented the link between the Commagenian and Achaemenid dynasties. The two inscriptions dedicated to Orontes [I], the sixth in the row of Persian forebears, from both the West and East terraces, read as follows:

Orontes on the West Terrace	*Orontes on the East Terrace*
[β]ασιλεὺς μέγας Ἀντίοχος Θεὸς Δίκαιος Ἐπιφανής Φιλο- ρώμαιος καὶ Φιλέλλην ὁ ἐγ βασ[ι]λέως Μιθραδάτου Καλλι- νίκου καὶ βασιλίσσης Λαοδίκης Θεᾶς Φιλαδέλφου	[βασιλεὺς μέ]γας Ἀντίοχ[ος] [Θεὸς] Δίκ[αιος] Ἐπιφανής [Φιλορώμαιος κ]αὶ Φιλέ[λλην] [ὁ] ἐ[γ βασιλέως Μιθραδάτου] Καλλινί[κου καὶ βα]σιλίσ[σης] Λαοδίκης Θεᾶς Φιλαδέ[λφου] τῆς ἐγ βασιλέως Ἀντιό[χου] Ἐπιφανοῦς Φιλομήτορ[ος] Καλλινίκου
Ἀροάνδην Ἀρτασούρα τὸν γαμήσαντα βασίλισσαν Ῥοδογούνην τήν Ἀρταξέρξου Θυγατέρα [64]	Ἀροάνδην Ἀρτασούρ[α τὸν] γαμήσαντα βασίλισσα[ν] [Ῥο]δ[ο]γούνην τήν βασ[ιλέως] [Βα]σιλέων μεγά[λου Ἀρτα-] ξέρξου του κα[ὶ Ἀρσάκου] Θυγατέρα[65]

Orontes on the West Terrace	*Orontes on the East Terrace*
"The great King Antiochus, God, the Righteous, the Manifest, friend to Romans and Hellenes,[66] son of King Mithradatēs Kallinikos (the Victorious), and Queen Laodikē, Goddess, brother-loving,	"[The gr]eat [King] Antioch[us], [God], the Right[eous], the Manifest, [Friend to Romans a]nd Hellenes, [son of King Mithradatēs] Kallinik[os (the Victorious), and Q]uee[n] Laodikē, Goddess, [brother-lo]ving, who is the daughter of Antioch[us] Epiphanēs Philomētōr (mother-loving) Kallinikos,
Aroandas (Orontes), son of Artasyras, who married Queen Rhodogune, daughter of Artaxerxes [II]."	Aroandas (Orontes), son of Artasyr[as], [who] married Quee[n] [Rho]dogune, daughter of the ki[ng of] [k]ings, the Gre[at Arta] xerxes [II], who is a[lso Arsakēs]."

What is at first glance striking is that the royal forebear, Artaxerxes II, who in the Commagenian genealogical construct serves as a link to the Achaemenid house and Dareios I, fulfills this very function for the early Arsacids. If Synkellos's aforesaid notice[67] were to be trusted, then the ancestor to whom the brethren Arsaces and Teridates (Ἀρσάκης τις καὶ Τηριδάτης ἀδελφοὶ τὸ γένος ἕλκοντες ἀπὸ τοῦ Περσῶν Ἀρταξέρξου) referred would be the selfsame Artaxerxes II. One possible reason why the Arsacids may have chosen Artaxerxes as their Achaemenid ancestor *par excellence* may have resided in the latter's given name being Arses (< **Ṛšan*-), whose hypocoristic Arsaces (< **Ṛšaka*-) happened to be the patronymic of the Arsacid house. Artaxerxes II is indeed attested in the *Astronomical Diaries*, either under his given name Arses: *Aršu šarru* "king Arses",[68] or with the use of both his given and throne names: [*Ar*]*šu ša Artakšatsu šar mātāti šumšu nabû* "[Ar]ses who is called Artaxerxes [II], king of the lands".[69] Granted, Artaxerxes's preeminence in the Commagenian *Ahnenkult* owes to the *reported* marriage of his daughter Rhodogune with the eponymous Orontes, but if the reconstruction of the final lines in the inscription dedicated to Orontes [I] were to be substantiated: [Ῥο]δ[ο]γούνην τήν βασ[ιλέως Βα]σιλέων μεγά[λου Ἀρτα]ξέρξου του κα[ὶ Ἀρσάκου] Θυγατέρα, "[Rho]dogune, daughter of the ki[ng of k]ings, the Gre[at Arta]xerxes [II], who is a[lso Arsakēs]," then we would have a formula known to us not only from Achaemenid Babylonia, as we have seen above, but also from the Mesopotamian literary tradition under Arsacid dominion.[70]

Indeed, during the reigns of Gōdarz (Gotarzes) I (fall–winter? 91–*ante* early spring 79) and Urūd (Orodes) I (early spring 79–winter 76/75 [*a quo*]), the *Astronomical Diaries* make use for the first time after the Achaemenid period of formulae that are reminiscent of Achaemenid practices, and, as we have argued elsewhere,[71] served the purpose of equating the neo-Iranian Arsacid empire with that of the Achaemenids:

> Aršakâ/Aršakam (šarru/šar šarrāni) *ša iṭṭarridu* Gutarzâ/Urudâ (šarru)
> Aršakâ šarru *ša šumšu* Gutarzâ
>
> "Arsaces (king/king of kings) *who is called* Gōdarz/Urūd, (king)"
> "Arsaces (king/king of kings) *whose name is* Gōdarz, (king)"

Thus, on the strength of this elusive token, it is possible guardedly to surmise that the use of a comparable formula in Commagene (βασ[ιλέως Βα]σιλέων μεγά[λου Ἀρτα]ξέρξου του *κα*[ὶ Ἀρσάκου] "ki[ng of k]ings, the Gre[at Arta]xerxes [II] *who is a[lso* Arsakēs]"), if indeed this restoration of Orontes I's stele proves tenable, may owe a debt to the impact of the Arsacid world, rather than being a testament to the direct Commagenian reception of Mesopotamian practices, as has been recently argued.[72] Thus, if parallels in the use of formulae from Achaemenid Mesopotamia, reintroduced by Babylonian scholars under the early Arsacids, and possibly attested in Commagene, should prompt us to look for possible sources of influence, and the direction thereof, then it ought to be that of Arsacid Iran on Commagene in the restricted confines of this equation.

But could we expand this first conclusion to other ideological elaborations of the Orontids as well, and submit that their genealogical constructions, especially the binary reference to Dareios I and Alexander of Macedon – which in his *nomos* inscription at Nemrud Dağı, Antiochus I so exquisitely calls καθ᾽ ἃ παλαιὸς λόγος Περσῶν τε καὶ Ἑλλήνων ἐμοῦ γένους εὐτυχεστάτη ῥίζα παραδέδωκε ("in so far as the ancient tale of the Persians and the Hellenes, *the most fortunate root of my ancestry*, has handed down [to us]")[73] – could have been directly influenced by Arsacid practices. Or, alternatively, would it be conceivable that the Orontids themselves may have inspired the Arsacids in their allusion to the dual source of their ancestry? Before we may address this question, we should have a glance at the epigraphic remains of Antiochus I's ancestors. The first one belongs to Dareios I the Great, the first and most consequential of the Persian forebears:

Dareios I on the West Terrace[74]	*Alexander I on the West Terrace*
βασιλεὺς μέγας Ἀντίοχος Θεὸς Δίκαιος Ἐπιφανής Φιλορώμαιος καὶ Φιλέλλην ὁ ἐγ βασιλέως Μιθραδάτου Καλλινίκου καὶ βασιλίσσης Λαοδίκης Θεᾶς Φιλαδέλφου βασιλέα βασιλέων μέγαν Δαρείου τὸν Ὑστάσπου[75]	Βα[σιλεὺς μέγα]ς [Ἀ]ντίοχος [Θεὸς Δίκαιος Ἐπιφα]νής [Φιλο-] [ρώμαιος καὶ Φιλέ]λ[λ]η[ν ὁ ἐγ] [βασιλέως Μιθραδάτου] [Καλλινίκου καὶ βασι-] [λίσσης Λαοδίκης Θεᾶς] [Φιλαδέλφου τῆς ἐκ βασιλέ-] [ως Ἀντιόχου Ἐπιφανοῦς Φιλο-] [μήτορος Καλ]λιν[ίκου] [βα]σιλέ[α] μέγ[αν Ἀλέ-] ξανδρον τὸν [βασιλέ-] ως Φιλίππου[76]
Dareios I on the West Terrace "The great King Antiochus, God, the Righteous, the Manifest, Friend to Romans and Hellenes, son of King Mithradatēs Kallinikos (the Victorious), and Queen Laodikē, Goddess, Brother-loving. King of Kings, the Great Dareios, son of Hystaspes."	*Alexander on the West Terrace* "The [great Ki]ng [A]ntiochos, [God, the Righteous, the Manifest, Friend] [to Romans and Hellenes, son of] [King Mithradatēs] [Kallinikos (the Victorious), and Queen] [Laodikē, Goddess,] [Brother-loving, daughter of King] [Antiochus Epiphanes Philo-] [mētōr (mother-loving) Kal] lin[ikos]. [The [Gre]at [Ki]ng [Ale]xander (or: the King, the Great Alexander),[77] son of [Kin]g Philip."

Noteworthy, at least judging from the extant source material, is the absence of Cyrus within the framework of Commagenian elaborations,[78] whereas, as we have seen above, Cyrus is well anchored in the constructs of Pontic and Arsacid dynasts. The omission of Cyrus in Commagene is not surprising. The house of Commagene had established its legitimacy on the strength of its connection with the political order created by Dareios I and his six helpers (the Seven), who had eliminated in a daring *coup-d'état* Bardiya, son of Cyrus, the last scion of the Anšanite line in Persia.[79] With Dareios I a different house was to govern over Persian affairs, and hence it does not astound that the satraps of the new order, either descendants of, or claiming to derive from, the Seven, having eventually become dynasts in their own right, would deem Dareios I the source of their legitimacy, and their association with the Seven's seizure of power as constitutive for their legitimacy.[80]

In this light, it is the Pontic (and Arsacid) policy of including Cyrus that stands out and requires further explanation.[81] There are sundry reports of the Mithridatids of Pontos having behaved like their Commagenian counterparts by alluding to the story of Dareios I and his six helpers. Indeed, Appian, while describing the origins of the house of Mithridates Eupator, mentions a certain Mithridates [I], a scion of the Persian royal house (Μιθριδάτης ἀνὴρ γένους βασιλείου Περσικοῦ "Mithridates, a man of the Persian royal house"),[82] as its founder. This Mithridates, thus continues the account, would eventually escape together with six horsemen from his overlord Antigonos (ὁ δ' ἐξέφυγε σὺν ἱππεῦσιν ἕξ "he escaped together with six horsemen"), and in time establish his reign in Cappadocia and the adjacent countries.[83]

Polybius reports the claim by another Pontic king, Mithridates II – whose daughter Laodike was Antiochus III's wife[84] – to descend from the Seven who had killed the magus: ὁ δὲ Μιθριδάτης εὔχετο μέν ἀπόγονος εἶναι τῶν ἑπτὰ Περσῶν ἑνὸς τῶν ἐπανελομένων τὸν μάγον "Mithridates [II] boasted of being the descendant of one of the Seven who had killed the magus". Polybius's note is echoed a century later in Diodorus's *Bibliotheca*, who recounts the same claim by Mithridates II: "There was also present with them Mithridates, the son of Ariobarzanes, and a descendant of one of the seven Persians who slew the Magian Smerdis, a man remarkable for courage and trained from childhood as a soldier."[85]

And for good measure, there is another note by Appian on the occasion of Mithridates Eupator's demise, taking his ancestry back to Dareios, son of Hystaspes: καὶ ὁ Μιθριδάτης ἀπέθνησκεν ἑκκαιδέκατος ὢν ἐκ Δαρείου τοῦ Ὑστάσπου Περσῶν βασιλέως, "so died Mithridates who was the sixteenth descendant of Dareios, son of Hystaspes, king of the Persians."[86]

Aside from unequivocally substantiating Achaemenid pretenses by the Mithridatids throughout the centuries, these passages are also testimony to the prevalence of the legend of the Seven, and consequently of Dareios, in Pontic ideological constructs. Thus, whence the allusion to Cyrus, when, and for what purpose? Since it appears that before Mithridates Eupator, the house of Pontos like other Irano-Hellenistic rulers legitimised sovereign power by attaching the dynastic eponym to Dareios I's line,[87] we have to locate the reason for the change of paradigm, from Dareios I to Cyrus, in the hegemonic aspirations of Eupator during the Mithridatic wars. Indeed, Eupator, who in his opposition to Rome sought a source of emulation to sustain the imperial design of his house, regarded the heroic figure of Cyrus – whose presence would create symmetry with the figure of the world conqueror Alexander – as a more formidable Persian forebear, of more consequent bearing upon Mithridates's thrust to hegemonic grandeur in Asia Minor than Dareios I, who even in more remote antiquity was regarded as an administrator rather than an exalted victor.

It is thus possible that the binary structure of Pontic ideology forged prior to 89 BC, wherein Cyrus's prestige had eclipsed Dareios's pertinence, may have influenced the Arsacids, awaiting an opportune moment – when comparable pressures and stimuli in the Arsacid realm necessitated drawing back on the Cyrus symbolism – to express itself. As far as the extant documentation permits judgment, we find the first *explicit* use of Cyrus in Arsacid ideological elaborations on the occasion of Artabān (Artabanus) II's design on Armenia in the first half of the first century of the Common Era.

The Commagenian example, however, seems to have had little or no bearing on early Arsacid ideology, as Cyrus seems an elusive presence therein. It is, however, not excluded that Arsacid practices may have impacted Commagene, if we were to take into account the use, in the inscription dedicated to the Orontid eponym in Nemrud Dağı, of Artaxerxes II's throne and given names, a practice reintroduced, after the Achaemenid period, on cuneiform documents of the Arsacid age, and attested for Gōdarz (Gotarzes) I and Urūd (Orodes) I for the years 90–87/86 and 80/79 BC respectively, thus a short period before the beginning of Antiochus I's reign.

Notes

1 See Panitschek 1987.

2 See Shayegan 2011, with preliminary conclusions on p. 291–292.

3 On the Arsacid conquest of Babylonia, see Shayegan 2011, p. 67–72.

4 See Shayegan 2011, p. 42–44; 232–233; 394–409.

5 For the use of the title of "King of Kings" by Mithridates Eupator of Pontus and Tigranes II of Armenia, see Shayegan 2011, p. 228; 240–241; 244–245; 316–330.

6 See Shayegan 2011, p. 287–292.

7 On the Arsacid "Achaemenid Program," see Panitschek 1990, p. 459–461; Wolski 1990a, p. 8–9; Wolski 1990b, p. 15; Wolski 1991, p. 53–55; Wolski 1993, p. 152–160; see also Dąbrowa 1983, p. 103–117, and Dąbrowa 2012b, p. 33–34; on Artabān (Artabanus) II's letter, see Wiesehöfer 2005, p. 120; Fowler 2005, p. 125–155; also Shayegan 2011, p. 41–331.

8 Tac. *Ann.* 6.31.

9 Just. 38.7.

10 On this question, see Shayegan 2004 [2008].

11 Cass. Dio 80.3.4.

12 Amm. Marc. 17.5.5.

13 On the entire dossier of the Alexander reception in pre- and early Islamic Iran, see Briant 2003, p. 443–521; and now authoritatively Wiesehöfer 2011, p. 124–128 (negative image), and 128–131 (positive image), especially 125–126, where the author describes the historical circumstances that may have caused the negative reception of Alexander already in Iranian antiquity: "No, the emergence and the broad and enduring effect of the negative Alexander-image may only be understood, if the Zoroastrian allegations, despite all exaggerations and elaborations, could be substantiated by the historical fact of atrocities committed by Alexander in Iran. This does not mean that the concrete allegations had to have their respective origin in Alexander's own time; it only means that the image of Alexander as evildoer had to have arisen in Zoroastrian circles in Iran during his lifetime." For the reason behind the positive appraisal of Alexander in Iran, see still

Frye 1985, p. 187–188. For further literature, see Shayegan 2011, p. 295–307.

14 *Bundahishn* 33.14, ed. Pakzad 2005.

15 Khaleghi-Motlagh 1997, 562, ll. 415–419.

16 On the Alexander romance in Iran, see discussion in Shayegan 2011, p. 304–305, n. 866, with ample literature.

17 See Frye 1985, p. 187–188: "More likely is the folkloric tendency to assimilate Alexander to the Iranian national tradition, such that one may postulate two Iranian traditions side by side, one of folklore which made Alexander a scion of the Achaemenid kings and an Iranian hero, while the priestly tradition maintained the historic picture of Alexander as the destroyer of not only the Iranian kingdoms, but also of the Iranian culture and sacred writings." Also Wiesehöfer 2011, 123–124.

18 On ideological exchanges between Eupator and Arsacid Iran, see Shayegan 2011, p. 307–311, with further literature; also more recently Olbrycht 2009; and McGing 2009; on the Roman association of Mithridates with Xerxes, see now Ballesteros Pastor, 2011.

19 On the seven conspirators who plotted against the alleged magus Gaumāta – that is, Dareios and his six helpers, who in time would become the heads of the most powerful families within the empire – see Briant 1996, p. 119–127, 140–149. More recently, see Shayegan 2012, p. 127–138.

20 See Frye 1984, p. 206; also Wolski 1993, p. 56.

21 Photios 58: Ἀρσάκης καὶ Τιριδάτης ἤστην ἀδελφὼ Ἀρσακίδαι, τοῦ υἱοῦ Ἀρσάκου τοῦ Φριαπίτου ἀπόγονοι. Οὗτοι Φερεκλέα τὸν ὑπὸ Ἀντιόχου τοῦ βασιλέως (θεὸν αὐτὸν ἐπίκλην ὠνόμαζον), ἀλλ᾽ οἵ γε Ἀρσακίδαι τὸν ὑπὸ Ἀντιόχου σατράπην αὐτῶν τῆς χώρας καταστάντα Φερεκλέα, ἐπεὶ τὸν ἕτερον τῶν ἀδελφῶν αἰσχρῶς ἐπείρασε βιασάμενος, οὐκ ἐνεγκόντες τὴν ὕβριν ἀνεῖλόν τε τὸν ὑβρίσαντα, καὶ ἑτέροις πέντε τὴν πρᾶξιν ἀνακοινωσάμενοι καὶ τὸ ἔθνος Μακεδόνων ἀπέστησαν, καὶ καθ᾽ ἑαυτοὺς ἦρξαν, καὶ ἐπὶ μέγα δυνάμεως ἤλασαν, ὡς καὶ Ῥωμαίοις ἀντιρρόπους μάχας θέσθαι, ἐνίοτε δὲ καὶ μεθ᾽ ἑαυτῶν τὴν νίκην ἔχοντας τοῦ πολέμου ἀπελθεῖν. See Henry 1959, I, [17a]:34–[17b]:5.

22 On the elusive Tiridates, see already Wolski 1979, p. 67–74; Wolski 1993, p. 56, n. 7; and Wiesehöfer 1996, p. 131–132; and Dąbrowa 2012a, p. 169; also Dąbrowa 2012b, p. 27.

23 Already Bevan 1902 II, p. 286: "Of what province, however, Pherecles was satrap the abstract of Arrian given by Photios does not specify; we may presume he was really eparch or hyparch of the district in which Asaak was situated."

24 On possible reasons for the Arsacid choice of Artaxerxes (II) as the Achaemenid ancestor *par excellence*, see below p. 13f.

25 See also Lerner 1999, p. 18–31.

26 Synkellos 539; see Mosshammer 1984, 343, ll. 7–9.

27 See Wolski 1993, p. 55–57; and Wiesehöfer 1996, p. 130–132.

28 Since this version suppresses the role of the Macedonian satrap of Parthia Andragoras (of whom, among others, Justin [41.41.5–9] knows to report), who is superseded by Arsaces, we may assume that Βακτριανός actually referred to a Macedonian settler of Bactria.

29 Str. 11.9.3.

30 See Sellwood 1980, types 3.1–2 and 4.1; also Alram 1986, 122–123.

31 *Kāren* <krny> is attested both in Parthian Nisa documents as <kryn> and in Sasanian inscriptions with the same spelling (and <kʾlny>). It most likely derives from **kārā̆-na-* (with **-(h)no-* the "Führer-Suffix") (Haebler 1982, 81–90; Rix 1982, 76; and Schmitt 2002, 58n48), and may be read either **kārān* (< **kāra-Hna-*), or more likely *kāren* (< **kāra-na-*), in western Middle Iranian, although the ambiguity of the Aramaic script permits either reading. For further reading, see Shayegan 2011, p. 170, n. 533.

32 See Shayegan 2011, p. 176, n. 552.

33 *Kwpdt* is related to Parthian *Kōfzāt* < **kaufa-zāta* "born to the mountain". The expected Old Persian form of *zan-/zā-* (< **ǰanH-/ǰn̥H-*) "give birth; procreate", namely, *dan-/dā-* had been hitherto only attested in the Elamite *Nebenüberlieferung*; other cognates of *zan-*, such as *°zana-* "people; race" (e.g., *vispa-zana-*; *paru-zana-*), are well attested in royal inscriptions.

34 For the text of (reproduced below), and commentary on, C2, see Naveh and Shaked 2012, p. 187–191:

Inside:

C2: 1 bšnt 1 wštʾsp krny ʾzgmʾ mn kwpdt npq qn

C2: 2 ʿl mrʾy wdywr qn 40

Outside:

C2: 3 kwpdt

Translation

Inside:

1: In the year 1. Vishtaspa Karanya. The disbursement from Kaufadāta: sheep came out

2: to my lord Vaidyura, 40 sheep.

Outside:

3: Kaufadāta.

35 Curt. 6.2.7.

36 Ibid.: "*Ergo interrogata quaenam esset, neptim se Ochi qui nuper regnasset in Persis filio eius genitam esse respondit, uxorem Hystaspis fuisse.*"

37 Arr. 3.19.4.

38 Curt. 6.2.7.

39 *Ibid.*

40 Arr. 7.6.5.

41 On Hystaspes, see also Shayegan 2007 [2012], p. 109.

42 Compare now Hyland 2013.

43 Naveh and Shaked 2012, p. 191: "The full name given here, **wštʾsp krny**, suggests that the Vishtaspa in question belongs to a family well known in later Iranian history, that of Kāren."

44 On this episode and more descriptions, see Shayegan 2011, p. 168–178. On the *fratrakā* and early rulers of Persis, see Wiesehöfer 1994; Wiesehöfer 1998, p. 36–37; Wiesehöfer 2007, p. 37–49; and Wiesehöfer 2011b, which proposes a late dating of the rulers of Persis, and following Hoover 2008, p. 213–215, offers a new sequencing of the *frataraka* rulers, to which we subscribe: Ardaxšahr, Wahbarz, Baydād, Wādfradād I, and Wādfradād II. For another recent study with a late dating (published prior to Hoover's novel sequencing), encompassing a thorough discussion of the archaeological, epigraphic and literary material, see Callieri 2007, p. 115–146. For an early dating, compare the excellent study of Sarkhosh Curtis 2010, p. 379–394, who synthesises the findings of Hoover 2008, and Klose and Müseler 2008. Also favouring

an early dating of the *fratarakā* are Hoover 2008, p. 213–215; Klose 2005, p. 93–103; and Klose and Müseler 2008, p. 11, 15; the works by Klose and Müseler that precede that of Hoover still subscribe to the traditional regnal sequence. See also Panaino 2003, p. 265–268. On the titulary of the *fratarakā* and their successors in Persis, the *Dāryānids*, see Shayegan 2005 [2009], p. 169–171.

45 See Alram 1987, p. 154; and most recently *apud* Wiesehöfer 2013, p. 723.

46 See Alram 1987, p. 147, 150; Bivar 1998, p. 39–40, figs. 25a/b and 26a/b; and Klose and Müseler 2008, p. 27, figs. 17 and 18.

47 See Shayegan 2011, p. 170.

48 Polyaen. 7.40.

49 See Wiesehöfer 1994, p. 110; Wisehöfer 2007, p. 39; Callieri 2007, p. 117; and Wiesehöfer 2011b, p. 113–114.

50 See Sellwood 1980, types 1–2; Alram 1986, 122–123; Sarkhosh Curtis 2007, 8; see also Weber 2010, 634–635.

51 Compare more recently Sinisi 2012, p. 280, who erroneously states the Middle Iranian term *kāren* written in Aramaic script was "the Aramaic equivalent of *autokrator*"; and Rezakhani 2013, p. 767. See also Weber 2010, p. 634–635.

52 See still Meillet 1911, p. 109–112: "On est donc conduit à se demander si les Parthes de l'époque arsacide n'auraient pas calqué sur le grec [αὐτοκράτωρ] un mot nouveau"; also Shayegan 1998, p. 32.

53 On the use of αὐτοκράτωρ among the Seleucids, a case in point is the usurper commander Tryphon, who systematically used the title (βασιλέως Τρύφονος αὐτοκράτορος) on his coins from Antioch and Phoenicia; see de Callataÿ and Lorber 2011, p. 425.

54 Compare recently Olbrycht 2011, p. 229–231, and 240.

55 For the use of the proper name *kāren* on the Nisa Ostraca, see Schmitt 1998, p. 187, no. 30. See also the use of *kāren* in Sasanian inscriptions, such as *Pērōz Kāren* (ŠKZ, Pth., 23); *Gōk Kāren* (ŠKZ, Pth., 24); *Ardaxšahr Kāren* (ŠKZ, Pth., 26), that is, "Pērōz (from the house of) Kāren," "Gōk (from the house of) Kāren," and "Ardaxšahr (from the house of) Kāren."

56 On the importance of the Iranian element in the Commagenian syncretism, as the end-point of an evolutionary process, whose beginnings suggest Antiochos I's cultic conception to have been solidly anchored in Greek conceptions – attested by Antiochos I's stele (and inscription) at Sofraz Köy depicting him solely with Apollo Epēkoos; over syncretic forms at the τέμενος sites of Zeugma and Samosata, where Zeus-Oromasdēs and Mithra-Helios-Apollo-Hermes are attested (at Zeugma, Apollo is depicted in the Greek fashion, nude; Crowther and Facella 2003, p. 65; Crowther 2003, p. 66), as well as at the ἱεροθέσιον of Arsameia on the Nymphaios, where we encounter the amalgamated Mithra-Helios-Apollo-Hermes shown in Iranian accoutrement; to the fully evolved syncretism of Nemrud Dağı – see Jacobs 2002a; also Crowther and Facella 2003, p. 62–65; compare also Messerschmidt 2011, p. 296–304; in particular, 302–304, who, while conceding to the presence of the Iranian element in the Commagenian cult, is intent on de-emphasising it, and argues for a reevaluation of the pre-Persian "autochthonous" cultic forms of the region(s), such as the Hittite, as sources of inspiration for Antiochos I: "Die Versuche, an existierende Kulte anzuknüpfen, werfen die Frage auf, ob nicht vorgriechische wie nichtiranische Traditionen, die in der religiösen Vorstellungswelt des südostanatolischen Raumes verwurzelt sind, bei der Konzipierung der kommagenischen Herrschervergöttlichung und Ahnenverehrung eine wesentlich größere Rolle spielten als lange Zeit angenommen wurde." Similarly, see Crowther and Facella 2003, p. 65; for other regional cults in the Commagene, see Schütte-Maischatz 2003. For Hittite parallels, still Börker-Klähn, especially 56–357. Arguing for the impact of Iranian traditions, among others by contrasting the tenor of Old Persian epigraphy with that of Commagenian inscriptions, see still Petroff 1998; and more recently the excellent pages of Panaino 2007.

57 On the *nomos* inscription at Nemrud Dağı, see Dörner and Young 1996, p. 207–217; on the remains of the *nomos* text from the temenos site at Samosata, see Crowther and Facella 2011; and Crowther and Facella 2003, p. 68–70; for the inscriptions of the *temenē* at Zeugma and Sofraz Köy, see Crowther and Facella 2003, p. 44–61, and 71–74; and Crowther 2003 (Zeugma); for the temenos site at Ancoz, see Wagner and Petzl 2003.

58 On the Commagenian ruler cult, and the distribution of the *hierothesia* (ἱεροθέσια) and *temenē* (τεμένη), see Wagner 2012, especially p. 46–47; and Wagner 1983; on Antiochos I's religious policy, and his binary (Greek/Persian) syncretistic religious system being not only a response to the particular power constellation, which followed upon the new order established by Pompey in the East – with Armenia reduced to a Roman vassal state, and Commagene entangled between the Arsacid and Roman empires – but also as a means to introduce equilibrium into the relations of Macedonian and Persian constituencies in Commagene itself, see Jacobs 2012b, especially p. 107: "Vielmehr dürfte der 'östlischer' Bezug, der … an Bedeutung gewann … innenpolitische Gründe gehabt haben. Anlass mag insbesondere ein Konkurrenzverhältnis innerhalb der kommagenischen Gesellschaft zwischen alteingesessener Oberschicht und den Nachkommen der makedonischen Eroberer gewesen sein, dem durch ein einseitig griechisch geprägtes Repräsentationsprogramm eher eine Verschärfung drohte." Also Mittag 2011, especially p. 150–160, whose exciting and careful analysis of the terminology used of honours for the gods, ancestors, and Antiochos I shows the limits of Antiochos I's dynastic cult: although these honours introduced the ruler into the sphere of the divine as a privileged interlocutor and partner of the gods, they still refrained from equating him with the divine essence. In this, the Commagenian cult, although indebted to Hellenistic precedents, nonetheless distinguishes itself from them, mainly in its reluctance to cross over wholly into the divine sphere. In this one might be tempted to recognise the sway of the Iranian element: "Deutlich wird, dass die Vorfahren immer stärker in die göttliche Sphäre gerückt werden und dass der König selbst eine größere Nähe zu den Göttern sucht, aber zu keinem Zeitpunkt selbst zum Gott wird. Beide Entwicklungen stehen in der Tradition hellenistischer Herrscher- und Dynastiekulte … Im religiösen Kern bleiben sie aber letztlich bis zum Schluss iranisch-persische Vorstellungen"; Mittag 2011, p. 160.

59 On Nemrud Dağı, its topography, review of the

Forschungsgeschichte, survey of past excavations, architecture, sculptures and epigraphic remains, see Sanders 1996; also Jacobs 2012a; Facella 2006, p. 261–270.

60 For a succinct review of the construction policy of Antiochos I (and Mithradates II), see Jacobs 2012a, p. 77–86; also Jacobs 2003, especially p. 120, who argues that Antiochos might have striven to lend a cultural identity to the nascent Commagenian polity on the Euphrates with the help of monumental sculptures within a region, where such tradition has been indigenous, and hence a predisposition for its receptivity was present.

61 For a discussion of (the epigraphic evidence on) the *Ahnengalerie* at Nemrud Dağı, see Messerschmidt 2012, p. 87–98; Facella 2006, p. 270–279; Facella 2009, p. 379–392; Dörner and Young 1996, p. 254–355; Dörner 1996, p. 361–377; Jacobs 2002b, especially p. 83–85, and 87, where the author rightly suggests that the *Ahnengalerie* was not originally part of Nemrud Dağı's holistic composition, but would acquire in time, in particular as it eventually encompassed contemporaneous family members, a more pronounced biographical dimension: "Im Verlauf der Arbeiten am Heiligtum rückte der gleichsam biographische Charakter des Programms deutlicher in den Vordergrund. Das ursprüngliche Vorhaben, die Vorfahren abzubilden, wurde dahingehend abgewandelt, daß Antiochos Verwandte und schließlich sogar lebende Familienangehörige abbilden ließ." On the women in the *Ahnengalerie*, especially on the maternal side, see Jacobs 2000, p. 297–306.

62 On this Orontes (I), see Facella 2006, 95–135; Facella 2009, 388–389; Dörner and Young 1996, 261–263; Dörner 1996, 364–366.

63 This Orontes (II) was a Persian nobleman who along with Mithraustes led the Armenian contingent at Gaugamela (Arr. 3.8.5), attached to the right wing (Arr. 3.11.7). Whether he is the same Orontes who held the satrapy of Armenia (and was a friend of Peukestes, satrap of Persis), and whom Diodorus mentions (ἡ δ᾽ ἐπιστολὴ … ἀπέσταλτο παρὰ Ὀρόντου τοῦ σατραπείαν μὲν ἔχοντος Ἀρμενίας φίλου δὲ ὄντος Πευκέστῃ "a letter … was sent by Orontes, who held the satrapy of Armenia, and was a friend of Peukestes"; D.S. 19.23.3; see also Polyaen. 4.8.3) remains uncertain. See Messerschmidt 2012, p. 91, who seems to identify this Orontes [II] with the one ruling over the Armenian satrapy in the aftermath of Alexander's demise: "Nach der Niederlage des Dareios konnte sich Orontes in Armenian behaupten … 317 v. Chr. wird er als Satrap – nicht König – von Armenien und freund des Peukestas … erwähnt." Undecided Facella 2006, p. 139: "Se si vuole infatti identificare questo Orontes con quello di Gaugamela, è necessario presupporre o che Orontes II sia figlio di Orontes I … oppure che Orotes II fosse nipote del satrapo." Strabo (Str. 11.531) also knows of a certain Orontes, the descendant of Hydarnes, one of the Seven (Ὀρόντης ἀπόγονος Ὑδάρνου τῶν ἑπτὰ Περσῶν ἑνός), identical with the Herodotean Intaphernes (Her. 3.70–71), in Armenia. This evidence taken together with the account of his command over the Armenian contingent at Gaugamela may support the hypothesis of him having been the satrap of Armenia.

64 Dörner and Young 1996, p. 294. Also Facella 2006, p. 95–96; and Facella 2009, p. 388.

65 Dörner and Young 1996, p. 261. Also Facella 2006, p. 96; and Facella 2009, p. 388.

66 For an excellent discussion of the evolving meaning of Φιλορώμαιος καὶ Φιλέλλην during the reigns of Antiochos I and Antiochos IV, as well as the reality of these conceptions in light of changing political exigencies, see Facella 2005, p. 87–103; also Facella 2010, especially p. 182–186.

67 See above, p. 11.

68 See Sachs and Hunger 1988, I, no. **–384** lower edge 1? (70–71); no. **–382** right edge 1–2 (76–77); no. **–381** A upper edge 1? (80–81).

69 See Hunger and van der Spek 2006, no. **–362** obv. 1, rev. 9' (= 3–7). This particular diary, recently dated by the authors to 29.xi.–28.xii.363 BCE (month ix of year 42 of Arses), was not originally included by Hunger in the edition of the *Astronomical Diaries*. On the names Arsaces and Arses, see Schmitt 2011, nos. 50 and 53.

70 See already Facella 2009, p. 387, n. 33.

71 Shayegan 2011, p. 291–292.

72 Compare Facella 2009, p. 386–387: "The possibility that Babylonian tradition was reflected in shaping the succession line of Antiochus' Achaemenid ancestors is not so remote, when considering the influence Babylonian culture might have had on the astronomical astrologers and in general intellectuals of the Commagenian royal court."

73 See Dörner and Young 1996, 208, N 28–31.

74 See also the severely damaged inscription dedicated to Xerxes (Dörner and Young 1996, p. 285; also Facella 2006, p. 88–89):

[βασ]ιλεὺς μέγα[ς Ἀ]ντίοχος
[Θεὸς] Δίκαιος Ἐ[πιφα]νής
[Φιλ]ορώμαιος κ[αὶ Φι]λέλλην
[ὁ ἐγ βα]σιλέως [Μιθ]ραδάτου
[Καλλ]ινίκου καὶ [βα]σιλίσ[σ]ης
[Λαοδ]ίκης Θε[ᾶς Φιλαδέλφ]ου
[βασιλ]έ[α] β[ασιλέων μέ]γα[ν]
[Ξέρξην τὸν ἐγ βασιλέως]
[βασιλέων μέγάλου Δαρείου]

75 Dörner and Young 1996, 282; also Facella 2006, 87.

76 Dörner and Young 1996, 323.

77 For a discussion on how to translate Alexander's title: [βα]σιλέ[α] μέγα[ν Ἀλέ]ξανδρον τὸν, namely as "the Great King Alexander," or "King, the Great Alexander," see Dörner and Young 1996, p. 324–325.

78 See already Panitschek 1987, p. 81.

79 On more recent interpretations of Cyrus' Anšanite lineage, resulting from Elamite and Persian acculturation, in contrast to Dareios I's Achaemenid house, see the excellent articles of Waters 2004; Potts 2005; Henkelman 2011.

80 See also Panitschek 1987, p. 80.

81 It is worthwhile mentioning that according to Diodorus (31.19.1), Cappadocian rulers also seem to have derived their ancestry from the Seven and indirectly also from Cyrus – Ὅτι λέγουσιν ἑαυτοὺς οἱ τῆς Καππαδοκίας βασιλεῖς εἰς Κῦρον ἀναφέρειν τὸ γένος τὸν ἐν Πέρσαις διαβεβαιοῦνται δὲ καὶ τῶν ἑπτα Περσῶν τῶν τὸν μάγον ἐπανελομένων ἑνὸς

ὑπάρχειν ἀπόγονοι "the kings of Cappadocia say that they take their ancestry back to Cyrus, and also maintain strongly that they are descendants of the seven Persians who took on the magus" – but, intriguingly their desire for anteriority to legitimise their rule in Cappadocia reaches back to the time preceding Cyrus and the Persian empire, for as Diodorus further recounts Cappadocians claim to be from the seed of Cyrus's aunt, Atossa, daughter of Cambyses, father of Cyrus the Great. Thus, although this genealogical construct provides indubitable anteriority, by bypassing and transcending the founder of the Persian empire, it fails to claim Cyrus as a direct ancestor.

82 App. *Mith.* 9.

83 *Ibid.*

84 Plb. 5.43.1–4.

85 D.S. 19.40.2.

86 App. *Mith.* 112.

87 See Panitschek 1987, p. 78: "Die überwiegende Mehrzahl der Pontos betreffenden Quellen berichtet von einem engen Zusammenhang zwischen der Beseitigung des 'falschen Smerdis' durch die Sieben Perser und der Einsetzung des Ahns der Dynastie."

Bibliography

Alram, M. (1987). "Eine neue Drachme des Vahbarz (Oborzos) aus des Persis (?)", *Litterae Numismaticae Vindobonensis* 3: p. 147–155.

——— (1986). *Nomina propria iranica in nummis: Materialgrundlagen zu den iranischen Personennamen auf antiken Münzen,* 2 vols (I, text; II, plates), Iranisches Personennamenbuch IV, Vienna.

Ballesteros, P.L. (2011). "*Xerxes redivivus.* Mitrídates, rey de Oriente frente a Grecia", in J.M. Cortés, E. Muñiz, R.C. Hervás (eds), *Grecia ante los Imperios: Actas de la V Reunión de Historiadores del Mundo Griego Antiguo*, Spal Monografías 15, Seville: p. 253–262.

Bevan, E.R. (1902). *The House of Seleucus,* (2 vols), vol. I, London.

Bivar, A.D.H. (1998). *The Personalities of Mithra in Archeology and Literature*, Biennial Yarshater Lecture Series, University of California, Los Angeles (December 5–9, 1994), No. 1, New York.

Börker-Klähn, J. (1994). "Ahnengalerie und letzte Dienste derer von Hattuša", in H. Gasche (ed.), *Cinquante-deux reflexions sur le Proche-Orient ancien: Offertes en hommage à Léon De Meyer,* Mesopotamian History and Environment, Occasional Publications 2, Leuven: p. 355–367.

Briant, P. (1996). *L'histoire de l'empire perse: de Cyrus à Alexandre,* Paris.

——— (2003). *Darius dans l'ombre d'Alexandre*, Paris.

Callataÿ, F. de, and Lorber, C.C. (2011). "The Pattern of Royal Epithets on Hellenistic Coinages", in P.P. Iossif, A.S. Chankowski, C.C. Lorber (eds), *More than Men, Less than Gods: Studies on Royal Cult and Imperial Worship: Proceedings of the International Colloquium Organized by the Belgian School at Athens (November 1–2, 2007)*, Studia Hellenistica 51, Leuven, Paris and Walpole, MA: p. 417–455.

Callieri, P. (2007). *L'Archéologie du Fārs à l'époque hellénistique: Quatre leçons au Collège de France 8, 15, 22 et 29 mars* 2007, P. Briant (ed.), Persika 11, Paris.

Crowther, C. (2003a). "Inscriptions of Antiochos I of Commagene and other Epigraphical Finds", in R. Early (ed.), *Zeugma: Interim Reports,* J. H. Humphrey (ser. ed.), Journal of Roman Archaeology Supplementary Series 51, Portsmouth, Rhode Island: p. 57–68.

Crowther, C., and Facella, M. (2003b). "New Evidence for the Ruler Cult of Antiochos of Commagene from Zeugma", in G. Heedemann, E. Winter (eds), *Neue Forschungen zur Religionsgeschichte Kleinasiens: Elmar Schwertheim zum 60. Geburtstag gewidmet,* Asia Minor Studien 49, Bonn: p. 41–80.

——— (2011). "A New Commagenian *Nomos* Text from Samosata", in E. Winter (ed.), *Von Kummuḫ nach Telouch: Historische und archäologische Untersuchungen in Kommagene,* Asia Minor Studien 64, Dolicher und Kommagenische Forschungen IV, Bonn: p. 355–366.

——— (2012). "Die Heiligtümer des Antiochos I. im Spiegel neuer epigraphischer Funde", in J. Wagner (ed.), *Gottkönige am Euphrat: Neue Ausgrabungen und Forschungen in Kommagene*, Darmstadt and Mainz am Rhein: p. 71–76.

Curtis, V.S. (2007). "The Parthian Revival in the Parthian Period", in V.S. Curtis, S. Stewart (eds), *The Age of the Parthians*, *The Idea of Iran, Vol. II*, London: p. 7–25.

——— (2010). "The Frataraka Coins of Persis: Bridging the Gap between Achaemenid and Sasanian Persia", in J. Curtis, St J. Simpson (eds), *The World of Achaemenid Persia: History, Art and Society in Iran and the Ancient Near East: Proceedings of a Conference at the British Museum 29th September – 1st October 2005,* London: p. 379–394.

——— (2012). "Parthian Coins: Kingship and Divine Glory", in P. Wick, M. Zehnder (eds), *The Parthian Empire and its Religions: Studies in the Dynamics of Religious Diversity. Das Partherreich und seine Religionen: Studien zu Dynamiken religiöser Pluralität,* Pietas 5, A. Gutsfeld, P. Villard (ser. eds), Gutenberg: p. 68–81.

Dąbrowa, E. (1983). *La politique de l'État parthe à l'égard de Rome — d'Artaban II à Vologèse I (ca 11 - ca 79 de n.è.) et les facteurs qui la conditionnaient,* Rozprawy Habilitacyne 74, Krakow.

—(2012a). "The Arsacid Empire", in T. Daryaee (ed.), *The Oxford Handbook of Iranian History,* New York: p. 164–186.

——— (2012b). "The Arsacids and their State", in R. Rollinger, G. Schwinghammer, B. Truschnegg, K. Schnegg (eds), *Altertum und Gegenwart: 125 Jahre Alte Geschichte in Innsbruck: Vorträge der Ringvorlesung,* Innsbrucker Beiträge zur Kulturwissenschaft, Neue Folge 4. Innsbruck: p. 21–52.

Dörner, F.K. (1996). "Epigraphy Analysis", in D.H. Sanders (ed.), *Nemrud Dağı*: The Hierothesion of Antiochus I. of Commagene: Results of the American Excavations Directed by Theresa B. Goell, 2 vols, Vol. I: Text, Winona Lake, Ind.: p. 361–377.

Dörner, F.K., and Naumann, R. (1939). *Forschungen in Kommagene*. Istanbuler Forschungen 10, Berlin.

Dörner, F.K., and Young, J.H. (1996). "Sculpture and Inscription Catalogue", in D.H. Sanders (ed.), *Nemrud Dağı*: The Hierothesion of Antiochus I. of Commagene: Results of the American *Excavations Directed by Theresa B. Goell,* 2 vols, Vol. I: *Text*. Winona Lake, Ind.: p. 175–360.

Facella, M. (2005). "Φιλορώμαιος καὶ Φιλέλλην: Roman Perception of Commagenian Royalty", in O. Hekster, R. Fowler (eds), *Imagining Kings: From Persia to Rome,* Oriens et Occidens: Studien zu antiken Kulturkontakten und ihrem Nachleben, Band 11, P. Briant, A. Kuhrt, F. Millar, R. Rollinger (ser. eds), Stuttgart: p. 87–103.

Facella, M. (2006). *La dinastia degli Orontidi nella Commagene ellenistico-romana,* B. Virgilio (ed.), Studi Ellenistici XVII, Pisa.

——— (2009). "Darius and the Achaemenids in Commagene", in P. Briant, M. Chauveau (eds), *Organisation des pouvoirs et contacts culturels dans les pays de l'empire achéménide: Actes du colloque organisé au Collège de France par la 'Chaire d'histoire et civilisation du monde achéménide et de l'empire d'Alexandre' et le 'Reseau international d'études et de recherches achéménides' (GDR 2538 CNRS), 9–10 novembre 2007,* Persika 14, Paris: p. 379–414.

——— (2010). "Advantages and Disadvantages of an Allied Kingdom: The Case of Commagene", in T. Kaizer, M. Facella (eds), *Kingdoms and Principalities in the Roman Near East,* Oriens et Occidens 19, Stuttgart: p. 181–198.

Fowler, R. (2005). "Most Fortunate Roots: Tradition and Legitimacy in Parthian Royal Ideology", in O. Hekster, R. Fowler, *Imaginary Kings: Royal Images in the Ancient Near East, Greece and Rome,* Oriens et Occidens: Studien zu antiken Kulturkontakten und ihrem Nachleben, Band 11, P. Briant, A. Kuhrt, F. Millar, R. Rollinger (ser. eds), Stuttgart: p. 125–218.

Frye, R.N. (1985). "Two Iranian Notes", in *Papers in Honour of Prof. M. Boyce,* 2 vols. Vol. I, Acta Iranica 24, Hommages et Opera Minora X, Leiden: p. 185–190.

Gariboldi, A. (2007). "Antioco I di Commagene sulle monete", in T. Gnoli, F. Muccioli (eds), *Incontri tra culture nell'oriente Ellenistico e Romano: Ravenna 11–12 marzo 2005,* Milan: p. 133–138.

Haebler, C. (1982). "καράνος: Eine sprachwissenschaftliche Betrachtung zu Xen. Hell. I 4, 3", in J. Tischler (ed.), *Serta Indogermanica: Festschrift für Günter Neumann zum 60. Geburtstag,* Innsbrucker Beiträge zur Sprachwissenschaft 40, Innsbruck: p. 81–90.

Henkelman, W.F.M. (2011). "Cyrus the Persian and Darius the Elamite: A Case of Mistaken Identity", in R. Rollinger, B. Truschnegg, R. Bichler (eds), *Herodot und das persische Reich / Herodotus and the Persian Empire: Akten des 3. Internationalen Kolloquiums zum Thema 'Vorderasien im Spannungsfeld klassischer und altorientalischer Überlieferungen, Innsbruck 24.–28. November 2008,* Classica et Orientalia 3, R. Bichler, B. Jacobs, G.B. Lanfranchi, R. Rollinger et al. (ser. eds.), Wiesbaden: p. 577–634.

Henry, R. (1959). *Photius Bibliothèque*, Vol. I: *Codices 1–84*, Collection Byzantine, Paris.

Hoover, O.D. (2008). "Overstruck Seleucid Coins", in A. Houghton, C. Lorber, O. Hoover, *Seleucid Coins: A Comprehensive Catalogue: Part 2: Seleucus IV through Antiochus XIII*, 2 vols: Vol. II, New York, Lancaster, PA, and London: p. 209–217.

Hunger, H., and van der Spek, R.J. (2006). "An Astronomical Diary Concerning Artaxerxes II (Year 42 = 363–2 BC): Military Operations in Babylonia", *Arta* 1–16 (note 2).

Hyland, J. (2013). "Vishtaspa *krny*: An Achaemenid Military Official in 4th-Century Bactria", *Arta* 1–7 (note 2).

Jacobs, B. (2000). "Die Reliefs der Vorfahren des Antiochos I. von Kommagene auf dem Nemrud Dağı: Versuch einer Neubennenung der Frauendarstellung in den mütterlichen Ahnenreihen", *Istanbuler Mitteilungen* 50: p. 297–306.

——— (2002a). "Bergheiligtum und heiliger Berg: Überlegungen zur Wahl des Nemrud Dağı-Gipfels als Heiligtum und Grabstätte", in J. Hahn, C. Ronning (eds), *Religiöse Landschaften*, Alter Orient und Altes Testament 301, Veröffentlichungen des Arbeitskreises zur Erforschung der Religions- und Kulturgeschichte des Antiken Vorderen Orients (AZERKAVO) 4, Münster: p. 31–47.

——— (2002b). "Die Galerien der Ahnen des Königs I. von Kommagene auf dem Nemrud Dağı", in J.M. Højte (ed.), *Images of Ancestors*, Aarhus: p. 76–88.

——— (2003). "Überlegungen zu Ursachen und Gründen für die Konzeption von Heiligtumsausstattungen in der späthellenistischen Kommagene", in K.S. Freyberger, A. Henning, H. von Hesberg (eds), *Kulturkonflikte im Vorderen Orient an der Wende vom Hellenismus zur römischen Kaiserzeit,* Orient-Archäologie 11, Rahden: p. 117–124.

——— (2012a). "Das Heiligtum auf dem Nemrud Dağı: Zur Baupolitik des Antiochos I. von Kommagene und seines Sohnes Mithradates II", in J. Wagner (ed.), *Gottkönige am Euphrat: Neue Ausgrabungen und Forschungen in Kommagene,* Darmstadt and Mainz am Rhein: p. 77–86.

——— (2012b). "Die Religionspolitik des Antiochos I. von Kommagene", in J. Wagner (ed.), *Gottkönige am Euphrat: Neue Ausgrabungen und Forschungen in Kommagene,* Darmstadt and Mainz am Rhein: p. 99–108.

Khaleghi Motlagh, D. (ed.) (1997). *Abu'l Qasem Ferdowsi: The Shahnameh (The Book of Kings)*, 8 vols: Vol. V, Persian Text Series, n.s. 1–8, E. Yarshater (ser. ed.), New York.

Klose, D.O.A., and Müseler, W. (2008). *Statthalter, Rebellen, Könige: Die Münzen aus Persepolis von Alexander dem Großen zu den Sasaniden,* Munich.

Lerner, J.D. (1999). *The Impact of Seleucid Decline on the Eastern Iranian Plateau: The Foundations of Arsacid Parthia and Graeco-Bactria,* Historia Einzelschriften 123, Stuttgart.

McGing, B.C. (2009). "Mithridates VI Eupator: Victim or Aggressor?" in J.M. Højte (ed.), *Mithridates VI and the Pontic Kingdom*, Black Sea Studies 9, Aarhus: p. 203–216.

Messerschmidt, W. (2011). "Grabstelle eines Herrschers v on Kummuḫ: Zu den späthethitischen Wurzeln des kommagenischen Königs- und Ahnenkultes", in E. Winter (ed.), *Von Kummuḫ nach Telouch: Historische und archäologische Untersuchungen in Kommagene,* Asia Minor Studien 64, Dolicher und Kommagenische Forschungen IV, Bonn: p. 283–307.

——— (2012). "Zwischen Tradition und Innovation: Die Ahnengalerie des Antiochos I. von Kommagene", in J. Wagner (ed.), *Gottkönige am Euphrat: Neue Ausgrabungen und Forschungen in Kommagene,* Darmstadt and Mainz am Rhein: p. 87–98.

Metzler, D. (2012). "Kommagene von Osten her gesehen", in J. Wagner (ed.), *Gottkönige am Euphrat: Neue Ausgrabungen und Forschungen in Kommagene,* Darmstadt and Mainz am Rhein: p. 109–116.

Mittag, P.F. (2012). "Zur Entwicklung des 'Herrscher-' und 'Dynastiekultes' in Kommagene", in L.-M. Günther, S. Plischke (eds), *Studien zum vorhellenistischen und hellenistischen*

Herrscherkult, Oikumene: Studien zur antiken Weltgeschichte 9, Berlin: p. 141–160.

Mosshammer, A.A. (ed.) (1984). *Georgius Syncellus: Ecloga chronographica,* Bibliotheca Scriptorum Graecorum et Romanorum Teubneriana, Leipzig.

Olbrycht, M.J. (2009). "Mithridates VI Eupator and Iran", in J.M. Højte (ed.), *Mithridates VI and the Pontic Kingdom,* Black Sea Studies 9, Aarhus: p. 163–190.

——— (2011). "The Titulature of the First Arsacids and its Religious Connotations [Tytulatura pierwszych Arsakidów i jej polityczno-religijne konotacje]", in L. Mrozewicza, K. Balbuzy (eds), *The World of Antiquity, its Polish Researchers and the Cult of the Ruler,* Studia Europaea Gnesnensia, Seria Monografie, t. 4, L. Mrozewicz (ser. ed.), Poznań: p. 229–241.

Pakzad, F. (2005). *Bundahišn: Zoroastrische Kosmogonie und Kosmologie,* Vol. I: *Kritische Edition,* H.R. Baghbidi (ed.), Ancient Iranian Studies, Series 2, Tehran.

Panaino, A. (2003). "The Bayān of the Fratarakas: Gods or 'Divine' Kings?", in C.G. Cereti, M. Maggi, E. Provasi (eds), *Religious Themes and Texts of pre-Islamic Iran and Central Asia: Studies in Honour of Professor Khale Gnoli on the Occasion of his 65th Birthday on 6th December 2002,* Beiträge zur Iranistik 24, N. Sims-Williams (ser. ed.), Wiesbaden: p. 265–288.

——— (2007). "Τύχη e χαρακτήρ: del sovrano fra Iranismo ed Ellenismo nelle inscrizioni di Antiocio I di Commagene", in T. Gnoli, F. Muccioli (eds), *Incontri tra culture nell'oriente Ellenistico e Romano: Ravenna 11–12 marzo 2005,* Milan: p. 117–131.

Panitschek, P. (1987). "Zu den genealogischen Konstruktionen der Dynastien von Pontus und Kappadokien", *Revista Storica dell'Antichità* 17–18: p. 73–95.

——— (1990). "Zur Darstellung der Alexander- und Achaemenidennachfolge als politische Programme in kaiserzeitlichen Quellen", *Klio* 72: p. 457–492.

Petroff, P. (1998). "Die griechisch-persische Tradition in Kultordnung und Herrscherrepräsentation des Antiochos I. von Kommagene", in L. Schumacher (ed.), *Religion-Wirtschaft-Technik: Althistorische Beiträge zur Entstehung neuer kultureller Strukturmuster im historischen Raum Nordafrika / Kleinasien / Syrien,* Mainzer Althistorische Studien 1, St. Katharinen: p. 21–97.

Petzl, G. (2012). "Die Königsinschriften von Kommagene", in J. Wagner (ed.), *Gottkönige am Euphrat: Neue Ausgrabungen und Forschungen in Kommagene,* Darmstadt and Mainz am Rhein: p. 61–70.

Potts, D.T. (2005). "Cyrus the Great and the Kingdom of Anshan", in V.S. Curtis, S. Stewart (eds), *Birth of the Persian Empire, The Idea of Iran,* vol. I, London: p. 7–28.

Primo, A. (2010). "The Client Kingdom of Pontus between Mithridatism and Philoromanism", in T. Kaizer, M. Facella (eds), *Kingdoms and Principalities in the Roman Near East,* Oriens et Occidens 19, J. Wiesehöfer (ser. ed.), Stuttgart: p. 159–179.

Rezakhani, K. (2013). "Arsacid, Elymaean and Persid Coinage", in D.T. Potts (ed.), *The Oxford Handbook of Ancient Iran,* New York: p. 766–777.

Rix, H. (1985). Review of: *Serta Indogermanica: Festschrift für Günter Neumann zum 60. Geburtstag,* J. Tischler (ed.) (1982), Innsbrucker Beiträge zur Sprachwissenschaft, Band 40, Innsbruck, in *Kratylos* 30: p. 69–78.

Sachs, A.J., and Hunger, H. (1988). *Astronomical Diaries and Related Texts from Babylonia,* 6 vols: Vol. I: *Diaries from 652 BC to 262 BC* (1988), Österreichische Akademie der Wissenschaften, phil-hist. Klasse, Denkschriften, Band 195, Vienna.

Sanders, D.H. (ed.) (1996). *Nemrud Dağı*: The Hierothesion of Antiochus I of Commagene: Results of the American Excavations Directed by Theresa B. Goell, 2 vols (Vol. I: Text; vol. II: Illustrations), Winona Lake, Ind.

Schmitt, R. (2002). *Die iranischen und Iranier-Namen in den Schriften Xenophons (Iranica Graeca Vetustiora. II),* H. Eichner, R. Schmitt (eds), Österreichische Akademie der Wissenschaften, phil-hist. Klasse, Sitzungsberichte, Band 692 — Österreichische Akademie der Wissenschaften, Veröffentlichungen der Iranischen Kommission 29, Vienna.

——— (2011). *Iranische Personennamen in der griechischen Literatur vor Alexander d. Gr.* Vol. V: *Iranische Namen in der Nebenüberlieferungen indogermanischer Sprachen,* Faszikel 5A, R. Schmitt, H. Eichner, B.G. Fragner, Velizar Sadovski (eds), *Iranisches Personennamenbuch – Iranische Onomastik* 9, Vienna.

Schütte-Maischatz, A. (2003). "Götter und Kulte Kommagenes: Religionsgeographische Aspekte einer antiken Landschaft", in E. Schwertheim, E. Winter (eds), *Religion und Region: Götter und Kulte aus dem östlichen Mittelmeerraum,* Forschungsstelle Asia Minor im Seminar für Alte Geschichte der Westfälischen Wilhelms-Universität Münster, Asia Minor Studien 45, Bonn: p. 103–114.

Schwertheim, E. (2000). "Die Kommagene: Ein Königreich am Rande des Imperium Romanum: Zur Bedeutung des Nemrud Dag", in H.-P. Müller, F. Siegert (eds), *Antike Randgesellschaften und Randgruppen im östlichen Mittelmeerraum: Ringvorlesung an der Westfälischen Wilhelms-Universität Münster,* Münsteraner Judaistische Studien, Wissenschaftliche Beiträge zur christlich-jüdischen Begegnung, Band 5, Münster: p. 75–86.

Sellwood, D.G. (1980, 2nd ed.). *An Introduction to the Coinage of Parthia,* London.

Shayegan, M.R. (1998). "The Evolution of the Concept of *xwadāy* in Middle Persian", *Acta Orientalia Academiae Scientiarum Hungaricae* 51, no. 1–2: p. 31–54.

——— (2004 [2008]). "On the Rationale behind the Roman Wars of Šābuhr II the Great", *Bulletin of the Asia Institute* 18: p. 111–133.

——— (2005 [2009]). "Nugae epigraphicae", in C.A. Bromberg, N. Sims-Williams, U. Sims-Williams, *Iranian and Zoroastrian Studies in Honor of Prods Oktor Skjærvø, Bulletin of the Asia Institute* 19, Bloomfield Hills, MI: p. 169–179.

——— (2007 [2012]). "Prosopographical Notes: The Iranian Nobility during and after the Macedonian Conquest", *Bulletin of the Asia Institute* 21: p. 97–126.

——— (2011). *Arsacids and Sasanians: Political Ideology in Post-Hellenistic and Late Antique Persia,* Cambridge.

——— (2012). *Aspects of History and Epic in Ancient Iran: From Gaumāta to Wahnām,* Gregory Nagy (ed.), Hellenic Studies Series 52, Washington, DC, and Cambridge, Mass.

Sinisi, F. (2012). "The Coinage of the Parthians", in W.E. Metcalf (ed.), *The Oxford Handbook of Greek and Roman Coinage,* New York: p. 275–294.

Wagner, J. (1983). "Dynastie und Herrscherkult in Kommagene: Forschungsgeschichte und neuere Funde", *Istanbuler Mitteilungen* 33: p. 177–224.

——— (2012). "Die Könige von Kommagene und ihr Herrscherkult", in J. Wagner (ed.), *Gottkönige am Euphrat: Neue Ausgrabungen und Forschungen in Kommagene,* Darmstadt and Mainz am Rhein: p. 43–60.

Waldmann, H. (1973). *Die kommagenischen Kulturreformen unter König Mithradates I. Kallinikos und seinem Sohne Antiochos I.,* M.J. Vermaseren (ed.), Études préliminaires aux religions orientales dans l'empire romain 34, Leiden.

——— (1991). *Der kommagenische Mazdaismus,* Deutsches Archäologisches Institut – Istanbuler Mitteilungen 37, Tübingen.

Waters, M.W. (2004). "Cyrus and the Achaemenids", *Iran* 42: p. 91–102.

Weber, Dieter (2010). "Iranica auf arsakidischen Münzen", in U. Hackl, B. Jacobs, D. Weber (eds), *Quellen zur Geschichte des Partherreiches: Textsammlung mit Übersetzungen und Kommentaren.* Vol. II: *Griechische und lateinische Texte, Parthische Texte, Numismatische Evidenz*, Novum Testamentum et Orbis Antiquus / Studien zur Umwelt des Neuen Testaments 84, Göttingen: p. 633–639.

Wiesehöfer, J. (1994). Die "dunkelen Jahrhunderte" der Persis: Untersuchungen zu Geschichte und Kultur von Fārs in frühhellenistischer Zeit (330–140 v. Chr.), Zatemata: Monographien zur Klassischen Altertumswissenschaft 90, Munich.

——— (1998). "Discordia et Defectio - Dynamis kai Pithanourgia: Die frühen Seleukiden und Iran", in B. Funck (ed.), *Hellenismus: Beiträge zur Erforschung von Akkulturation und politischer Ordnung in den Staaten des hellenistischen Zeitalters: Akten des Internationalen Hellenismus-Kolloquiums 9.—14 März 1994 in Berlin,* Tübingen: p. 29–56.

——— J. (2005). *Iraniens, Grecs et Romains,* P. Huyse (ed.), Studia Iranica, Cahier 32, Paris.

——— (2007). "Fars under Seleucid and Parthian Rule", in V.S. Curtis, S. Stewart, *The Age of the Parthians, The Idea of Iran*, vol. II, London and New York: p. 37–49.

——— (2011a). "The 'Accursed' and the 'Adventurer': Alexander the Great in Iranian Tradition", in Z.D. Zuwiya (ed.), *A Companion to Alexander in the Middle Ages,* Brill's *Companions to the Christian Tradition*, vol. 29, Leiden: p. 113–132.

——— (2011b). "Frataraka Rule in Seleucid Persis: A New Appraisal", in A. Erskine, L. Llewellyn-Jones, *Creating a Hellenistic World,* Swansea.

——— (2013). "Frataraka and Seleucids", in D.T. Potts (ed.), *The Oxford Handbook of Ancient Iran*, New York: p. 718–727.

Winter, E. (2008). "Stadt, Herrschaft und Territorium in der Kommagene: Siedlungs- und Polisstrukturen in hellenistisch-römischer Zeit", in E. Winter (ed.), *PATRIS PANTROFOS KOMMAGHNH: Neue Funde und Forschungen zwischen Taurus und Euphrat,* Asia Minor Studien 60, Bonn: p. 37–49.

Wolski, J. (1990a). "Alexandre le Grand et l'Iran: Contribution à l'histoire de l'époque séleucide at arsacide", in J. Harmatta (ed.), *From Alexander to Kül Tegin: Studies in Bactrian, Pahlavi, Sanskrit, Arabic, Aramaic, Armenian, Chinese, Türk, Greek, and Latin Sources for the History of Pre-Islamic Central Asia*, Budapest: p. 1–9.

——— (1990b). "Le titre de 'Roi des Rois' dans l'idéologie monarchique des Arsacides", in J. Harmatta (ed.), *From Alexander to Kül Tegin: Studies in Bactrian, Pahlavi, Sanskrit, Arabic, Aramaic, Armenian, Chinese, Türk, Greek, and Latin Sources for the History of Pre-Islamic Central Asia,* Budapest: p. 11–18.

——— (1991). "L'époque parthe entre l'hellénisme et l'iranisme", in P. Bernard, F. Grenet, *Histoire et cultes de l'Asie centrale préislamique: sources écrites et documents archéologiques: Actes du colloque international du CNRS (Paris, 22–28 novembre 1988)*, Paris: p. 49–55, pl. 1.

——— (1993). *L'empire des Arsacides,* Acta Iranica 32, Textes et Mémoires XVIII, Leuven.

3

Dynastic Connections in the Arsacid Empire and the Origins of the House of Sāsān

Marek Jan Olbrycht
University of Rzeszów

Sinatrucids versus Artabanids

In the history of later Parthia there were many branches of the Arsacids, descended from various kings and close relatives of kings who were high up in the hierarchy. The House of Arsaces was broad and ramified enough to be troubled by a multitude of internal conflicts. Moreover, the power of the Arsacids was dependent on great aristocratic clans.[1] The aim of this study is to analyse the causes and results of the conflicts between different branches of the Arsacids, especially between the scions of Sinatruces in the male line and the so-called Younger Arsacids stemming from Artabanus II (8/9–39/40 AD). These conflicts had important consequences for Arsacid history, including the emergence of the Indo-Parthian dynasty. I shall show that the rise of the House of Sāsān in Iran resulted mainly from internal Parthian struggles.

The predominant Arsacid branch on the Parthian throne in the first century BC (from 78/77 BC to 11/12 AD) was the line descended from Sinatruces, known as the Sinatrucids. This line ousted another group of Arsacids with a claim to power, the descendants of Mithradates II the Great (122–87 BC).[2] Sinatruces was eighty when he ascended the throne;[3] hence he must have been born around 158 BC, in the reign of Mithradates I (165–132 BC).[4] Presumably he was one of Mithradates I's sons. His accession created a singular situation, since it blocked the succession of the much younger line descended from Mithradates II. Thus it is not surprising that some Arsacid princes challenged the Sinatrucid claim to the throne and that pretenders like Tiridates I and Mithradates IV appeared, who tried to depose Phraates IV.[5] The anti-Sinatrucid opposition managed to depose Phraataces (Phraates V).[6]

The Sinatrucid line was marked by a strong parricidal and fratricidal inclination. Phraates III was murdered by his sons, Mithradates III and Orodes II. The latter, supported by the Sūrēn clan, murdered his brother, and then, following the Parthian victory at Carrhae (53 BC), had his ally Sūrēn executed. Then Orodes II was probably murdered by his son Phraates IV, who eliminated his numerous brothers to secure the throne.[7] Thus rivalry between sons to succeed their father the king was a common problem in Parthia in the first century BC and later on.

The assassination of Orodes II sparked a series of conflicts, inevitably leading to a change in the balance of power within Parthia itself. Orodes II's reign had been relatively stable, as evidenced by frequent Parthian engagement in offensive warfare against Rome from 51–38 BC. After the execution of Surenas (Sūrēn), Orodes II managed to neutralise the powerful Sūrēn clan, but there must have been a strong residual hostility left. The death of Pacorus, the heir to the throne, in 38 BC, shook Parthian affairs. It cannot be ruled out that the force behind the rapid rise to power of Phraates IV in 38–37 BC was the Sūrēn clan, which wanted to restore its former strength and influence and made use of the crisis of the monarchy. But Phraates IV's coronation was met with defiance by many of the Parthian clans and vassals.

In the reign of Phraates IV the conflict within the Parthian elite was already firmly established and in the opening decades of the first century AD led to the crystallisation of three main factions: the "legitimists" along with the Sūrēn and part of the Kārin clan, who supported the descendants of Phraates IV; the Median-Atropatenian faction; and the Dahian-Hyrcanian faction. The two latter groups were united for a time, rallying in their support of Artabanus II against the Phraatids.[8] In his domestic policy Phraates IV was extremely cruel to his relatives and made sudden dynastic changes, such as the appointment of Phraataces as his heir, which caused commotion in the Parthian empire.

His reign was ended by a *coup d'état* carried out by his son Phraataces (3/2 BC–4 AD) and his consort Musa. When there were no more descendants of Sinatruces left in Parthia itself following the deposition of Phraataces, the adherents of this line embarked on bringing back those Sinatrucids who were living in Rome. It was to this faction, which I call the Phraatids (in that it united the supporters of the House of Phraates IV), that the powerful clans of Kārin and Sūrēn belonged.

The aftermath of the struggle between Vonones I, the last Sinatrucid of any significance in western Parthia, and Artabanus II (8/9–39/40 AD), was to prove critical for the Imperium Parthicum. The fall of the Sinatrucid line, a branch of the Arsacid dynasty, marked an important caesura in the history of the Parthian empire. Artabanus II fought for the throne of Parthia against the descendants of Phraates IV in the male line: Vonones I, Phraates (VI) and Tiridates II.

Artabanus's reign marked the coming to power of a rival branch of the Arsacids, descended most probably from Mithradates II through the male line.[9] The Artabanids (8/9–51 AD) and the monarchs descended from Artabanus II's brother Vonones, conventionally known as the House of Vologases I or the Vologasids (51–226 AD), restored Parthia to the status of a great power. These two lines make up the Younger Arsacids.[10]

The fall of the Sinatrucids in Parthia and the rise to power of Artabanus II and his dynastic branch of the Arsacids led to a change in the balance of power in the Parthian empire. Meanwhile the Sinatrucids split off the eastern satrapies of Sakastan, Drangiana and Arachosia from the Younger Arsacid state and set up their own Indo-Parthian kingdom. Their ruling dynasty, named the Gondopharids after its founder, enjoyed the support of the Parthian Sūrēn clan and part of the Kārin clan.

Gondophares and the Indo-Parthian ruling house

In 19 AD when the Romans killed the Sinatrucid ruler Vonones I and revoked their support for the Sinatrucids,[11] the split in the Parthian ruling class became obvious. The death of Vonones meant the inevitable supremacy of Artabanus II in the Imperium Parthicum. At this time, around 20 AD, a certain Gondophares declared himself king in the eastern Parthian satrapies of the territory of Sakastan, Drangiana and Arachosia, what we now call Indo-Parthia. The concurrence of these events was probably not a coincidence. The dates of Gondophares' reign – *c.* 20–50 AD – have been established on the basis of the Takht-i Bahi inscription and references in the apocryphal *Acts of Thomas*.[12] We know of Gondophares chiefly from his coinage.[13] He availed himself of bombastic titles: "Great King of Kings" (ΒΑΣΙΛΕΥΣ ΒΑΣΙΛΕΩΝ ΜΕΓΑΣ), and "Autokrator" (ΑΥΤΟΚΡΑΤΩΡ), or "Self-appointed", an epithet applied to an individual who exercised absolute power, unrestrained by superiors.[14]

The coins of Gondophares that show him wearing a diadem allude overtly to western Arsacid issues. Their reverse presents the monarch seated on his throne with Nike crowning him. The title "Autokrator" and the figure of Nike imply that Gondophares must have proclaimed himself king in defiance of an enemy, and most probably one of the enemies in question was Artabanus II. The title "Great King of Kings" suggests that he saw himself as the equal of the Artabanids.

"Gondophares" passed into the title used by the rulers of Indo-Parthia, just like the honorific Arsaces in Parthia and Augustus in Rome. Similarly, the *tamga* became a dynastic mintmark on Gondopharid coinage.[15] This so-called Gondopharid symbol occurred on coins in the eastern marches of Parthia in the first century BC. It was used as a countermark on Parthian issues and their imitations in Bactria and perhaps in neighbouring areas. In particular, it occurs on the coins of Orodes II and Phraates IV.[16] Later on it appears on the Firuzabad relief of the Sasanian king Ardashir I, where it decorates the caparison of the horse of a prince accompanying Ardashir.[17]

There is a particular group of coins attributed to Gondophares, consisting of drachms of typical Arsacid format. On the obverse there appears a royal portrait with a high tiara, while the reverse depicts the ruler being crowned by Nike, and gives his name and titles. One of the legends reads: "Great King of Kings Hyndopherres, who is surnamed Sā[s]e"[18] (ΒΑΣΙΛΕΥΣ ΒΑΣΙΛΕΩΝ ΜΕΓΑΣ ΥΝΔΟΦΕΡΡΗΣ Ο ΕΠΟΝΟΜΑΖΟΜΕΝΟΣ ΣΑ[Σ]Η). The decipherment of the name Sāse, or Sāses, allows us to conclude that Gondophares' personal name was Sāses.[19] Among Gondophares' successors was a ruler called Sāses.[20] The Indo-Parthian name Sāses, attested as the surname of Gondophares, contains the same core element as the Parthian name Sāsān. In Sanskrit the genitive form is *Sasasa*, and the Greek legends offer ΣΑΣΟΥ.[21] Significantly, the last known Indo-Parthian ruler was Farn-Sāsān, son of Ādūr-Sāsān (see below).

We may draw some conclusions regarding the dynastic connections of the House of Gondophares on the grounds of the Gondophares-Sāses coins. The monarch's tiara depicted on them, which is decorated with stags and horns, copies the tiaras of Sinatruces and Phraates III (71/70–57 BC), the first kings of the Sinatrucid line.[22] No tiaras of this kind had appeared on Parthian coinage for nearly a hundred years until Vologases I (51–79 AD). This fact suggests that Gondophares and his scions, by referring to Sinatruces and his son, were highlighting their origins and their royal claims.

A substantial role in the rise of Indo-Parthia must have been played by the Sūrēn clan, whose principal lands lay in Sakastan.[23] This clan, a staunch supporter of the Sinatrucids against Artabanus II in the west, came out in favour of Gondophares after Vonones I's disaster. Perhaps this development neither happened overnight, nor was immediately flaunted. Nonetheless when Artabanus II crushed a rebellion of the Sūrēn leader Abdagases in 36 AD (see Tac. *Ann.* 6.31, 36–37, 42–44),[24] the clan's hitherto privileged position in western Parthia must have declined. The name Abdagases is not recorded anywhere else in the history of Iran except for two Indo-Parthian rulers (Abdagases I and II).[25] The fact that a nephew of Gondophares and one of his successors in Indo-Parthia bore the name Abdagases (II) implies that the Sūrēn were close kinsmen of Gondophares. Thus the close kinship between Abdagases II and Abdagases Sūrēn mentioned by Tacitus is very probable.

In view of the fact that dynasties representing different branches of the Arsacids ruled in Parthia and Indo-Parthia, we may speak of two Parthian states in the later Arsacid period. The Gondopharid state survived until the early third century AD. Its relations with the western Parthians under the Vologasids (51–226 AD) took varied courses. At certain times the Indo-Parthians appear to have acknowledged the hegemony of their western cousins.

The coins of the later Indo-Parthians[26] are of low weight and quality. Most of them are imitations of the issues of Pakores, a Gondopharid ruler of the beginning of the second century AD. Greek and Kharosthi legends became corrupted. Coins bear portraits of several rulers wearing diadems or different tiaras, some of which are adorned with the Gondopharid symbol. This symbol also appears elsewhere on the coins. Some of these issues have Parthian inscriptions in front of the face or around the head. Many coins are counterstruck imitations of Kushan issues of Vasudeva with OESHO (Shiva) written on both sides. This feature dates the coins to the second half of the second century AD. The quality of monetary output improved under the last known Indo-Parthian prince, Farn-Sāsān, whose name used to be misread as Ardamitra until recently the name was correctly read by A.B. Nikitin.[27] Farn-Sāsān's coins show a ruler wearing a diadem on the obverse, while the reverse depicts a fire altar flanked by two incense burners. Identically shaped fire altars occur on coins of the Sasanian king Ardashir I. The inscription on the Indo-Parthian coins reads: "Farn-Sāsān, son (of) Ādūr-Sāsān, grandson of Tiridat, great-grandson of Sānabar, King of Kings" (*prnssn – BRY 'twrssn - BRY BRY tyrdty BRY – npy s'nbry MLKYN MLK'*).

Nothing is known about Tiridat[es] and Ādūr-Sāsān, the ancestors of the Farn-Sāsān named on the coins. The main point of reference for Farn-Sāsān is Sānabar, an Indo-Parthian king ruling about 100 AD. The altar motif suggests a close connection between the coinages of Farn-Sāsān and Ardashir. But who was imitating whom? M. Alram believes that Farn-Sāsān was Ardashir's contemporary and copied the latter's coinage.[28] But the title King of Kings indicates that Farn-Sāsān had substantial political claims which would have conflicted with the even more ambitious plans of Ardashir I. Sakastan was annexed by Ardashir around 224–225 AD, shortly after the death of Artabanus IV.[29] After 224/225 AD issues by Farn-Sāsān of coins with the King of Kings honorific would be unlikely, whereas Ardashir commenced issuing coins with the fire altar motif once he had declared himself King of Kings in 224 AD or even later in 226/227.[30] It is probable that Farn-Sāsān's reign in Sakastan ended in 224/225 AD, if not slightly earlier, and his chief successor there was a prince called Ardashir (see below). Taking into account historical circumstances and chronological limits, the conclusion to be drawn is that it was Ardashir I who borrowed the fire altar motif from Farn-Sāsān.

The Parthian name "Sāsān"

The main component of the name Farn-Sāsān is the word *ssn*/Sāsān, which was in widespread use in eastern Parthia, including the Nisa texts. The etymology of Sāsān is controversial. D.N. McKenzie and V.A. Livshits derive it from Old Iranian **Sāsāna*, "Defeating enemy".[31] Documents from Parthian Nisa, Merv (Marw) and Kosha-depe in Turkmenistan (Parthia proper and Margiana) contain many instances of the name Sāsān.[32] It is extant in numerous composita like Sāsāndāt and Sāsānbuxt. These composite names show that Sāsān was in fact the name of a regional Zoroastrian deity worshipped in eastern Parthia and also in Khwarezm (Chorasmia).[33] The name Sāsān also occurs in Armenia and Sogdiana, evidently as a result of Parthian influence.[34] Bearing the distribution of its incidence in mind, we have to conclude that it was most prevalent in Parthia proper, and therefore it was a Parthian name.

Recently M. Schwartz has proposed another etymology of Sāsān.[35] He sees a continuum from the ancient Syrophoenician form **Sasm* to the Late Antique Greek and Aramaic form *Sæsæn/Sesen*. But his alleged Parthian *Sesen* for *ssn* is not convincing, for linguistically no links are discernible between **Sasm* or *Sæsæn/Sesen* and Parthian *ssn*. Moreover, the occurrence of the non-Persian name *ssn* spelled in Greek Σασαν or Σασάνης in the ŠKZ inscription clearly implies that this is actually the Parthian name Sāsān. This name was borne by several Parthian grandees, including members of the Sūrēn clan. Thus, Livshits's explanation remains valid.

The Genealogy of Sāsān

It is well known that a character named Sāsān occurs in Ardashir's genealogies as recorded in various major sources.[36] There is no evidence for the occurrence of the name Sāsān in Persis before the third century AD. The appearance in Persis of the Parthian name Sāsān, previously known only from its occurrence in the eastern regions of Parthia and Indo-Parthia, is by no means a random event. There must have been a special political connection with the Indo-Parthians from Sakastan as well as Arachosia and Persis. Ardashir's controversial genealogy includes a character named Sāsān and another ancestor called Pābag. The evidence consists of several informative works, including the *Shahnameh*, the *Kārnāmag ī Ardašir ī Pābagān*, Tabari's *History*, early Sasanian inscriptions and coins, western sources (Agathias, Synkellos) and Armenian evidence. There are substantial differences between some of them.

Sāsān in the Shahnameh *and the Pahlavi sources*

In the *Shahnameh* Sāsān[37] is a scion of the Kayanid kings Dārā (II), Dārā (I)/Dārāyan, Ardashir Bahman, Esfandiyar and Goshtasp. Dārā II, the last Kayanid king before Alexander, is a distant echo of the Achaemenid king Darius III (336–330 BC), who was vanquished by the Macedonian king.[38] In the story of Bahman and Homay, Sāsān (the Elder) is the son of Ardashir Bahman,[39] called Ardaxšīr ī Kay (the Kayanid), who also appears in the *Zand ī Wahman Yasn*.[40] Ardashir Bahman has been identified with various Achaemenid kings.[41] It seems that an identification with Artaxerxes II Mnemon (404–359 BC) is the most convincing.[42] This prince also appears in Parthian genealogies as the ancestor of the Arsacids.[43] The inclusion of the Kayanids in Sāsān's genealogy was intended to prove Ardashir I's descent from the Kayanids (as a kind of reminiscence of the Achaemenids) and thus to create a connection between the Sasanians and the mythical kings of the past. *Shahnameh* represents "genuine Persian tradition", based on the Sasanian chronicle *Xwadāy-nāmag*.[44]

Ferdowsi maintains that Sāsān (the Elder), son of Dārā, was a Persian prince who fled to India and lived there as a shepherd.[45] He died in obscurity in India, but left behind a son who bore his name, "which continued in the family for four generations".[46] His descendant, also called Sāsān, worked for Babak (Pābag), the ruler of Estakhr in Persis (Fars). Pābag gave him his daughter in marriage. The princess gave birth to Ardashir Babakan (Pābagān). Afterwards Sāsān (the Younger) disappears from the story.

The *Shahnameh* tradition suggests that the ancestral seat of Sāsān's forebears was in India, where they had fled in apprehension of the arrival of Alexander. This item of data calls for special attention, as it seems to have been intended as the approved explanation of Sāsān's Indo-Parthian origins.

A genealogy of Ardashir is preserved in the *Kārnāmag* in the formula: *ardaxšīr ī kay ī pābāgān ī az tohmag ī sāsān ud nāf ī dārāy šāh*[47] – "Ardaxšīr, the Kayānid, son of Pābag from the parentage of Sāsān and from the lineage of King Dārā". In the *Bundahishn* (35.36, A232) the genealogy of Ardashir is given as *Artaxšahr ī Pābagān kē-š mād duxt ī Sāsān ī Weh-āfrīd*[48] – "Ardashir son of Bābak whose mother (was) the daughter of Sāsān son of Weh-āfrīd". Thus the Pahlavi evidence shows differences in detail concerning the position of Sāsān. Pābag is deemed to be Ardashir's father, while Sāsān appears as the grandfather or unspecified forebear of Ardashir I. But the common point is that this tradition names both Pābag and Sāsān in Ardashir's genealogy.

Sāsān in Roman and Armenian sources

The third-century Roman records call Ardashir a Persian and use the name *Artaxerxes*, copying the variant of a well-known Achaemenid name. They note that Ardashir recovered the kingdom of the Persians (Herodian 6.2.6–7; Dio 80.3.1–2). These records bear tell-tale signs of the propaganda the first Sasanians addressed to the Romans: both Ardashir I and Shapur I endeavoured to portray themselves as successors to the ancient Persians, not as an offshoot of the Arsacids. This was the message they disseminated among the Persians too.

Paradoxically, later Roman records turned out to be better informed on Ardashir's real family connections than the third-century authors. A very interesting tradition is preserved in the chronicle of Agathias II, 27, 1–5: *1.*

> *It is said that Artaxares'* [i.e. Ardashir's] *mother was married to a certain Pabak, who was quite obscure, a leather worker by trade, but very learned in astrology and easily able to discern the future. 2. It so happened that a soldier called Sasanus, who was travelling through the land of the Cadusaei, was given hospitality by Pabak and lodged in his house. 3. The latter recognized somehow, in his capacity as a seer, I presume, that the offspring of his guest would be splendid and famous and would reach great good fortune. He was disappointed and upset that he had no daughter or sister or any other close relative. But finally he yielded his own wife to him and gave up his marriage bed, nobly enduring the shame and preferring the future good fortune to the present disgrace and dishonour. 4. And so Artaxares was born, and was reared by Pabak. But when he grew up and boldly seized the throne, a bitter quarrel and dispute immediately broke out between Sasanus and Pabak. Each of them wanted him to be called his son. 5. Finally, and with difficulty, they agreed that he should be called the son of Pabak, though born from the seed of Sasanus. This is the genealogy of Artaxares given by the Persians, and they say it is true since it is actually recorded in the Royal Archives.*[49]

A similar story is preserved in Synkellos [p. 440.11–441.2 (p. 677.11–678.7 *CSHB*)]:

> *After Artabanus, the family of Chosroes* [i.e. the Sasanians] *began to rule. It began as follows: Artaxerxes* [i.e. Ardashir], *an unknown and undistinguished Persian, gathered a body of irregular troops, destroyed Artabanus and assumed the crown. And he once more restored the Kingship to the Persians. He was a Magian and through him the Magians have become prestigious in Persia. They say that the mother of Artaxerxes lived with a man called Pambecus, who was a shoe-maker by profession, but an astrologer and in this respect versed in the dark arts or stuff and nonsense. And a soldier by the name of Sananus* [sic] *was marching through the land of the Cadusaei*

and was entertained in the house of Pambecus, and Pambecus had "foreknowledge", we suppose, through his astrology, that the offspring of Sananus would be raised to a high level of good fortune. But not having a daughter or a sister or any female relative, he shut in his own wife with Sananus, and she conceived and brought forth Artaxerxes. Chosroes' family, therefore, was descended from this Artaxerxes, also called Artaxares.[50]

Agathias claims that Ardashir's biological father was Sāsān, whereas Pābag was his adoptive father. This tradition reflects the attempts the first Sasanians made to present their ancestry in compliance with their legitimising dynastic policy, in which the role of Sāsān was deliberately relegated to a backstage position. Agathias's harangue is prejudiced against the Sasanians but as far as Ardashir's genealogy is concerned, his data partly coincide with the image propagated by Ardashir I and Shapur I. This comes as no surprise, since Agathias or his informant Sergius had access to the Sasanian archives.[51]

Contrary to Agathias and Synkellos, the Armenian authors Moses Khorenatsi (2.67) and Agathangelos (Armenian version, 18–20) call Ardashir the son of Sāsān without hesitation. They do not name Pābag. Furthermore the Greek version of Agathangelos calls Ardashir *"son of Sasanus, which is the origin of the Sasanian name of the Persian kings descended from him"*.[52]

Sāsān in the *History* of Tabari

Tabari gives Ardashir three genealogies which differ on details but all say that Sāsān married a princess Rāmbihisht of the Persian Bāzrangid/Bāzranjīn family, the minor vassal dynasty of Persis/Fars (Tabari 813–814), and was the father of Pābag (Babak) and the grandfather of Ardashir (cf. the table below). Tabari emphasises Sāsān's links with Estakhr and the temple of Anahid. Tabari 813–814 says that Sāsān was the custodian of the temple of Anahid at Estakhr. He was also a devotee of the chase and equestrian pursuits, customs typical of Iranian aristocracy. Perhaps Sāsān was both priest and prince, like Tiridates, the Arsacid king of Armenia crowned by his brother Vologases I in 53 AD and then by Nero in Rome in 66 AD.[53] Assuming that Sāsān came from Sakastan, a country exceptionally important for the preservation and development of Zoroastrianism,[54] one may easily understand that he was deemed also as a person capable of taking on a cultic function. This may suggest that Sāsān's position as temple custodian in Fars was a result of his priesthood competences.

After the accession of Ardashir, the Bāzrangids disappear from historical testimonies.[55] Sāsān and Rambihisht's son Pābag (Babak) consolidated his power with the help of his own sons, Shapur and Ardashir. Ardashir made himself the castellan (*argbed*) of Dārābgerd. He induced his father to join a plot to kill the Bāzrangid king of Estakhr and rose in open rebellion against the Parthians (Tabari 813, 815–16).

Table 3.1: Genealogies of Sāsān in the History *of Tabari*

Version I, Tabari 813	*Version II, Tabari 813*	*Version III, Tabari 823*
Ardashir	Ardashir	Ardashir
Babak Shah, King of Khīr	Babak	Babak
Sāsān	Sāsān	Sāsān the Elder
Babak	Babak	Ardashir
Sāsān	Zarar	Bahman
Babak	Bihafridh	Isfandiyar
M.h.r.m.s	Sāsān	
Sāsān	Bahman	
King Bahman	Isfandiyar	
Isfandiyar	Bishtasb	
Bishtasb	Luhrasb	
Luhrasb		
Kaywaji		
Kaymanush		

Tabari's genealogy for Sāsān is patently defective, for it gives no historical characters bridging the gap between Sāsān and the Kayanids; it does not even cite Dārā, who is enumerated in the *Shahnameh*. A common point of Sāsān's genealogies in the *Shahnameh* and Tabari is the fact that Sāsān was a newcomer in Persis/Fars; he had no ancestors there. Tabari's Sāsān may be defined as an impoverished prince of foreign origin (a fact passed over in silence by Tabari) who established himself in Persis. The first recognisable character in Tabari's genealogies of Sāsān is Bahman. Tabari says nothing about Sāsān's forebears living in India as related in the *Shahnameh* tradition.

Sāsān versus Pābag in early Sasanian inscriptions and coinage

Ardashir I calls himself son of the "divine Pābag, the king", on his Naqsh-e Rostam inscription[56] and on his coins.[57] In his inscriptions at Naqsh-e Rajab, Shapur I is designated as son of Ardashir I and grandson of Pābag.[58] In his genealogy recorded in the Ka'ba-ye Zardosht (ŠKZ) inscription, Shapur I goes only as far as "divine king Pābag" (*bay Pābag šāh*) and no Sāsān is mentioned at all (ŠKZ § 1.10).[59] The ŠKZ inscription names as the first prince a Lord (*xwadāy*) Sāsān among the rulers who lived in the reign of Pābag (ŠKZ § 40).[60] The list of Shapur's ancestors in ŠKZ § 36, which enumerates offerings for members of the royal family, is significant. In this section, Sāsān the Lord (*xwadāy*) comes first in the list, while Pābag is called king (*šāh*). "King" Shapur (Ardashir's brother) is called the son of Pābag.

Generally, Shapur I is called in the ŠKZ the grandson of Pābag and son of Ardashir I.

Characters named Sāsān occur several times in the ŠKZ inscription, but none of them is referred to as related to the house of Ardashir. We know of two Sāsāns at the court of Ardashir I, Sūrēn Sāsān and Sāsān Andēgān, among the few named potentates. Both are representatives of great Parthian clans. The dominions of Andēgān are difficult to locate but it seems that their core lay in eastern Iran. Samʿani in *Kitab al-Ansab* knows a village called Andukan near the city of Sarakhs.[61] The name implies that the location was the stronghold of the Andēgān, maybe even their heartland. The presence of Sūrēn Sāsān at the court of Ardashir is perfectly understandable, as the Sūrēn clan was one of the mainstays of Ardashir's rebellion against Artabanus IV.

At Shapur I's court we discern a eunuch Sāsān, son of Sāsān, and a judge named Sāsān. There is also one Winnār, son of Sāsān (Winnār ī Sāsānīgān). These individuals hold fairly minor offices. In later centuries the name Sāsān is rare in Persia.[62]

In face of the fact that in a number of ancient testimonies Sāsān is closely linked to Ardashir, his omission from Shapur's official genealogy tells its own story. There was apparently something that Shapur I intended to pass over in silence. As a matter of fact, the dynasty was called Sāsānian, not Pābagian/Bābakian. Significantly, Narseh's inscription from Paikuli (NPi) speaks directly of the glory and rulership of the clan of Sāsān. The phrase "since the gods gave glory and rulership to the family of Sāsān" (*yazdān farrah šahr-xwadāyīf ō tōhm čē Sāsānagān dād*)[63] demonstrates that for Narseh I, Sāsān is the main point of reference as an ancestor.

The "Heir Apparent" coins

Ardashir's coinage provides a salient source for his reign.[64] One of his last issues is the so-called "Heir Apparent" coins, showing the king and the head of a young man wearing a tiara. They were minted in the last decade of the reign, i.e. between 229/230 and 239/240 AD.[65] Ever since the time of F.D.J. Paruck, these coins have been regarded as presenting an image of Ardashir with his son and heir, Shapur. Apart from the name Ardashir the rest of the legend is indecipherable. Michael Alram analysed the coins recently and stated that chemical analysis of Farn-Sāsān's coinage has given results which are in accord with those for the Heir Apparent coins;[66] in other words, the Heir Apparent coins were minted in Sakastan. Perhaps, as suggested by Alram, the young prince on them is the king of Sakastan, Ardashir, mentioned in the Shapur I's inscription.

The coins showing Ardashir I with his heir provide evidence that most probably his son (?), the ruler of Sakastan, was intended to be his successor. But as we know, it was Shapur I who succeeded to the throne. If Shapur's accession meant the failure of another candidate's bid for the throne, he would have been interested in concealing the facts regarding Ardashir's connection with Sakastan and the succession plans he had made. Hence the machinations in the ŠKZ inscription and the cover-up of the fact that Ardashir's real father was Sāsān, who had come from Sakastan.

Ardashir versus the Younger Arsacids

Ardashir's conquests have been analysed frequently.[67] Here I am interested in the strategic situation in Iran when Ardashir started to transcend the borders of Persis/Fars, that is around 220 AD. At that time the Parthian empire was divided into two parts ruled by Walagaš/Vologases V and Ardavan/Artabanus IV. Vologases ruled in Babylonia and Maishan, while his brother Artabanus IV controlled western Iran, Kirman, Parthia proper, Media, Susiana/Khuzestan, Mesopotamia (Asuristan) and Atropatene/Adhurbaigan. Khosrov, ruler of Armenia, was a member of a collateral line of the same House of the Younger Arsacids. The House of the Gondopharids or Indo-Parthians, represented by Farn-Sāsān, as it seems, had an alliance with Ardashir I, resulting from blood ties and, more importantly, a common political interest based on the intention of defeating or even destroying the western Arsacids.

At first, Ardashir made consistent efforts to conquer Persis/Fars. He subdued Estakhr and Darabgird, two of the five regions of Persis/Fars. Only then did he attack Kirman.[68] He vanquished king Balash (Vologases) and made one of his own sons, Ardashir, governor there (Tabari 817). Ardashir, son of Ardashir I, is listed in the ŠKZ as the king of Kirman. Only later did Ardashir conquer the coastland of Fars.[69] In 224 AD Ardashir overcame Artabanus IV at the battle of Hormuzgan. Two years later he captured Ctesiphon, thus eliminating Vologases V. By and large Ardashir managed to defeat the western Arsacids and to kill the legitimate male heirs in Parthia. But even after 226 AD there were still some residual foci of opposition left in Armenia and Atropatene, the bastions of the western Arsacids. Another unsubdued hotbed was Hatra, a powerful city with a dynasty whose members were kinsmen of the Arsacids.

In Tabari's life of Shapur I, Ardashir I is presented as an intransigent enemy of the Parthians. Remarkably the motif of a strong antipathy to the Arsacids comes in Tabari in the biography of Shapur I, who must have been interested in disseminating the story of vengeance on the Arsacids. Of course, this would mean the western Arsacids, not the Sakastan line, from which Shapur himself probably derived. Tabari (823) gives a reason why Ardashir I could have adopted such an attitude. In his chapter on Shapur I (Sābūr al-Junūd) he refers to the vow of Sāsān the Elder: "*When Ardashīr b. Bābak had attained the royal power, he wrought great slaughter among the Arsacids (al-Ashakāniyyah), to whom belonged the "Party Kings", until he had exterminated them, in accordance with an oath which Sāsān the Elder (...) had sworn: that, if at some point, he should attain the royal power, he would not spare a single one of the progeny of Ashak, son of Khurrah.*"[70]

Ardashir's eastern campaigns and the role of Armenia

An examination of Ardashir's military campaigns in eastern Iran will help to obtain a clearer picture of his political strategy. There is an ongoing debate as to when Ardashir conducted what is known as his eastern campaign. The data in the records seem to be at odds with each other. According to Tabari, after the battle of Hormuzgan Ardashir invaded Atropatene, Adiabene and Asuristan. Then, after taking Ctesiphon in 226/227 AD, he prepared his eastern campaign. But according to the *Nihayat*, the eastern campaign was fought *before* the capture of Ctesiphon. Some scholars date the eastern campaign even after 233.[71]

In my opinion Ardashir conducted two eastern campaigns – one in 224/5 AD, and another in *c.* 233 AD. They had completely different strategic aims. The first campaign reached Marw and Sakastan and could indeed be described as "collecting up" the lands of the Parthians. The second campaign went further, perhaps up to Bactria and Chorasmia, beyond the borders of the former Parthian state. After the victory at Hormuzgan, Ardashir wanted to settle matters in the east in order to rally reinforcements for an attack on Hatra and Armenia, the powerful bastions of the western Arsacids. He must have realised that large-scale operations in the vicinity of the border with Rome would provoke a conflict with the western power. As a consequence of the changes which had ensued in the balance of power in Iran, Rome was now an ally of the Arsacids in Armenia and Hatra. Therefore, what Ardashir needed was to secure his rear, that is eastern Iran, and to assemble his armed contingents. In view of Ardashir's strategic goals, the version which sounds the most consistent and reliable is presented in the *Nihayat*'s account.

According to the *Nihayat*, after Hormuzgan Ardashir marched into Khorasan and spent a year in Marw until all the kings of Khorasan offered their submission. In all likelihood, the years 224–225 AD are precisely when Sakastan acknowledged the authority of Ardashir I and was incorporated into the empire. The King of Kings is credited with founding the city of Zarang in Sakastan.[72] The next stage was the conquest of Atropatene/Adhurbaigan and the fighting against Armenia. Ardashir failed in his war with Armenia, just as his assaults on Parthian Hatra came to nothing.

While some of the western provinces of the Parthian empire put up fierce resistance against Ardashir, the eastern regions of Iran acquiesced without much ado. Except for Kirman, where Ardashir's son was installed, the princes of this region acknowledged Ardashir's hegemony without putting up any opposition. Kirman fought against Ardashir I because it was one of the mainstays of the Younger Arsacids. It is to be noted that the founder of the Younger Arsacids, Artabanus II, was closely linked to Kirman.[73]

Significantly the rulers of eastern Iran held the chief offices in the imperial hierarchy under Ardashir I. These princes were, apart from Ardashir, king of Kirman, Sadaluf, king of Abrenag (in Khorasan), Ardashir, king of Marw, and Ardashir, king of Sakastan. We do not know the exact identity of Ardashir, king of Sakastan/Sagestan under the King of Kings Ardashir I.[74] He may have been Ardashir I's son, known from the "Heir Apparent" coins.

In the third century AD Sakastan was one of the chief provinces of Iran, and it was commonly governed by an heir to the throne, including a son of Ardashir, who was removed from the political stage by Shapur I, and then Narseh I, son of Shapur I, who later became King of Kings (293–302 AD). In Sakastan Narseh was followed by Wahram III.[75]

Sakastan (Sagestan) occurs in Shapur I's inscription as a land connected with Turan and Hindustan/Hindestan, in other words Sind.[76] The title King of Hindestan, Sagestan and Turan occurs in an inscription from Persepolis dated to 310/311 AD in relation to a ruler called Shapur.[77] Sakastan, earlier known as Drangiana/Zarangiana or the land of the Ariaspi, had been an important centre for Zoroastrianism already in Achaemenid times. In the third century AD religious and cultural matters acted as a firm bond linking Persis and Sakastan.[78] Sakastan's religious connections with Persis were by no means coincidental and ran parallel to political affiliation.

The Armenian sources provide invaluable and unique information on the fall of the Younger Arsacids in Iran and the attitudes of the Parthian clans. Armenia was governed by a branch of the Younger Arsacids, the scions of Tiridates I (*c.* 52–80 AD), the brother of Vologases I. This put the Armenian Arsacids in the position of adversaries of Ardashir and Shapur I. The first Sasanians appreciated Armenia's signal importance, but were not able to subdue it permanently. Shapur I temporarily conquered Armenia, where, as in Sakastan, a dominion was set aside for Sasanian heirs apparent.

In compliance with the facts, the Armenian author Moses Khorenatsi writes that Ardashir I was defeated by the Armenian King Khosrov (Chosroes) and was ready to make substantial concessions (2.71–73).[79] According to another historian Agathangelos, Khosrov anxiously tracked the rise of Ardashir (Artasiras) in Iran:[80] "*These events were reported to Chosroes the Arsacid ruler of Great Armenia, that Artasiras the son of Sasanus had gained the throne of Persia and had destroyed Artabanus his brother. There was an additional report that the Parthians preferred the kingship of Artasiras to that of their own countryman.*"

Parthian clans against Artabanus IV

One of the most astonishing phenomena in the career of Ardashir I is the fact that he enjoyed the support of the chief Parthian clans Sūrēn, Kārin and Andēgān. The origin of another family, the Wārāz – mentioned in early Sasanian inscriptions – is not clear. The Armenian author, Moses Khorenatsi (2.71), claims that the great Parthian clans supported the rebellion of Ardashir: "*After Artashir, son of Sāsān, had killed Artavan and gained the throne, two branches of the Pahlav family called Aspahapet and Surēn Pahlav were jealous that their own kinsman Artashes should rule, and willingly accepted the rule of Artashir, son of Sāsān.*"[81] Moses also writes that the House of Kārin Pahlav stood in opposition to "Artashir" (Ardashir), but this claim must have referred to one of the subsidiary branches of the clan, since we know that members of the clan called Peroz Kārin and Gog Kārin held prominent offices at Ardashir's court (ŠKZ § 42). Agathangelos (Greek version) knows of a certain Karinas, sent along with Zekas as Ardashir's envoys to Artabanus IV: they are called "the most important clan leaders and generals".[82] Karinas was clearly a member of the Parthian Kārin clan. Zekas (Ζηκᾶς) is mentioned in ŠKZ § 40.7 as Zīk – he probably represented a Persian family.[83]

The ancient sources speak of the law generally recognised throughout Iran that only Arsacid blood was eligible for the throne. Adherence to and respect for the Arsacid dynasty was an extremely strong and enduring factor in Parthian Iran. Only an Arsacid could be invested with *khvarenah/farr*, the royal glory which qualified him to exercise power (Strab. 16.1.28; Amm. 23.6.6). The Parthians in opposition to Artabanus IV regarded him as a king whose rule was "unlawful". Ardashir and the rebels were said not to tolerate "a despotic attitude".[84] The arguments Agathangelos uses here are not directed against the Arsacids as a whole, but specifically against Artabanus IV. The allegations of his despotism are reminiscent of similar charges laid in the first century AD, when the Sūrēn and Kārin clans attempted to overthrow Artabanus II and Gotarzes II. The Parthian conspirators against Gotarzes acted in Rome and went to great lengths to make it clear that they did not intend to abjure the House of Arsaces, but only wanted to put the son of Vonones and grandson of Phraates IV on the throne, spurning the rule of Gotarzes. We are left with the impression that Gotarzes belonged to the *familia Arsacidarum* (Tac. *Ann.* 12.10.1–2). In the *Annales* 12.14.3 Tacitus appears to suggest that Meherdates, the grandson of Phraates IV, was a relative of Gotarzes from the same Arsacid stock, but Gotarzes looked down on him, regarding him as a foreigner and a Roman (*atque ille non propinquum neque Arsacis de gente, sed alienigenam et Romanum abcrepans*).

According to Moses Khorenatsi the Armenian king Khosrov was saddened because his relatives had submitted to Ardashir. Khosrov sent messengers asking his Parthian relatives "in the lands of the Kushans", i.e. in eastern Iran, to come to his aid against the Persians. But the Sūrēn and Aspahapet clans did not agree (2.71–72). Khosrov was informed that his "kinsman Vehsachan with his branch of the Karēn (Kārin) Pahlav had not given obeisance to Artashir" (2.72).[85] Ardashir is said to have slaughtered all the branch of the Karēn Pahlav. One child was rescued – the ancestor of the Armenian family Kamsarakan (2.73). The Parthian clans, especially the Sūrēn, had lent their support to Ardashir in return for far-reaching concessions. Moses Khorenatsi maintains that Ardashir promised to return to the Pahlavs [Parthians] *"their original homeland called Pahlav, the royal city Bahl, and all the country of the Kushans. Similarly he promised the form and splendour of royalty, half of [the empire of] the Aryans, and second place under his own authority. Attracted by this, Anak, who was from the Surēn Pahlav line, undertook to kill Khosrov."* (2.74)[86]

The accounts of Moses and Agathangelos show that Ardashir I won over the great clans of Parthia to his side. In the struggles against the Younger Arsacids the Sūrēn represented to some extent the Indo-Parthian realm. On the whole we may speak of a coalition comprising Ardashir, the Sūrēn and part of the Kārin, along with the later Gondopharids, against the western Arsacids, who after the capture of Ctesiphon in 226 AD were still defending their positions in Armenia and Hatra. The final outcome of the war was in 226 not yet apparent. Khosrov's assassination by Anak, a Sūrēn clansman, shows how committed the clan's support was (see the Armenian version of Agathangelos 24–32).

It is to be supposed that Ardashir's claims to the Arsacid throne were treated by the most powerful Parthian clans of the East as legitimate demands, for the prince was actually an Arsacid through his father's line. The rebellion led by Ardashir was just another phase of a long-lived conflict between the Younger Arsacids and the Indo-Parthian rulers, who stemmed from the Sinatrucid line. Ardashir's rebellion against Artabanus IV would have had no chance of success without Ardashir's claim to Arsacid descent. My hypothesis attempts to explain the reasons for the Parthian clans taking this view.

Sāsān, Pābag and Ardashir I – facts and manipulations

The key figure in the history of the downfall of the Arsacids was Sāsān, an Indo-Parthian prince who married a Persian princess, who then gave birth to Ardashir I. For reasons of propaganda Ardashir I, and later Shapur I, endeavoured to downplay Sāsān's role, so as not to be perceived in Persis as a foreign dynasty. We do not know whether it was Pābag who hid Sāsān away from the full glare of public view. After his takeover, Ardashir himself, fearing that the local aristocracy in Persis might perceive him as a foreign prince, might have been interested in such a move. While in Persis, Ardashir preferred to stress his Persian roots, rather than present himself as originating from Sakastan. This is why Ardashir's coins call Pābag his father. The first Sasanians manipulated the official accounts about their origin and connection to Sāsān. Later Shapur I had additional reasons to deny his connection with Sakastan. For him it was a case of obliterating the memory of his rival who ruled in Sakastan and had been designated by Ardashir I to succeed to the Iranian throne. This is why Ardashir and Shapur highlight on their coins their origin from Pābag and omit Sāsān. In the preamble of the ŠKZ the original point of reference in Shapur's genealogy is Pābag. Narseh, on the contrary, had Sāsān mentioned as his eponym; he became King of Kings in 293 AD after dynastic quarrels[87] and spent many years in Sakastan. This difference in genealogical records implies that some kings deliberately forged the facts and both the first Sasanians arouse the greatest suspicion in this respect.

By and large, the exact relationship between Sāsān and Pābag is obscure.[88] In the ŠKZ the mother of Pābag is given as Dēnag, but it is not stated whether she was married to Sāsān. It seems that Pābag was Ardashir's father-in-law, and maybe his adoptive father. If Pābag had been Ardashir's biological father and the son of the Persian Sāsān, the first Sasanians would have had no reason to be reticent about fundamental facts concerning their lineage. However, in the official propaganda Sāsān was pushed from view and mentioned only cursorily, without a clear indication of his ancestral relation to later generations, as may be seen in the ŠKZ inscription. That is why the data from the Armenian sources and the *Shahnameh* may be treated as trustworthy. The Armenian Arsacids were well informed on Ardashir's family relationships and kinship. Starting with Narseh's account, which names Sāsān as the dynasty's founding ancestor and passes over Pābag in silence, the Sasanians did not promote the figure of Pābag, instead acknowledging Sāsān. By this time their power was consolidated enough for them not to have worried about such measures to bolster their genealogy with bogus data. More reliable information on Ardashir's ancestry is not to be had until the late Sasanians, and that is why the tradition of Sāsān as the progenitor of Ardashir survived in the *Shahnameh* as well as in the account of Agathias.

It is to be noted that the Gondopharid symbol appears on the coat of arms used by a companion of Ardashir I, as depicted on the Firuzabad relief. This may be explained by the assumption that Ardashir's family had close ties to the Gondopharid branch of the Arsacids.

It is not a coincidence that one of the best ancient experts on early Sasanian Iran, Ammianus Marcellinus, does not see any break in Partho-Sasanian history and that he speaks of the rule of the house of Arsaces as lasting until his days in the fourth century AD. In his *Res gestae* (23.6.5–6) Ammianus claims:

> *(5) Hence to this very day the over-boastful kings of that race suffer themselves to be called brothers of the Sun and Moon, and just as for our emperors the title of Augustus is beloved and coveted, so to the Parthian kings, who were formerly low and obscure, there fell the very greatest increase in distinction, won by the happy auspices of Arsaces. (6) Hence they venerate and worship Arsaces as a god, and their regard for him has been carried so far, that even down to the memory of our time only a man who is of the stock of Arsaces (if there is one anywhere) is preferred to all in mounting the throne. Even in any civil strife, which constantly arises among them, everyone avoids as sacrilege the lifting of his hand against an Arsacid, whether he is bearing arms or is a private citizen.*[89]

Hence Ammianus implies that Arsaces was an ancestor of Shapur II (309–379 AD). In the extant fragments of his *Res gestae* there are no references to Sāsān and the early Sasanians.[90] Ammianus was well informed and must have heard of Ardashir's rebellion, but evidently he considered him an Arsacid *de facto*. The reigns of the descendants of Sāsān could be seen as comparable to the rule of the junior lines of the Arsacids, in bitter conflict with each other in the first and second centuries AD. For example, the Phraatids were at enmity with the Artabanids, and later the Hyrcanian-Dahian faction feuded with the Atropatenian branch.

Some Persians sided with Artabanus IV against Ardashir: "He had a large number of Persians who were not confederates of the council of their own countrymen."[91] However, it was the victors, not the vanquished, who wrote the history, readily manipulating the facts.

Conclusions

The old rivalry between branches of the Parthian royal house and clans, including the Younger (western) Arsacids, the Gondopharids in Indo-Parthia, the Sūrēn and Kārin, revived when a rebellion broke out in Persis under the leadership of Ardashir I, son of the Gondopharid prince Sāsān. The connections between the Gondopharids of Sakastan and the Sūrēn with Persis under Ardashir eventually led to the overthrow of the Younger Arsacids.

A comparison of the diverse traditions about Sāsān shows that the Persian writings and Sasanian inscriptions were manipulated for specific political reasons. The *Shahnameh* tradition traces Sāsān's ancestry to the late Kayanids, harking back to the historical Achaemenids. The same tradition suggests that the ancestral seat of Sāsān's forebears was in India, where they had fled in fear of Alexander. Sāsān was in fact a member of the Arsacid Gondopharid line, the ruling dynasty of Indo-Parthia, who reigned in Afghanistan and the north-western regions of India. Even under Farn-Sāsān they held Sakastan, Arachosia and probably part of Sind.

Most probably Sāsān was the father of Ardashir, as indicated by the *Shahnameh,* Agathias and the Armenian authors, and as implied by Narseh's inscription at Paikuli. The coins and inscriptions of Ardashir I and Shapur I say Ardashir I was the son of Pābag. Tabari, *Kārnāmāg* and *Bundahishn* give a version that Ardashir's father was Pābag, but include Sāsān in the genealogy.

How can these traditions be reconciled? In the history of Iran there were instances of monarchs adopting dignitaries who later acceded to the throne. This happened with Gotarzes II, the adopted son of Artabanus II. For Ardashir I we may assume that the *Shahnameh* and *Kārnāmag* tradition is closer to the truth, and that Ardashir's genuine father was Sāsān. The assumption that Sāsān was the biological father of Ardashir I leads to the conclusion that Ardashir was in fact an Arsacid on the male line.

In the case of Sāsān or his sons, adoption may have been involved; the law and customary practices offered a range of possibilities. The ŠKZ 45 inscription mentions two princes named Sāsān under Shapur I. One prince Sāsān was adopted by the Farragan family, the other by the Kidugan family.[92] Here adoption presumably means the admission of Parthians into the noble families of Persis. Adoption was regulated in Sasanian legislation, as evidenced by the *Mādayān ī hazār dādestān* (32, 11–33, 17, par. 28). That is how Pābag became the "adoptive" father of Ardashir.

For reasons of propaganda Ardashir I, and later Shapur I, endeavoured to downplay Sāsān's role, so as not to be perceived in Persis/Fars as a foreign dynasty. The paradox is that, assuming Sāsān was Ardashir's father, the Sasanian dynasty in fact had a Parthian, and perhaps even an Arsacid ancestry. Moreover, the early Sasanians built up their empire thanks to the support of the chief clans of Parthia including the Sūrēn and Kārin. That is why the Sasanian *Ērānšahr* has been referred to as "the empire of the Persians and Parthians".[93] And that is why Ammianus perceived the royal house of Persia as the Arsacids.

Notes

1 On Parthian clans, see Wolski 1989; Olbrycht 2003. On internal struggles in Parthia, see Olbrycht 2013 and 2013a.
2 On Mithradates II, see Olbrycht 2010b.
3 Lucian, *Makrob.* 15. On Sinatruces, see Debevoise 1938, p. 52–53; Karras-Klapproth 1988, p. 161–163; Olbrycht 1998, p. 110–112.
4 Olbrycht 2010a.
5 On Phraates IV and his rivals, see Karras-Klapproth, p. 137–145.
6 On Phraataces, see Debevoise 1938, p. 143–151; Ziegler 1964, p. 51–57.
7 For details, see Debevoise 1938, p. 70–149.
8 Olbrycht 1997; 2013.
9 More on this in Olbrycht 2013.
10 Olbrycht 1998a.
11 Vonones I's death: Debevoise 1938, p. 155.
12 Indo-Parthians: Fröhlich 2006; 2008. Gondophares: Bivar 1981; 2002; 2007.
13 Coins of Gondophares: Mitchiner 1975–6, types 1067–1071; NPIIN 1158–1175.
14 On the epithet "Autokrator", see Callataÿ and Lorber 2011, p. 450.
15 Mitchiner 1975/1976, type 1071; Cribb 1985, p. 295.
16 Sellwood 1980, 91.7–11.
17 von Gall 1990, Abb. 3; Daryaee 2010, p. 242; Frye 1984, p. 200.
18 Senior 2001, II, type 240.2D.
19 Fröhlich 2008, p. 56 maintains that coins in the name of Gondophares were issued by two rulers.
20 NPIIN 1203–1211; Senior 2001, type 244; coins b, e.
21 NPIIN 264–266.
22 Sellwood 1980, types 33, 37 and 39. On the attribution of Sellwood's type 33 to Sinatruces, see Olbrycht 1997a, p. 52; Loginov and Nikitin 1996. Coins of the Sinatrucids circulated in Bactria in the nomadic principalities and were imitated there very often.
23 See al-Tabari 1.683; Nöldeke 1879, p. 437.
24 Olbrycht 2013b.
25 Brunner 2011.
26 Senior 2001, p. 271–279.
27 Nikitin 1994.
28 Alram 2007, p. 234.
29 Alram 2007, p. 235 assumes that Ardashir I conquered Sakastan in about 233 AD, but the political circumstances point to an earlier dating around 224/5 AD, see the discussion below.
30 See Alram in Alram and Gyselen 2003, p. 24–25. On the title King of Kings as Ardashir's honorific, see Alram in Alram and Gyselen 2003, p. 22–23. Cf. Wiesehöfer 1987.
31 MacKenzie 1986, p. 114; Livshits 2010, p. 254.
32 The most detailed study is Livshits 2010, p. 251–254, first published in 1977. Cf. Gignoux 2003, p. 64; Nikitin 1994, p. 170, n. 15.
33 Livshits 2010, p. 253–254.
34 Huyse 1999, II, p. 115.
35 Schwartz 1996; 1998. Likewise Huyse 1999, II, p. 115.
36 On Sāsān and his genealogy, see Frye 1989; Shaki 1990; Gignoux 1998; Daryaee 2007, p. 5–6; 2010; Huyse 1999, II, p. 115.
37 Ferdowsi 1984, lines 4011ff. For the English translation, see Davis 2006, p. 530–531.
38 See Tafazzoli 1994; Olbrycht 2004; Olbrycht 2010; Daryaee 2006, p. 48. Dārā II was the son of Dārā I and the last king of the Kayanid dynasty. His name is recorded as Dārā in the Pahlavi literature. In some Islamic sources (*Dārāb-nāma)* it is given as Dārāb.
39 Davis 2006, p. 440.
40 Cereti 1995, p. 152.
41 On the identifications of Bahman with Artaxerxes I or even with Cyrus the Great and on the intermixture of various traditions concerning Bahman, see Yarshater 1971, p. 521f.; Khalegi-Motlagh 1988, p. 489–490.
42 Boyce 1991, p. 385; Daryaee 2006, p. 495; Arjomand 1998, p. 245–248.
43 See, e.g. Gutschmid 1888, p. 30; Wolski 1993, p. 56.

44 Daryaee 2006, p. 496.
45 "When Dara was killed in battle and his family fell upon dark times, a wise, brave son, who was called Sasan, survived him." Davis 2006, p. 530.
46 Davis 2006, p. 530.
47 *KNP* in Nyberg 1964, 6.18–19; Grenet 2003, III.19, p. 68–69.
48 Frye 1989; Daryaee 2010, p. 243.
49 Translation after Cameron 1969/70, p. 87–88.
50 Translation after M.H. Dodgeon in: Dodgeon, Lieu 2002, p. 9–10.
51 Cameron 1969/1970; Gariboldi 2005.
52 *History of the Armenians*, Greek version, 3. Translation after Dodgeon, Lieu 2002, p. 14.
53 On Tiridates, see Karras-Klapproth 1988, p. 179–183.
54 Sakastan played a significant role in the history of Zoroastrianism, see, e.g., Gnoli 1993.
55 See Bosworth 1999, p. 4, n. 9; Shahbazi 2005.
56 Back 1978, 281.
57 Alram, Gyselen 2003, 21,
58 Back 1978, 282–283.
59 See Huyse 1999, II, p. 15.
60 Remarkably, each of the different language versions gives a different name for Sāsān's father; in the Greek version it is Arnekan, and in the Persian text Orsig.
61 See Pugachenkova 1961, p. 21. On the location of Andēgān, see Chaumont 1975, p. 138–139. Huyse 1999, II, p. 136 (on ŠKZ § 42.6) proposes a location near Maishan which is possible but only for one of the dominions held by Andēgān. The main seat must have been in Khorasan and not in Babylonia.
62 Livshits 2010, p. 251; Justi 1895, s.v. Sāsān.
63 Humbach, Skjærvø 1983, III1, p. 65 § 80, Parth. l.36, and p. 122–123; Shayegan 2011, p. 14; Frye 1989.
64 The coinage of Ardashir I can be divided into three major phases, see Alram and Gyselen 2003; Alram 2007, p. 227–231.
65 Alram 2007, p. 235.
66 Alram 2007, p. 238. The inscriptions of the "Heir Apparent" coins are similar to those of the coins minted by Farn-Sāsān (Skjærvø in Alram and Gyselen 2003, p. 55–56).
67 See Widengren 1971; Wiesehöfer 1987; Daryaee 2009, p. 2–6; 2010.
68 Widengren 1971, p. 736.
69 Widengren 1971, p. 737–739.
70 Translation by Bosworth 1999.
71 See a detailed discussion in Alram 2007, p. 232.
72 See *Šahrestānīhā ī Ērānšahr* 38 (ed. Daryaee); Gnoli 1993, p. 10.
73 Artabanus II: *quia Hyrcanis Carmaniisque per adfinitatem innexus erat* (Tac. *Ann.* 6.36.4).
74 On Ardashir, King of Sakastan, see ŠKZ § 41 with Huyse 1999, II, p. 131. On Sasanian Sakastan, see ŠKZ § 3.7 with Huyse 1999, I, p. 29–30.
75 Humbach, Skjærvø 1983, III1, p. 110. Cf. Agathias 4.24.8.
76 ŠKZ § 34 (mpI24, paI 19, grI 42).
77 Back 1978, p. 492–495.
78 Gnoli 1989, p. 134ff.; 1993.
79 Widengren 1971, p. 780.
80 *History of the Armenians,* Greek version, 9. Translation after Dodgeon, Lieu 2002, p. 14.
81 Translation after Thomson 1978.
82 *History of the Armenians*, Greek version 6, ed. Lafontaine.
83 See Huyse 1999, II, p. 128.
84 *History of the Armenians*, Greek version 6, ed. Lafontaine.
85 Vehsachan is usually identified with the Kushan king Vasudewa, but this seems too far-fetched a speculation.
86 Translation after Thomson 1978. Moses's account is based on Agathangelos's *History of the Armenians* §§24–36.
87 Daryaee 2009, p. 10–13.
88 On Pābag see: Huyse 1999, II, p. 14–15.
89 *Quam ob rem numinis eum vice venerantur et colunt ea usque propagatis honoribus ut ad nostri memoriam non nisi Arsacides is sit, quisquam in suscipiendo regno cunctis anteponatur, et in qualibet civili concertatione, quae adsidue apud eos eveniunt, velut sacrilegium quisque caveat ne dextra sua Arsaciden arma gestantem feriat vel privatum.* Translation by J.C. Rolfe.
90 Drijvers 1999, p. 195.
91 Agathangelos, *History of the Armenians,* Greek version 7 (Dodgeon, Lieu 2002, 13).
92 See Huyse 1999 II, p. 152–154.
93 See MacKenzie 1993, p. 106–108.

Bibliography

Adhami, S. (2003). "A Question of Legitimacy: The Case of Ardašīr I (Dēnkard IV)", *Indo-Iranian Journal* 46: p. 223–230.
Agathias (1975). *The Histories*, translated by J.D.C. Frendo, Berlin.
Alram, M. (1999). "The Beginning of Sasanian Coinage", *Bulletin of the Asia Institute* 13: p. 67–76.
——— (2003). "Numismatics and History – An Outline. A) Ardashir I", in M. Alram, R. Gyselen (eds), *Sylloge Nummorum Sasanidarum*, Band I, Vienna: p. 21–31.
Alram, M., and Gyselen, R. (2003). *Sylloge Nummorum Sasanidarum Paris–Berlin–Wien*, Band I, Vienna.
Arjomand, S.A. (1998). "Artaxerxes, Ardašīr, and Bahman", *Journal of the American Oriental Society* 118: p. 245–248.
Back, M. (1978). *Die Sassanidischen Staatsinschriften, Studien zur Orthographie und Phonologie des Mittelpersischen der Inschriften zusammen mit einem etymologischen Index des mittelpersischen Wortgutes und einem Textcorpus der behandelten Inschriften*, Leiden.
Bivar, A.D.H. (1981). "Gondophares and the Shāhnāma", *Iranica Antiqua* 16: p.141–150.
——— (2002). "Gondophares", in *Encyclopaedia Iranica* online.
——— (2007). *"Gondophares and the Indo-Parthians", in V.S. Curtis, S. Stewart (eds), The Age of the Parthians, The Idea of Iran, vol. II*, London: p. 26–36.
——— (2009). "Kushan Dynasty I. Dynastic History", in *Encyclopaedia Iranica* online.
Boyce, M., and Grenet, F. (1991). *A History of Zoroastrianism. Zoroastrianism under Macedonian and Roman Rule*, Leiden.
Brunner, C.J. (2011) "Abdagases", in *Encyclopaedia Iranica* online.
Callataÿ, F.de, and Lorber, C.C. (2011). "The Pattern of Royal Epithets on Hellenistic Coinages", in P. Iossif, A.S. Chankowski, C.C. Lorber (eds), *More than men, less than gods. Studies*

on royal cult and imperial worship. Proceedings of the international colloquium organized by the Belgian School at Athens (November 1–2, 2007), Studia Hellenistica 51, Leuven: p. 417–455.

Cameron, A. (1969–70). "Agathias on the Sasanians", *Dumbarton Oaks Papers* 23–4: p. 67–183.

Cereti, C. (1995). *The Zand ī Wahman Yasn. A Zoroastrian Apocalypse*, Serie Orientale Roma 75, Rome.

Chaumont, M.L. (1975). "États vassaux dans l'empire des premiers Sassanides", in *Monumentum H.S. Nyberg*, Acta Iranica 4, Leiden: p. 89–156.

Cribb, J. (1985). "New Evidence of Indo-Parthian Political History", in *Coin Hoards* VII, London: p. 282–300.

CSHB: Corpus Scriptorum Historiae Byzantinae, Bonn, 1828–1878.

Daryaee, T. (2002). *Šahrestānīhā ī Ērānšahr: A Middle Persian Text on Late Antique Geography, Epic and History,* Costa Mesa.

——— (2003). "The Ideal King in the Sasanian World: Ardaxšīr ī Pābagān or Xusrō Anōšagruwān?", *Nāme-ye Irān-e Bāstān, The International Journal of Ancient Iranian Studies* 3.1: p. 33–45.

——— (2006). "The Construction of the Past in Late Antique Persia", *Historia, Zeitschrift für Alte Geschichte* 55: p. 493–503.

——— (2008). "Kingship in Early Sasanian Iran", in V.S. Curtis, S. Stewart (eds), *The Age of the Sasanians: The Idea of Iran*, London: p. 60–70.

——— (2010). "Ardashir and the Sasanians' Rise to Power", in M.J. Olbrycht (ed.) (2010): p. 237–256.

Davis, D. (2006). *Shahnameh. The Persian Book of Kings, A New Translation*, New York.

Debevoise, N.C. (1938). *A Political History of Parthia*, Chicago.

Dodgeon, M.H., and Lieu, S.N.C. (1994): *The Roman Eastern Frontier and the Persian Wars AD 226–363*, London and New York.

Drijvers, J.W. (1999). "Ammianus Marcellinus' Image of Arsaces and Early Parthian History", in J.W. Drijvers, D. Hunt (eds), *The Late Roman World and its Historian: Interpreting Ammianus Marcellinus,* London and New York: p. 193–206.

Ferdowsi (1984). Firdousi, *Shahname*, vol. V, translated by Ts.B. Banu-Lakhuti, V.G. Berznev, Moscow.

——— (2005). *The Shahnameh (The Book of Kings),* D. Khaleghi Motlagh, M. Omidsalar (eds), vol. 6, New York.

Fröhlich, C. (2006) "Indo-Parthian Dynasty", in *Encyclopaedia Iranica* 10: p. 100–103.

——— (2008). *Monnaies indo-scythes et indo-parthes du département des Monnaies, Médailles et Antiques: catalogue raisonné*, Paris.

Frye, R.N. (1975). "The Rise of the Sasanians and the Uppsala School", in *Monumentum H.S. Nyberg,* Acta Iranica 4, Leiden: p. 237–245.

——— (1984). *The History of Ancient Iran,* Munich.

——— (1989). "Bābak", in *Encyclopaedia Iranica* 3: p. 298–299.

Gariboldi, A. (2005). "Agathias e l'origine di Ardašir", in M. Bernardini, N.L. Tornesello (eds), *Scritti in onore di Giovanni M. D'Erme*, Naples: p. 489–503.

Gignoux, Ph. (1994). "Denāg", in *Encyclopaedia Iranica* 7: p. 282.

——— (1998). "Sāsān ou le dieu protecteur", in N. Sims-Williams (ed.), *Proceedings of the Third European Conference of Iranian Studies, Part 1: Old and Middle Iranian Studies*, Wiesbaden: p. 1–7.

——— (2003). *Iranisches Personennamenbuch, Mitteliranische Personennamen, Faszikel 3: Noms propre sassanides en moyen-perse épigraphique*, Vienna.

Gnoli, G. (1989). *The Idea of Iran*, Rome.

——— (1993). "Pars i Sagestan v sasanidskoi religioznoi politike", *Vestnik drevnei istorii* 1993/4: p. 9–13.

Grenet, F. (translated by) (2003). *La geste d'Ardashir fils de Pābag*, Die.

Gutschmid, A.v. (1888). *Geschichte Irans und seiner Nachbarländer von Alexander dem Großen bis zum Untergang der Arsaciden*, Tübingen.

Humbach, H., and Skjærvø, P.O. (1983). *The Sassanian Inscription of Paikuli* III/1, Wiesbaden.

Huyse, Ph. (1999). *Die dreisprachige Inschrift Šāburs I. an der Ka'ba-I Zardušt (ŠKZ)*, Corpus Inscriptionum Iranicarum, III Pahlavi Inscriptions, vol. I, London.

Justi, F. (1895). *Iranisches Namenbuch*, Marburg.

Karras-Klapproth, M. (1988). *Prosopographische Studien zur Geschichte des Partherreiches auf der Grundlage antiker literarischer Überlieferung*, Bonn.

Khaleghi Motlagh, D. (1988). "Bahman", *Encyclopaedia Iranica* 3, p. 489–490.

Khaleghi Motlagh, D., and Omidsalar, M. (2005). *The Shahnameh (Book of Kings)*, vol. 6, New York.

Livshits, V.A. (2010). *Parfyanskaya onomastika*, St. Petersburg.

Loginov, S.D., and Nikitin, A.B. (1996). *Parthian Coins from Margiana: Numismatics and History*, *Bulletin of the Asia Institute* 10: p. 39–51.

MacKenzie, D.N. (1993). "The Fire Altar of Happy *Frayosh", *Bulletin of the Asia Institute* 7: p. 105–109.

——— (1986). "Names from Nisa", in *Peredneaziatskii sbornik* IV: *Drevniaia i srednevekovaia istoriia i filologiia stran perednego i srednego vostoka*, Moscow: p. 105–115 [repr. in Idem, *Iranica diversa*, C.G. Cereti and L. Paul (eds), Rome, 1999: p. 209–215].

Macuch, M. (1981). *Das sasanidische Rechtsbuch "Mātakdān i Hazār Dātistān",* Teil II, Wiesbaden.

Mitchiner, M. (1975–1976). *Indo-Greek and Indo-Scythian Coinage*, vol. 1–9, London.

Nikitin, A.B. (1994). "Die Münzen des letzten indo-parthischen Königs von Sīstān. Ein Abschied von 'Ardamitra'", *Numismatische Zeitschrift* 102: p. 167–170.

Nöldeke, T. (1879). *Geschichte der Perser und Araber zur Zeit der Sasaniden. Aus der arabischen Chronik des Ṭabarī*, Leiden.

NPi = Inscription of Narseh in Paikuli.

NPIIN = M. Alram, *Nomina Propria Iranica in Nummis. Materialgrundlagen zu den iranischen Personennamen auf antiken Münzen*, Vienna 1986 (IPNB IV).

Nyberg, H.S. (1964). *A Manual of Pahlavi*, Part I, Wiesbaden.

Olbrycht, M.J. (1997). "Vardanes contra Gotarzes II. Einige Überlegungen zur Geschichte des Partherreiches ca. 40–51 n. Chr.", *Folia Orientalia* 33: p. 81–100.

——— (1997a). "Parthian King's Tiara - Numismatic Evidence and Some Aspects of Arsacid Political Ideology", *Notae Numismaticae* 2: p. 27–65.

——— (1998). *Parthia et ulteriores gentes. Die politischen Beziehungen zwischen dem arsakidischen Iran und den Nomaden der eurasischen Steppen* (Quellen und Forschungen zur Antiken Welt, Bd. 30), Munich.

——— (1998a). "Das Arsakidenreich zwischen der mediterranen Welt und Innerasien. Bemerkungen zur politischen Strategie der Arsakiden von Vologases I. bis zum Herrschaftsantritt des Vologases III. (50–147 n. Chr.)", in E. Dąbrowa (ed.), *Ancient Iran and the Mediterranean World* (Electrum 2), Krakow: p. 113–159.

——— (2003). "Parthia and Nomads of Central Asia. Elements of Steppe Origin in the Social and Military Developments of Arsakid Iran", in I. Schneider (ed.), *Mitteilungen des SFB "Differenz und Integration" 5: Militär und Staatlichkeit*, Halle/Saale: p. 69–109.

——— (2004). *Aleksander Wielki i świat irański*, Rzeszów.

——— (2009). "Mithradates VI Eupator and Iran", in: J.M. Hoejte (ed.), *Mithridates VI and the Pontic Kingdom*, Aarhus: p. 163–190.

——— (2010). "Macedonia and Persia", in J. Roisman, I. Worthington (eds), *Blackwell Companion to Ancient Macedonia*, Malden: p. 342–369.

——— (2010a). "Mithradates I of Parthia and his Conquests up to 141 B.C.", in M. Dzielska et al., *Hortus Historiae. Studies in Honour of Professor Jozef Wolski on the 100th Anniversary of His Birthday*, Krakow: p. 229–245.

——— (2010b). "The Early Reign of Mithradates II the Great in Parthia", in M.J. Olbrycht (ed.) (2010): p. 144–158.

——— (2013). *Artabanos II's Genealogy* (forthcoming).

——— (2013a). *Parthian Strategy* (forthcoming).

Olbrycht, M.J. (ed.) (2010). *Orientis Splendor. Studies in memory of Józef Wolski = Anabasis.* Studia Classica et Orientalia 1, Rzeszów.

Panaino, A. (2002). "The bayān of the Fratarakas: Gods or 'divine' Kings?", in C. Cereti, M. Maggi, E. Provasi (eds), *Religious themes and texts of pre-Islamic Iran and Central Asia: Studies in honour of Professor Gherardo Gnoli on the occasion of his 65th birthday on 6 December 2002*, Wiesbaden: p. 283–306.

Pugachenkova, G.A. (1961). "Yarty-Gumbez", *Epigrafika Vostoka* 14: p. 12–22.

Schwartz, M. (1996). "*Sasm, Sesen, St. Sisinnios, Sesengen Barpharangès, and... 'Semanglof'", *Bulletin of the Asia Institute* 10: p. 253–257.

——— (1998). "Sesen: a Durable East Mediterranean God in Iran", in N. Sims-Williams (ed.), *Proceedings of the Third European Conference of Iranian Studies held in Cambridge, 11th to 15th September 1995, Part 1, Old and Middle Iranian Studies*, Wiesbaden: p. 9–13.

Sellwood, D. (1980, 2nd ed.). *An Introduction to the Coinage of Parthia*, London.

Senior, R.C. (2001). *A Catalogue of Indo-Scythian Coins*, Glastonbury.

Shahbazi, S. (1990). "On the Xwadāy-nāmāg", in *Papers in Honor of Professor Ehsan Yarshater*, Leiden: p. 208–229.

——— (2002). "Shapur I. History", in *Encyclopaedia Iranica* online.

——— (2005). "Sasanian Dynasty", in *Encyclopaedia Iranica* online.

Shaki, M. (1990). "Sasan ke bud?", *Iranshenasi* 2.1: p. 78–80.

Shayegan, R. (2011). *Arsacids and Sasanians. Political Ideology in Post-Hellenistic and Late Antique Persia*, Cambridge.

ŠKZ = Inscription of Shapuhr on Ka'ba-ye Zardosht.

Tabari (1999). *The History of al-Ṭabarī,* translated by C.E. Bosworth, New York.

Tafazzoli, A. (1994). "Dārāb", in *Encyclopaedia Iranica* 7: p. 1–2.

Thomson, R.W. (1976). *Agathangelos, History of the Armenians*, Albany.

——— (1978). *Moses Khorenatsi, History of the Armenians*, Cambridge, MA.

von Gall, H. (1990). *Das Reiterkampfbild in der iranischen und iranisch beeinflussten Kunst parthischer und sasanidischer Zeit*, Berlin.

Widengren, G. (1971). "The Establishment of the Sasanian Dynasty in the Light of New Evidence", in *La Persia nel medioevo*, Rome: p. 711–782.

Wiesehöfer, J. (1987). "Ardašīr I", in *Encyclopaedia Iranica* 2: p. 371–376.

——— (1999). "Fārs II. – History in the Pre-Islamic Period", in *Encyclopaedia Iranica* 9: p. 333–337.

——— (2007). "Fars under Seleucid and Parthian Rule", in V.S. Curtis, S. Stewart (eds), *The Age of the Parthians, The Idea of Iran, vol. II*, London: p. 37–49.

Wolski, J. (1989). *Die gesellschaftliche und politische Stellung der großen parthischen Familien*, Tyche 4: p. 221–227.

——— (1993). *L'Empire des Arsacides*, Acta Iranica 32, Leuven.

Yarshater, E. (1971). "Were the Sassanians Heirs to the Achaemenids?", in *La Persia nel medioevo*, Rome: p. 517–531.

Ziegler, K.-H. (1964). *Die Beziehungen zwischen Rom und dem Partherreich*, Wiesbaden.

4

From Terror to Tactical Usage: Elephants in the Partho-Sasanian Period*

Touraj Daryaee
University of California, Irvine

Clear examples of the elephant's connection with kingship in the Iranian world come from the literary and iconographic evidence of the Sasanian era sources. This is interesting, as it is assumed that it was in Late Antiquity that Zoroastrianism was established as an organised religious tradition. It is according to this same tradition (through the evidence of Pahlavi texts) that elephants are classified as demonic beasts.[1] Consequently, a dichotomy exists about this fabulous animal in royal and clerical circles. This paper concentrates on the numismatic and textual evidence, suggesting that there is much continuity in the use of elephants between the Parthian and the Sasanian periods. It is further posited that elephants were not only important as a symbol of kingship, but also that their demonic outward appearance was used against the opponents of the Parthians and the Sasanians, namely the Roman empire.

Two sets of textual evidence for the use of elephants by the Sasanians are dated to the third century AD. Both literary sources are suspect, but come from divergent traditions. Ardaxšīr (Ardashir) Pābagān, the founder of the Sasanian dynasty, is mentioned as having used war elephants against the Romans under Severus Alexander. Alexander addresses the Senate in his victory speech (*Historia Augusta* 56.2–3):

> Conscript Fathers, we have conquered the Persians. There is no need of lengthy rhetoric; you should know, however, this much, namely, what their arms were, and what their array. First of all, there were seven hundred elephants provided with turrets and archers and great loads of arrows. Of these we captured thirty, we have left two hundred slain upon the field, and we have led eighteen in triumph.[2]

It is true that perhaps the *Historia Augusta* is using established literary themes when mentioning the war between the Persians and the Romans, borrowing from the wars of Darius III and Alexander III of Macedon, where elephants were used.[3] Still, I think this testimony is worth some attention, as there are other sources that point to the third century for the use of elephants as war machines by the Sasanians. In the *Shahnameh* (*Book of Kings*), Pābag, instead of dreaming of a white elephant, dreams:

> Sāsān was riding a war elephant, and in his hand was an Indian sword ...[4]

The connection between Iran and India is clear here as both the elephant and the sword point to India. But one can argue that the *Shahnameh* is a late source, perhaps reflecting a late Sasanian use of the elephant as a beast of war. Another piece of textual evidence comes from the Middle Persian *Kārnāmag ī Ardāxšīr ī Pābagān* (*The Testament of Ardašīr, son of Pābag*), a story about the founder of the Sasanian dynasty, Ardashir I. In this famous text, parts of which are studied by all students of Middle Persian, there appears the episode of the three dreams of Pābag, the local ruler of Pārs or Persis. On the second night the following dream was made manifest (KAP I.9):

> Another night he saw in this manner that Sasan is sitting on an adorned white elephant and everyone in the country is standing around him and all are saluting him and worshipping and praising him ...[5]

* I would like to thank Dr Vesta Sarkhosh Curtis for her many helpful comments on the paper.

Figure 4.1: Lower panel of the Arch of Galerius (after Canepa 2009)

Pābag asks his dream interpreters to decode its meaning (KAP I.13):

> The dream interpreters said that that person whom you saw in these dreams, either he or from the offspring of that man, someone will become the king of the world, since the sun and a white adorned elephant (symbolize) bravery and power and victory ...[6]

Here we do not have a war elephant, but rather a white elephant which in this context is associated with regal power, a notion that comes from India.[7]

Shapur I (240–270 AD) may also have used elephants in his war with the Roman Emperor Valerian. This we hear at least from the Persian side, where in the *Book of Kings*, Shapur faced Baranush/Varanush/Valaranus/Valerian in battle in 259 AD in the following manner:

> Drums and trumpets were sounded on each side, and the new Persian king, stationed in the centre of his troops, felt the thrill of battle. There was such a wailing of trumpets and clashing of Indian bells that the moon and the vault of the heavens shook; there were war drums strapped to the elephants, and their thundering noise carried for two miles.[8]

The battle takes place on a plain which the text calls *altouyaneh* (northern Mesopotamia/Armenia?), where Valerian is defeated and captured, according to the text (Davis p. 575). Here we see that elephants are used as a means of terrorising the Roman forces, something that we shall encounter in the Roman sources as well.

In the late third and fourth centuries AD, as the Sasanians and Romans faced one another, elephants were continually used by the Sasanian forces. This time we have information from the Roman side, when a heavy defeat was inflicted on the Persians and the king's wife captured during the battle between Galerius and Narseh in 298 AD. The Arch of Galerius in Thessaloniki commemorates his victory. On it both rulers are shown facing one another.[9] Two panels depict elephants used by the Sasanians being exhibited as part of the gifts sent to the emperor by the Sasanians.[10]

Figure 4.2: Persian elephant corps at Bishapur (Photo by M. Vandaee)

But in the fourth century the Sasanians struck back, and again, elephants were used by the Sasanian army. During the reign of Shapur II (309–379 AD), when Nisibis was put under siege (337/338, 346, 350 AD), the use of the beast is mentioned (Julian's *Orations* 2.63b/66a).

Ammianus Marcellinus is another important source for elephants and the Late Antique Iranian army. In his description of the war between Shapur II and Julian, he states that the Persians appeared at a location called Maranga, where the Persian general of the cavalry, Meren (Mehrān?), along with the king's two sons came to battle. The Persian army is described thus (Amm. Marc. XXIV.6.8):

> The Persians opposed to us serried bands of mail-clad horsemen in such close order that the gleam of moving bodies covered with densely fitting plates of iron dazzled the eyes of those who looked upon them, while the whole throng of horse was protected by coverings of leather. The cavalry was backed up by companies of infantry, who, protected by oblong, curved shields covered with wickerwork and raw hides, advanced in very close order. Behind these were elephants, looking like walking hills, and, by the movements of their enormous bodies, they threatened destruction to all who came near them, dreaded as they were from past experience.[11]

It is interesting that elephants were used by the Sasanians in the Caucasus, especially in Armenia. In the fifth century, Armenia suffered terribly from Persian assaults and many of its nobles perished in 451 AD at the battle of Avarayr.[12] The war was waged by order of the king of kings, Yazdigird II, but the architect behind it was the *Wuzurg-framadār*, Mihr-Narseh. Ełishe mentions the large Persian army's march to Armenia with many "companies of elephants" (Ełishe, p. 140). The Persian attack formation was arranged thus (Ełishe p. 114):

> He summoned many of the generals under his authority and ordered them to bring forward the companies of elephants. These he divided into various groups, and he assigned to each elephant three thousand armed men in addition to all the other troops.[13]

Figure 4.3: Tāq-ī Būstān (Photo by Ali Matin)

Thus, as time went on, we begin to understand the way in which elephant formations were organised in the Sasanian period and how they were used in battle against their enemies. Images of elephants and their use in Sasanian hunting grounds (Tāq-ī Būstān) are best known from the time of Xusrō (Khusrau) II (590–628 CE), and as we shall see below, Perso-Arabic texts provide evidence for their appearance at the court of the most opulent king of the Persians.

The most detailed information on the use of elephants by the Sasanian military comes from the time of Yazdigird III at the battle of Qadisiyyah in 634 AD. Here we are given a full treatment of the tactical use of elephants in various ways by the Sasanian forces. By the seventh century elephants were not only used for direct attack, but also as the centre of operations for command and logistics. The number of elephants at the battle of Qadisiyyah is uncertain as there are variant traditions, but one account has it that some thirty elephants were used by Rustam Farrokhzād, the Sasanian general. The elephants were divided into three sections, eighteen at the centre and fifteen on the two wings.[14] But it is said that field commanders also stood on elephants,[15] surveying the battle. The most interesting information is the number of people who were on the elephants (Tabari Events of Year 14):

> They confronted the elephants so that the drivers turned them in another direction. Every elephant was ridden by twenty men.[16]

This number seems too high, but it suggests that at least several people were stationed on the elephants during the war. Needless to say, the Muslims found a way to defeat the Sasanian army with their elephants, which ushered in the end of the Sasanian Empire. Still, elephants continued to be used in warfare, a practice which was revived under the Qaznavids in the tenth century.

The use of elephants as a symbol of kingship and as a weapon of war has a longer history with which the numismatic evidence can aid us.

From the Achaemenids to Alexander III and his successors

We know that the Achaemenids used elephants in their army, no doubt as a result of Darius's venture into India. According to Arrian, at Gaugamela Darius III used fifteen elephants in battle against the Macedonian forces:

> In front of Darius's royal squadron of cavalry stood the elephants and fifty chariots. (Arrian, Book III.11)

With Alexander III of Macedon and his successors, elephants are used and appear on coinage as well. Alexander is shown on a silver coin battling the Indian king Porus, who is sitting on an elephant. This is part of a larger series of silver coins. In addition, a gold coin appeared a few years ago bearing a riderless elephant on the reverse, which has been attributed by some scholars to the same series.[17] The most important coin to compare in iconographic terms with this gold coin is that of Ptolemy I of Egypt (305–283 BC), where on the obverse Alexander is shown wearing an elephant scalp. But the meaning of this portrait is unclear, perhaps referring to the conquest of India.

Parthia: The Missing Link

The most comprehensive work on the use of elephants in the ancient Iranian world is by Michael B. Charles who states "... one might well ask why the Parthians did not use elephants for military purposes; or at least why they were not attracted to the royal symbolism which the elephant seems to have had for the [Sasanians]."[18] But it is in the Parthian period that we have both representational and literary evidence for the importance and use of elephants. The Greco-Bactrians placed

Figure 4.4: Bronze coin of Demetrius I (© The Trustees of the British Museum)

Figure 4.5: Bronze coin of Mithradates I (©The Trustees of the British Museum)

elephants on their coinage, for example that of Demetrius I (*c.* 200–180 BC).[19]

It is possible that it was with the Mithradates I's (138/136 BC) defeat of the Greco-Bactrian ruler Eucratides that elephants began to appear on Parthian coinage. Some of the bronze coins of Mithradates I show an elephant on the reverse accompanied by the inscription "of the Great King, Arsaces", perhaps in commemoration of his conquest of Bactria. This is thus the first time that we see elephants struck on Parthian coinage of eastern mints, perhaps symbolising rule over Bactria.

Similar literary evidence is also furnished both by classical and Parthian sources. The classical source is from an event in the first century AD, namely the Battle of Rhandeia in 62 AD. The Roman general Paetus had taken over the Armenian command and wanted to place Armenia under direct Roman rule.[20] His forces in the valley of Arsanias or Murad Su were repeatedly defeated and were placed under siege. Before Corbulo was able to bring help from Syria, Paetus made a humiliating treaty with the Parthian king of kings, Vologases (Wālxš), in which he agreed to evacuate Armenia. The Romans agreed to build a bridge across the Arsanias (Murad Su) for the Arsacids before their departure.[21]

Tacitus, our main source for this event, provides some very interesting details on the mode of humiliation and the representation of Parthian power over the Romans. He states:[22]

> Meanwhile Paetus threw a bridge over the river Arsanias ... apparently with the view of facilitating his march. It was the Parthians, however, who had required this, as an evidence of their victory; for the bridge was of use to them ...

Furthermore, the Roman forces were made to march under a "yoke" (Lat. *iugum*), which was part of the Roman cultural imagery of subjugation. While the Romans were on the march, the Armenians took some of them as slaves and even took the clothes off their backs for further humiliation. But what symbolically made the event momentous was the king of kings' march over the bridge in the following manner (Tacitus, *Annals* XV.15):

> Seated himself on an elephant, he [Vologases] crossed the river Arsanias, while those next to his person rushed through it at the utmost speed of their horses; for a rumour had gained ground that the bridge would give way, through the trickery of its builders. But those who ventured to go on it found it to be firm and trustworthy.

The other literary evidence comes from the Parthian epic, *The Testament of Zarēr* (*Āyādgār ī Zarērān*), which is a tale about the war between the Iranians who had become Zoroastrian and the Turānians, who were keeping their pagan religion and challenging the new converts. The scene of war and the way the Iranian army is depicted are similar to that of Ammianus's description of the Sasanian army (ĀZ 27–31):

> Then the army (*Kārwān*) was on the move. Elephant drivers went to the elephants and the horse groomers to the horses and tower-watcher to the tower. There are many swords of Rustam, many quivers full of lances, many bright armours and many four-fold armours. The army (*Kārwān*) of Iranshahr is such that its noise reaches the sky and its vibration to hell. When they move the road will be cut and the water of the rivers will be in commotion that for one month it cannot be drunk and for fifty days it will not be clear ..."[23]

Based on the evidence furnished, we can draw several conclusions. First, elephants were used as a psychological weapon of terror against their enemies by successive ancient Iranian dynasties. Early on, they were used as a sort of tank of the ancient world. This trend appears to have been the case from the Achaemenid period onwards in the Iranian domains. On the other hand, by the beginning of the first century AD, the symbolic nature of elephants as a representation of kingship is evident in Iran. This notion, however, was inherited from India and the Indo-Iranian borderland kingdoms (the Greco-Bactrians). Secondly, elephants became more important tactically as time passed in Late Antique Iran. The early Sasanians may have used these beasts as a scare tactic, but by the late Sasanian period they were more than a mere psychological weapon against the enemy's army. Elephants were then used as a logistical tool, from which the battle scene was surveyed by the army commanders and the movements of forces observed. For the very same reason their use outlasted the ancient Iranian dynasties and continued into pre-Modern times in Iran.

Notes

1 H.-P. Schmidt 1980, p. 215; M. Moazami 2005, p. 313.

2 *Scriptores Historiae Augustae*, 56.2–3: *Persas, patres conscripti, vicimus. longae eloquentiae opus non est, tantum scire debetis, quae illorum arma fuerint, qui apparatus. iam primum elephanti septingenti idemque turriti cum sagittariis et onere sagittarum. ex his triginta cepimus, ducenti interfecti iacent, decem et octo perduximus.*

3 M.B. Charles 2007, p. 306–308. For a survey of Late Antiquity, see P. Rance 2003, p. 355–384.

4 *The Shahnameh: The Persian Book of Kings*, trans. D. Davis 2007, p. 530.

5 F. Grenet 2003, transcription p. 56: *any šab-ēw ēdōn dīd čiyōn ka sāsān pad pīl-ēw ārāstag ī spēd nišāst estād ud hark ē andar kišwar pērāmōn ī sāsān estēnd ud namāz awiš barēnd ud stāyišn ud āfrīn hamē kunēnd.*

6 *Ibid.*, p. 56: *xwamn-vizārān guft kū ān kē ēn xwamn padi-iš dīd ōy ayāb az frazandān ī ān mard kas-ēw ō pādixšāyīh ī gēhān rasēd čē xwaršēd ud pīl ī spēd ī ārāstag čērīh ud tuwānīgīh ud pērōzīh.*

7 T. Daryaee 2014.

8 Davis, *ibid.*, p. 575.

9 M.P. Canepa 2009, p. 93–94.

10 *Ibid.*, p. 97.

11 Amm. Marc. XXIV, 6.8: *contra haec Persae obiecerunt instructas cataphractorum equitum turmas sic confertas, ut lamminis coaptati corporum flexus splendore praestringerent occursantes obtutus, operimentis scorteis equorum multitudine omni defensa, quorum in subsidiis manipuli locati sunt peditum, contecti scutis oblongis et curvis, quae texta vimine et coriis crudis gestantes densius se commovebant. post hos elephanti gradientium collium specie motuque inmanium corporum propinquantibus exitium intentabant documentis praeteritis formidati.*

12 For the circumstances and sources see S.J. McDonough 2006, p. 74–75.

13 Ełishē, trans. R.W. Thomson, 1982, p. 166–167.

14 *The History of Al-Tabari*, trans. Y. Friedmann 1992, p. 62–63.

15 *Ibid.*, p. 89

16 *Ibid.*, p. 91.

17 F. Holt and O. Bopearachchi 2011, p. 10–11. The authenticity of this gold coin has, however, been questioned by many scholars: for a review of Holt and Bopearachchi's book and an overview of the views of other scholars, see R. Bracey (2011).

18 M.B. Charles, *op. cit.*, p. 339.

19 E. Errington and V. Sarkhosh Curtis 2007, p. 51, fig.6.

20 A.D.H. Bivar 1983, p. 84.

21 *Ibid.*, p. 84.

22 Tacitus, *Annals*, XV.15.

23 *uš kārwān ēwarz kunēnd ud pīlbān pad pīl rawēnd ud stōrbān pad stōr rawēnd ud wardyūndār pad wardyūn šawēnd was ēstēd *šafšanj ī rōdstahm was kantigr ī purr tigr ud was zrēh ī rōšn ud was zrēh ī0020ahārkard ud kārawān ī ērānšhar ēdōn bē ēstēnd ka wāng bē ō asmān šawēd ud pattān bē ō dušox šawēd pad rāh kū šawēnd widarag ēdōn bē brīnēnd ud rōd-iz āb bē šēbēnd ī tā ēw māh āb xwardān nē šāyēd tā panjāh rōz rōšn nē bawēd*; for the transcription see B. Gheiby 1999, p. 2–3; for the reading of *šafšanj* see T. Daryaee 2005, p. 95–98.

References

Ammianus Marcellinus. *The Roman History of Ammianus Marcellinus*, translated by J.C. Rolfe (1939–1950), Loeb Classical Library, Cambridge, Mass.

Bivar, A.D.H. (1983). "The Political History of Iran under the Arsacids", in E. Yarshater (ed.), *The Cambridge History of Iran*, Cambridge.

Bracey, R. (2011). "Reviews: Holt, F. and Bopearachchi, O. (eds), *The Alexander Medallion: Exploring the Origins of a Unique Artefact*, Imago Lattara, 2011", NC 171: p. 487–494.

Canepa, M.P. (2009). *The Two Eyes of the Earth. Art and Ritual of Kingship between Rome and Sasanian Iran*, California: p. 93–94.

Charles, M.B. (2007). "The Rise of the Sassanian Elephant Corps: Elephants and the Later Roman Empire", *Iranica Antiqua* XLII: p. 306–308.

Daryaee, T. (2005). "The 'Bow of Rustam' and the 'Gleaming Armor' of the Parthians: Notes on the Parthian Epic *Ayādgār ī Zarērān*", *Electrum* 10: p. 95–98.

——— (in press). "Between India and Iran: The Elephant as the Symbol of Kingship", in T. Daryaee and A. Patel (eds), *India and Iran through the Longue Durée*, Costa Mesa, California.

Davis, D. (trans.) (2007). *The Shahnameh: The Persian Book of Kings*, Penguin Classics.

Ełishē, *History of Vardan and the Armenian War*, translated by R.W. Thomson (1982), Harvard: p. 166–167.

Errington, E., and Curtis, V.S. (2007). *From Persepolis to the Punjab. Exploring Ancient Iran, Afghanistan and Pakistan*, London.

Gheiby, B. (1999). *Ayādgār ī Zarērān*, Bielfeld.

Grenet, F. (2003). *La Geste d'Ardashir fils de Pâbag*, Paris.

Holt, F., and Bopearachchi, O. (eds) (2011). *The Alexander Medallion. Exploring the origins of a unique artifact*, Rouqueyroux.

McDonough, S.J. (2006). "A Question of Faith? Persecution and Political Centralization in the Sasanian Empire of Yazdgard II (438–457 CE)", in H.A. Drake (ed.), *Violence in Late Antiquity: Perceptions and Practices*, Farnham, Surrey: p. 74–75.

Moazami, M. (2005). "Evil Animals in the Zoroastrian Religion," *History of Religions* 44.

Rance, P. (2003). "Elephants in Warfare in Late Antiquity", *Acta Antiqua Academiae Scientiarum Hungaricae* 43: p. 355–384.

Schmidt, H.-P. (1980). "Ancient Iranian Animal Classification," in *Studien zur Indologie und Iranistik*, vols. 5–6: p. 215.

Scriptores Historiae Augustae, translated by D. Magie (1993), 2 vols, Loeb Classical Library, Cambridge, Mass.

Tabari. *The History of Al-Tabari. The Battle of al-Qādisiyyah and the Conquest of Syria and Palestine*, vol. XII, translated by Y. Friedmann (1992), New York.

Tacitus. *The Annals*, translated by A.J. Church and W.J. Brodribb (1864), Cambridge and London: available on-line at http://www.perseus.tufts.edu/hopper/text?doc=Perseus:text:1999.02.0078.

5

Remarks on the Location of the Province of Parthia in the Sasanian Period*

Mehrdad Ghodrat-Dizaji
Urmia University

Compared with later eras, the historical geography of Iran during the Sasanian period has not attracted the attention of scholars. This is possibly due to the fact that, for a long time, the available sources for this period were either post-Sasanian or else came from countries neighbouring the Sasanian empire. Based on these sources, more than a century ago J. Olshausen and J. Marquart illuminated Iranian geography during this dynasty. Fortunately, in recent decades the discovery of Sasanian inscriptions, coins, seals and seal impressions and their scholarly publication have provided valuable sources for studying Iran's geography under the Sasanians. However, the ongoing publication of these new sources has not yet been adequately used to shed fresh light on Sasanian historical geography. Since the location of the province of Parthia in this period is controversially identified in modern studies, the present paper aims at illustrating the location of the province of Parthia in the Sasanian period by taking advantage of these sources. It is almost superfluous to remark that ambiguity about the geographical location of Parthia not only hinders clear description of the administrative geography of this and other related provinces, but also it has an impact on the description of historical events and, in turn, the analysis of their consequences.

The province of Parthia (Παρθία) was one of the prominent regions in the historical development of ancient Iran. In the Achaemenid period and in Old Persian, Parθava was an important province (satrapy), which appears for the first time along with other provinces in inscriptions. Darius I (522–486 BC), for instance, named Parthia in his Bisitun inscription along with the satrapies of Drangiana, Areia, Chorasmia, Bactria, Sogdiana and Gandara.[1] This is similar to the location of Parthia in Herodotus's *Histories*. In a list the latter offered about the satrapies during the reign of Darius, he included the Parthians, Chorasmians, Sogdians and Areioi as a single satrapy.[2] Thus, according to these sources from the Achaemenid period on the Parθava, it can be concluded that the province ended in Gorgān to the north-west, Khwārazm to the north, Sogdiana to the north-east, Balkh to the east, Herat to the south-east and Kirmān to the south. Its area approximately equalled today's Khurāsān province and the southern part of Turkmenistan. Achaemenid sources and Herodotus's information on the location of Parthia in the Achaemenid period have been accepted widely by modern scholars.[3]

Although sometimes, as under Alexander III of Macedon, Parthia formed a single satrapy along with Gorgān,[4] it can be surmised that Arsacid Parthia occupied the same location as Achaemenid Parthia. This idea was quite clearly mentioned in the *Geography* of Strabo, as he distinguished between Parthia as a province and Parthia as an empire, and placed the province in the region of modern-day Khurāsān in north-eastern Iran.[5]

Most historians, however, both past and present, usually consider that the same was true of Parthia in the Sasanian period as well, and believe that this is the very area which was later called Khurāsān.[6] It is even stated that the

* I would like to thank Dr Vesta Sarkhosh Curtis and Dr Michael Alram for inviting me to the conference *Parthian and Early Sasanian Empires: Adaptation and Expansion* (Kunsthistorisches Museum, Vienna, 14–15 June, 2012), and to the other conference attendees for their helpful comments and suggestions. I would also like to thank Dr Elizabeth Pendleton for her reading the manuscript and helpful comments.

elimination and demise of the Parthian language was a process that started with the rise to power of the Sasanians, and its abolition was so thorough that nowadays no dialect can be found in Khurāsān that retains any trace of the Parthian language.[7] However, it is interesting that according to linguistic studies, Parthian was one of the north-western Iranian languages (and Middle Persian belongs to the south-western group).[8] Since the only linguistic evidence remaining comes from Middle Parthian, which coincides with both the Arsacid and Sasanian periods, there remains an unanswered question: how is it possible for the province of Parthia to be located in north-eastern Iran in the period when Middle Iranian languages were spoken (i.e. the Parthian and Sasanian periods), while its language is considered to be one of the north-western languages of Iran?[9]

The remaining sources and evidences from the Sasanian era refute the idea that the province of Parthia in this period was located in north-eastern Iran. From among the local and contemporary sources from the early Sasanian period, the important trilingual inscription of Shapur I (240–272 AD) on the Ka'be-ye Zardusht (ŠKZ) at Naqsh-i Rustam in Fārs (Persis) provides the most illuminating data regarding the administrative divisions of Iran at that time. Its list of provinces defines the extent of the Sasanian empire under Shapur I in clockwise geographic enumeration. The empire's north-eastern provinces in this inscription consist of Gorgān, Marw, Harēw, Abaršahr, Kirmān, Sagestān, Tūrān etc.[10] All the provinces mentioned here were located in eastern Iran, and it should be understood that Abaršahr is mentioned as a province, not as a city. As the inscription lists before and after Abaršahr other provinces, the position of which is known, the location of Abaršahr can be determined to a large extent. Thus we may definitively place Abaršahr in the north-east of present-day Iran, which comprised most of Khurāsān province, and which ended in Gorgān to the north-west, to the north-east in Marw, to the east in Harēw, to the south-east in Sagestān, and to the south in Kirmān.

The list of the eastern provinces from the Ka'be-ye Zardusht inscription is confirmed by other sources. Tabarī, for instance, when referring to the campaign of Ardashir I (224–240 AD), founder of the Sasanian empire, in eastern Iran, named Sagestān, Gorgān, Abaršahr, Marw and Khwārazm as eastern provinces of Iran.[11] Also later on, during the reign of Khusrau I (531–579 AD), when the Sasanian empire was divided into four *Kust*s or quarters, Abaršahr was listed along with Herat, Marw, Balkh and so on as provinces governed by the *spāhbed* (commander) of the east (*xwarāsān*).[12] According to Islamic geographers, Nishāpūr (the capital of Abaršahr), Herat, Marw and Balkh were four important cities of Khurāsān, each of which was at some time the capital of Khurāsān.[13] Thus, based on the inscription of Ka'be-ye Zardusht, which is also confirmed by literary sources, it can be stated that there was no province called Parthia in the Khurāsān region during the early Sasanian period.

In the rest of the inscription, the provinces of Parthia and Abaršahr are differentiated from one another, each being separately mentioned.[14] There are also other sources and sufficient evidence left from the early Sasanian period which when pieced together, allow us to determine the location of this province. In his inscription at Ka'be-ye Zardusht Shapur I lists Parthia as one of the provinces of his empire in the order as stated before (Middle Persian version): Pārs, Pahlaw, Khuzistān, Mēšān and so on.[15] Kirdēr, the prominent Zoroastrian priest in the early Sasanian period, commissioned an inscription at Naqsh-i Rustam, which lists the provinces in the following order: Pārs, Pahlaw, Āsuristān, Mēšān and so on.[16] Manichean writings, which provide evidence for their rituals in Abaršahr, Pārs, Khuzistān and Parthia, confirm what is found in the inscriptions.[17] Additionally, Ammianus Marcellinus (fourth century AD) mentions Parthia after Persis and before Kirmān. According to Ammianus, Parthia was located to the north of Persis.[18]

Thanks to these sources, a clearer picture of the position of Parthia in the early Sasanian era emerges. By examining its location in the inscriptions with respect to that of other provinces whose location is known, one can assert that at this time Parthia was located in the central part of the Iranian plateau, neighbouring Pārs and Khuzistān: that is to say, it was bounded by Pārs to the south, by Khuzistān to the south-west, by Media to the west and north-west, by the Alborz Mountains to the north, by Abaršahr to the north-east, and by Kirmān to the east.[19]

Since the administrative organisation in the early Sasanian era was not that much different from that under the late Arsacids, one may assume that the location given in the early Sasanian sources for Parthia is a reflection of administrative divisions in late Arsacid times. It has been suggested that the name Abaršahr was attributed to the north-east of Iran after the Parni tribes settled there, and the name Parthia was attributed after the gradual transfer of Parthian capitals and settlements to the west of Iran.[20] We know that the central parts of Iran were under the rule of Arsacid emperor Ardavān (Artabanus) IV (213–224 AD), and that Hamadan, Qom and Ray were probably the first cities conquered by Sasanian king Ardashir I after his defeat of Artabanus.[21] This can be interpreted as showing the importance of Parthia for the Persian founder of the Sasanian dynasty, an importance which is also evident in the later sources. As mentioned earlier, Shapur I in his Ka'be-ye Zardusht inscription lists the province of Parthia in second place after Pārs.[22] According to Shapur, Parthia was also the second province chosen for settlement by Roman prisoners of war.[23] Parthia was also mentioned in second place after Pārs in the inscription of Abnun, who was in charge of the ceremonies of Shapur's harem. This is also the case in the above-mentioned inscription of Kirdēr.[24] The importance of Parthia was reflected even in the writings of the Roman author Ammianus Marcellinus in the fourth century

Table 5.1: Regions of fahla *according to early Islamic authors.*

Regions / *Authors*	*Azarbaijan*	*Māsabadhān*	*Mihrajāngadhaq*	*Kirmānshāh*	*Dīnawar*	*Nihāwand*	*Hamadan*	*Qazvīn*	*Ray*	*Qom*	*Isfahan*
Ibn al-Muqaffa	■					■	■		■		■
al-Khwārazmī	■					■	■		■		■
al-Dīnawarī		■	■	■	■	■	■				
Ibn al-Faqīh		■	■	■	■	■	■			■	
Ibn Khurradhābih		■	■		■	■	■	■	■		■
al-Mas'ūdī	■	■			■	■	■				
Hamza al-Isfahānī	■					■	■		■		■
al-Maqidisī		■	■		■	■	■				
Yāgut		■	■	■	■	■	■			■	

AD. It is worth mentioning that Sasanian emperor Narseh (293–302 AD) in his Paikuli inscription mostly referred to Persians and Parthians when listing those who played a role in the early years of his reign.[25] It must be noted that determining the exact location of events related to Parthia in these inscriptions depends heavily on the geographical location of Parthia. Clearly where in the Abnun inscription Romans attack (Pārs and) Parthia, the writer did not want to say that the Romans invaded north-eastern Iran.

Gay, Goyman and Ray, which were mentioned in the Ka'be-ye Zardusht inscription and on late Sasanian seals,[26] were located in this area. Having compared these regions with those cited on seals of the late Sasanian era and in early Islamic books, it can be concluded that they correspond to present-day Isfahan, Qom and Ray respectively. Ray, headquarters of the Parthian Mehrān family,[27] and Gay (Arabic Jay, later Isfahan), headquarters of the Vaspuragan (seven Parthian nobles),[28] were located in central and north-central Iran. There was, however, no mention of Isfahan in the Ka'be-ye Zardusht inscription. But Isfahan appears in Kirdēr's inscriptions at Sar Mashhad and Naqsh-i Rustam, written some thirty years after Shapur,[29] as a province along with Parthia, Persis and so on.

Does this indicate a change in the administrative divisions of Sasanian Iran which led to Parthia's expansion to western parts? What makes this likely is that according to Sasanian-based Arabic and New Persian sources, in the late Sasanian era the Parthian region[30] not only embraced central and north-central areas of Iran but also extended to western parts of its plateau.[31] Based on these sources, a large part of central and western Iran was called *fahla* or *pahla*. The earliest source in this respect is that of Ibn al-Muqaffa, which is mentioned in *al-Fihrist* of Ibn al-Nadīm, based on which the regions of Isfahan, Ray, Hamadan, Māh-i Nihāwand and Azarbaijan were called *fahla*.[32] The same evidence can also be found in the works of al-Khwārazmī and Hamza al-Isfahānī.[33] In *al-akhbār-al-tiwāl*, al-Dīnawarī, without mentioning the name *fahla*, considered the realm of Ardavān/Artabanus (presumably Ardavān IV, the last Arsacid king) to be confined to *jibāl* – i.e. Nihāwand, Dīnawar, Hamadan, Māsabadhān, Mihrajānqadhaq and Hulwān (Kirmānshāh and Qasr-i Shīrīn).[34] However, referring to the *pahlav* regions in his book entitled *Mukhtasar Kitāb al-buldān*, Ibn al-Faqīh, Dīnawarī's contemporary, believed that they were the same areas mentioned in Dīnawarī, in addition to Qom.[35] In his book, *Kitab al-Masālik wa al-mamālik*, Ibn Khurradhābih holds that *pahlav* incorporated Ray, Isfahan, Hamadan, Dīnawar, Nihāwand, Mihrjānqadhaq, Māsabadhān and Qazvīn.[36] Al-Maqidisī in his book entitled *Ahsan al-taqāsim* believed that the *pahlav* region encompassed Hamadan, Māsabadhdān, Mehrajānqadhaq, Nihāwand and Dīnawar.[37] Al-Bīrunī in his work *Āsār al-bāqia* considered that the land included Isfahan and Ray.[38] Eventually, Yāgut in *Mu'jam al-buldān* assumed the land of *fahla* to comprise Hamadan, Māsabadhān, Qom, Māh-i Basra (Nihāwand), Sīmara (Mihrajānqadhaq), Māh-i Kufa (Dīnawar), and Kirmānshāh.[39]

Most of the Muslim historians who referred to *fahla* also stated that in this region *fahlavī* was a common language. Even today, some old poems known as *fahlavīyāt* can still be found in Islamic sources. The available examples mostly come from the areas which were considered to be part of *fahlav*, such as Nihāwand, Avroman, Ray, Hamadan, Isfahan and Qazvīn. According to new studies, the available poems in *fahlavī* reveal the characteristics of oral literature. Thus we may say that the *fahlavī* poems continued the oral traditions of the Parthian *gosan*s and Sasanian minstrels, following the principles of Middle Iranian prosody. The *fahlavīyāt* have certain linguistic affinities with Parthian, although in their existing forms they have been much influenced by New Persian.[40]

Based on the aforementioned statements, and relying on Persian and Arabic sources, *fahla* areas can be summed up in Table 5.1.

Now, if one compares this information with the list offered in early Sasanian inscriptions, some differences come to the surface. These are the result of changes in both the position and extent of Parthia in the late Sasanian and early Islamic periods. Consequently, Parthia covered the western part of Iranian plateau. All the authors cited above described Hamadan and Nihāwand as parts of Parthia. Moreover, regardless of the differences among Islamic writers as to the boundaries of *fahla*, they all unanimously believed that Khurāsān was not part of Parthia, a view which is supported by the early Sasanian inscriptions.

To sum up, the province of Parthia in the Achaemenid period included the north-eastern parts of Iran. Nevertheless, there is evidence indicating that in the late Arsacid period the term was applied to the central and north-central regions of Iran. Sources from the early Sasanian period categorically demonstrate that Parthia was located in this part of Iranian plateau. However, Islamic sources reveal that in the late Sasanian period, Parthia now encompassed in addition the western part of Iran. In other words, from the Achaemenids to the Sasanians, there was a change in the location of Parthia from north-east to western Iran. Having considered the evidence and reasons set out above, it can be concluded that, if Middle Parthian has features of the north-western Iranian languages, this is due to the fact that the Parthian region was located in the northern and western part of Iranian plateau during those times.

Notes

1 Schmitt 1991, p. 49–50.
2 Herodotus 3.93 (tr. p. 121, 123).
3 *Cf.* e.g. Dandamaev 1989, p. 85.
4 Debevoise 1938, p. 7.
5 Strabo 11.9.1 (tr. p. 271, 273); *cf.* Drijvers 1998, p. 282. Later references in Strabo (*ibid.*), however, apparently show that during the Arsacid period, Parthia extended to central parts of Iran with the capital city Hekatompylos.
6 *Cf.* Lazard 1995, p. 50; Pourshariati 2008, p. 4, 6, 42, 222, 263, 275, 392–393, 419–420.
7 Lazard 1995, p. 50. Sundermann (1989, p. 115) explains the points as follows: "Ihrer ostiranischen Heimat zum Trotz gehört die parthische Sprache zu den nordwestiranischen Mundarten und Sprachen. In Sprachen und Mundarten dieser Gruppe müssen daher die Verwandten des Parthischen gesucht werden, wenn auch keine derselben sich bisher als Nachkomme des Parthischen hat identifizieren lassen."
8 Sundermann *loc. cit.*
9 Eastern Iranian languages were spoken in present-day Afghanistan and beyond.
10 Huyse 1999, p. 23–24. The name of Abaršahr appears in the Middle Persian version as *hamag Abaršahr*. Abaršahr also appeared on Sasanian coins with the mint abbreviation AP; *cf.* Schindel 2006, p. 675.
11 Nöldeke 1879, p. 17; *cf.* also Alram 2007, p. 233.
12 *Cf.* e.g. Y'aqūbī 1883, p. 201.
13 Marquart 1901, p. 47; Le Strange 1905, p. 382.
14 Bivar (1983, p. 26) stated that it was likely that the Sasanians had intentionally built Abaršahr apart from Parthia. There is, however, no evidence to confirm such a claim. The available sources mostly indicate that the Iranian name of Abaršahr was applied to the Achaemenid satrapy of Parthia after the settlement of Parni tribes in the region: *cf.* Henning 1958, p. 95; Brunner 1983, p. 767; Shahbazi 1389/2011, p. 243–244.
15 Huyse 1999, p. 22–23.
16 Gignoux 1991, p. 61, 71.
17 Sarkarati 1378/1999, p. 149, 157–170, 177–178.
18 Ammianus Marcellinus 23.6.14 (tr. p. 357).
19 A brief description of this location is provided by Brunner 1983, p. 752–753; *cf.* also Gyselen 1989, p. 73.
20 Brunner 1983, p. 767.
21 Schippmann 1990, p. 16.
22 Huyse 1999, p. 22–23.
23 Huyse 1999, p. 43.
24 Tavoosi & Frye 1989, p. 25–38; Gignoux 1991, p. 71.
25 Skjærvø 1983, p. 29, 31, 34, 43, 63–64, 67–68.
26 Gyselen 1989, p. 73.
27 Marquart 1901, p. 124.
28 Marquart 1901, p. 29.
29 Gignoux 1991, p. 61, 71.
30 Persian form: *pahla*, Arabic: *fahla, bahla*, *cf.* Lazard 1995, p. 50.
31 Olshausen (1876) cited most of these sources and their contents about the geography of Parthia; *cf.* also Tafażżolī 1999, p. 158–162.
32 Ibn al-Nadīm 1953/1974, p. 15.
33 al- Khwārazmī 1895, p. 117; Hamza al-Isfahānī 1412/1992, p. 23.
34 al-Dinawarī 1969, p. 40; also *cf.* al-Mas'ūdī in *Mururj al-Dhahab* (1861–1877, p. 133) who calls the Arsacids the kings of *jibāl* i.e. Dīnawar, Nihāwand, Hamadan, Māsabadhān and Azarbaijan. Also *cf.* Tabarī's *History* (Nöldeke 1879, p. 7) who assumes the Arsacid king Ardawān was king of *jibāl*.
35 Ibn al-Faqīh 1885, p. 296.
36 Ibn Khurradādhbīh 1889, p. 57.
37 al-Maqdisī 1906, p. 373–374.
38 al-Biruni 1879, p. 34.
39 Yāqūt 1397/1977, p. 42.
40 Tafażżolī 1999, p. 159.

References

Alram, M. (2007). "Ardashir's Eastern Campaign and the Numismatic Evidence", in J. Cribb and G. Herrmann (eds), *After Alexander. Central Asia before Islam* (Proceedings of the British Academy 133), Oxford: p. 227–241.

Ammianus Marcellinus. *Rerum gestarum libri*, translated by J.C. Rolfe (1950), vol. 2, London and Cambridge, Mass.

al-Biruni, Muhammad b. Ahmad. *The Chronology of Ancient Nations*, translated and edited by E. Sachau (1879), London.

Bivar, A.D.H. (1983). "The Political History of Iran under the Arsacids", in E. Yarshater (ed.), *The Cambridge History of Iran*, vol. 3.1, Cambridge: p. 21–99.

Brunner, Chr. (1983). "Geographical and Administrative Divisions: Settlements and Economy", in E. Yarshater (ed.), *The Cambridge History of Iran*, vol. 3.2, Cambridge: p. 747–777.

Dandamaev, M.A. (1989). *The Political History of the Achaemenid Empire*, Leiden.

Debevoise, N.C. (1938). *A Political History of Parthia*, Chicago.

al-Dīnawarī, Ahmad b. Dāwūd. *al-Akhbār al-tiwāl*, edited by 'A.M. 'Āmir (1969), Cairo.

Drijvers, J.W. (1998). "Strabo on Parthia and Parthians", in J. Wiesehöfer (ed.), *Das Partherreich und seine Zeugnisse (The Arsacid Empire: Sources and Documentation)*, Stuttgart: p. 279–293.

Ibn al-Faqīh, Ahmad b. Muhammad al-Hamadānī. *Mukhtasar Kitāb al-Buldān*, edited by M.J. de Goeje (1885), Leiden.

Ibn Khurradādhbih, Abu 'l-Qāsim 'Ubaydallāh. *Kitāb al-Masālik wa 'l-mamālik*, edited by M.J. de Goeje (1889), Leiden.

Ibn al-Nadīm, Muhammad b. Ishāq. *al-Fihrist*, edited by R. Tajaddud (1353/1974), Tehran.

Gignoux, Ph. (1991). *Les quatre inscriptions du mage Kirdēr*, Studia Iranica, Cahier 9, Leuven.

Gyselen, R. (1989). *La géographie administrative de l'empire sassanide. Les témoignages de sigillographie* (Res Orientales 1), Bures-sur-Yvette.

Hamzat al-Isfahānī. *al-Tanbīh 'ala Hudūth al-Tashīf*, edited by As'ad Talas (1412/1992), Beirut.

Herodotus. *Histories*, translated by A.D. Godley (1960), vol. 2, London and Cambridge, Mass.

Huyse, Ph. (1999). *Die dreisprachige Inschrift Šābuhr I. an der Ka'ba-i Zardušt (ŠKZ)*, Corpus Inscriptionum Iranicarum, Part III, vol. I, London.

al-Khwārazmī, Abu 'Abdallāh Mohammad b. Ahmad. *Mafātīh al-'ulūm*, edited by G. van Vloten (1895), Leiden.

Lazard, D. (1995). *La Formation de la langue persane*, Paris.

Le Strange, G. (1905). *The Lands of the Eastern Caliphate: Mesopotamia, Persia, and Central Asia from the Moslem Conquest to the Time of Timur*, Cambridge.

al-Maqdisī, Muhammad b. Ahmad. *Ahsan al-taqāsīm fī ma'rifat al-aqālīm*, edited by M.J. de Goeje (1906), Leiden.

Marquart, J. (1901). *Ērānšahr nach der Geographie des Ps. Moses Xorenac'i*, Berlin.

al-Mas'ūdī, Abu 'l-Hasan 'Alī b. Husayn. *Murūj al-dhahab wa-ma'ādin al-jawāhar*, vol. 2, edited and translated by Barbier de Meynard and Pavet de Courteille (1861–1877), Paris.

Nöldeke, Th. (1879). *Geschichte der Perser und Araber zur Zeit der Sasaniden aus der arabischen Chronik des Tabari*, Leiden.

Olshausen, J. (1876). *Parthava und Pahlav, Mâda und Mâh*, Berlin.

Pourshariati, P. (2008). *Decline and Fall of the Sasanian Empire: The Sasanian–Parthian Confederacy and the Arab Conquest of Iran*, London and New York.

Sādigī, 'A.A. (1357/1978). *Takvīn-i zabān-i Fārsī* (in Persian), Tehran.

Sarkārātī, B. (1378/1999). "Akhbār-i tārikhī dar āsār-i Mānavī" (in Persian), *sāyehā-ye šekār šodeh*, Tehran: p. 133–211.

Schindel, N. (2006). "The Sasanian Eastern Wars in the 5th Century: The Numismatic Evidence", in A. Panaino and A. Piras (eds), *Proceedings of the 5th Conference of the Societas Iranologica Europae, vol. 1, Ancient & Middle Iranian Studies*, Milan: p. 675–689.

Schippmann, K. (1990). *Grundzüge der Geschichte des sasanidischen Reiches,* Darmstadt.

Schmitt, R. (1991). *The Bisitun Inscription of Darius the Great. Old Persian Text*, Corpus Inscriptionum Iranicarum, Part I, London.

Shahbazi, A., Shapur (1389/2010). *Tārīkh-i Sāsāniān* (in Persian), Tehran.

Skjærvø, P.O. (1983). *The Sassanian Inscription of Paikuli*, Part 3.1, Wiesbaden.

Strabo. *The Geography*, translated by H.L. Jones (1928), vol. 5, London and Cambridge, Mass.

Sundermann, W. (1989). "Parthisch", in R. Schmitt (ed.), *Compendium Linguarum Iranicarum*, Wiesbaden: p. 114–137.

Tafażżolī, A. (1999). "Fahlavīyāt", *Encyclopaedia Iranica*, vol. 9, New York: p. 158–162.

Tavoosi, M., and Frye, R.N. (1989). "An Inscribed Capital Dating from the Time of Shapur I", *Bulletin of the Asia Institute* 3: p. 25–38.

Yāqūt, Abī 'Abdallāh. (1397/1977). *Mu'jam al-buldān*, vol. 4, Beirut.

Ya'qūbī, Ahmad b. Abī Ya'qūb. (1883). *Tārīkh*, edited by M.Th. Houtsma, Leiden.

6

The Birth of the Sasanian Monarchy in Western Sources

Andrea Gariboldi
University of Bologna

The last notable political achievement of Arsacid foreign policy was the peace signed with the Romans in 218 AD.[1] Although some years later Cassius Dio (LXXX 3–4) and Herodian (VI 2, 1–2) wrote about serious trouble on the eastern border of the Roman empire, reporting the murder of Artabanus and Ardashir's ascent to the throne, which should be dated to 224 AD,[2] the Romans did not immediately realise the revolutionary character of the new Sasanian empire.

The territorial claims (supposedly) advanced by the Persians created apprehension on the Roman side.[3] Herodian, who says that he was a contemporary of Artabanus (Hdn VI 2, 7), is very clear on one point at least: a bold protagonist in the Orient, called Artaxerxes/Ardashir, the king of the Iranians, seized power from the Parthians and killed their Great King Artabanus, who wore the double diadem (Hdn VI 2, 1).[4] These remarks are scanty but correct. The title of *basileus megas* (of Babylonian and Achaemenid origin) was characteristic of the Parthian dynasty but was never officially adopted by the Sasanian kings,[5] while the double diadem sometimes adorns the king's head in the late Parthian and Elymaian art.[6]

Yet in Roman literary texts there is no single term used to describe the Sasanians, who are generally defined as Persians, Medians or even Parthians (not always for purely rhetorical reasons), even by very competent historians, like Ammianus Marcellinus.[7] Modern historiography has usually emphasised that his digression about the Persis region, in particular, is very generic and imprecise.[8] One might even think that Ammianus, who should have been well informed about the difference between Parthians and Sasanians, was not the author of this *excursus*. He was personally present during the campaigns of Constantius II against Shapur II. Moreover, he was a direct witness of the siege of Amida in 359 AD and a contemporary witness of the great Persian expedition of Julian in 363 AD.[9] Ammianus was a native of Antioch and served with the Roman army as *protector* (a kind of military attaché): this important position gave him access to secret documents and official letters, and he also participated in delicate missions behind the Roman *limes*. Nevertheless, in his *Histories* we do not find a single reference to the dynastic change in Persia, when Ardashir brought to an end a regime which had lasted five centuries.

How can we explain this surprising omission? Ammianus was an enthusiastic supporter of Julian's aggressive policy against the barbarians. He thought that a strategy mainly based on military containment along the Mesopotamian border was not sufficient to meet the Persian threat. Julian, who was welcomed by the Phoenician community on the eve of the Persian campaign as *barbarorum extinctor*, "the terminator of the barbarians",[10] once proclaimed to his troops: *abolenda nobis natio molestissima, cuius in gladiis nondum nostrae propinquitatis exaruit cruor* (*H.* XXIII 5, 19) – "We must destroy this pernicious people, on whose swords the blood of our relatives is not yet dry." Julian's references to recent Roman defeats clearly alluded to the catastrophic Oriental campaigns of Gordian III, Philip the Arab and Valerian. Julian visited Gordian's tomb at Zaitha, where he celebrated sacrifices in his honour.[11] He was anxious to fight and desired to add to his official titles the cognomen *Parthicus*.[12] The Roman emperor represented himself as the avenger of the soldiers killed at Carrhae; the final solution thunders in the threatening words (echoing those of Cato), *abolenda nobis natio*.

Julian, like a tragic actor, was confronted by a host of ill omens: the strange and sudden deaths of soldiers, unexpected thunderbolt strikes and, in particular, the discovery of a huge dead lion pierced by javelins, which the Etruscan haruspices (who used to accompany the Roman emperor in battle) explicitly interpreted as the impending death of *one* king. Without listening to his advisers, Julian rushed against the Persians, led by Shapur II. Ammianus has harsh words for the Persian king; in addition to describing him (correctly) as an old man, *longaevus ille Sapor* (*H*. XXVII 12, 1), he calls him *efferatus, truculentus, irritabilis, asperrimus, astutus* and *immaniter arrogans*, "enormously arrogant". Yet the Roman historian knows the meaning of some Sasanian royal titles, such as *saansaan*, "King of Kings" (*šāhān šāh*), and *pirosen*, "victor in wars" (*pērōz*).[13] In the *Histories*, setting aside the generic digression on the usages and customs of the Persians (*H*. XXIII 6), which is clearly based on the sixth book of the *Geography* of Ptolemy, there is little information about the Persian nobility or the administration of the Sasanian empire. The short sketch of the Magi and Zoroaster's religion openly derives from classical Greek sources, such as Herodotus and Plato. Nevertheless, Ammianus never defines the Persians as "barbarians" but adopts the terms *natio* or *gentes*.

In general, the ethnic *Persae* is more commonly used in the *Histories* than *Parthi*. It is important to note that Ammianus links the Parthian dynasty to the Sasanians, about whom, in practice, he has nothing of note to say; as Willem Drijvers correctly pointed out, Ammianus does not actually distinguish between Parthians and Sasanians.[14] He completely omits to explain how the Sasanians came to power in Iran (but was this included in one of the lost books?), and curiously confers on Shapur II the royal title of the deified Arsaces, *Solis frater et Lunae*, "brother of the Sun and Moon".[15] Ammianus's historical anachronism is evident when he writes: "Hence they venerate and worship Arsaces as a god, and their regard for him has been carried so far, that even down to the memory of our time (*ad nostri memoriam*) only a man who is of the stock of Arsaces, if there is one anywhere, is preferred to all in mounting the throne."[16] Ammianus's principal intent was to prove an historical continuity, and even a genealogical one, between the Parthians and the Sasanians, in order to distort the facts. The falsification is manifest when he affirms that *in his time* only an Arsacid man could ascend to the throne. This misrepresentation of history cannot be casual in Ammianus, and especially in the fourth century AD, when the Roman emperors no longer bore the official title *Parthicus* but the more correct *Persicus/Persikos*.[17]

The first emperor to employ the epithet *Persicus Maximus* (rather than *Parthicus Maximus*) was Philip the Arab (attested in an inscription from Rome).[18] Philip optimistically celebrated on some of his coins the *pax fundata cum Persis*,[19] although in fact he had to ransom his army and was forced to renounce the Roman protectorate over Hatra and part of Armenia. The Romans tried to conceal the disastrous campaigns of Gordian III, even if in Zonara (XII 17) the memory of the young emperor "falling from his horse" during a pitched battle with the Persians still survives. Santo Mazzarino has shown that the Greco-Roman historiography concerning the Persian wars of the third century, including Ammianus's account, is completely altered.[20] The historic deformation of the traditional version, the so-called "vulgate", attributes Gordian's death to an internal plot of Philip, rather than admitting Shapur's responsibility.

In Roman inscriptions up to the reign of Probus both *Parthicus* and *Persicus* are attested interchangeably as Roman imperial titles, but from Carus onward, the correct term *Persicus* became popular also in literary texts. If so, why did Julian, along with Ammianus, insist on *Parthici cognomentum*? Julian aimed at revitalising the old Roman anti-Parthian tradition, going back to the battle of Carrhae and to Trajan's victories over the Parthians, and of course he dreamed of becoming a new Alexander the Great. Julian even confessed, in his letter addressed to Themistios, that he feared that he would not be able to equal the military virtues of Alexander. But were the dream of emulating Alexander and the model of Trajan sufficient to generate a desire to obtain an anachronistic title, thus cancelling the Sasanians from history?

Alain Chauvot, in an important study on the Roman perception of the barbarians, observed that in Julian's orations we can detect an ambiguous attitude towards the Parthians. In the first panegyric dedicated to Constantius, which was written around 356/7 AD, the "Asiatic" barbarians were deemed as one single Oriental nation that fought first Alexander and then the Romans; the Persians were considered as simply the remains of the Macedonian empire. We find in this text the confusing classical conflation of Medians, Parthians and Persians. The Romans were the natural successors of Alexander in the Persian wars. In the second panegyric for Constantius (358/9 AD), Julian's opinion rapidly seems to change: he mentions only the Parthians, as though the Sasanians never existed.[21] It is worth citing a passage from the *Second Oration*, which should be seriously considered in the historiographical debate conducted by many Iranologists on the subject of the Sasanians' memory (real or presumed) of their Achaemenid past.[22] According to Julian, the Sasanians were terribly afraid of being mistaken for Parthians, hence they tried to exalt many aspects deriving from the Achaemenid tradition, such as, for instance, their style of dress and military tactics. Julian describes the Persian siege of Nisibis in 350 AD by the troops of Shapur II (Iul. *Or*. III 63a-b):

> Ἐνταῦθα κοσμεῖ τὴν στρατιὰν τὸν Περσικὸν τρόπον· διασώζουσι γὰρ καὶ ἀπομιμοῦνται τὰ Περσικὰ οὐκ ἀξιοῦντες, ἐμοὶ δοκεῖ, Παρθυαῖοι νομίζεσθαι, Πέρσαι δὲ εἶναι προσποιούμενοι. Ταῦτά τοι καὶ στολῇ Μηδικῇ χαίρουσι καὶ ἐς μάχας ἔρχονται ὁμοίως ἐκείνοις ὅπλοις τε ἀγαλλόμενοι τοιούτοις καὶ ἐσθήμασιν ἐπιχρύσοις καὶ ἁλουργέσι. Σοφίζονται δὲ ἐντεῦθεν τὸ μὴ δοκεῖν ἀφεστάναι Μακεδόνων, ἀναλαβεῖν δὲ τὴν ἐξ ἀρχαίου βασιλείαν προσήκουσαν. Οὐκοῦν καὶ ὁ βασιλεὺς Ξέρξην μιμούμενος ἐπί τινος χειροποιήτου καθῆστο γηλόφου, προσῆγε δὲ ἡ στρατιὰ ξὺν τοῖς θηρίοις. Ταῦτα δὲ ἐξ Ἰνδῶν εἵπετο, καὶ ἔφερεν ἐκ σιδήρου πύργους τοξοτῶν πλήρεις.[23]

"Thereupon [Shapur II] arrayed the army in the Persian fashion. For they keep up and imitate Persian customs, it seems to me, because they do not wish to be considered Parthians, and so they pretend to be Persians. That is surely why they prefer the Median manner of dress; and when they march to battle they look like them, and take pride in wearing the same armour and dress adorned with gold and purple. By these means they try to evade the truth and to make it appear they have not revolted from Macedon, but are merely resuming the empire that was theirs of old. Thus their king, imitating Xerxes, took position on an artificial elevation; then the army advanced with wild beasts (it is said that they came from India); they brought onward the iron towers full of archers."

These words of Julian are paradigmatic, in my opinion, not only for understanding the terminological oscillation between Parthians and Persians in the Roman sources, but also because they indicate that the disappearance of the Sasanians from both Julian's speeches and Ammianus's *Histories* was a deliberate choice of political anti-propaganda. In substance, as much the Sasanians presented themselves as natural heirs of the Achaemenids, avoiding any mention of their Parthian heritage, so by contrast Julian, a true master of rhetoric, insisted on the fact that the Sasanians were merely Parthians disguised as Persians. This anti-rhetoric technique employed by Julian may explain why the Sasanians disappear from Ammianus's digression on Persia (which was purposely inserted in his work between Julian's speeches and the narration of the Persian expedition), where it is claimed that the Sasanians descend from Arsaces. The error of Ammianus cannot be accidental. In the above-mentioned passage, Julian describes precisely the manner in which his enemies besieged towns, and, notwithstanding some allusions to Herodotus in the way Shapur is likened to Xerxes, who admired his fleet from the heights of Abydos[24] (although Nisibis compares poorly with Athens), it clearly emerges that Sasanian propaganda was aimed at producing evidence for the ancient Achaemenid origins of the new Iranian empire.

The Parthian era was perceived by Zoroastrian historiography as a very negative period, linked to the deeds of the "accursed Alexander" (*gizistag Aleksandar*), who set on fire the sacred books of the *Avesta*, killed many religious authorities and caused the fragmentation of Persian political power.[25] The propaganda invented by the Sasanians themselves, embedded in the *Stories* of Agathias and also reported by later Muslim historians, deliberately shortened the duration of the Parthian kingdom, saying that the reign of the Arsacid (*Aškānid*) rulers lasted only for 266 (or 270) years, which is roughly half of the real period.[26]

Julian, by contrast, stressed that the Macedonian realm passed from the Seleucids to the Romans, thus the neo-Persian power should be considered subject to Rome; he does not mention, like other classical sources, the territorial claims of the Sasanians, who, it was said, were restoring the old dimensions of the Achaemenid empire that stretched from India to the Aegean Sea. (Was this a Roman exaggeration, suggested by Herodotus?) Julian enters into the deep motivations of those revisionist ambitions. Thus the "Apostate" was fully aware of the new political form that grew in Persia, and combatted this problem by denying it. I surmise that the philosopher emperor wanted to be called *Parthicus* in order to frustrate the ideological aspirations of his enemies, because the Sasanians deemed the Parthian kingdom as the political descendent of the Seleucids. In the event of Roman success, the Romans planned to hand over the Sasanian kingdom, after the death of Shapur II, to the Persian prince Hormisdas/Ohrmazd (the elder brother of Shapur), who was living in Rome as an exile.[27] Julian relied on this Ohrmazd, who served in the Roman cavalry, when he conferred on him the command of the Roman army during the transfer from Constantinople to Antioch.

The modern historians who strongly denied any possibility that the Sasanians could remember, at least to some extent, their Achaemenid past (the famous *historical amnesia*),[28] stating that it was just an *interpretatio romana*,[29] useful to the publicity of the Roman emperors, grasped, in my opinion, only one important side of this intricate question. Julian, in fact, distorted the meaning of the propaganda of his enemies, insisted on the hetero-ethnic of "Parthians" and connected his campaigns to Trajan's wars; indeed, in a rare moment when the mask of the historical fiction falls away, he admits that the Sasanians wanted to be called Persians, because they were not Parthians: Πέρσαι δὲ εἶναι προσποιούμενοι, "they pretend/simulate/presume to be Persians".

It is important that Julian informs us that the Sasanians considered the Achaemenids as their ancestors, in opposition to the Parthian background. What kind of direct or indirect knowledge they had about the Achaemenids is another unresolved problem. In any case, it is doubtful that the idea of the Sasanians as heirs of the Achaemenids could exist *only* in the western historiographical paradigm of the *imitatio Alexandri*,[30] because the Sasanian national epic/history, for instance, attested in the *Kārnāmag* of Ardashir, elaborated the assumption that Ardashir was descended *az tōhmag ī Sāsān ud nāf ī Dārāy šāh*, "from the seed of Sāsān and from the lineage of king Darius".[31] Similarly, Tabari writes that "he arose in Fārs seeking, as he alleged, to avenge the blood of his paternal cousin Dārā, son of Bahman, son of Isfandiyār, on whom Alexander had made war and had killed two of the latter's chief commanders".[32]

The contradictory and derogatory genealogy of Ardashir, collected by Agathias (II 27), states that Ardashir was actually the son of a σκυτοτόμος, a "cobbler" or shoemaker, by name Pābag, but Agathias also reports that he stemmed ἐκ σπέρματος Σασάνου, "from the seed of Sāsān", which is the correct Greek translation of the formula that we find in the inscription of Narseh (NPi § 80), *ō tōhm čē Sāsānagān*, "to the family of Sāsān".[33] In the Zoroastrian texts, the

Parthian Dark Age was connected with a process of political disintegration, also weakened by the Hellenistic influence, which only Ardashir could reunify and revitalise with his nationalistic Iranian pride. There is a significant passage of the *Bundahishn* (XXXIII 19–20), in which the birth of the Sasanian dynasty is clearly joined to the former periods:

> *pas andar xwadāyīh ī Dārā(y) ī Dārāyān Aleksandar ī kēsār az Hrōm dwārist ō Ērānšāhr āmad ud Dārā(y)-šāh ōzad ud hamāg dūdag ī xwadāyān ud mow-mardān ud paydāgān ī Ērānšāhr abesīhēnīd ud was marag ātaxš afsārd ud dēn ī mazdēsnān ud zand stad ō Hrōm frēstād ud abestāg sōxt ud Ērānšāhr pad nawad kardag-xwadāy baxt. Pas andar ham hazārag Arda(x)šīr ī Pābagān ō paydāgīh āmad ud ān kardag-xwadāyān ōzad ud xwadāyīh win(n)ārd ud dēn ī mazdēsnān rawāgēnīd ud ēwēnag ī was wirāst ī pad tōhmag ī ōy raft.*[34]

> "Then during the reign of Dārā, the son of Dārā, Alexander the Caesar moved from Rome and came to the Iranian kingdom, he killed king Dārā and destroyed all the families of the rulers, the Magi and the notables of the Iranian kingdom; he extinguished a great number of fires and took away the *Zand* of the Mazdean religion and sent it to Rome; he set on fire the *Avesta* and divided the Iranian kingdom among ninety house-rulers. Then, in the same millennium, came Ardashir, the son of Pābag, he killed those lords and restored the sovereignty, promoted the religion of the Mazdeans, established many customs and went with his own stock."

Ardashir, restoring the good religion that was dispersed by the accursed Alexander, restored the mythical Iranian tradition and presented himself as the natural continuator of a millenary royal saga. Thus, the Sasanian monarchy found its legitimation among the members of Sāsān's family, whose historical origin is unfortunately lost in myth. Sasanian inscriptions do not say explicitly that Sāsān was Ardashir's father or grandfather; this was assumed by later historians. But there is the possibility that the "lord" (*xwadāy*) Sāsān claimed royal blood from some Indo-Parthian dynasty.[35] In any case, it is unlikely that all these peculiar aspects of Sasanian kingship could be really understood outside the Iranian context. We cannot exclude *a priori* that all the abundant mentions, both in the Greco-Roman and in the Iranian sources, that refer to the rights of the Persian "ancestors" (πρόγονοι/*maiores*) could have something to do with the Achaemenid past, even if confused. Rahim Shayegan has recently demonstrated that the tradition of evoking one's forebears in royal inscriptions, always within the selfsame dynasty, is typical of the Iranian conception of kingship. As a matter of fact, the ancestors are mentioned in Old-Persian texts (*apaniyāka-*), in Middle-Persian and Parthian inscriptions (*ahēnagān*/*hasēnagān*), and also the inscription of Rabatak offers a reconstruction of Kanishka's genealogy.[36] What we can maintain is that all this convergence of sources mentioning the forefathers of the kings was not a pure invention of the western authors, but an integral part of the mythical elaboration of the Sasanian State. This mythical elaboration was then picked up by the Romans.

In the end, we still lack clear evidence about the identity of these venerable ancestors: were they the Achaemenids, the Frataraкās or mythical kings, like the Kayānids, who never existed in history? We receive different answers according to each source. As we have seen, Ardashir was not presented in the *Bundahishn* as a direct descendant from the Achaemenid family, but rather as the legitimate restorer of kingship over the Iranian lands, and this exactly corresponds to the Roman view.

The ancient debate that flourished on the true origin of the Persian kings indicates that the Romans did in fact realise that a new era had started with Ardashir, once one looks beyond their strongly denigrating propaganda against their Oriental enemies. Unfortunately, it is impossible to find out just one monolithic truth, but I hope to have shown that sometimes terminological confusions may conceal more recondite political motivations.

Notes

1 Dąbrowa 1984, p. 160.
2 Felix 1985, p. 25–42, collects the ancient sources about Ardashir's reign; see also Dodgeon, Lieu 1991, p. 9–15; Hackl, Jacobs, Weber 2010, p. 169; Alram, Gyselen 2003, p. 21–31; Frendo 2002, with further bibliography.
3 Kettenhofen 1984; *idem* 2002; Wiesehöfer 1986; Gnoli 1996; Huyse 2002; Shayegan 2011, p. 30–38.
4 Alföldy 1989, p. 229–237.
5 Shayegan 2011, p. 41–45; Muccioli 2013, p. 403–409.
6 Wiesehöfer 2006, p. 401–408; von Gall 1980.
7 Paratore 1966; Pugliese Carratelli 1971, p. 598–599.
8 Feraco 2004, p. 110–111; Drijvers 1999, p. 195; Brok 1975, p. 49–50.
9 Bowersock 1978, p. 105–119; Drijvers 2006, p. 46: "In 363 he took part in the disastrous Persian expedition of Julian, of which he presents an elaborate description in Books 23–25 of the *Res Gestae*". On Julian's *Perserfeldzug*, see also Brodka 2009, p. 78–88; Blockley 1988; Fornara 1991; Barnes 1998; Smith 1999.
10 Bowersock 1978, p. 122–123; Chauvot 1998, p. 174–175.
11 According to Ammianus, Gordian's tomb was at Zaitha (*H.* XXIII 5, 7), while Zosimus says that it was near Dura (Zos. III 14, 2). See Fornara 1991, p. 8; Edwell 2008, p. 69.
12 *Ornamentis inlustrium gloriarum inserere Parthici cognomentum ardebat* (*H.* XXII 12, 2); Potter 2004, p. 517–518; Drijvers 1999, p. 203.
13 *Persis Saporem saansaan appellantibus et pirosen, quod rex regibus imperans et bellorum victor interpretatur* (*H.* XIX 2, 11). See Drijvers 2006, p. 53.
14 Drijvers 1999, p. 195; *idem* 2006, p. 52–61.
15 *Unde ad id tempus reges eiusdem gentis praetumidi appellari se patiuntur Solis fratres et Lunae* (*H.* XXIII 6, 5). Cf. XVII 5, 3: *Rex regum Sapor, particeps siderum, frater Solis et Lunae*. Drijvers 1999, p. 198; *idem* 2006, p. 60; Muccioli 2009, p. 89.
16 *Quam ob rem numinis eum vice venerantur et colunt eo usque propagatis honoribus, ut ad nostri memoriam non*

nisi Arsacides, si sit usquam, in suscipiendo regno cunctis anteponatur (*H.* XXIII 6, 6).

17 Chauvot 1992, p. 116–117.

18 *CIL* VI 1097. Ziegler 1964, p. 142–143.

19 Alram, Blet-Lemarquand, Skjærvø 2007, p. 12–13.

20 Mazzarino 1971; Edwell 2008, p. 171–173.

21 Chauvot 1998, p. 164–169; *idem* 1992, p. 118–119: "A la confusion inorganisée du premier *Eloge* se substitute une confusion délibérée. Tout se passe comme si les Perses sassanides n'existaient pas [...] Aux Sassanides, qui se présentent comme les héritiers des Achéménides, dont ils revendiquent les anciens territoires, Julien oppose implicitement qu'ils ne sont que des Parthes déguisés en Perses".

22 Shayegan 2011, p. 361–368; Gariboldi 2011, p. 42–50.

23 Lacombrade 1964, p. 133.

24 Hdt. VII 44.

25 Daryaee 2007.

26 Gnoli 2013, p. 43–47; Gariboldi 2011, p. 78–81; Cameron 1969–70, p. 105 (Agath. II 26, 1).

27 Amm. Marc. XVI 10, 16; XXIV 1, 2; Zos. II 27; Zos. III 11, 3; Zon. XIII 5. John of Antioch (F266), tells the curious story of Ohrmazd's flight from his Persian prison, with the help of his mother and wife who prepared for him iron chains full of pearls (as a symbol of royalty); he fled to Licinius. But according to Zosimus, Ohrmazd found a knife-file inside a fish brought by his wife. There are interesting similarities between the romantic stories of Kawād and Ohrmazd, who were both able to escape from prison with the help of their women. About the role of Hormisdas in Roman strategy, see Shayegan 2011, p. 367–368. (Libanios *Ep.* 1402); Gariboldi 2011, p. 44; Potter 2004, p. 517; Mosig-Walburg 2000, p. 78–82; Blockley 1992, p. 9–12.

28 Yarshater 1971; Daryaee 2002.

29 Kettenhofen 1984; Straub 1986; Huyse 2002; Shayegan in this volume.

30 Huyse 2002, p. 307: "Il est possible, même vraisemblable, que les Sassanides aient revendiqué des territoires jadis en la possession de leurs ancêtres. Il est en revanche hautement improbable qu'ils aient circonscrit le territoire revendiqué d'une façon aussi précise que les revendications formulées par les auteurs gréco-romains le laissent à supposer. Il est de surcroît tout à fait exclu qu'ils aient fait référence à Cyrus ou à d'autres rois achéménides, encore moins au maudit Alexandre le Grand." Yarshater 1971, p. 519, evidenced that a real *historical amnesia* of the Achaemenid past started in Iran during the Parthian period; the question was debated also by Gnoli 1989, p. 124: "Some sort of memory, however vague, of the Achaemenian past must have existed anyway during the Parthian period and, to some extent, must have been less vague in Fars, the cradle of the ancient dynasty"; Shayegan 2011, p. xiv: "The portrayal of the Sasanians as heirs to the Achaemenids thus existed as an intrinsic part of the Roman *imitatio*, which not only sought to evince the historical continuity of the Greco-Roman world by vindicating Alexander's legacy, but also to bestow a similar perception of permanence upon the history of the east by depicting the Sasanians as cognizant heirs of the Achaemenids."

31 Daryaee 2002, p. 5.

32 Ṭabarī 814: Bosworth 1999, p. 3.

33 Gariboldi 2005; Shayegan 2011, p. 14–17.

34 Pakzad 2005, p. 366–367.

35 There are coins of a certain Farn-Sāsān who ruled in Sakastān in the late Parthian and early Sasanian period, but he was an enemy and not a vassal of the Sasanian kings. See Nikitin 1994; Alram 2007, p. 234–235; Olbrycht in this volume.

36 Shayegan 2008; *idem* 2011, p. 14–29 and *passim;* also in this volume.

References

Alföldy, G. (1989). "Cassius Dio und Herodian über die Anfänge des neupersischen Reiches", in G. Alföldy (ed.), *Die Krise des Römischen Reiches. Geschichte, Geschichtsschreibung und Geschichtsbetrachtung*, Stuttgart: p. 229–237.

Alram, M. (2007). "Ardashir's Eastern Campaign and the Numismatic Evidence", in J. Cribb, G. Herrmann (eds), *After Alexander. Central Asia before Islam*, Proceedings of the British Academy 133, Oxford: p. 227–242.

Alram, M., Blet-Lemarquand, M., and Skjærvø, P.O. (2007). "Shapur, King of Kings of Iranians and non-Iranians", in R. Gyselen (ed.), *Des Indo-Grecs aux Sassanides: données pour l'histoire et la géographie historique*, Res Orientales XVII, Bures-sur-Yvette: p. 11–40.

Alram, M., and Gyselen, R. (2003). *Sylloge Nummorum Sasanidarum. Paris – Berlin – Wien,* I. *Ardashir I. – Shapur I*, Phil.-hist. Kl., Denkschriften 317, Vienna.

Barnes, Th. D. (1998). *Ammianus Marcellinus and the Representation of Historical Reality*, Ithaca and London.

Blockley, R.C. (1988). "Ammianus Marcellinus on the Persian Invasion of 359", *Phoenix* 42: p. 244–260.

——— (1992). *East Roman Foreign Policy: Formation and Conduct from Diocletian to Anastasius*, Leeds.

Bosworth, C.E. (1999). *The History of al-Ṭabarī, Vol. V: The Sāsānids, the Byzantines, the Lakhmids, and Yemen*, Albany.

Bowersock, G.W. (1978). *Julian the Apostate*, Cambridge, MA.

Brodka, D. (2009). *Ammianus Marcellinus. Studien zum Geschichtsdenken im vierten Jahrhundert n.Chr.*, Electrum 17, Kraków.

Brok, M.F.A. (1975). "Die Quellen von Ammians Exkurs über Persien", *Mnemosyne* 28: p. 47–56.

Cameron, A. (1969–70). "Agathias on the Sassanians", *Dumbarton Oaks Papers* 23/24: p. 67–183.

Chauvot, A. (1992). "Parthes et Perses dans les sources du IVe siècle", in M. Christol (ed.), *Institutions, société et vie politique dans l'empire Romain au IVe siècle AP. J.-C.*, Collection de l'Ecole française de Rome 159, Rome: p. 115–125.

——— (1998). *Opinions Romaines face aux barbares au IVe siècle ap. J.-C.,* Paris.

Dąbrowa, E. (1984). "Le programme de la politique en Occident des derniers Arsacides", *Iranica Antiqua* 19: p. 149–165.

Daryaee, T. (2002). "Memory and History: The Construction of the Past in Late Antique Persia", *Nāme-ye Irān-e Bāstān* 2: p. 1–14.

——— (2006). "Sasanians and their Ancestors", in A. Panaino, A. Piras (eds), *Proceedings of the 5th Conference of the Societas Iranologica Europœa. Ravenna, 6–11 October 2003*. Ancient and Middle Iranian Studies, Milan: p. 387–393.

Daryaee, T. (2007). "Imitatio Alexandri and its Impact on Late

Arsacid, Early Sasanian and Middle Persian Literature", in E. Dąbrowa (ed.), *Studies on the Late Roman History*, Electrum 12, Kraków: p. 89–97.

Dodgeon, M.H., and Lieu, S.N. (1991). *The Roman Eastern Frontier and the Persian Wars (AD 226–363). A Documentary History*, London and New York.

Drijvers, J.W. (1999). "Ammianus Marcellinus' Image of Arsaces and Early Parthian History", in J.W. Drijvers, D. Hunt (eds), *The Late Roman World and its Historian: Interpreting Ammianus Marcellinus*, London and New York: p. 193–206.

——— (2006). "Ammianus Marcellinus' Image of Sasanian Society", in J. Wiesehöfer, Ph. Huyse (eds), *Ērān ud Anērān. Studien zu den Beziehungen zwischen dem Sasanidenreich und der Mittelmeerwelt. Beiträge des Internationalen Colloquiums in Eutin, 8.-9. Juni 2000,* Oriens et Occidens 13, Munich: p. 45–69.

Edwell, P.M. (2008). *Between Rome and Persia. The Middle Euphrates, Mesopotamia and Palmyra under Roman Control*, London and New York.

Felix, W. (1985). *Antike literarische Quellen zur Außenpolitik des Sāsānidenstaates, I (224–309)*, Phil.-hist. Kl., Sitzungsberichte 456, Vienna.

Feraco, F. (2004). *Ammiano geografo: la digressione sulla Persia (23, 6),* Naples.

Fornara, Ch.W. (1991). "Julian's Persian Expedition in Ammianus and Zosimus", *Journal of Hellenic Studies* 111: p. 1–15.

Frendo, D. (2002). "Cassius Dio and Herodian on the First Sasanian Offensive against the Eastern Provinces of the Roman Empire (229–232)", *Bulletin of the Asia Institute* 16: p. 25–36.

Gall, H. von (1980). "Relieffragment eines elymäischen Königs aus Masǧed-e Soleiman", *Iranica Antiqua* 15: p. 241–250.

Gariboldi, A. (2005). "Agathias e l'origine di Ardašir", in M. Bernardini, N.L. Tornesello (eds), *Scritti in onore di Giovanni M. D'Erme*, Series Minor LXVIII, Naples: p. 489–503.

——— (2011). *La monarchia sasanide tra storia e mito*, Indo-Iranica et Orientalia, Series Lazur 2, Milan and Udine.

Gnoli, Gh. (1989). *The Idea of Iran. An Essay on its Origin*, Serie Orientale Roma LXII, Rome.

——— (1996). "Il pericolo persiano: Ardashir e Shapur I", in M.G. Angeli Bertinelli, G.P. Desideri, D. Foraboschi (eds), *Storia della società italiana, 3. La crisi del principato e la società imperiale*, Milan: p. 399–433.

——— (2013). *Da Alessandro ad Ardašir. Storiografia e cronologie arabo-persiane*, Conferenze ISMEO 1, Rome.

Greatrex, G., and Lieu, S.N. (2002). *The Roman Eastern Frontier and the Persian Wars. Part II: AD 363–630. A Narrative Sourcebook*, London and New York.

Hackl, U., Jacobs, B., and Weber, D. (2010). *Quellen zur Geschichte des Partherreiches. Textsammlung mit Übersetzungen und Kommentaren*, 1, Göttingen.

Huyse, Ph. (2002). "La revendication de territoires Achéménides par les Sassanides: une réalité historique?", in Ph. Huyse (ed.), *Iran: questions et connaissances*, I. *La période ancienne*, Studia Iranica, Cahier 25, Paris: p. 297–311.

Kettenhofen, E. (1984). "Die Einforderung des Achämenidenerbes durch Ardašīr: Eine *interpretatio romana*", *Orientalia Lovaniensia Periodica* 15: p. 177–190.

——— (2002). "Die Einforderung der achämenidischen Territorien durch die Sāsāniden: Eine Bilanz", in S. Kurz (ed.), *Yādnāme-ye Iradj Khalifeh-Soltani. Festschrift Iradj Khalifeh-Soltani zum 65. Geburtstag*, Aachen: p. 49–75.

Lacombrade, Ch. (1964). *L'empereur Julien: œuvres complètes*, Paris.

Mazzarino, S. (1971). "L'anonymus post Dionem e la 'topica' delle guerre romano-persiane: 242/4 d.C.–283/(4?) d.C.", in *La Persia nel Medioevo*, Problemi attuali di scienza e di cultura 160, Rome: p. 655–678.

Mosig-Walburg, K. (2000). "Die Flucht des persischen Prinzen Hormizd und sein Exil im römischen Reich: Eine Untersuchung der Quellen", *Iranica Antiqua* 35: p. 69–110.

Muccioli, F. (2009). "Il problema del culto del sovrano nella regalità arsacide: appunti per una discussione", in E. Dąbrowa (ed.), *Orbis Parthicus. Studies in Memory of Professor Jósef Wolski,* Electrum 15, Kraków: p. 83–104.

——— (2013). *Gli epiteti ufficiali dei re ellenistici*, Historia 224, Stuttgart.

Nikitin, A.B. (1994). "Die Münzen des letzten indo-parthischen Königs von Sīstān. Ein Abschied von 'Ardamitra'", *Numismatische Zeitschrift* 102: p. 167–170.

Pakzad, F. (2005). *Bundahišn. Zoroastrische Kosmogonie und Kosmologie*, Tehran.

Paratore, E. (1966). "La Persia nella letteratura latina", in *La Persia e il mondo Greco-Romano,* Problemi attuali di scienza e di cultura 76, Rome: p. 505–558.

Potter, D.S. (2004). *The Roman Empire at Bay: AD 180–395*, London and New York.

Pugliese Carratelli, G. (1971). "La Persia dei Sasanidi nella storiografia romana da Ammiano a Procopio", *La Persia nel Medioevo,* Problemi attuali di scienza e di cultura 160, Rome: p. 597–604.

Shayegan, M.R. (2008). "On the Rationale behind the Roman Wars of Šābuhr II the Great", *Bulletin of the Asia Institute* 18: p. 111–133.

——— (2011). *Arsacids and Sasanians. Political Ideology in Post-Hellenistic and Late Antique Persia*, Cambridge.

Smith, R. (1999). "Telling Tales. Ammianus' Narrative of the Persian Expedition of Julian", in J.W. Drijvers, D. Hunt (eds), *The Late Roman World and its Historian: Interpreting Ammianus Marcellinus*, London and New York: p. 89–104.

Straub, J. (1986). "Die Sassaniden als 'aemuli imperii' im Urteil des Ammianus Marcellinus", in J. Straub (ed.), *Regeneratio imperii, II: Aufsätze über Roms Kaisertum und Reich im Spiegel der heidnischen und christlichen Publizistik*, Darmstadt: p. 218–222.

Wiesehöfer, J. (1986). "Iranische Ansprüche an Rom auf ehemals achämenidische Territorien", *Archäologische Mitteilungen aus Iran* 19: p. 177–185.

——— (2006). "Das elymäische Doppeldiadem", in R. Rollinger, B. Truschnegg (eds), *Altertum und Mittelmeerraum: Die antike Welt diesseits und jenseits der Levante. Festschrift für Peter W. Haiden zum 60. Geburtstag*, Oriens et Occidens 12, Stuttgart: p. 401–408.

Yarshater, E. (1971). "Were the Sasanians Heirs to the Achaemenids?", in *La Persia nel Medioevo,* Problemi attuali di scienza e di cultura 160, Rome: p. 517–533.

Ziegler, K.-H. (1964). *Die Beziehungen zwischen Rom und dem Partherreich. Ein Beitrag zur Geschichte des Völkerrechts*, Wiesbaden.

7

Kirdēr and the Re-organisation of Persian Mazdeism

Antonio Panaino
University of Bologna

The ascent of the Sasanian dynasty had an enormous impact on the future development of Zoroastrianism, particularly in western Iran. This assumption is based on objective evidence, which is unfortunately not always fully considered by historians in all its heavy implications. This evidence consists of ritual and theological Mazdean sources organised according to patterns established and fixed in Persia, during and after the establishment of Sasanian power. This includes the written Avestan tradition, in particular its ritual texts, which preserved not only the two earlier Mazdean liturgies, the long and short versions, but also the later exegetical and priestly commentaries such as the *Nērangestān*, as well as, finally, the Pahlavi *Zand*.[1] On the other hand, and by way of contrast with this rich western tradition, we possess only very superficial data about the contemporary liturgy of eastern Zoroastrianism – I mean that form of Mazdean religion rooted among the communities of Sogdia, Bactria, Choresmia, Sistan and so on. Thus, apart from a Sogdian fragment of the *Aṣ̌əm Vohū* and few other debated references,[2] we do not have direct access to Avestan sources and liturgies presented according to a Late Antique eastern *recensio*, independent of that developed within the framework of the western (i.e. Persian) schools of Mazdean priests. We are therefore compelled to refer to archaeological data in the form of pictorial cycles. These have been thoroughly investigated by Russian and European scholars, among whom I must mention in particular Fr. Grenet (and his collaborators), who has often focused on Zoroastrian religious content in a number of Sogdian paintings in his research.[3] Our current knowledge of ancient Mazdeism is in fact mostly based on a number of ritual texts whose *Vorlage* was established in western Iran under the authority of the Sasanian kings and by their priestly staff. Furthermore, our views are based on evidence from regions where Sasanian control was direct, and where Persian influence was very important. I want to be precise about this. As we know, the Sasanians were extremely active also in eastern Iran, but the impact of their presence there was balanced and countered by prominent and rich local traditions, which unfortunately did not achieve any consistent attempt to produce a written version of the Avestan liturgy. Consequently, we do not now possess any Avestan manuscript or ritual source that was fixed according to a written system or that simply followed a tradition based on a direct continuity, either from the ancestral Avestan communities in eastern Iran or else from the communities that later lived in more or less the same geographical areas. The legacy of the earliest Zoroastrian tradition was fixed only after its liturgy had been transmitted (probably in Achaemenid times) from eastern to western Iran, most likely in Persia, and there it was finally transcribed during the Sasanian period.[4] This does not mean we can state that other versions belonging to an earlier and genuine Avestan heritage were unknown or never fixed, but evidence of their existence remains an historical and philological *desideratum*, a dream, not a reality. It is a paradox, but the most important cultural heritage of the pre-Islamic eastern Iranian linguistic and spiritual tradition, that represented by Avestan literature, is a material (but at the same time also an intellectual) production that we have today thanks to the active role of religious elites formed and educated in western Iran, more specifically in the framework of Late Antiquity and early mediaeval Persia.

The additional fact that the Avestan alphabet was derived from the Pahlavi model shows the absolute importance of the western Iranian cultural context. This is further supported by certain influences recognisable in the characters and conventions adopted also in the Pahlavi Psalter, which follow patterns such as the distinction between short ("closed") and long ("open") vowels, as attested in Greek and Syriac scripts (and it is from the Greek alphabet that at least three Avestan signs derive more or less directly).[5]

For these reasons, the role of the Sasanians was surely essential in many respects. In the present contribution, I would like to focus on some facts relating to the first century of Persian domination, in close connection with the documentation left by the priest Kirdēr about the re-organisation of "Persian" Zoroastrianism.[6] This mission of Kirdēr proved to be not only very efficient but also seminal for its future development, notwithstanding the eventual collapse of the Sasanian empire and the change of religion after the Muslim conquest. In fact, it is my personal belief that without the Sasanians we would probably lack access (albeit limited and unilateral) to Avestan sources themselves. Instead our knowledge of Zoroastrianism would be based mostly on Western (Greek and Latin), Arabic and Syriac sources, or fragmentary archaeological materials of a local nature, such as bullae, seals, etc., along with other "concrete" scattered remains. We should bear in mind that we do not have from Sasanian times a single important liturgical (and textual) document concerning a Mazdean ritual (with the exception of the two inscriptions commissioned by Kirdēr concerning his "vision").[7] Therefore without the evidence from (later) Avestan and Pahlavi manuscripts (none of which has come from an archaeological context but rather from the mediaeval collections of Mazdean temples), our picture of Zoroastrianism would have been severely mutilated, if not totally ruined.

As part of this paper, I want to reflect on the career of Kirdēr.[8] He was already mentioned among the dignitaries of Šābuhr (Shapur) in ŠKZ § 49, an inscription probably composed between 260 and 262 AD, as noted by Huyse.[9] He then obtained two further promotions, as we can deduce from the titles[10] which he attributed to himself under four different kings.[11] As Skjærvø[12] has summarised, his official titles were as follows:

> §4: Under Šābuhr (Shapur) (r. 239/40?-72?): *Kirdēr ī ēhrbed* (M-P. 34 <'yhrpt>, Parth. 28 <'hrpty>, Gr. 66 ΜΑΓΟΥ; then: *Kirdēr ī mowbed ud ēhrbed*;
>
> §6: under Ohrmazd I (r. 272?-73): *Kirdēr ī Ohrmazd mowbed Ohrmazd bay pad nām* "Kirdēr the *mowbed* of Ohrmazd, after the name of Ohrmazd the god";
>
> §8: under Wahrām I (r. 273–76): *Kirdēr ī Ohrmazd mowbed*;
>
> §10: under Wahrām II (r. 276–93): *Kirdēr ī bōxt-ruwān-Warahrān ī Ohrmazd mowbed.*

As is well known, the last appearance of this priest is in the Paikuli inscription (293 AD), where he is described as *Kirdēr Ohrmazd maγ[bed]* (Parth. line 14 <mgw[pt]>).[13]

If the idea of an ascent, of an official progress, in function, authority and power, is clear in the wording of Kirdēr's titles, I must nevertheless underline the fact that his decision to publish four personal inscriptions showed the new and prominent social role he dared to assume. Although written texts were probably accessible to a limited number of people, I cannot assume that the emission of these inscriptions had no public importance. Nor can I accept that illiterates did not know the contents of these documents (if we presume, although I am not completely sure of this, that powerful people had no access to written texts either directly or through personal scribes in their service). This act, because of its public effect, assumed an intrinsic political force. With it, Kirdēr made it clear that his religious authority, although placed at the service of the king and his dynasty, carried its own role and prestige. Perhaps it would be too far-fetched to say that Kirdēr asserted the autonomy of religious power as opposed to that of the royal family. It is, however, certain that he (deliberately?) did not exactly follow royal protocol in the way he set forth the titles of the various kings, but used instead more prosaic formulations. Furthermore, we must not forget that at the beginning of his inscriptions he expressed his wish to be, in this specific order, "well disposed" firstly towards the gods, then towards Ardaxšīr (Ardashir) and Šābuhr (Shapur). The gods take first place, and his obligations lie firstly towards them, and only secondly towards the crown. Nothing strange, apparently; but it is one thing for a priest to think in this way, another to write down his thought.

Very many scholars have underlined the intolerant character of Kirdēr, in particular with reference to the persecution of religious minorities. Here I think that we should be more prudent in proposing a definitive reconstruction of the historical data in the light of the inevitable religious propaganda promoted by this priest *pro domo sua*. We can entertain some doubt, for instance, as to whether the new Sasanian rulers had any interest in promoting a systematic persecution of all the religious communities living inside the borders of the conquered territories, especially when the new *Šāhān Šāh* assumed the title of king not only of the *Ērān*, but also of the *Anērān*. It is possible that Kirdēr referred merely to his own bold attempts and actions, through which he aimed at imposing a limit on the influence and diffusion of other religious communities. It is also possible that his personal desire to repress, persecute and expel them remained to a certain extent in all probability in his mind. It is possible that not everything lay within his power, at least as he would have desired. It is true that the Manicheans were persecuted, but this happened only at a particular period and not systematically throughout Kirdēr's long career. Some scholars have, in fact, seen a change in the foreign policy of the Sasanians away from an optimistic universalism towards a more prudent nationalism,[14] although the details are not sufficiently documented. I would prefer not to speak of "liberalism" in the case of Šābuhr (Shapur) I,[15] just as I would prefer not to attribute an overwhelmingly aggressive policy to Kirdēr himself. The truth should probably stay in the balance between political and military interests in asserting control over the newly conquered territories and the religious zealotry of some priests who desired to enlarge their own authority and influence. It is not improbable that Kirdēr too had to wait before it was possible to enforce his "religious" power. This period of waiting was probably necessary, as he needed to increase his religious authority. And of course, the legitimacy of any power is based on facts – or sometimes on fiction. We may thus suspect that the inscriptions offer a sort of self-hagiographic representation of his religious life.

Many researchers have shown that the technical terminology used by Kirdēr has correspondences or linguistic and theological similarities in the Avestan and Pahlavi texts.[16] Textual references to specific sources have been suggested with a high degree of probability, so that we can trust that Kirdēr knew his job very well, and that he saw himself as following an historical tradition from which the pillars of the attested Mazdean literature derive. We must also consider the evidence that certain patterns used by Kirdēr apparently correspond to earlier Iranian models;[17] it is possible that these striking correspondences reflect a common Iranian heritage and lore, but they could also be the final result of a long oral priestly tradition, already present in ancient Persia. What we see here is his strong anti-Ahremanic enthusiasm and determination, a characteristic fully understandable in an authoritative person, whose main intention was the establishment of a new moral standard and a sort of orthodoxy. But the direction taken by Kirdēr should be seen within the context of the Sasanian conquest, and not independently from it.

In fact, on seizing power the new royal dynasty began to elaborate a fresh ideology, in which the religious element was essential, so that a new line of propaganda was adopted. As I have shown in another contribution,[18] we must imagine that a sort of "*conseil du roi*" was working on the choice of the titles and on the political messages to be sent out by the highest authority of the empire. Nothing was merely the fruit of improvisation or happened simply by chance. The kings were declared to be followers of Ohrmazd (*măzdēsn*), to possess the same image/brightness of their gods, to represent the most ancestral values of the *Ērān*, although they were not so blind as to pretend a conversion to Zoroastrianism of all the conquered people. They tried to distinguish themselves sharply from the past dynasty, thus creating a dark image for the Parthians.

The same arguments should be considered if we look at the iconography of Sasanian coins, where various items of religious *regalia* were chosen and engraved, to say nothing of the representation of the sacred fires on the reverse. It is difficult to imagine that these symbols were adopted without any discussion between the most senior members of the royal family, the most important officers, and the religious élite of the kingdom. But this was propaganda, and normal, as happens today. We can, however, suppose that the priests who supported and flanked the Sasanian innermost royal circle offered many suggestions. It would be inconceivable that the royal family had elaborated and developed a full plan of political theology concerning the monarchy without consulting its own clergy. Kirdēr and other priests were part of an elite, which framed and shared a common project, and they in turn supported the plans of the royal clan by creating a more elaborated hierarchy, in which it was possible to follow an ascending sacerdotal career. This also meant that it was necessary to coordinate the different temples, which in part already existed, but which probably did not answer to a unified authority and leadership. On the one hand, this kind of development was a religious issue but, on the other hand, it was also a matter of political interest, because the most important temples had huge properties and inevitably they played not only a spiritual but also a very significant economic and social function. The progress towards religious standardisation of the empire was paralleled by that of its military and administrative control. This also explains why the priestly class assumed an ever more pervasive role in the administration of justice. It is difficult to believe that this role was obtained by the priests without the support of those who wielded political power.

We cannot avoid some consideration of Kirdēr's emphasis (§16) on his zealous activity against the *ahlomōys*, or "heretics", an action that assumed not only religious but also political implications. Skjærvø[19] has rightly recalled the Avestan background of this term (*Y*. 9, 18, etc.). It refers not only to evil-doers, but also to special enemies of the priests.

We also find in Kirdēr's inscriptions references to the moral pillars of Zoroastrianism with regard to marriage (with open support for the *xwēdōdah*, or "next-of-kin marriage") and sexual practice, so that it is impossible to deny that he was in absolute agreement with what we know about common Mazdeism according to its written ritual and exegetical sources.

I want also to draw your attention to the fact that Kirdēr in the systematic description of his career underlines his active role in controlling the territory covered by the priestly community (*mowestān* or *mogestān*),[20] both at court and throughout the empire. He insists on the fact that divine services and rituals were increased and that many new fires of Wahrām were founded. Such a process must be seen in connection with the parallel statements presented by Šābuhr (Shapur) I in his *Res Gestae*, §§ 32–35,[21] when he emphasises the fires restored or founded by him and the rituals he put in order. The two descriptions refer to a common plan, probably decided in the same rooms and by the same leadership. The fact that Kirdēr openly states that the conditions of the priests were improved and that many agreements or contracts were signed for their own advantage confirms the economic and political background to his actions.

It is also interesting to note that the high priest writes that he was established already under Šābuhr (Shapur) I as "independent and sovereign" (§ 2; *k'mk'ly W p'thš'y* [*kāmgār ud pādixšā*]) over the *mogestān* (§ 2). This same statement was confirmed under the later kings. This kind of autonomy must carry a certain meaning and cannot be just an empty pretension. We can probably see here the basis of an alliance, but also the origin of an impending dichotomy in the political history of the Sasanian kingdom.

Just before concluding this brief reflection on the first steps of the interaction between politics and religion at the beginning of the Sasanian empire, I would like to share with you a last series of remarks on the function of the so-called "vision" expressed in two inscriptions by Kirdēr. Its contents are a matter of debate and polemics. Recently I have also entered the discussion, simply making a few critical remarks.[22]

1. The vision cannot be the description of something that happened in a trance. This kind of ritual is not attested in the Mazdean liturgical tradition. In addition, when scholars assume that the trance was collective and that it was shared by a group of people or, worse, of children, I simply ask how this is possible. I understand that a person can fall into a trance and then start to speak, but how can two or more people fall into a trance and say the same thing at the same time? As for children, it is known that they were not admitted to official rituals in the whole Indo-Iranian tradition.
2. The main idea strongly rooted in the speculative conception of the Avestan ritual was that of opening an esoteric path, where Ohrmazd and the priests could meet. In other words the *Yasna* and other rituals were an instrument to obtain a mental vision, an anticipation in life of the afterlife, a means through which the priests became *saošiiaṇt*s, as recently underlined by Kellens.[23] We also know that one of the titles used by Kirdēr is *Ohrmazd mowbed*. As Skjærvø has written:[24] "It is known also in Pahlavi; in *Dēnkard* 4.22 (ed. Dresden, p. [322]; ed. Madan, p. 413) we are told that it was applied to persons who had been revealed to have the ability to see in(to) the other world (*mēnōy-wēnišnīh*; Zaehner 1955: 8; Gignoux, 1968: p. 413, n. 19)."

This was exactly what Kirdēr did. In other words, I suggest that Kirdēr organised a ceremony in which he framed a sort of ritual drama, a representation of the journey to paradise of his own double or, literally, "Kirdēr's likeness" (*hangerb*), and his meeting with the female double of his future *dēn*, there represented as a "woman" (*zan* [NYŠE]),[25] probably a reflex of the Av. *carāiti-* (*H.N.* 2, 10; *čarāydīg* in the Pahlavi translation).[26] But I have already offered in detail my arguments on this subject and there is not time to repeat them here.[27]

What I did not clarify earlier is that the high priest Kirdēr installed a special ritual. Its target was not to perform his anticipated death, but to show himself (in his quality of person in whose favour the ritual was organized, i.e. like a Vedic *yájamāna-*) his final destiny. At the time of the ritual, Kirdēr was not dead, and therefore it is his double, his *hangerb*, who meets the *dēn*, which is presented simply as a superb woman. This description of the *dēn* (although differently denominated) is in agreement with that attested in the Avestan source. In addition, the simple reference to a woman, who helps the *ruwān* (soul) to cross the Činwad bridge, not expressly called *dēn* but rather *kanīg-kirb* (literally "having the body of a woman"), is mentioned in a later Pahlavi book, the *Anthology of Zādspram*. This source dedicates all chapter 31 to the *mard-kirb* ("the form of man") and the *kanīg-kirb* ("the form of woman").[28] This particular passage presents clear eschatological implications. The functions of the *kanīg-kirb* are patently those of the *dēn*, exactly as in the inscriptions of Kirdēr. The role of the *mard-kirb*, however, remains mostly unclear, although indisputably eschatological. (In 31, 1, the *ruwān* can reach the garden of paradise with his help and that of the "form of woman", who are presented as the father and the mother of the soul itself.) My impression is that Zādspram still had a distant memory of a tradition in which both these doubles played a specific role, but he was not conversant with that esoteric tradition. In fact, it is evident that the *mard-kirb* corresponds to Kirdēr's *hangerb* (where *gerb* is equivalent to *-kirb*, both being a derivation from Av. *kəhrpa-* "body"), while the *kanīg-kirb* corresponds to the "superb" *zan*, who meets him. Furthermore, Kirdēr's likeness, his *hangerb*, represented the living person, which, as in Zādspram, is different from the *ruwān*. In fact, in the afterlife, according to the Mazdean doctrine, it is only the masculine soul, the *ruwān* (Av. *uruuan-*), which meets the *dēn* (Av. *daēnā-*). Thus, the masculine soul finally meets the feminine one. But here, according to the inscriptions of Kirdēr, nobody was dead. Kirdēr is alive and wants to know his destiny. Consequently we must deduce that in this context a special carefully controlled terminology was adopted; it is only the double of the individual who wants to see his final destiny that is employed (and his name is therefore repeated with *hangerb*), and not his masculine soul, which can be separated from the living person and his/her body only after a true physical death. The terminology attested is, then, not that of children, but of well-trained priests, who know precisely what they are doing. In the later tradition preserved by Zādspram only fragments of a more complex doctrine survive, but its survival is a remarkable witness to an ancient doctrine, no longer practised or properly understood.

I have only one thing left to say. The presence of this apparently strange reference to a very esoteric ritual was also a political act. The high priest showed that he was worthy of his dignity, that he had an extraordinary ritual competence for a ceremony in which his final ascent was enacted. He was a witness of the complete truthfulness of his religion and of his own eschatological power. All those who were able to read or hear the contents of this text of Kirdēr probably formed different impressions. The uninitiated admired his courage and the superb description of a terrifying and dramatic journey. They should repent of their sins and were perhaps inspired to follow the rules of the religion in the final hope of approaching the paradise of Ohrmazd less fearfully. The few who were fully initiated knew that Kirdēr had been the protagonist in a ritual in which the destiny of his double was celebrated and its entrance to the realm of the afterlife in company of the female double was revealed. Such people probably kept the secret and, if properly qualified, passed through the same ritual themselves at the appropriate time.

But for us, the most important aspect of Kirdēr's "vision" is that it provides us with an account of a sacred ceremony in scriptural form. Although we may have different views about this source, we can all share the objective observation that it contains something which had not only a political force, but also a religious dimension.

We can all furthermore agree that by committing it to textual form, Kirdēr provided us with a document that can open seminal perspectives for further investigations. And this in spite of the fact that the subject of that "vision" was deeply esoteric. But any true power is also full of secrets or else it would appear naked. A naked power cannot last very long, and when its final moment comes, it will not leave, at least, an enduring legacy.

Notes

1 On the present status of Avestan studies, see the volume edited by A. Cantera (*The transmission of the Avesta*, Iranica 21, Wiesbaden 2012), containing a number of very pertinent articles on this subject by the best specialists in the field.

2 See Gershevitch *apud* Sims-Williams 1976, p. 74–82; *cf.* also Tremblay 2001, *passim*.

3 See de la Vaissière & Riboud 2003, p. 127–135.

4 It is commonly assumed, although the subject is still open to discussion, that, as Hoffmann (1989, p. 53 = 1992, p. 870) stated: "YAv. *i̯i* and *u̯u* may have developed in West Iran under the influence of Old Persian, where every postconsonantal *i̯* and *u̯* became *iy* and *uv* respectively"; *cf.* Kellens (1989, p. 35), who doubts the Arachosian alteration against Hoffmann 1979 (= 1992, p. 736–740).

5 See Hoffmann 1971 (reprinted in 1975); 1989; Panaino 1997a.

6 This should not be interpreted as confirmation that Kirdēr played a unique role in the foundation of Sasanian Zoroastrianism, as, for instance, it was assumed by Sprengling (1940, p. 215). Sprengling thought that Ardaxšīr (Ardashir) "had little time and opportunity" for such things. On the contrary, I believe that already in the earliest phases of their ascent to power the Sasanians paid great attention to propaganda and to the construction of an ideological and religious programme, which was, obviously, developed and improved under Šābuhr (Shapur).

7 On this subject see the discussion in Panaino 2011, with a large bibliography. *Cf.* also Skjærvø 2011, p. 611–613, *passim*.

8 *Cf.* U. Weber 2009; 2010.

9 Huyse 1999, I, p. 10–14.

10 They appear "both in the description of his career in the first part of the longer inscriptions and in the summary at the end of the inscriptions (§38), including KNRb" (after Skjærvø 2011, p. 610).

11 See Henning 1954, p. 40–42; MacKenzie 1989, p. 62.

12 Skjærvø 2011, p. 610–611.

13 Ed. Humbach – Skjærvø 1983, pt. 3.1, p. 41–43); *cf.* the Manichean Parthian form <qyrd[y]r mgbyd> (M6031 I Bi 5: Henning, 1942, p. 948–949; Sundermann 1981, p. 71).

14 See in particular Gnoli 1984.

15 *Cf.* Skjærvø 2011, p. 620.

16 See Skjærvø 2011, p. 612, p. 617.

17 See Gnoli 1979, p. 425–432.

18 Panaino 2009.

19 2011, p. 617.

20 See MacKenzie 1998, p. 61–62. *Cf.* Back 1979, p. 230; Gignoux 1972, p. 28; 1991, p. 66, n. 123.

21 Huyse 1999 I, p. 45–48; II, p. 102–110. *Cf.* Mariq 1965, p. 56–59.

22 Panaino 2011; Panaino in press.

23 See the *Résumée* of J. Kellens' lecture of 20 January 2012, now accessible on the web site of the Collège de France.

24 2011, p. 613.

25 See, e.g., chapters 30 and 31 of the inscription of Naqš-e Rostam, etc.; MacKenzie 1989, p. 50, 56. *Cf.* also Kellens 1975, p. 462–465. For the "beauty" of the *dēn*, see Gnoli 1993, p. 81–82.

26 *Cf.* Skjærvø 1983, p. 281; Kellens 1975, p. 462–465; 1995a; 1995b; Piras 2000, p. 53, 60, 66, 79, 93; Gnoli 1994, p. 295–297. *Cf.* again Kellens 1995a; Panaino 1997b. *Cf.* Bartholomae 1904, p. 581, n. 1. With regard to *H.N.* 2, 24 and additional Pahlavi sources see Lecoq 1972, p. 130.

27 Panaino 2011; Panaino in press.

28 Gignoux – Tafazzoli 1993, p. 112–113.

References

Back, M. (1978). *Die sassanidische Staatsinschriften*, Studien zur Orthographie und Phonologie des Mittelpersischen der Inschriften zusammen mit einem etymologischen Index des mittelpersischen Wortgutes und einem Textcorpus der behandelten Inschriften, Acta Iranica 18, Tehran and Liège.

Bartholomae, Chr. (1904). *Altiranisches Wörterbuch*, Strasburg.

Dresden, M.J. (1966). *Dēnkart. A Pahlavi Text: Facsimile Edition of the Manuscript B of the K.R. Cama Oriental Institute*, Bombay.

Gignoux, Ph. (1968). "L'inscription de Kartir à Sar Mašhad", *Journal Asiatique*: p. 387–418.

——— (1972). *Glossaire des inscriptions Pehlevies et Parthes*, Corpus Inscriptionum Iranicarum, Supplementary Series, Vol. I, London.

——— (1991). *Les quatre inscriptions du mage Kirdir. Textes et concordances*, Studia Iranica, Cahier 9, Paris.

Gignoux, Ph., and Tafazzoli, A. (1993). *Anthologie de Zādspram. Édition critique du texte pehlevi traduit et commenté*, Studia Iranica, Cahier 13, Paris.

Gnoli, Gh. (1979). "*Ašavan*, Contributo allo studio del libro di Arda Wirāz", in Gh. Gnoli, A.V. Rossi (eds), *Iranica*, Naples: p. 387–452.

——— (1984). "Universalismo e Nazionalismo nell'Iran del III secolo", in L. Lanciotti (ed.), *Incontro di Religioni in Asia tra il III e il X secolo d.C. Atti del Convegno internazionale di studi storico-religiosi promosso e organizzato dalla Fondazione Giorgio Cini e dall'Istituto Italiano per il Medio ed Estremo Oriente (Is. M.E.O.), Venezia, 16–18 novembre 1981*, Civiltà Veneziana, Studi 39, Florence: p. 31–54.

——— (1994). "A Sassanian iconography of the *Dēn*", *Bulletin of the Asia Institute* N.S. 7, *Iranian Studies in Honor of A.D.H. Bivar* (1993 [1994]): p. 79–85.

Henning, W.B. (1942). "Mani's last Journey", *Bulletin of the School of Oriental and African Studies* 10: p. 941–953.

——— (1954). "Notes on the Great Inscription of Šāpūr I", in *Prof. Jackson Memorial Volume. Papers on Iranian Subjects*, Bombay: p. 40–54.

Hoffmann, K. (1971). "Zum Zeicheninventar der Avesta-Schrift", in W. Eilers (ed.), *Festgabe deutscher Iranisten zur 2500 Jahrfeier Irans*, Stuttgart: p. 64–73.

——— (1975). *Aufsätze zur Indoiranistik*, Band III, J. Narten (ed.), Wiesbaden.

——— (1979). "Das Avesta in der Persis", in J. Harmatta (ed.), *Prolegomena to the Sources on the History of Pre-Islamic Central Asia*, Budapest: p. 89–93.

——— (1989). "The Avestan Language", in E. Yarshater (ed.), *Encyclopaedia Iranica*, Vol. III, London. and New York: p. 47–62.

——— (1991). *Aufsätze zur Indoiranistik*, Band III, S. Glauch, R. Plath, S. Ziegler (eds), Wiesbaden.

Humbach, H., and Skjærvø, P.O. (1983). *The Sassanian Inscription of Paikuli*, III.1 *Restored text and translation*, Wiesbaden.

Huyse, Ph. (1999). *Die dreisprachige Inschrift Šābuhrs I. an der Ka'ba-i Zardušt (ŠKZ)*, 2 Vols, Corpus Inscriptionum Iranicarum, Part III, Pahlavi Inscriptions, London.

Kellens, J. (1975). "Mythes et conceptions avestiques sous les Sassanides", in *Monumentum Henrik Samuel Nyberg*, Vol. 1, Acta Iranica 4, Leiden, Tehran, Liège: p. 457–470.

——— (1989). "Avestique", in R. Schmitt (ed.), *Compendium Linguarum Iranicarum*, Wiesbaden: p. 32–54.

——— (1995a). "L'âme entre le cadavre et le paradis", *Journal Asiatique* 283: p. 19–56.

——— (1995b). "Y a-t-il une âme osseuse?", in R. Gyselen (ed.), *Au carrefour des religions: Mélanges offerts à Philippe Gignoux*, Res Orientales 7, Bures-sur-Yvette: p. 157–160.

Lecoq, P. (1972). "Remarques sur l'inscription de Sar Mašhad", *Studia Iranica* 1: p. 127–131.

MacKenzie, D.N. (1989). "Kerdir's Inscription", in G. Herrmann, D.N. MacKenzie (eds), *The Sasanian Rock Reliefs at Naqsh-i Rustam*, Iranische Denkmäler, Iranische Felsreliefs I, Berlin: p. 35–72.

Madan, Dh.M. (1911). *The Complete Text of the Pahlavi Dinkard*, Bombay.

Mariq, A. (1965). *Classica et Orientalia* (Extrait de *Syria* 1955–1962 revu et corrigé, augmenté d'un article inédit et d'un index), Paris.

Panaino, A. (1997a). "Philologia Avestica V. The Origin of Avesta Letters *ẏ* and *v*", *Münchener Studien zur Sprachwissenschaft* 57: p. 81–96.

——— (1997b). "*nāirikā-* e *jahikā-* nell'aldilà zoroastriano", in R. Arena, M.P. Bologna, M.L. Mayer Modena, A. Passi (eds), *Bandhu. Scritti in onore di Carlo Della Casa*, Vol. II, Alessandria: p. 831–843.

——— (2009). "The King and the Gods in the Sasanian Royal Ideology", in R. Gyselen (ed.), *Sources pour l'histoire et la géographie du monde iranien (224–710)*, Res Orientales 18, Bures-sur-Yvette: p. 209–256.

——— (2011a). "Apocalittica, Escatologia e Sciamanismo nell'opera iranologica di Philippe Gignoux con una nota sulla 'visione' del Mago Kirdēr", in R. Gyselen, Chr. Jullien (eds), *Rabbo l'olmyn. "Maître pour l'Eternité", Florilège offert à Philippe Gignoux pour son 80e anniversaire*, Studia Iranica, Cahier 43, Paris: p. 205–243.

——— (in press). "A Sasanian Esoteric Ritual. Remarks about the Symbolic Ascent to Paradise of the High Priest Kirdēr", in Fl. Badalanova Geller (ed.), *Knowledge to die for. Transmission of Prohibited and Esoteric Knowledge through Space and Time*, Max Planck Institute, *Topoi*, Berlin.

Piras, A. (2000). *Hādōxt Nask II. Il racconto zoroastriano della sorte dell'anima. Edizione critica del testo avestico e pahlavi, traduzione e commento*, Serie Orientale Roma 88, Rome.

Sims-Williams, N. (1976). "The Sogdian Fragment of the British Library", *Indo-Iranian Journal* 18: p. 43–82.

Skjærvø, P.O. (1983). "Kirdir's Vision: Translation and Analysis", *Archäologische Mitteilungen aus Iran* N.S. 16 (1983 [1985]): p. 269–306.

——— (2011). "Kartīr", in E. Yarshater (ed.), *Encyclopaedia Iranica*, Vol. 15, New York: p. 608–628.

Sprengling, M. (1940). "Kartīr, founder of Sasanian Zoroastrianism", *The American Journal of Semitic Languages and Literatures* 57: p. 197–228.

Sundermann, W. (1981). *Mitteliranische manichäische Texte kirchengeschichtlichen Inhalts*, Berliner Turfantexte 11, Berlin.

Tremblay, X. (2001). *Pour une histoire de la Sérinde. Le manichéisme parmi les peuples et religions d'Asie Centrale d'après les sources primaires*, Veröffentlichungen der Kommission für Iranistik 28, Vienna.

Vaissière, E. de la, and Riboud, P. (2003). "Les livres des Sogdiens (avec une note additionelle par Frantz Grenet)", *Studia Iranica* 32: p. 127–136.

Weber, U. (2009). "Wahrām II., König der Könige von Ērān und Anērān", *Iranica Antiqua* 44: p. 559–643.

——— (2010). "Wahrām III., König der Könige von Ērān und Anērān", *Iranica Antiqua* 45: p. 353–393.

Zaehner, R.Ch. (1955). *Zurvan. A Zoroastrian Dilemma*, Oxford (reprinted New York 1972).

LINGUISTIC

the Nunnery between 2009 and 2012 (Monaghan 2011–12). Some 500 sherds examined from an as yet unidentified site on Longis Common, thought to have been excavated in the 1950s, included 'legionary' type pottery and other wares of the late 1st to 2nd century (Monaghan and de Jersey 2014–15).

The Bonded Store and La Plaiderie assemblages

Methods and condition

The La Plaiderie assemblage was used to establish a series of codes for fabric, form and decoration (see Appendix). These were applied a decade later to the Bonded Store.

Brenda Dickinson and Kay Hartley have commented on the samian and mortaria respectively. Certain diagnostic amphorae sherds from La Plaiderie were also identified by David Williams. The Roman pottery from both sites is particularly fragmentary, indicating the heavy disturbance these sites have undergone. The acidic nature of the soils in Guernsey has also affected the condition. Rounded water-worn sherds are frequent among the assemblages from both sites, as well as badly abraded and soil-stained ones. There is a fresh water stream with a fluctuating water table at the Bonded Store and both sites lay close to the ancient shoreline, and thus were particularly exposed to weathering. Although the majority of the Roman sherds appear to be residual in later levels, both assemblages have been studied in as much detail as possible due to their significance for Roman studies both within and beyond Guernsey. Coarse pottery was quantified by sherd count (Table 4), with samian quantified separately. Coarse pottery and amphorae were also weighed at the Bonded Store, as were some groups at La Plaiderie. It was decided not to use estimated vessel equivalents (EVEs) due to the small size of deposits and the scrappy nature of much of the pottery. Guernsey has not yet yielded stratified deposits of sufficient size to produce a firm ceramic phasing.

Dating of the sites

The Bonded Store offers the best evidence for the late Iron Age to Roman transition, and has a stronger 1st-century component. The combined evidence of the coins, samian and mortaria attest to activity at La Plaiderie mainly from the later 1st through to the mid-/late 3rd century AD, while the samian and mortaria alone suggest there was a broadly contemporary period of activity at the Bonded Store. La Plaiderie has significantly more east Gaulish samian in the 3rd century, and more activity in the later Roman period. From the 1st century AD through to the end of the Roman period, both assemblages share essentially the same range of fabrics.

The late Iron Age and late Iron Age/Roman transition

During the late Iron Age, the imported pottery consists of Italian wine amphorae and Armorican wares alongside locally made copies of the latter.

i) La Plaiderie

Activity at La Plaiderie cannot certainly be said to have taken place on the site itself until sometime around the second half of the 1st century BC/early 1st century AD. A few scraps of coarse pottery were found in poor condition and were indistinguishable on the basis of fabric alone either from pottery dating to the Roman period (fabrics

Table 4 The Bonded Store and La Plaiderie: summary of coarsewares.

	Bonded Store				*La Plaiderie*	
	sherds	*%*	*weight/g*	*%*	*sherds*	*%*
Iron Age or late Iron Age	264	5.6	3094	7.1	4	<0.1
Gallo-Belgic wares	204	4.3	1174	2.7	65	1.2
all finewares	149	3.2	861	2	374	6.6
céramique fumigée	284	6	2710	6.2	254	4.5
all BB and Durotrigan wares	154	3.3	1341	3.1	722	12.8
all North Gaulish grey fabrics	841	17.9	6733	15.5	838	14.9
tripod bowl fabric	558	11.9	10,768	24.7	523	9.3
all other grey and sandy wares	552	11.8	5103	11.7	550	9.7
oxidised wares	1588	33.7	10,440	24	2175	38.6
white wares	67	1.4	436	1	50	0.9
others	40	0.8	919	2.1	85	1.5
Total	4706	100	43,579	100	5640	100

TBF1 and AQR) or indeed the prehistoric (Bronze Age) material also found on the site. However, a solitary body sherd from a corrugated bowl, in a different and distinctive vesicular fabric, definitely does date to the late Iron Age. Such suspected local products have been found associated with a few Dressel 1 amphorae (Williams 1996, 51) and pottery types imported from Armorica (along with copies of these in local fabrics other than vesicular ware) on the site at King's Road on the western edge of St Peter Port (Burns *et al.* 1996).

Although no late Iron Age Armorican imports are present in the assemblage from La Plaiderie, the Dressel 1B amphora and the sherd of distinctive vesicular ware represent intriguing evidence for activity (the precise nature of which is unclear) dating to the late Iron Age. Allowing for the fact that the earlier Dressel 1A type may be present among the other four Italian amphorae from the assemblage, this late Iron Age activity can only be dated loosely to the period *c.*120–10 BC. A few scraps of vessels of Aquitainian origin in *céramique fumigée* (fabric SCFR) were also present. The third type of Armorican import also usually found associated with Italian Dressel 1 species amphorae is graphite-coated ware. This ware is probably also present but not immediately recognisable due to the graphite-coating having been worn away during deposition. Late Iron Age La Plaiderie therefore remains enigmatic, and it is likely that intensive Roman use of the site has destroyed much evidence of what went before, and is responsible for the poor state of the pottery.

ii) The Bonded Store

The late Iron Age presence at the Bonded Store is markedly more emphatic than that at La Plaiderie. Pottery from trenches excavated in Areas C and D in particular shows that activity began on the site during the late Iron Age. The range in date of the Roman wares in the site assemblage and evidence for their use suggest that the site was then occupied without any discernible break through to the end of the Roman period.

Associated with Italian Dressel 1 amphorae are numerous examples of pottery imports from Armorica, particularly black-cordoned and rilled micaceous wares. Added to the presence of locally made copies of these Armorican imports, a picture emerges of activity on the site that was directly linked with other sites on the island and beyond. The one sherd of vesicular ware at La Plaiderie, along with the Italian amphorae from that site, assumes greater significance in view of the substantial material of late Iron Age date from the nearby site at the Bonded Store.

Occupation on the site at King's Road, where Italian amphorae, Armorican imports and local copies of these wares are all present (Burns *et al.* 1996), was clearly contemporary with that at the Bonded Store during the late Iron Age. Both of these sites have significant quantities of local wares (including vesicular ware) but the imported Italian amphorae and Armorican wares are present in greater numbers at the Bonded Store. Over 16kg of briquetage, including some briquetage 'furniture', is present at the Bonded Store and this appears to be mostly associated with the late Iron Age activity on the site although some undoubtedly belongs with the subsequent early Roman activity.

The apparent absence of other early Roman amphorae types and other early Roman imported wares from the site at King's Road is intriguing. The briquetage at the Bonded Store could indicate that initial activity on or near the site was seasonal. Assuming that there was more than just a redistribution/exchange of goods connection between these two sites during the late Iron Age, it is possible that the focus of activity moved from King's Road to St Peter Port (illustrated by the Bonded Store) in the early Roman period. There is then some evidence suggested by the pottery for activity recurring at King's Road from around the mid-1st century AD and continuing during the 2nd century AD (Wood 1996, 52–5).

As at La Plaiderie, potentially the earliest of the early Roman period amphora types present at the Bonded Store are 16 body sherds of Camulodunum 185A/Haltern 70 (dated mid-1st century BC to the mid-1st century AD), followed by at least eight Pascual 1 amphorae of probable Augustan date. The remaining early Roman amphorae from the Bonded Store are not numerous and mostly date between the later 1st century BC and the early 2nd century AD. Apart from the Dressel 20 and Gauloise 4 amphorae, these other types include nine sherds of Dressel 7–11, three sherds of Camulodunum 189 ('carrot amphora'), and a handful of sherds that represent further types, the most important of which are a possible (Spanish) Dressel 2–4, Dressel 28, Beltran IIB and Richborough 527.

The material associated with the earliest of these amphora types is much the same as at La Plaiderie, except for the fact that there is both a greater variety of forms and quantity of semi-fine table wares, as well as the presence of two particular coarsewares not found at La Plaiderie. One of the latter was imported from Gaul (fabric MDER) and the other (fabric DUR) is the earliest import from pre-Roman Britain. Aquitainian *céramique fumigée* (fabric SCFR) is more noticeable than at La Plaiderie; this includes at least three *vases bobines* (dating between 20 BC and AD 40), a jar (Santrot and Santrot 1979, form 221, dating to the last decade of the 1st century BC), and a bowl dating from the latter decade of the 1st century BC through to around AD 70. Pompeian Red ware dishes are also present at the Bonded Store but only one is probably Augustan in date. A greater range of largely 1st-century AD Gallo-Belgic wares (fabrics GB and GB/TR) are present at the Bonded Store with sherds from at least nine vessels, including beakers (mainly), cups and plates. Central Gaulish terra nigra and Armorican *céramique fumigée* (fabrics MCF and SCFO) are also well-represented with three further *vases bobines*, four plates, several cups, bowls (some from Rennes) and jars dating to the 1st century AD. A particularly aesthetically pleasing form is a cordoned bowl (fabric SCFO), imitating a late Iron Age form, that would appear to have been produced in Armorica where the form originated. As at La Plaiderie, further terra nigras (fabrics EGGS, SCFO, STN, STNR, MCF and GCF) from various Gallo-Roman sources appear to be more common at the Bonded Store from the early/mid-1st century AD onwards.

The distinctive jars with an internally-grooved rim (fabric MDER; Cam. 262) are typically very late 1st century BC/early 1st century AD. Around seven of these vessels are present at the Bonded Store, most of which came from central Gaul, but one is in a different fabric and may be Armorican in origin. Central Gaul also supplied many of the flagons of early Roman date at the Bonded Store, represented largely by body sherds and ribbed handles with a cream slip. Other sherds from flagons in a distinctive orange/red fabric and an off-white slip identical to flagon sherds found at the native site of the Tranquesous (see below) appear to be Gallo-Roman (Mougon) products of around the mid-1st century AD. The direct link with the Tranquesous is further strengthened by the five non-spill bowls (fabric DUR) from the Bonded Store as well as the terra nigras present on both sites. One example of the same DUR bowl form is present at the Tranquesous (Wood 1990, 57). These bowls from the Bonded Store and the Tranquesous are significant as they represent the only pottery imports from pre-Roman Britain. They are indicative of 'return loads' as well as continuing contact with central-southern Britain seemingly post-dating the late Iron Age links epitomised by the Armorican wares and Italian wine.

In summary, it would appear that La Plaiderie was probably founded slightly later in date than the site at the Bonded Store, but otherwise both sites were occupied continuously through to the end of the Roman period, while only La Plaiderie seems to have had a slim early medieval (or 'Dark Age') component.

The early Roman period

By the early Roman period, virtually all of the pottery was imported and, with the exception of the wine amphorae from the Catalan coastal region of north-eastern Spain, all but two of the other pottery imports were semi-fine table wares. The latter are mainly *céramique fumigée* and related terra nigra and terra rubra, imported initially from south-west Gaul then central and northern Gaul (*i.e.* Gallia Belgica) as well as Armorica. Coarsewares represent the two further imported wares: one is also from central Gaul (jars with moulded rims) while the other is the only known import from pre-Roman Britain (Dorset; fabric DUR non-spill bowls). There are also a few Pompeian Red ware plates/dishes of Mediterranean origin.

Semi-fine table wares from the areas described above continued to be imported during the course of the 1st century AD. Camulodunum 185A amphorae, Spanish olive oil amphorae and southern Gallic wine (Gauloise 4 amphorae) are present and while most were imported from the early 1st century AD onwards, some types could have been imported earlier. Fine wares from south Gaul also appear at around the same time with samian from Montans and La Graufesenque, but no Arretine wares have been identified. Flagons from Mougon were presumably imported along with other central Gaulish wares including further flagons and terra nigra. Accompanying the later Gallo-Belgic wares from northern Gaul are coarse greywares, terra nigra-type wares and the first imported mortaria from Picardy.

A handful of sherds represent the remaining early Roman amphora types present at La Plaiderie, and while their periods of production collectively span some 200 years, the majority of them were probably imported during the second half of the 1st century BC and the remainder during the 1st century AD. These include Camulodunum 185A/Haltern 70, Pascual 1, Camulodunum 186A, Gauloise 5 and Dressel 28. Potentially the earliest of these are the few sherds of Camulodunum 185A/Haltern 70 amphorae (mid-1st century BC to mid-1st century AD) followed by two Pascual 1 amphorae of probable Augustan date.

La Plaiderie was also receiving small quantities of semi-fine table wares during the earlier Roman period. Initially, these were imported from south-west and then western and northern Gaul, and to a lesser extent central Gaul. A few cups and bowls of Aquitainian origin in *céramique fumigée* (fabric SCFR) were imported from Augustan times. At least three of the four Pompeian Red ware dishes from the site, fabric PRW2, could belong to this period. Probably slightly later in date are the body sherds from four or five Gallo-Belgic drinking vessels (fabric GB) and some featureless sherds of central Gaulish terra nigra (fabrics CF and MCF). Armorican *céramique fumigée* and allied terra nigras in a variety of other fabrics (EGGS, SCFO, STN, STNR, MCF and GCF) from a number of Gallo-Roman sources appear to be more common from the early/mid-1st century AD, around the time that the earliest (Tiberio-Claudian) samian was being imported from south Gaul. There are undoubtedly flagons dating to this period (body sherds in white, pink and red fabrics) but particular types cannot be determined due to the complete absence of diagnostic sherds and the largely indistinct range of fabrics. Signs of use of these imported wares (see below), along with other evidence, suggests that occupation occurred at La Plaiderie during the early Roman period.

Around the mid-1st century AD, possibly from the early Claudian period, jars and other vessels in a terra nigra-type ware were being imported from northern Gaul. These grey/black jars (fabric GCF), with crudely burnished horizontal bands on the short neck of the vessels, are the forerunners of the *gobelet à col tronconique* form that is particularly common at La Plaiderie and the Bonded Store during the 2nd and 3rd centuries AD (fabrics NGGW 1–2). An identical earlier jar in the same fabric (GCF) is present at King's Road along with a sherd from the later, developed greyware type (Wood 1996, 52, nos 228 and 245 respectively). From the mid-/late 1st century AD the growing diversity and quantity of imported wares is more marked, suggesting that occupation at La Plaiderie was by then well-established. The supply of south Gaulish samian and terra nigra continued, amphorae continued to be imported (Dressel 20, Gauloise 4, Gauloise 5 and Dressel 28) and the first mortaria from northern Gaul appeared.

The earliest pottery of potentially local origin in the early Roman assemblage consists of just three vessels: a bowl, a reeded-rim jar and a cheese press (fabric AR). It is not even certain that these were local products, and all the other early Roman pottery found at La Plaiderie appears to have been imported. Excavation on the native site at the Tranquesous in St Saviour's parish produced a number of vessels including reeded-rim jars in a fabric (identical to fabric AR from La Plaiderie) which the excavator thought might be local, but was more probably imported (Burns 1978, 202, fabric type IV). The Tranquesous vessels appear to derive from the latest phase of activity on that site which is contemporary with the early Roman phase of activity at La Plaiderie. Pottery of 1st-century date which was indisputedly imported at the Tranquesous (mostly dating to the latter part of the century) included samian, terra nigras and greywares, demonstrating a clear link between these two sites.

A small amount of early Lezoux samian imported from central Gaul in the later 1st century AD was found at La Plaiderie. Other colour-coated fine wares from central Gaul began to appear from the later 1st century/early second century AD in the form of 'hairpin' beakers. These, like the 2nd- and early 3rd-century AD colour-coated drinking vessels from Gaul (fabrics CC and CGCC) and Germany (fabrics KOLN, RHT and RC) were presumably imported along with the samian of the period from these areas. Dating to around the same time as the 'hairpin' beakers are the two Dressel 20 amphorae mentioned above and the first import from Roman Britain (a stamp-decorated bowl from the potteries in the Little and Much Hadham region; fabric LEST). North Gaulish greywares (NGGW 1–2 series of fabrics) also started to appear on the site during the later 1st century AD; principally jars decorated with distinctive horizontal lustrous bands, although the majority of vessels from this source are later (see below).

The early Roman activity at the Bonded Store would appear to have continued on from the preceding late Iron Age activity. The imported wares of early Roman date testify to further significant activity on the site that was contemporary with that at La Plaiderie. Gallo-Belgic wares make up much of the fineware, with south Gaulish samian contributing only some 1% of the pottery. Greywares, *ceramique fumigée* and oxidised flagons make up much of the rest.

High Empire

During the High Empire period the differences between the Bonded Store and La Plaiderie assemblages are chiefly in the respective quantities of a given fabric.

The bulk of the samian at both sites is 2nd century AD in date and principally from Lezoux. Both sites (especially La Plaiderie) were also receiving samian from sources in east Gaul during the 2nd century AD, as well as a few vessels during the first half of the 3rd century AD. At the Bonded Store, central Gaulish samian makes up over 6% of the total assemblage of all periods (excluding amphorae), indicating how important the ware was.

From the later 1st century up to the early 3rd century AD, fine wares from central Gaul (Lezoux) predominate, including 'hairpin' beakers, samian and black colour-coated wares. East Gaulish samian of Antonine and early 3rd-century AD date, mainly from the Argonne and Rheinzabern, is present in remarkable quantities. Other colour-coated wares from the Argonne, Trier and Cologne are also present and were accompanied by coarsewares from Urmitz and the Rhineland/Tavernay mortaria.

A significant range of mainly 2nd- and 3rd-century AD semi-fine wares and coarsewares were imported from a number of production centres in the Nord/Pas-de-Calais/Somme Valley area of Gallia Belgica. These include *vases tronconiques*, pentice beakers, pinch-neck flagons and hooked-rim jars along with other greywares. The neighbouring area of the Seine Valley supplied both Gauloise 12 amphorae and a range of flagons including 'pulley-wheel' types.

Jars, pentice beakers and flagons were imported from northern Gaul in the 2nd and 3rd centuries (fabrics NGGW and NGWO). These later imports from north Gaul constitute around one quarter of the entire assemblage from La Plaiderie, and are associated with further wares of the period from the same general area of northern Gaul and Germany (samian, mortaria, plus fabrics NGGW 3–4, EIFL, MARB and see below). Various other greywares, coarse and semi-fine wares also appear to have been imported from the general area of northern Gaul from at least the late 1st century AD and throughout the remainder of the Roman period, although the quantities diminish significantly during the later 3rd and 4th centuries AD. Similarities between their fabrics and the NGGW series of fabrics, as well as the presence of types of distinctive form known to have been produced in this area, leave no room for doubt that the majority of kitchen/table wares (excluding samian) found on the site prior to the later Roman period came from sources in northern Gaul.

It is not possible to date vessels in some of these fabrics (e.g. CCB) more closely than 2nd to 4th century AD. Vessels in fabrics NGSG and MG certainly began to appear during the 1st century AD and continued to be imported up to the 3rd century, but the number of vessels concerned is no more than thirty or so in all. First- and 2nd-century vessels in these fabrics and certain varieties of the QT series of fabrics (particularly QTG) were also found at both the Tranquesous and King's Road sites. Prior to the detailed study of the La Plaiderie and Bonded Store assemblages it was considered that some greywares from King's Road could have been produced locally (Wood 1996, 54), but this now seems very unlikely as far greater quantities and a wider range of forms would be present on all the sites concerned; Gaul is the more likely source for most of the greywares.

The pottery from both La Plaiderie and the Bonded Store establishes the fact that there were some surprisingly strong links with the general area of northern Gaul. An interesting aspect of both assemblages is the lack of hard evidence for High Empire period pottery from sources in Brittany (Armorica) and western Normandy, in contrast to the late Iron Age and late Roman periods. While there are a number of unsourced Roman fabrics (GG, MR, FOXO, and QTW), some of which may originate from these areas, on present evidence only fabric GOW would seem to be a (western) Normandy product and even then the solitary small two-handled flask from La Plaiderie in this fabric is mid-/late 3rd century AD in date. Also, the Normandy amphorae (and flagons) are more characteristic of the area of Haute-Normandie around the Seine estuary, further to the east. Even if products of these areas are present among the unassigned fabrics (and Kay Hartley believes some unsourced mortaria may be Breton in origin), the number of vessels concerned is quite small.

Weak links with eastern Roman Britain are suggested at La Plaiderie by the presence of the solitary stamp-decorated bowl (fabric LEST) and at least three black-burnished ware 2 (fabric BB2) vessels; one of these is probably 2nd century AD in date while the rest are 3rd century. BB2 also occurs at the Bonded Store and in finds from the harbour, but is clearly unimportant compared to its prominence in eastern Britain in the 2nd and 3rd centuries. Pottery does not seem to be shipped in any great quantity from the Thames estuary sites (see Monaghan 1987) to Guernsey, indicating this material probably arrived on the back of other trade or the movement of people. Intriguingly, a significant amount of BB2 and 2nd-century Thames estuary products have in contrast been found in Alderney (Monaghan and de Jersey 2014–15).

In the 2nd century AD, black-burnished ware 1 (fabric BB1) from Dorset also began to be imported to the site. Initially, it appears only in very small numbers as the vast majority of vessels (83 out of a total of around 90) are later than AD 270 in date. BB1 appears to have been imported throughout the late 3rd and 4th century AD. The presence of these and other Romano-British wares is significant as they testify to a change in the character of the La Plaiderie assemblage that became more marked from around the later 3rd century AD and continued through to the end of the Roman period. This is also the case in the Bonded Store assemblage, and BB1 is prominent amongst the few sherds found in Alderney.

Both sites were receiving some mortaria during the later 1st century AD, but Kay Hartley dates the majority to the 2nd/mid-3rd century AD with sources of supply principally within the area of northern Gaul/Germany.

Late Roman (after AD 270)

While pottery from Gallo-Roman sources continued to be imported, both the quantities and number of sources concerned were far less than previously. Sources in Roman Britain were supplying much of the pottery imported to both sites during the late Roman period (or much of the pottery that can be confidently dated to after *c*. AD 270). Contemporary occupation on both sites, though still significant, may have been less substantial than it was during the High Empire.

Of all the Romano-British wares found at La Plaiderie, BB1 is by far the most common although there are fairly significant but lesser quantities of further Romano-British black-burnished type wares (fabric BBT series). Sherds from some 20 Alice Holt and New Forest greywares (fabric AH/NF) are present that together appear to span the 4th century AD. Late 3rd/4th-century AD colour-coated wares from both the New Forest and Oxfordshire potteries (fabrics NFCC and OXRC) are also represented by at least 12 vessels: beakers, cups and flagons in the main. A solitary sherd from a late Romano-British parchment ware bowl/dish decorated with brown paint is also present. The dating of a New Forest mortarium to probably the second half of the 4th century AD (Monaghan 1990, 68), dredged off the seabed to the north of the harbour, provides external evidence suggesting the continued importation of wares from southern England to Guernsey during the same period.

Imports from Gaul during the later Roman period derive from three areas. Most of the hooked-rim jars and bowls (fabric NGGW 3) from north Gaul, along with the greyware vessels (fabrics NGGW 1–2), are certainly mid- to late Roman in date, but some products could have continued to be imported during the late 3rd/4th century AD. Indeed, one further type from the same area in a distinctive range of forms (fabric NGLTN) belongs to the later occupation on La Plaiderie and suggests that other imports may have continued to come from northern Gaul. These strongly moulded jars and bowls with excised decoration mark a revival of the earlier terra nigra tradition. All told, these imports represent just a handful of vessels, far fewer than was previously imported from the same area during the High Empire period.

In the late Roman period, importation of pottery from western Gaul is more prominent. The 15 *céramique à l'éponge* (fabric EPON) bowls and (mostly) drinking cups found at La Plaiderie derive from an area where wine contained in barrels may also have been imported to Guernsey. The presence of *à l'éponge* bowls on the later 3rd-century Roman wreck recovered from the harbour mouth in St Peter Port (Rule and Monaghan 1993, 129) is significant. It establishes an early date for the importation of this ware, suggests a direct link with the town sites, and means that some of the pottery from them dates to the same period as the wreck. However, the later 4th-century AD date of other wares found at La Plaiderie, as well as the evidence from sites elsewhere both in Britain and in neighbouring Gaul, demonstrate that *céramique à l'éponge* continued to be imported throughout the 4th century AD (Wood 1994, 164).

Fine wares from the New Forest and Oxfordshire are present in roughly equal amounts to those from Gallia Belgica (fabric NGLTN) and western Gaul (fabric EPON) combined. Further fine wares from the Nene Valley (fabric NVCC) may be represented by sherds from a flagon/bottle.

La Plaiderie was also receiving some coarse pottery from the northern Cotentin region of western Normandy during the later Roman period. Although no production site has yet been located, it is believed that a local imitation of black-burnished ware was being made in the area due to the presence on a number of sites in the north of the region of certain forms in a characteristically local micaceous fabric (Blaszkiewicz 1992, 38). Six of the large cooking pots concerned (fabric WNMW) are present at La Plaiderie and presumably date within the same period as the Cotentin finds: from the second half of the 4th century to the early 5th century AD (Blaszkiewicz and Jigan 1994, 135).

An important coarseware (the TBF fabric series), representing around 10% of each of the La Plaiderie and Bonded Store assemblages, merits detailed comment at this point. On the basis of this ware at La Plaiderie, the possibility of significant local pottery production in Guernsey during the Roman period was suggested some years ago (Wood 1990, 53). Adding the caveat at the time that the Cherbourg region was also a possible source gave due consideration to a number of facts: finds of this ware principally occurred in these two areas, no production sites had been located, and given the similar geology of the island and neighbouring Normandy either area was possible as a source for the ware (*ibid*). Naturally, should it be proved that production did not occur in Guernsey, then by definition both the start date and amount of material that may otherwise have been imported from western Normandy assumes far greater significance. Conversely, should the ware indeed be a Guernsey product, it would be significant in both local terms and as a known export in the later Roman period. On present evidence, and in the continuing absence of a known production area, there are strong grounds for believing that the ware is a local Guernsey product.

The principal forms in this ware are tripod bowls, lids and jars which on the basis of fabric variations have been divided into three groups (fabrics TBF1, TBF1 GREY and TBF2). These divisions do not alter the fact that the fabrics are all broadly similar and indeed are indistinguishable from certain suspected local fabrics of late Iron Age date from sites elsewhere in Guernsey (cf. Burns *et al.* 1996, 48–9). Fabric TBF1 is by far the most common but all three fabrics, except for the range of forms involved, otherwise exhibit the same wide variations in colour, coarseness and inclusions of the more common fabrics of their potential local late Iron Age forebears.

Only the tripod bowl form is recorded as being found on sites in the Cotentin, as is also the case with the sparse finds from southern England (Wood 1994, 162); the full range of forms is only known at present on both town sites in Guernsey. All the finds outside Guernsey are late Roman in date (mid-/later 3rd to the end of the 4th century AD, *ibid*) but evidence from the town sites as well as two further sites in Guernsey suggests that production of the ware began during the mid-/late 2nd century AD. A foot sherd from a tripod bowl was found in 2000 at Route de Carteret near the west coast, associated with central Gaulish samian of Antonine date. Part of a lid and other pottery types of 2nd-century AD date are present at King's Road; this piece (Burns *et al.* 1996, 70, no. 244) is drawn as a base but is the handle part of a lid. There is no record in either the Cotentin or southern England of tripod bowls in this fabric being found on sites earlier than the late Roman period. Moreover, not only are examples of this ware found either in England or in the Cotentin limited to the tripod bowl form, all those finds are large-size examples of the form. The high percentage of this ware in the town assemblages, the variations in the size and profiles of the principal forms suggestive of chronological developments, and particularly the presence of the ware on Guernsey sites from the 2nd century AD onwards, point towards the ware being a local product with a period of production spanning some 200 years.

A reconsideration of the assemblage after the death of Mark Wood, when phasing became available, indicates that fabric TBF makes up a significant component of Phase 1 at the Bonded Store. This supports the assertion of an early start in Guernsey; indeed it may have been around in the 1st century AD, or even be the continuation of an Iron Age tradition. Sherds from lids of this fabric (if not over-washed) have traces of sooting on their interior surface, complementing the burning/burnt residue on the interior of the tripod bowl. This suggests the two vessels were used together, with the lid acting as a *couvre-feu*. Finds of tripod bowls outside Guernsey and Alderney (Wood 1990, 55) are not, to date, associated with either the lid or jar forms.

The Bonded Store has less late 3rd- and 4th-century AD imported pottery than La Plaiderie. BB1 is represented by around 25 vessels, one quarter of the amount found at La Plaiderie, while each of the remaining Romano-British wares are present in roughly half the amounts of those present at La Plaiderie. The Gallo-Roman imports are equally less-well represented, with five *céramique à l'éponge* drinking bowls and a flagon, around four vessels in NGLTN and two WNMW large cooking pots.

Late/post-Roman period

There is no apparent break in the occupation at La Plaiderie suggested by the pottery, but the date of the end of occupation is just as uncertain as the start of activity on the site. The same is true of the Bonded Store, but occupation seems to end earlier.

Two vessels from La Plaiderie illustrate the bottom end of the scale of the wide variation in coarseness of the potential local Guernsey fabrics. These vessels (fabric AQR) are either late Roman or sub-Roman in date and their fabric is akin to the local briquetage of late Iron Age/early Roman date found on sites in the Bailiwick (Burns *et al.* 1996, 120). Crude copies of a tripod bowl and a BB1 flanged bowl form are present in this 'briquetage type' fabric. The presence of these late or sub-Roman vessels is intriguing given the final amphora type (see below) found at La Plaiderie and the apparent presence of early medieval pottery as well. Their combined presence, along with the inability to date the majority of the late Roman pottery more closely than the period AD 270–400+, means that determining the end of occupation on the site is somewhat difficult to establish. Also, it is not possible to tell whether the scant early medieval material represents a continuation of occupation from the late Roman period or the nature of the activity it represents.

Together with the late Roman tripod bowls (fabric TBF1), the western Normandy cooking pots (fabric WNMW) represent the clearest dating evidence for occupation continuing on the site during the second half of the 4th century AD and with the latter, perhaps even into the early 5th century AD. The presence of at least two late Roman Palestinian amphorae only adds to the difficulty in determining the end of/a break in/continuation of occupation issue on the site during the late Roman period into the early medieval. Although usually dated 5th/6th century AD (Peacock and Williams 1986, 191), it is believed that this amphora type could have been imported into Britain from the late 4th century AD onwards (Holbrook and Bidwell 1991, 11). These Palestinian amphorae could therefore date anywhere from the late Roman period into the early medieval. Added to this, there is the handful of sherds of post-Roman coarsewares from the site that provide a tantalising glimpse of Guernsey during the 5th/6th century AD (Wood 1994, 163). These sherds (fabrics MG, PR? and a possible E Ware base), though scarce and of unknown significance, nevertheless represent a potential land-based counterpart to the Merovingian jugs of 6th-century AD date found on the seabed of the modern harbour (Monaghan 1988, 455). The La Plaiderie fabrics suggest that most derive from western Normandy, although the potential E Ware vessel is a product of western Gaul; the fact that the fabric of the latter is also similar to earlier Gallo-Roman (Petit-Niort) products from the same general region means that some doubt must remain as to its date in the absence of a more helpful diagnostic sherd. Whether or not this early medieval presence at La Plaiderie represents a continuation of occupation on the site from the late Roman period, it was certainly ephemeral compared with previous Roman occupation on the site.

It would appear that occupation at the Bonded Store continued into the late 4th/early 5th century AD, again best illustrated by the presence of the large-size tripod bowls in fabric TBF1, the WNMW vessels, and a possible sherd of a Kapitan II ('hollow foot') amphora. This type of amphora is not present at La Plaiderie, just as the late Roman Palestinian amphora type is not present in the Bonded Store assemblage. There are two roller-stamped greyware sherds (fabric MER?) from the Bonded Store that are possibly post-Roman in date but given their poor condition it has to be said that this is by no means certain. Evidence for early medieval activity at the Bonded Store is therefore slight.

La Plaiderie and the Bonded Store: comparisons

The pottery present in both assemblages provides clear evidence for domestic occupation on both sites (Table 5). This is evident from the outset at the Bonded Store, where the late Iron Age assemblage compares with that from King's Road, including prestigious imports of Italian wine alongside Armorican imports and local wares. The presence of briquetage 'furniture' suggests that salt-working took place on or near the site at the Bonded Store and the quantity of material present may indicate more than just provision for on-site consumption of salt. The late Iron Age local wares and briquetage signify that the site was initially a 'native' concern and it is tempting to suggest that Armorican Gauls themselves were involved in some way, given the imported wares present on the site from that area.

The purely 'Roman' nature, as opposed to a native undertaking, which has been suggested for the site at La Plaiderie would seem to be confirmed not only by the fine pottery present but also from an early date by the presence of high-status metal objects such as bronze mixing-bowls, one of which is Claudio-Neronian in date (cf. Frere *et al.* 1992, 308). Similarly, fine pottery is present at the Bonded Store from a very early date, as well as high-status glass vessels including some of Claudio-Neronian date. From the

Table 5 The Bonded Store and La Plaiderie: detailed breakdown of coarsewares.

	Bonded Store				*La Plaiderie*	
	sherds	*%*	*weight/g*	*%*	*sherds*	*%*
Iron Age or late Iron Age	264	5.6	3094	7.1	37	0.7
Gallo-Belgic *terra rubra*	43	0.9	160	0.4	–	–
Gallo-Belgic miscellaneous	–	–	–	–	9	0.2
Sandy *terra nigra*	156	3.3	973	2.2	56	1.0
Pompeian Red	5	0.1	41	0.1	–	–
Central Gaulish colour-coated	16	0.3	51	0.1	42	0.7
Rough Cast ware	13	0.3	30	0.1	20	0.4
Cologne colour-coated	8	0.2	33	0.1	8	0.1
Trier	11	0.2	37	0.1	50	0.9
New Forest	16	0.3	300	0.7	31	0.5
Oxford	5	0.1	15	0.0	10	0.2
Marbled ware	4	0.1	10	0.0	15	0.3
Nene Valley colour-coated	–	–	–	–	5	0.1
Early mica-dusted ware	32	0.7	181	0.4	9	0.2
Eggshell ware	2	0.0	3	0.0	–	–
Céramique à l'éponge	14	0.3	77	0.2	108	1.9
Miscellaneous colour-coated	28	0.6	124	0.3	40	0.7
Parchment ware	–	–	–	–	1	0.0
Céramique craquelée bleutée	–	–	–	–	35	0.6
Céramique fumigée	54	1.1	473	1.1	5	0.1
Grogged *céramique fumigée*	113	2.4	1358	3.1	114	2.0
Smooth *céramique fumigée*	33	0.7	150	0.3	85	1.5
Reduced smooth *céramique f.*	84	1.8	729	1.7	21	0.4
Misc. *céramique fumigée*	–	–	–	–	29	0.5
Durotrigan ware	6	0.1	80	0.2	–	–
BB1	105	2.2	935	2.1	604	10.7
BB2	5	0.1	26	0.1	11	0.2
BB2 type	38	0.8	300	0.7	107	1.9
North Gaulish greyware	685	14.6	4681	10.7	731	13.0
North Gaul late *terra nigra*	45	1.0	664	1.5	26	0.5
North Gaul sandy grey	111	2.4	1388	3.2	81	1.4
Tripod bowl fabric	558	11.9	10,768	24.7	523	9.3
Alice Holt/Farnham	15	0.3	182	0.4	13	0.2
Quartz-tempered	292	6.2	2997	6.9	175	3.1
Greywares	64	1.4	536	1.2	–	–
Grey scraps	100	2.1	196	0.4	–	–
Coarse quartz/granite greyware	68	1.4	1029	2.4	53	0.9
Eifelkeramik	3	0.1	34	0.1	19	0.3
Miscellaneous sandy	15	0.3	129	0.3	228	4.0
North Gaul oxidised	655	13.9	4272	9.8	1541	27.3
Oxidised, flagon-type fabric	659	14.0	5569	12.8	633	11.2
Sandy oxidised micaceous	17	0.4	99	0.2	1	0.0
Miscellaneous oxidised	257	5.5	500	1.1	–	–
Quartz-tempered white ware	15	0.3	154	0.4	50	0.9
White wares	52	1.1	282	0.6	–	–
West Normandy micaceous	31	0.7	830	1.9	82	1.5
Vesicular ware	9	0.2	89	0.2	1	0.0
	4706	***100***	***43,579***	***100***	***5609***	***100***

early Roman period onwards on both sites there are Spanish wine (Pascual 1) amphorae, then later wine amphorae from southern Gaul and Normandy, plus olive oil amphorae. These amphorae, or rather their contents, as well as the range of imported kitchen wares and fine table wares present throughout the Roman period, are indicative of a Romanised way of life of some standing. The Roman glass from both sites underlines this theme from the 1st century and into the 3rd/4th century AD.

Food preparation and consumption is also evident from an early date and throughout the Roman period. There are colanders from both sites, a cheese press from La Plaiderie, and a complete range of kitchen and table wares which bear signs of use; the trituration grits on some of the gritted samian and other mortaria have been worn away. All the Pompeian Red ware plates/dishes have traces of sooting on their external surface which is characteristic of use rather than a catastrophic fire, and the various greywares and late Roman BB1 cooking vessels continue that theme right through into the later Roman period. Sooting is also evident on the bases of some of the High Empire pinch-neck flagons (fabric NGWO) which suggests the heating of liquids. The large quantity of oxidised, off-white and 'white' sherds presumed to come from flagons is noticeable on both sites, and indeed is a common feature of sites included in the Gazetteer.

Stirring marks are present on samian vessels from the Bonded Store and a bowl (fabric GCF) from La Plaiderie. While the samian supply during the High Empire period was apparently sufficient for any broken vessels simply to have been replaced, life may not have been quite so simple either during the early Roman period or towards the end of the samian supply to the sites. A pre-Flavian form 27 from La Plaiderie and a late 2nd/1st half of the 3rd-century AD form 31 from the Bonded Store both have drill-holes which indicate the vessels were sufficiently prized for them to be mended with metal rivets.

The tripod bowls (fabric TBF series) are particularly interesting as a characteristic of these vessels is that they all have traces of burning/burnt residue on their interior surface (just as the lids are sooted on their interior surface). This is presumably the result of a cooking process where the tripod bowls could have served as portable stoves with lids acting as a *couvre-feu*. They may also have functioned as a light source in view of the absence of any evidence for lamps (cf. Wood 1993b).

The pottery from both sites also indicates other activities. In addition to late Iron Age and early Roman salt-working, there is evidence in the Bonded Store assemblage for other Roman period activity in the form of fragments of ceramic with a vitrified surface and evidence of smelting. 'Metal-working' appears to have occurred at La Plaiderie given the 3rd-century AD coin-counterfeiting moulds (Burns 1986, 96). Spindle whorls, fashioned from Pascual 1 amphorae and coarseware sherds (particularly fabric TBF1) are fairly numerous at the Bonded Store, although a fragment of a ground-down sherd from a drinking cup (fabric EPON) from La Plaiderie could either be a spindle whorl or a gaming piece. Further gaming counters ground down from a variety of wares are present on both sites.

Fragments of 2nd-century AD ceramic figurines from central Gaul are present including one statuette of Venus on each site showing the popularity of this cult. There is also one 'dea nutrix' figurine from the Bonded Store. While enough of this statuette survives to be able to type the piece (due to the basketry impression of the chair the matron sat in), there is insufficient remaining to know whether one or two infants were being suckled. A further figurine, this time of a household god (*lares*) was found at Fort Le Marchant in the north of the island (Burns 1987, 36, no. 43). This site has also produced 2nd/3rd-century AD samian and most notably north Gaulish greywares.

Only one piece of evidence survives for burial practice in the form of a cremation urn (fabric TBF1) at La Plaiderie of late 3rd-century AD date (cf. Burns 1987, 34, no. 22). It was the general Roman practice to bury adult dead away from habited areas, which raises the question of where the limits of Roman St Peter Port were at that date. Guernsey's Roman burial-grounds are yet to be located.

Other religious connotations are suggested by a *post-cocturam* graffito on a mid-3rd-century AD mortarium from La Plaiderie (*ibid*, 34, no. 25). Further examples of graffiti on pottery are present at the Bonded Store, including simple marks on a samian sherd as well as the remains of lettering on coarseware vessels that could represent names (p. 90).

The presence of a wide variety of fine imported Roman wares, Roman glass and metal vessels as well as commodities contained in amphorae suggest that the town sites were of some standing. It should be remembered, however, that the availability and variety of such material could be due more to the fortuitous location of the island than the sophistication of its citizens. St Peter Port could receive whatever was being transported along the Atlantic and Channel maritime routes, when cargo ships took advantage of Guernsey as a convenient stopping-off place (Monaghan 1990). Some rare items, like the LEST fabric bowl or the late Romano-British parchment ware vessels, were more likely to have been brought by their owners as personal possessions than via bulk trade. One can imagine these being swapped by sailors or travellers for goods or services in ancient St Peter Port. Additional considerations, such as state-controlled supply (whether or not directly in the hands of the military or their agents) set against shipping undertaken by civilian merchants would also have had a bearing (Wood 1990, 58).

With the exception of the late Iron Age local wares and (arguably) the TBF fabric series, all the other wares were imported by sea. This knowledge simplifies our assessment of the meaning of these wares (see Monaghan 1990, 63).

Assuming that the TBF fabric series is indeed a local product and not a further import, the remaining 90% of each assemblage by sherd count was imported: 82% and 85% by weight for the Bonded Store and La Plaiderie respectively. Should it be proven that the TBF fabric series was also imported, then both Roman assemblages would essentially consist of entirely imported material. It is clear from the range in date of all the imported pottery found on the town sites that visiting ships were using the ancient anchorage of St Peter Port not merely as a safe haven in times of dire need, but on a 'regular', purposeful basis from the late Iron Age onwards, throughout the Roman period. The number of suspected shipwreck sites in the approach to the port supports this.

It was suggested by the excavator of La Plaiderie that the site was a 'large trading establishment', a 'way station' (Burns 1986, 96). Analysis of the Roman pottery assemblage suggests that the activity on the site did not seem to have involved major 'warehousing' of large quantities of vessels for later sale, exchange or redistribution. Other, as yet undiscovered, sites in St Peter Port could, however, have fulfilled that function and the port as a whole certainly appeared to fulfil the role of a way station (Monaghan 1990, 68). Samian vessels that usually occur in sets are present at the Bonded Store, but Brenda Dickinson has commented that there is no way of knowing if they were bought in sets. The quantities of wares present at any given time during the centuries the sites were occupied would not seem to suggest anything other than the requirements of domestic occupation. Warehousing of items other than pottery cannot, however, be ruled out.

Overall, a familiar picture emerges of St Peter Port as an entrepôt. The town fulfilled this role during medieval and post-medieval times, and its general character can, without any difficulty, be projected back to the Roman period and into the late Iron Age. The more recent role of the Bonded Store to store alcohol in transit offers an interesting link with its ancient origins.

Amphorae

Amphorae were being traded for what they contained, rather than in their own right. They therefore illustrate Guernsey's trading networks much more directly than coarse and fine pottery, which could have arrived by more indirect routes.

At La Plaiderie, 20% of the amphorae assemblage consisted of a number of identifiable types of amphorae and unassigned sherds of early date (Table 6). While it is not possible to ascribe some of these sherds to a particular type with certainty, there are clearly Spanish, Gallo-Roman and (more significantly) Italian and other fabrics among them; the Italian sherds are mostly rounded and water-worn, suggesting they may have come up from the beach. There are nine body sherds in Italian fabrics, differences in which suggest that there are four different amphorae present that are best described as Dressel 1 species (as their poor condition prevents further distinction being made). Fortunately, there is also a diagnostic basal spike (and a body sherd in the same fabric) from a fifth amphora; the thickness of this spike suggests it is from a Dressel 1B amphora (as opposed to the earlier Dressel 1A type). These two sherds represent the earliest amphora from La Plaiderie that can be ascribed to a particular type with some certainty and date to the period 75–10 BC.

Table 6 La Plaiderie: summary of amphorae.

	Sherds	*% sherds*
Gallic, PW27, PW55 plus PW30, 31	246	58
Italian, PW2, 3, 4, 6	17	4
Spanish PW25 (Dressel 20)	71	16.7
Other Spanish, PW 6B, 15	43	10.1
Tunisian PW34	1	<1
Algerian? PW38	1	<1
Palestinian PW46	11	2.3
Unidentified and miscellaneous	34	8
Total	424	100
amphora/100 coarseware sherds = 7.5		

PW = Peacock and Williams (1986) types.

Some 50% of the amphora assemblage from the Bonded Store is late Iron Age or early Roman in date (Table 7). With the late Iron Age amphorae, diagnostic sherds (i.e. rims *etc*) are just as scarce as at La Plaiderie, but some body sherds are in better condition and the thickness of these can be taken as a reasonable indicator of the presence of a particular form type. Fifty-three sherds in Italian fabrics are present, representing around 14 Dressel 1 species amphorae on the basis of differences in the fabrics present and a few diagnostic sherds. Just over half of these would appear to belong to the earlier Dressel 1A type, with the remainder being the later Dressel 1B. It is clear from the presence of these amphorae types and other associated imported wares, as well as local copies of the latter, that significant activity occurred on the site from around 120 BC (as is indicated by the earliest date for the Dressel 1A type) and continued down to around 10 BC (on the basis of the latest date for the Dressel 1B type).

The remaining 80% of the amphorae from La Plaiderie date from the later 1st through to the mid-/late 3rd century AD. Gauloise 12 amphorae (PW55) produced in eastern Normandy are the most numerous (41%), followed by Spanish Dressel 20 (23%) and Gallo-Roman Gauloise 4 (PW27: 17%). These same amphorae types are also present at the Bonded Store where together they constitute around 50% of the identifiable amphorae from the site. Here, Dressel 20 sherds are more numerous (22%), with Gauloise types 4 and 12 being present in roughly equal but lesser quantities (15% each). Dressel 20 is the classic Spanish

Table 7 The Bonded Store: summary of amphorae.

	Sherds	% sherds	Weight (g)	% weight
'Carrot' type PW 12 (Cam. 189)	4	1	38	>1
Gallic (PW27 and PW55)	124	33.5	3109	19.1
Italian PW3/4 (Dressel 1A/1B)	32	8.6	2209	13.5
Other Italian, PW3 and PW10	33	8.6	1073	6.5
Spanish PW15 (Haltern 70)	17	4.5	658	4.0
Spanish PW16	8	2.1	358	2.2
Spanish PW25 (Dressel 20)	73	19.6	6285	38.6
Spanish PW6A and 6B (Dressel 1)	56	15	1940	11.9
Other Spanish (PW10, 19, 24?)	4	1	208	1.2
Aegean 'Kapitan II'? (PW47)	1	>1	12	>1
Unidentified and miscellaneous	19	5.3	372	2.4
Total	371	100	16,262	100

PW = Peacock and Williams (1986) types. Many sherds are burned or water-rolled. All uncertain identifications have been included with the type they are rated as 'probably' belonging to.

olive oil amphora of the period, whilst the two Gauloise types suggest the importation of wine.

Gauloise 12 amphorae are commonly dated to the mid-2nd/3rd century AD. In view of the highly residual nature of the site assemblages and the broad date-span of production of Gauloise 4 and Dressel 20, many of these amphorae types found could date anywhere between the 1st and the mid-/late 3rd century AD. Moreover, more precise dating of certain amphorae types is also restricted by the fact that the vast majority from both sites are represented by featureless body sherds. However, two rim sherds of Dressel 20 from La Plaiderie are from two different vessels, one dating to the late 1st to early 2nd century AD and the other to the later 1st to the mid-2nd century AD. A Dressel 20 rim from the Bonded Store would appear to be 3rd century AD in date.

Eleven sherds from two Palestinian amphorae from La Plaiderie, and the Kapitan II amphora from the Bonded Store are the only late Roman types present.

Mortaria

Mortaria are numerically unimportant at both land sites, with the best examples being found on the seabed and possibly therefore just being carried past the island. Kay Hartley has produced an archive report on 31 vessels – almost all of those found in Guernsey to date. The emphasis is on north Gaul, especially Taverney (Val-d'Oise) and Noyon (Oise). Taverney was the probable source of a number of vessels of form G255 and G272, whilst Noyon is the probable source of mortaria of forms G238 and G255. Some are of forms (if not always the fabric) made in the Rhineland. A number were unidentified and several are suspected to be from sources in Brittany. Marine finds include mortaria possibly originating in East Anglia, Essex and the New Forest (Hartley 1990, 66; 1993, 85).

Quantification and phasing

An analysis of the pottery assigned to the site phasing demonstrates the high level of residuality in the Bonded Store assemblage (Table 8). Even Roman Phase 1 contains 2nd-century material. An element of seriation can, however, be demonstrated by the tail-off of residual Iron Age material and Gallo-Belgic wares in Phases 2 and 3, and *céramique a l'éponge* appearing by Phase 3. A striking feature is the high preponderance of oxidised fabrics in all periods. Much undoubtedly originates in north Gaul, but oxidised fabrics are clearly more important than the miscellaneous greywares. The tripod bowl fabric is there from Phase 1 and although it increases in importance, the quantity in Phase 1 supports the idea of an early start. While not significant numerically, the supply of BB1 can, however, be seen to increase in the later phases. North Gaulish greyware peaks in Phase 2, reinforcing the evidence that it is Guernsey's signature imported coarseware during the High Empire period.

Conclusions

The Roman pottery from the Bonded Store and La Plaiderie has provided the opportunity to place all the known sites and finds in the island within a broader framework of Guernsey during the Roman period. The inescapable conclusion is that Guernsey was a significant port-of-call within the system that moved goods and people along the maritime routes of the Atlantic seaboard as well as along the length of the Channel.

The evidence also points to significant shifts in the trade routes. In the late Iron Age and early Roman period, the predominance of pottery from western Gaul – Armorica and Aquitaine – indicates that Guernsey is on the known trade route which heads up the Atlantic coast of Gaul, then across the Channel to landing points in south-west England such as Hengistbury Head in Dorset. After the invasion of Britain, the trade routes seem to shift to along the Channel. We see more pottery from north Gaul, Gallia Belgica, central and eastern Gaul plus the Rhineland reaching Guernsey during the High Empire. This is also when Guernsey receives the Gaulois amphorae from Normandy and has an imported

Table 8 The Bonded Store: key Roman pottery phasing.

Fabric group	*Sherd count by phase*				*% sherds by phase*			
	1	*2*	*3*	*all*	*1*	*2*	*3*	*all*
Oxidised wares	149	453	268	1588	27.7	34.6	34.1	33.7
North Gaulish greywares	84	237	128	841	15.6	18.1	16.3	17.9
Other greywares	65	138	118	544	12.1	10.5	15.0	11.6
Iron Age or late Iron Age	59	88	10	264	11.0	6.7	1.3	5.6
Gallo-Belgic wares	54	60	18	204	10.1	4.6	2.3	4.3
Céramique fumigée	48	105	39	284	8.9	8.0	5.0	6.0
Tripod bowl fabric	48	127	120	558	8.9	9.7	15.3	11.9
Finewares (except samian)	11	44	24	149	2.0	3.4	3.1	3.2
BB1	7	24	25	105	1.3	1.8	3.2	2.2
Durotrigan ware	5	1	–	6	0.9	0.1	0.0	0.1
White wares	3	17	9	67	0.6	1.3	1.1	1.4
BB2 type	2	6	21	38	0.4	0.5	2.7	0.8
BB2	1	1	–	5	0.2	0.1	0.0	0.1
Eifelkeramik	–	–	–	3	0.0	0.0	0.0	0.1
Others	1	10	5	40	0.2	0.8	0.6	0.8
Total	537	1311	785	4706				100

The 'all' figure for Iron Age or late Iron Age includes post-Roman and unstratified; 26 sherds were found in the Iron Age phase.

pottery suite similar to London. In the later Roman period, after the mid-3rd century, there seems to be a reversion to cross-Channel trade and for the first time there is a significant amount of Romano-British pottery in Guernsey. This may indicate that the eastern Channel became unsafe in the light of incursions by 'pirates' or 'barbarians'.

The imported pottery found in Guernsey and the connections suggested by the sources of origin should serve as a reminder not to underestimate either the frequency or the extent of the shipping involved. What occurred on Roman Guernsey is of direct significance to the broad scope of Roman studies, particularly regarding trading routes.

Catalogue of illustrated coarse pottery

by Mark Wood and Jason Monaghan

The coarse pottery catalogue has been compiled from an initial selection of pots for drawing by Mark Wood, including his fabric codes and identifications. Dating and descriptive information has been supplemented by Jason Monaghan. Vessels are listed by Area and trench, with the earliest contexts first and residual vessels at the end. The generic form description is followed by the colour, fabric description or code, then origin and dating information. The context number or find spot is given at the end. As this is the first substantial body of Roman pottery to be published from Guernsey we have illustrated a number of vessels which would not otherwise be drawn, either due to being fragmentary or of very familiar form (Figs 60–64). Dating information is provided entirely from external parallels.

The Bonded Store

AREA A, RESIDUAL (FIG. 60.1–3)

1. Stamped sherd, light grey MER, possibly Merovingian, 5th–6th century AD (A1203)
2. Pulley-wheel flagon, oxidised F55 (A2007)
3. Tripod bowl, grey WNMW, possibly Normandy, 3rd or 4th century AD (A2007)

AREA B, TRENCH 2 (FIG. 60.4–6)

4. Jar, dark grey surface on light grey core, NGGW2, 2nd or 3rd century AD (B2061)
5. *Vase tronconique*, lustrous grey exterior on light grey core with burnished lines, NGGW1, Picardy, 2nd or 3rd century AD (B2054)
6. Flagon, oxidised FOX (B1204)

AREA B, RESIDUAL (FIG. 60.7)

7. Jar, coarse grey QTG (B1032)

AREA C, TRENCH 1 (FIG. 60.8–16)

8. Jar with lid-seated rim, oxidised, mica-coated MDER, LIA/1st century AD (C1083)

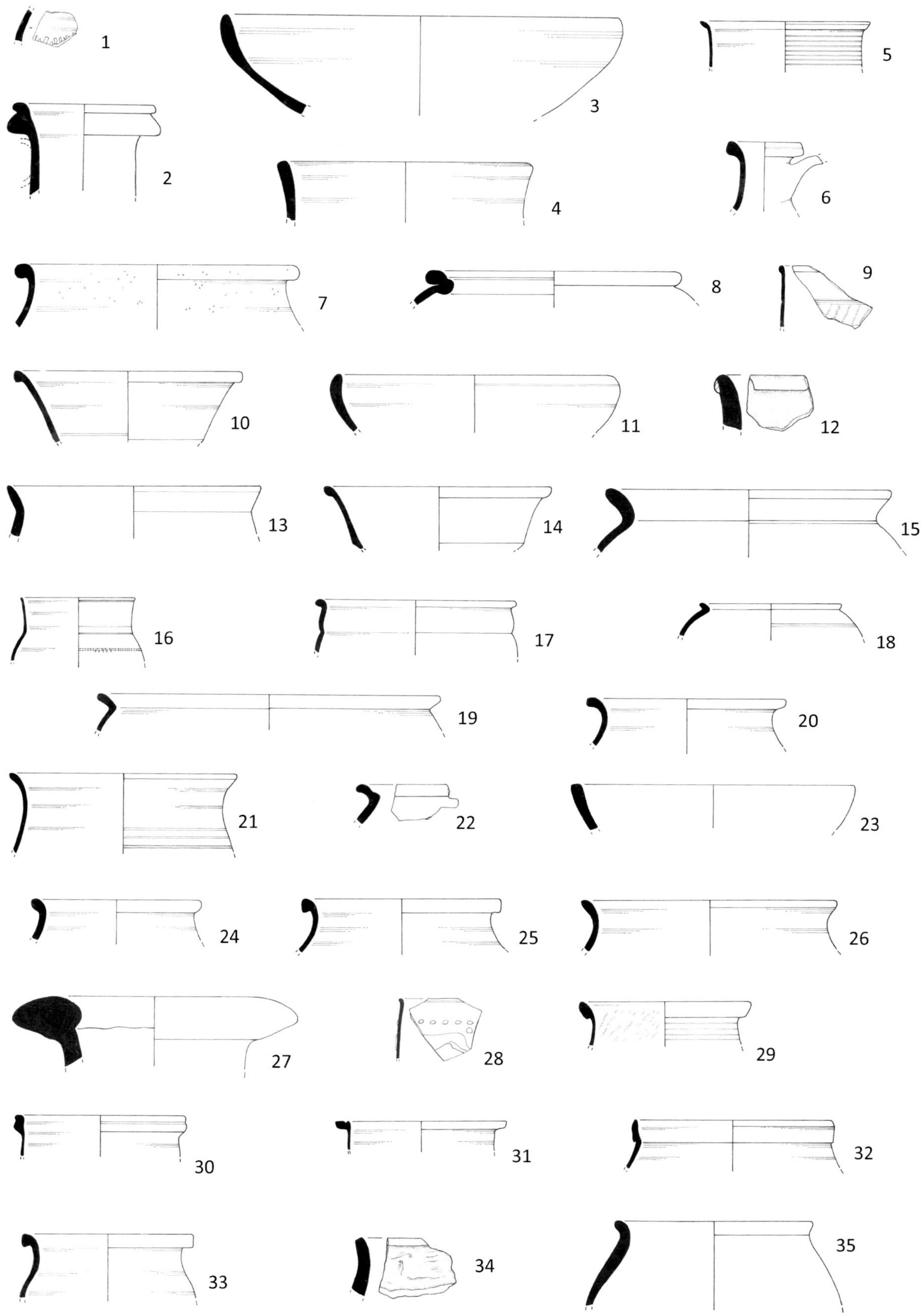

Figure 60 Coarsewares from the Bonded Store, areas A, B and C (trenches 1 and 2). Scale 1:4.

9. Bowl with stamp decoration, light grey sandwiched fabric, *céramique fumigée* SCFR (C1005)
10. Bowl, burnished light grey, *céramique fumigée* SCFR (C1005)
11. Dish, burnished grey on light grey core, NGGW2 (C1005)
12. Bead-rim jar, grey with brownish core, AQR (C1070)
13. Jar, light grey burnished QTG (C1006)
14. Bowl, light grey STN, probably 1st century AD (C1006)
15. Jar, grey with oxidised core QT/GCF (C1006)
16. Beaker, lustrous black-brown on sandwiched fabric, Rhenish (Trier), late 2nd to mid-3rd century AD (C1070)

AREA C, TRENCH 2 (FIG. 60.17–35)

17. Jar or bowl, light grey with near-white core, NGGW1/CF (C2094)
18. Small jar with subtle lid seating, oxidised, mica-coated MDER, 1st century BC to mid-1st century AD (C2080)
19. Jar, dark grey with light grey core, NGGW2 (C2097)
20. Jar, light grey NGGW2/QTW (C2097)
21. Bowl, dark grey surface on light grey fine *céramique fumigée* SCFR (C2097)
22. Bowl, grey fabric QT (C2094)
23. Bowl/dish, dark grey-black and burnished QT (C2094)
24. Jar, grey QT (C2094)
25. Jar, light grey with off-white core, coarse fabric QTG (C2094)
26. Jar, grey with mica at surface, NGGW or Alice Holt/New Forest (C2094)
27. Amphora rim, Spanish form Dressel 20, PW25, 2nd to mid-3rd century AD (C2094)
28. Beaker, 70–80mm rim diameter, hunt-cup design showing hindquarters of an animal, probably a deer; brown slip on white fabric, Cologne AD 120–200 (C2094)
29. Jar, lustrous grey with lighter core and burnished lines, burned and partly discoloured, NGGW (C2094)
30. Jar with bifid rim, light grey but sooted, NGGW3 (C2094)
31. Small bowl with flanged rim, grey NGGW (C2094)
32. Jar with lid-seated rim, grey NGGW3 (C2094)
33. Jar, light grey NGGW2 (C2094)
34. Jar, grey with grey-brown interior, handmade AQG/R (C2094)
35. Jar, grey TBF1 (C2094)

AREA C, TRENCH 3 (FIG. 61.36–46)

36. Cordoned jar, dark grey *céramique fumigée* SCFR, late 1st century BC to 1st century AD (C3034)
37. Jar, dark grey slip on exterior with burnished bands on lighter core, NGGW2/CF (C3030)
38. Jar or bowl, grey with light grey core, NGGW2 (C3030)
39. Small jar, diameter uncertain, dark grey with high silver mica in fabric and surface, possibly AQR (C3030)
40. Jar or bowl rim, light grey with lighter core, NGGW2 (C3021)
41. Jar, grey handmade TBF1, 1st century BC to 1st century AD (C3022)
42. Amphora PW25, Dressel 20, 2nd to mid-3rd century AD (C3036)
43. Bowl or jar, grey with light grey core, NGGW/CF, similar in form to no. 60 (C3023)
44. Small bowl, light grey with off-white core, NGGW1 (C3030)
45. Small bowl, grey lustrous surface on light grey core, NGGW1 (C3026)
46. Bowl with roulette decoration, grey, late TN/NGGW, later 1st century AD (C3033)

AREA C, TRENCH 4 (FIG. 61.47–49)

47. Dish, grey GCF/STNR (C4022)
48. Jar, dark grey with oxidised core, STNR (C4042)
49. Jar, grey with grey-white core, NGGW1 (C4015)

AREA C, RESIDUAL (FIG. 61.50–64)

50. Jar, dark grey burnished surface with light grey core, NGGW1 (C4014)
51. Flanged bowl, grey BB1, form Gillam 231 or similar, late 4th century AD (C4013)
52. Jar, burnt and discoloured grey on exterior else oxidised with golden mica; mica-coated MDER, late 1st century BC to early 1st century AD (C1004)
53. Jar of ‘cooking pot’ type, grey BB2 type BBTA, form Gillam 143 or 144, later 2nd to 3rd century AD (C2004)
54. Jar, dark grey handmade, LIA, probably 1st century BC to 1st century AD (C2071)
55. Wide-mouthed flagon or jug, rim approx. 120mm diameter, cream NGWO (C4014)
56. Jar or bowl with bifid rim, grey Alice Holt/New Forest (C2080)
57. Bowl, dark grey with light grey core, STN, 1st to early 2nd century AD (C1003)
58. Dish, dark grey with brown-grey core and burnished lines, TBF1 (C1004)
59. Flagon rim, oxidised, FOX (C3017)
60. Bowl/jar, grey with oxidised core (similar to no. 43), NGGW/CF (CT2/L3)
61. Bowl or jar, grey NGGW3 (C4013)
62. Body sherd, soft orange-painted decoration on cream fabric, probably New Forest (coarse) Parchment Ware, mid-3rd to mid-4th century AD (C3017)
63. Dish or bowl, light grey NGGW1/4 (C3017)

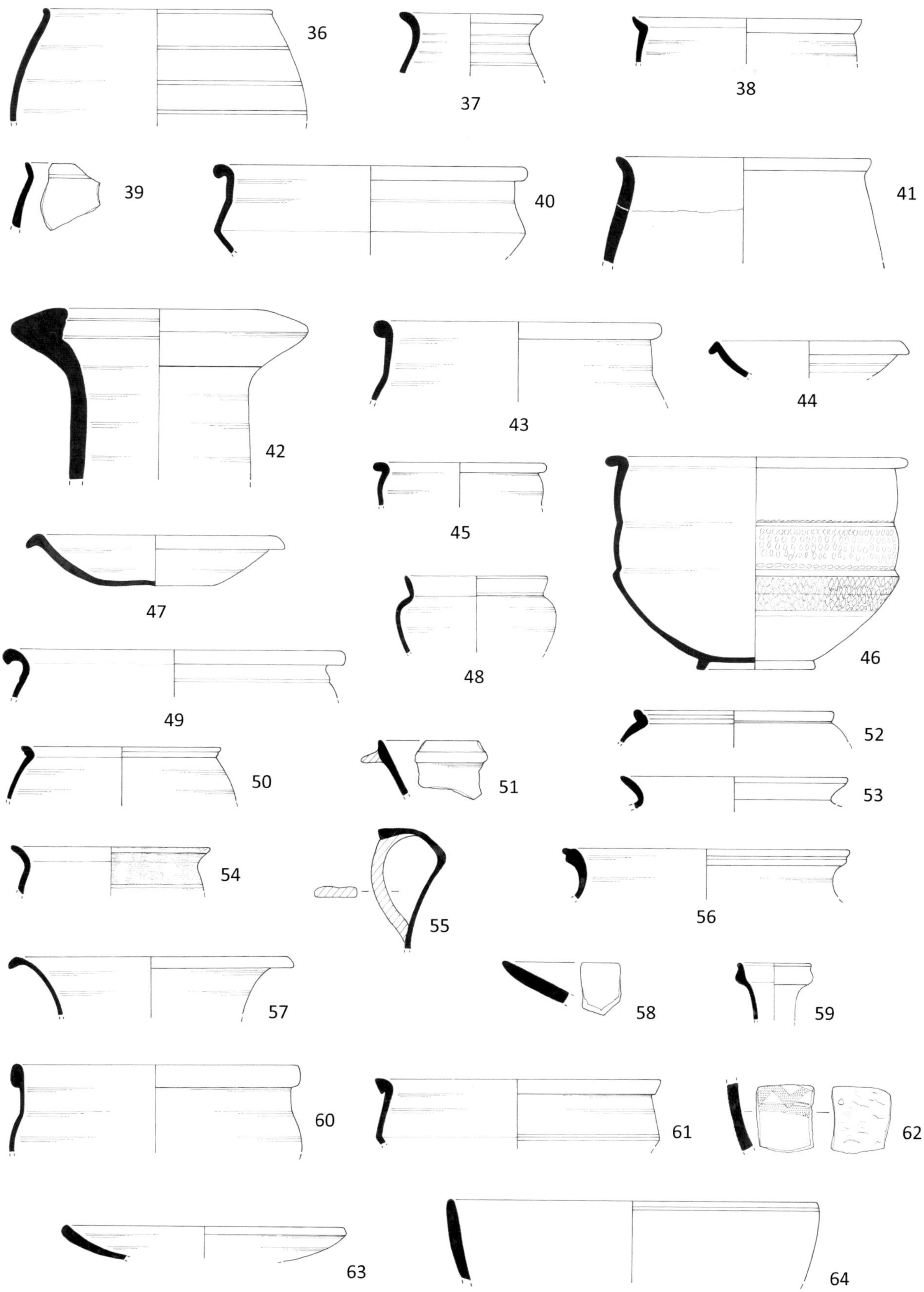

Figure 61 Coarsewares from the Bonded Store, area C (trenches 3, 4 and residual). Scale 1:4.

64. Dish, grey eroded BB1, form Gillam 234, 2nd century AD (C1003)

AREA D, TRENCH 1 (FIG. 62.65)

65. Bead-rim dish, black handmade Durotrigian BB1, 1st century BC to 1st century AD (D1007)

AREA D, TRENCH 2 (FIG. 62.66–69)

66. Jar, grey with sandwiched core, *céramique fumigée* SCFR, Santrot form 221, late 1st century BC to early 1st century AD (D2013)
67. Bead-rim bowl or dish, black handmade Durotrigian BB1, 1st century BC to 1st century AD. Small percentage of rim remaining so wall angle is approximate (D2013)
68. Jar rim and base, abraded dark grey exterior on light grey body, STN, possibly 1st century AD (D2010)
69. Jar, dark grey but surfaces abraded, possibly Durotrigan BB1, 1st century BC to 1st century AD (D2010)

AREA D, TRENCH 3 (FIG. 62.70–71)

70. Bowl, light grey, burnt and discoloured, *céramique fumigée* SCFO, Aquitaine, Menez form 126a, 20 BC – AD 40 (D3007)
71. Jar, light grey SCFR, 1st century BC to 1st century AD (D3006)

AREA D, RESIDUAL (FIG. 62.72–75)

72. Mortarium, cream fabric with flint and quartz grit, Rhineland-Taverney, MORHT, Gillam 255, 2nd century AD (D4103)
73. Jar neck, grey, possibly NGGW (D4103)
74. Dish or bowl, grey coarse QTG (D4007)
75. Small jar, grey with prominent mica, MG (D2009)

La Plaiderie

TRENCH 1 (FIG. 62.76–100)

76. Lid-seated jar, cream EIFL, probably Urmitz, Alzei form 27 (Tyers 174, no. 2), 3rd to 5th century AD (T1/L1)
77. Jar base, pinkish cream NGWO (T1/F29, F20/12, T1/2/Ext)
78. Bowl, grey-brown over oxidised fabric AQR/TBF1 (T1/L2)
79. Jar, dark grey burnished finish on grey NGLTN (T1/L2)
80. Mortarium or bowl, grey surface on coarse cream fabric QTW, appearing to be abraded on interior (T1/L2)
81. Jar, grey with light grey-brown core, STN (T1/L2)
82. Bowl, dark grey with oxidised sandwiched fabric, NGGW3 (T1/L2)
83. Jar, grey-brown with mica at surface, WNMW, 4th to early 5th century AD (T1/L2, T1/F47A)
84. Large jar or bowl rim (T1/L2)
85. Colander or strainer base, grey with grey-brown core (T1/L2)
86. Jar with reeded rim, grey wheel-made harsh fabric AR (T1/L2)
87. Small bowl, light grey metallic slip on grey fabric, NFGW (T1/L2)
88. Leg from tripod bowl, grey fabric with dribbles of white paint, identified as NFGW but would be a curious form from this source, probably 4th century AD (T1/L2)
89. Jar, grey NGGW3 (T1/B2/L3, T1/L3)
90. Jar, grey with grey-white core, possibly *céramique craquelée-bleutée* CCB (T1/L3)
91. Tripod bowl base, handmade, grey discoloured brown in parts, TBF1 (T1/L3)
92. Bowl, with uneven rim, grey NGGW (T1/L3)
93. Lid-seated jar, cream EIFL, possibly Paris Basin, Alzei form 27 (Tyers 174, no. 2), 3rd to 5th century AD (T1/F8)
94. Mortarium base, cream with quartz grits, probably Gallic MORTG (T1/F44)
95. Base with footring from bowl, unusual for this fabric, cream EIFL, 3rd to 5th century AD (T1/F48)
96. Jar or flagon base, cream NGWO (T1/F73)
97. Mortarium, cream, *post-cocturam* graffito DIV I. S and traces of burning, Rhineland-Taverny MORHT, 2nd or 3rd century AD (T1/F69)
98. Two-handled flagon, coarse cream fabric looking like a Roman version of medieval Normandy Gritty ware, GOW (T1/F69)
99. Jar, light grey NGGW (T1/F108)
100. Dish, oxidised micaceous PRW with sooted rim and no slip remaining, 1st century AD (T1/F85)

TRENCH 2 (FIG. 63.101–104)

101. Pulley-wheel flagon, oxidised with remains of white slip, FOXO/F55, probably 2nd or 3rd century AD (T2/L1)
102. Dish, brown surface on grey core, knife-trimmed profile, BBTB, 2nd to 4th century AD (T2/L4)
103. Jar of cooking-pot form, abraded grey-brown coarse fabric BBTB in the BB2 tradition, later 2nd to 3rd century AD (T2/L4)
104. Jar serving for cremation burial, handmade grey fabric sooted on neck and discoloured grey-white on one side, possibly local. Neck forming is quite uneven and there are indications of knife-trimming on lower body (T2/F124)

Other Roman sites (Figs 63.105–121, 64.122–129)

The finds from the St Peter Port harbour seabed have some abrasion, discolouration and marine growths on the surface.

105. Bowl, dark grey with grey core becoming light on interior margin, NGGW (St Peter Port harbour, Gazetteer C7)

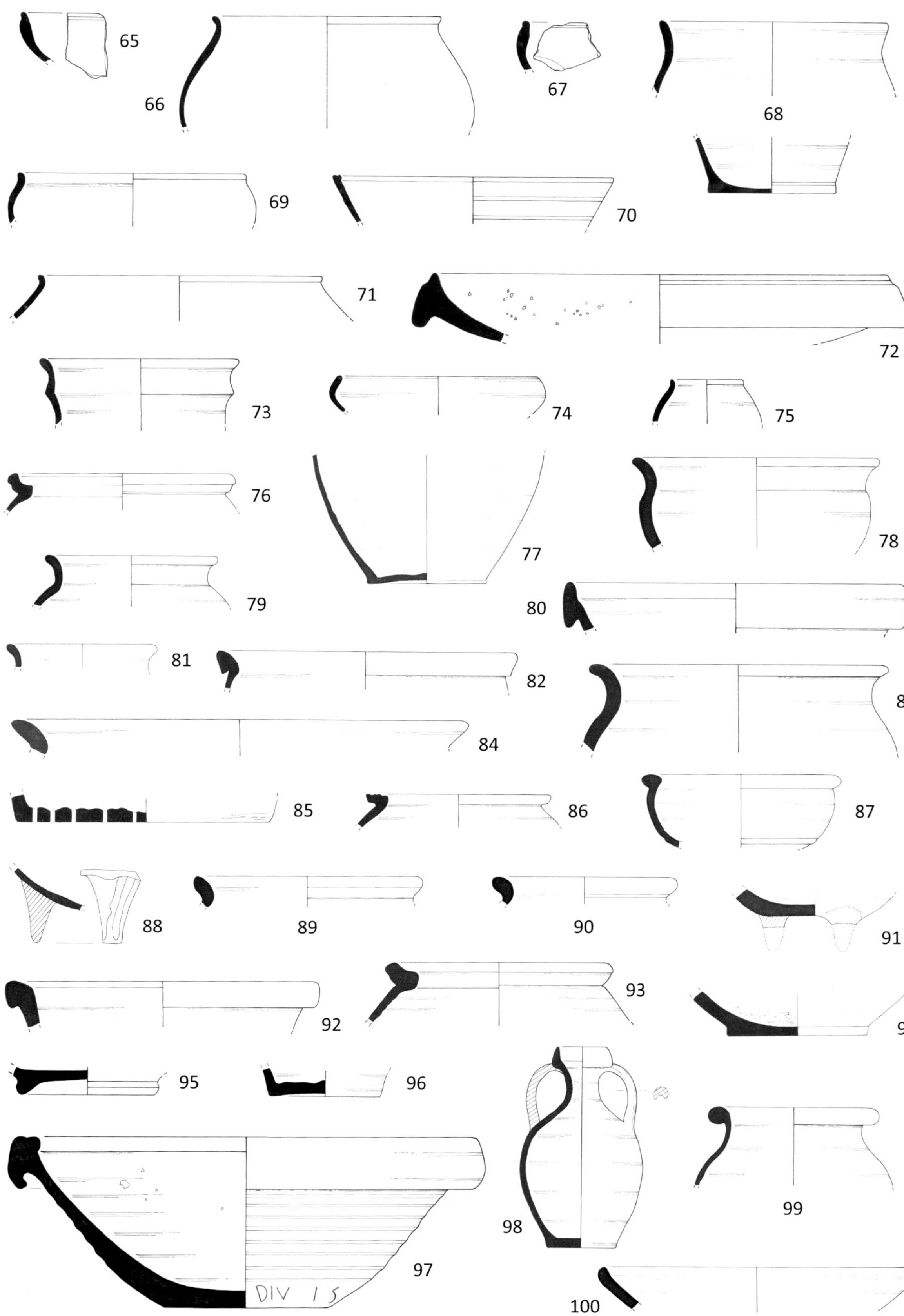

Figure 62 Coarsewares from the Bonded Store (area D) and La Plaiderie (trench 1). Scale 1:4.

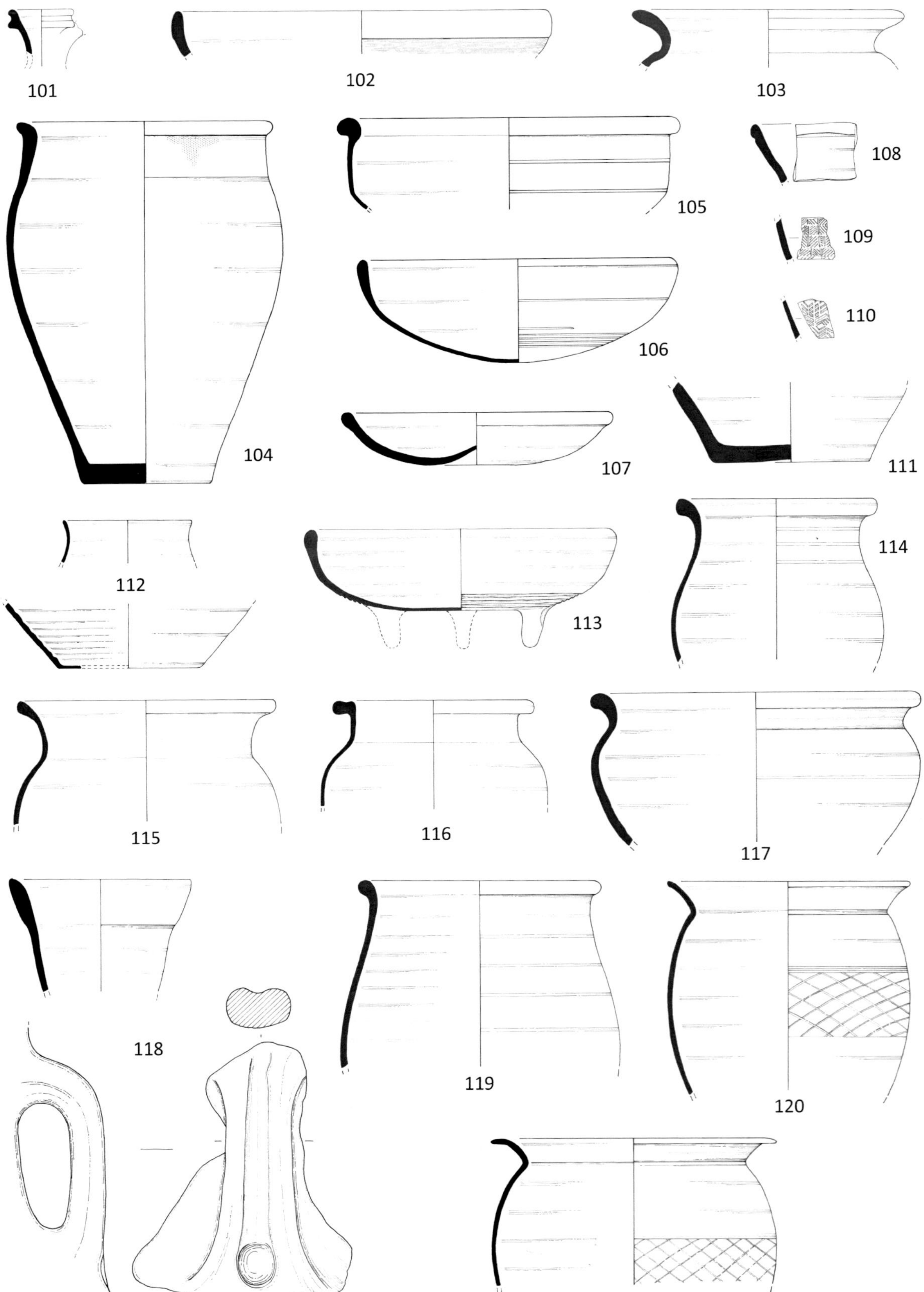

Figure 63 Coarsewares from La Plaiderie (trench 2) and other Roman sites. Scale 1:4.

106. Dish, dark grey surface discoloured white in places, white core, Gallo-Belgic TN, 1st century AD (St Peter Port harbour, Gazetteer C7)
107. Dish, grey to black with white core, Gallo-Belgic TN, 1st century AD (St Peter Port harbour, Gazetteer C7)
108. Dish, discoloured cream-grey surface with sandwiched section, BB2-type BBTA 'dog dish', mid-2nd to mid-3rd century AD (St Peter Port harbour, Gazetteer C7)
109. Body sherd from jar or bowl, discoloured a greenish-grey with grey slightly sandy fabric. Stamping resembles that of Argonne Ware in the 4th century AD (Cow Bay, Gazetteer B21)
110. Body sherd from jar or bowl, cream surface over off-white sandy fabric. Stamping resembles that of Argonne Ware in the 4th century AD (St Peter Port harbour, Gazetteer C7)
111. Bowl base, grey burnished with black bands over wheel-made sandy fabric and brownish core, much like TBF (St Peter Port harbour, Gazetteer C7)
112. Jar, grey with light grey core, STN or NGGW (St Peter Port harbour, Gazetteer C7)
113. Tripod bowl, light grey with traces of sooting, wheel-made fabric (but not TBF), deep incised grooves under base (St Peter Port harbour, Gazetteer C7)
114. Jar, dark grey with light grey core and lustrous burnished bands on neck, NGGW (St Peter Port harbour, Gazetteer C7)
115. Jar, grey handmade coarse sandy fabric. Although abraded the remains of diagonal scoring can be seen (St Peter Port harbour, Gazetteer C7)
116. Lid-seated jar, grey wheel-made quartz-tempered fabric (St Peter Port harbour, Gazetteer C7)
117. Jar or bowl, dark grey but discoloured by brown-black solidified pitch on interior and possibly exterior too. The pitch is very similar to that found on Roman wreck so the sherds making up this vessel may have originated from there (St Peter Port harbour, Gazetteer C7)
118. Amphora, buff fabric with orange core and grey margins, PW Class 15, Haltern 70, mid-1st century BC to mid-1st century AD (found 'one mile north of Tautenay', Gazetteer C2)
119. Jar, dark grey with light grey core and burnished bands, NGGW (St Peter Port harbour, Gazetteer C7)
120. Jar of cooking pot form, black BB1 with narrow band of obtuse burnished lattice typical of 3rd century after *c*. AD 225 (St Peter Port harbour, Gazetteer C7)
121. Jar of cooking pot form, black BB1 with narrow band of obtuse burnished lattice typical of 3rd century after *c*. AD 225 (St Peter Port harbour, Gazetteer C7)
122. Bowl, muddy grey sandy fabric with harsh feel, crudely decorated with burnished lines on exterior and burnished lines and starbust on interior (St Peter Port harbour, Gazetteer C7)
123. Bowl, grey with abraded surface, traces of vertical scoring on cordon, probably Thames-side/Upchurch late 1st–2nd century AD (Monaghan 1987, type 4A) (St Peter Port harbour, Gazetteer C7)
124. Small jar base, buff with gold mica at surface, grey interior, MDER, 1st century AD? (St Peter Port harbour, Gazetteer C7)
125. Flanged dish, grey-black abraded BB1 similar to Gillam 229, later 4th century AD (St Peter Port harbour, Gazetteer C7)
126. Bowl, oxidised sandy fabric with silver mica at surface although abraded (St Peter Port harbour, Gazetteer C7)
127. Jar, dark grey sandy handmade fabric patchily discoloured and sooted. Vessel interior very uneven due to finger impressions, exterior decorated by diagonal slashing (St Peter Port harbour,Gazetteer C7)
128. Small mortarium discoloured buff but once cream, quartz grit with some flint, Taverney (Vermeersch 1993). Kay Hartley comments that this is a 'Flanged mortarium with flange downturned almost to the body and thus something between a Gillam 255 (e.g. no. 72, above) and a collar type… probably late 2nd or 3rd century in date' (St Peter Port harbour, Gazetteer C7)
129. Mortarium, grey fabric with buff surface, no remaining grit, form Gillam 238. Kay Hartley comments that one production centre for these mortaria can be attributed to Noyon (Oise), but there will have been others in the Oise/Somme area of northern France (Hartley 1998, 200–6). It is securely dated to the period AD 65–100 (*e.g.* Cunliffe 1971, 171, nos 1 and 6). These mortaria are found throughout Britain and less commonly in northern France and Belgium. This sherd is discoloured to black, with magenta patches and has surface encrustation, all resulting from being in the sea; it would originally have been cream throughout and considerably lighter in weight. It would have had flint and quartz trituration grit (St Peter Port harbour, Gazetteer C7)

The samian ware

by B. R. Hartley and Brenda Dickinson

Editors' note: in the mid-1980s Brenda Dickinson and Brian Hartley examined the La Plaiderie samian, and in the late 1990s Brenda Dickinson examined the samian from the Bonded Store and a selection of other sites on Guernsey. Samian studies have advanced to the point where a detailed listing from such small sites might seem excessive. However, as these are the only samian assemblages of any size found to date in Guernsey, they are listed here in detail.

Abbreviations: CG = central Gaulish, EG = east Gaulish, SG = south Gaulish. Unless otherwise stated, CG = Lezoux and SG = La Graufesenque.

La Plaiderie

SUMMARY

The samian from La Plaiderie ranges from the Tiberio-Claudian period to the 3rd century. The material is divided

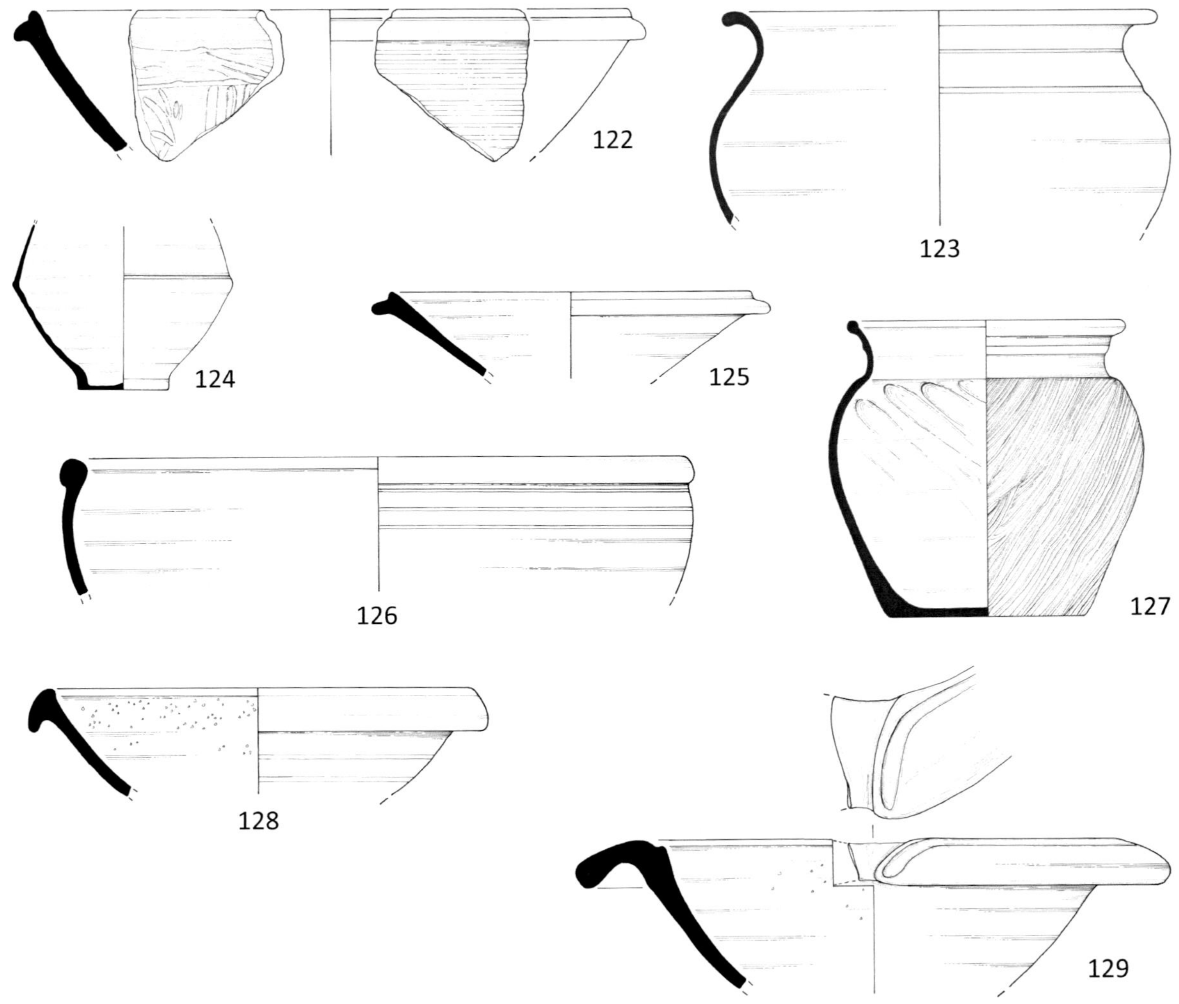

Figure 64 Coarsewares from other Roman sites. Scale 1:4.

into south Gaulish (12%), central Gaulish (1% from Les Martres-de-Veyre and 57% from Lezoux), and east Gaulish (31%) (Table 9). The 1st-century material comes mainly from La Graufesenque, but there are a few Montans vessels and two in characteristic 1st-century Lezoux fabrics. Montans ware, presumably shipped up the west coast, is common in north-west Gaul. First-century Lezoux ware also occurs in fair quantity in this area and is known from Jersey. The opening years of the 2nd century saw a little samian from La Graufesenque, Montans and Les-Martres-de-Veyre. However, the bulk of the 2nd-century material is obviously from Lezoux, though some of the remarkably high proportion of east Gaulish ware at the site will be contemporary with it. This includes material from Rheinzabern and the Argonne, with a little from Trier.

The extraordinary thing about the site is the overall percentage of east Gaulish ware, much of which is likely to be 3rd century, with Rheinzabern, the Argonne and Trier as the only identified sources. The problem is how and why such a high proportion of east Gaulish ware reached the Channel Islands, when comparable material seems to be largely lacking in Brittany and south-west Britain, as well as in Normandy west of the Seine. There are more unusual forms such as flagons, jars with 'cut-glass' decoration and 'black' samian than would normally be expected from one site. There is also a fairly high proportion of mortaria, but that is not uncommon on sites occupied in the late 2nd and 3rd century.

Catalogue

TRENCH 1

U/S	Material ranging from the 1st to the 3rd century, mainly central and east Gaulish and of mid- to late Antonine and 3rd-century date. It includes a sherd of form Dr. 30 in F.50
F.1	Dr. –, SG. A scrap in pale cream fabric, with maroon-brown glaze, typical of Tiberio-Claudian Montans ware
F.6	i) Dr. 27, SG, Flavian or Flavian-Trajanic

Table 9 La Plaiderie: summary of samian vessel sources.

Industry	*Min. no. of vessels*	*Period*	*% of whole*
South Gaul	*34*		*11.9*
Montans	15	4 Tibero-Claudian	5.2
		2 Flavian-Trajanic	
		1 Trajanic	
		5 Trajanic or Hadrianic	
La Graufesenque	19	4 first century	6.6
		2 Neronian/early Flavian	
		2 pre-Flavian	
		3 early Flavian	
		1 Flavian	
		5 Flavian or Flavian/ Trajanic	
		2 Flavian/Trajanic	
Central Gaul	*164*		*57.3*
Les Martres-de-Veyre	2	1 Trajanic or Hadrianic	0.7
		1 early Antonine	
Lezoux	162	1 Tibero-Claudian	56.6
		1 Flavian?	
		4 Hadrianic	
		17 Hadrianic or early Antonine	
		1 early Antonine	
		23 mid- to late Antonine	
		11 late Antonine	
		104 Antonine	
East Gaul	*88*		*30.8*
Rheinzabern	30		10.5
Trier	8		2.8
Argonne	9		3.1
Unassigned	41		14.3

ii) With F.48, F.90, T1 L2 (4) and probably F.76, Dr. 37, CG. The ovolo (Rogers B153) and zig-zag borders suggest the work of Servus iv (Rogers' Servus II). The panels include: 1B) an ornamental balustrade (Rogers U263); 1C) a Cupid (O. 508 variant); 2) Pan to right (D.419 = O.717), over a box; 3) the balustrade, over a 'propellor' and a vase (Rogers T29). Other sherds show two double-bordered arcades, one with the 'propellor', the other with a Pan (D. 412 = O.710), partly obliterated by an inserted panel with bead and zig-zag borders and containing a discus-thrower (D. 400 = O.673). To the right is a leaf (Rogers H133) on a zig-zag stem. Various devices are used to divide the panels and support the arcades, such as a pillar (Rogers P21), a striated spindle with double chevron ends and a caryatid (D. 656 = O. 1199). The relationship between the various sherds is not clear. The bowl is almost certainly by Servus; cf. Sauvaget 1970, pl. iv for the ovolo, border, Pan, discus-thrower, arcades, column and box. A bowl from Colchester may be from the same mould and, if so, the decoration is much more varied than appears here. *c.* AD 160–200

F.8 Dr. 79, CG, mid- to late Antonine

F.8A i) Dr. 31, 33 and –, CG. Antonine
ii) Dr. 45 (Trier), 30 or 37 rim (Rheinzabern), a gritted samian mortarium (Rheinzabern) and a scrap, EG. Late 2nd or early 3rd century

F.9 Dr. 68, CG. A jar with black, faintly iridescent coating over pink-brown fabric. The decoration includes a band of rouletting over panels: 1) a double festoon; 2) a trifid motif in a small double medallion. The medallion appears on jars in the styles of Namilianus-Croesus and the Paternus v group (Bémont 1977, 230 and 185, respectively). Mid- to late Antonine

F.11/15 i) Dr. 37, in the fabric of Les Martres-de-Veyre, possibly with the Mercury D. 290, used there by Cettus, *c.* AD 135–160
ii) Dr. 36, CG. Hadrianic or early Antonine
iii) With F.73. Dr. 37, CG. A bowl with a large vine leaf (Rogers H13) in a winding scroll, together with a bird to right. The leaf was used by potters in the Cerialis ii-Cinnamus ii group, *c.* AD 130–170
iv) Dr. 31, CG, stamped MATERNINI: Maternianus i of Lezoux, where the die (2a) is known to have been used. The name is not entirely certain and could be Maternianus, if the final leaning N is not intended to be AN ligatured. All the other examples noted are on cups of Dr. 33. One is in a burial at Astwick, Bedfordshire, together with stamped vessels of Aucella (1a), Do[v]eccus i (13c), Marcrinus iii (1a) and Sacrillus (3a), all mid- to late Antonine potters, *c.* AD 160–190. Slightly burnt with heavily-worn footring

F.14 i) (Joining F.101) Dr. 18/31R, SG. Probably late 1st- or early 2nd-century Montans ware.
ii) Dr. 31 and – (two, one burnt), CG. Antonine. One of the unidentified sherds (unburnt) is perhaps from a disc-necked flagon
iii) Dr. 30 or 37, CG. Mid- to late Antonine
iv) Curle 21, EG. Late 2nd or early 3rd century

F.14B Dish and –, EG. Late 2nd or early 3rd century

F.16 Dr. 79 *etc*. CG. Mid- to late Antonine

F.18 Dr. 37, CG. In the style of Servus iv (Rogers' Servus II), with one of his ovolos (Rogers B153), a zig-zag border and a Pan (D. 419 = O. 717) in a double arcade. The decoration recalls his bowl in F.6, *c*. AD 160–200

F.20 Dr. 45, CG, *c*. AD 170–200

F.22 Dr. 37, CG. Antonine

F.23 Inkwell, CG. Antonine

F.32 i) Dr. 29 rim, SG. Before *c*. AD 85
ii) Dr. 37, SG. Flavian or Flavian-Trajanic
iii) Dr. 30 or 37 rim, EG (Rheinzabern). Late 2nd or early 3rd century

F.41 i) Dr. 30, SG. Flavian or Flavian-Trajanic
ii) Two fragments of Dr. 37, SG. The fabric is not impossible for Montans, where detached spirals were often used as fillers in the field, as here. The animal, apparently unrecorded, but deeply impressed, appears to be a bear. Probably 2nd century, *c*. AD 100–145
iii) Dr. 33 and – (three), CG. Antonine

F.43 i) –, SG. The cream fabric and purple-brown glaze suggest Tiberio-Claudian Montans ware
ii) A scrap of Argonne ware. Second half of the 2nd century

F.44 *Plain*
i) –, SG. First century
ii) Dr. 18/31, probably from Les Martres-de-Vayre. Trajanic or Hadrianic
iii) Dr. Curle 11 and a scrap, CG. Hadrianic
iv) Dr. 15/31 (?), 33 (a minimum of three) a dish, at least two jars and a handle, burnt, which may belong to one, CG. Antonine
v) Dr. 45 collar and a base fragment of gritted samian mortarium (worn), CG, *c*. AD 170–200
vi) A gritted samian mortarium, EG. Late 2nd or early 3rd century
vii) CG (mainly) and EG scraps. Mostly Antonine, though some could be early 3rd century
Decorated
viii) Dr. 29, SG, *c*. AD 70–85
ix) Dr. 30 or 37 base (small) and a jar with a scroll decoration, CG. Hadrianic or Antonine
x) Dr. 37, CG. Hadrianic or early Antonine
xi) Two joining sherds of Dr. 37, heavily eroded, in Argonne fabric. The decoration, which is closed by three uneven grooves, involves animals to the left, chasing each other, and a small leaf, perhaps heart-shaped, *c*. AD 150–200
xii) Two or three sherds from jars with 'cut-glass' decoration, CG. Antonine
xiii) An unusual flagon form, perhaps similar to Oswald and Pryce 1920, pl. lxxxii, 6 and 10, or a colour-coated oil-flask. Probably CG and Antonine
xiv) Dr. 37, EG. Probably Trier ware, with an ovolo with straight tongue turned to the right at the bottom, in the manner of Censor ii, Criciro vii and Dexter ii. Late 2nd or early 3rd century
xv) Dr. 37, EG. The ovolo (Ricken and Fischer 1963, E42 and a dog to right (*ibid*, T146a) were used at Rheinzabern in the late 2nd and early 3rd century. There is also a vertical series of bifid (?) motifs, upside-down, *c*. AD 180–240. Also three black and one orange colour-coated sherds

F.47 i) Dr. 30, SG. The ovolo, with straight tongue swelling to the right at the end, resembles one used at Brive (Moser and Tilhard 1987), though the bowl is in La Graufesenque fabric and the ovolo seems to have been used there, too. A saltire panel has a trifid motif in the top, between striated spindles. Flavian
ii)Two jars, one in 'black samian' fabric, CG. Antonine
iii) Dr. 37, EG. Late 2nd or early 3rd century

F.48 i) Dr. 30, in pale fabric, with purple-brown glaze. Probably Montans ware, with panels showing: 1) a saltire; 2) a kneeling stag (a variant of Hermet, pl.27, no. 2.); 3) a basal wreath of trifid (?) motifs. The style is probably derived from the Germanus i school at La Graufesenque. Cf. Hermet, pl. 101, nos 22, 24, 26, 27, 29. Late 1st or early 2nd century
ii) See F.50, iii
iii) Dr. 37 (two), CG. Hadrianic or early Antonine
iv) Dr. 31, 33, Curle 21 and two sherds from one vessel, with external groove, CG. Antonine
v) Dr. 37 (two: in the styles of Servus iv (see F.6) and the Paternus v group) and 79, CG. Mid- to late Antonine
vi) Dr. 45 and a gritted samian mortarium, CG, *c*. AD 170–200
vii) Dr. 37, EG. The tongueless ovolo (Ricken and Fischer 1963, E67) and bear (*ibid*, M126a) were used at both Heiligenberg and Rheinzabern by Reginus vi. Cf. Ricken 1948, Taf. 142, 14F and 21F. The fabric does not help to decide the provenance. *c*. AD 150–180
viii) Dr. 31, 37 (two, one from Rheinzabern), 45 (in Trier fabric), two gritted samian mortaria and a jar, EG. Late 2nd or early 3rd century
ix) Many CG and a few EG scraps, the latter including a sherd of Trier ware. Late 2nd and/or early 3rd century

F.48B i) Dr. 15/17, SG. 1st century
ii) Dr. 37, CG. In orange, micaceous fabric with orange-brown glaze and a coarse wavy line below a rosette-tongued ovolo. Hadrianic-Antonine

iii) Dr. 31, 33, 36 (two), 37 (two, one burnt), Curle 15 or 23, a gritted samian mortarium and several scraps, CG. Probably all Antonine
iv) Dr. 31R, CG. Mid- to late Antonine
v) Dr. 37, in what at first sight appears to be Rheinzabern fabric. However, none of the motifs can be traced precisely in Rheinzabern ware and it remains possible that this is a late CG bowl. Apart from the rosette, matched in the work of Marcus v, the only clue is in the plant, which is similar to (but probably not identical with) one used by Banuus. The bird was originally a Lezoux type, but as variants were also used at Rheinzabern, it does not help greatly. Late Antonine or early 3rd century
vi) Dr. 30 or 37, 43 (?), 45, a gritted samian mortarium, a cup, a flagon and a sherd with cut-glass decoration, EG, late 2nd or early 3rd century

F.50 i) Footring, perhaps 2nd-century Montans ware. Trajanic or Hadrianic
ii) Dr. 29/37, SG. The rim is beaded like form 37, but has the internal grooving of form 29, though it lacks external rouletting. There are also three external grooves above the decoration. Second-century Montans ware. Trajanic or Hadrianic
iii) Two sherds, with others in F.48, T1 L1 and T1 L2 (7), some joining. Dr. 30, CG. The rosette-tongued ovolo is probably Rogers B24. The panels include: 1) a small double medallion; 2) Apollo (D. 55 = O. 92); 3A) a bird to right, looking back, in a chevron festoon (Rogers F60); 3B) a band of chevrons; a sphinx to left (D. 497 = O. 857), among leaf-tips (Rogers J122, or the like); 4A) a seated Diana (D. 68 = O. 111); 4B) (probably joining) a hare to right (O. 2057). Elsewhere are a bird (O. 2317?) in a double medallion, following 4A, and an erotic group (Oswald, pl. XC, M), following 4B. The decoration recalls Les Martres-de-Veyre, though the bowl itself is in Lezoux fabric. It is almost certainly in one of the less common, and probably earlier, styles of Sacer i, who is thought to have started work at Les Martres. The festoon is on a stamped Dr. 30 from Dragonby and the ovolo and rosette are on another, from Cannstatt (Knorr 1905, taf. V, 5). Unstamped bowls in Sacer's style include the bird and medallion (Melandra) and the erotic group and hare (Heronbridge), *c.* AD 125–140.
iv) A flagon neck, CG? Cf. Oswald and Pryce 1920, pl. LXXXIII, 2. Second century?

F.51 Dr. 33 (?), EG. Late 2nd or early 3rd century

F.57 Dr. 37 (?), EG, almost certainly Argonne ware. Second half of the 2nd century

F.58 i) Dr. 37, CG. Hadrianic or early Antonine
ii) Dr. 30 or 37 rim, CG. Antonine
iii) Dr. 37, CG or EG. Second century
iv) Dr. 37, 45 (Trier?), two gritted samian mortaria, two jars and two scraps, EG. Late 2nd or early 3rd century
v) Two fragments from an EG bowl, with barbotine scroll-work on the outer wall. It belongs to the range Ludowici SMa-c and is most probably SMc. The fabric suggests an origin at Trier, where such vessels were found in the Massenfund (Huld-Zetsche 1972, Abb. 4, 11a). First half of the 3rd century.

F.64 i) A jar base and a scrap, CG. Antonine
ii) A CG 'black samian' jar, with bung foot. Antonine

F.69 A scrap of 1st-century samian, probably from Montans

F.69/66 i) Dr. 36, in cream fabric with brown glaze, probably early 2nd-century Montans ware
ii) –, CG. Second century
iii) A disc-necked flagon, CG. Antonine?
iv) A gritted samian mortarium, burnt, CG, *c.* AD 170–200
v) Dr. 31, EG, from the Argonne or Rheinzabern. Late 2nd or early 3rd century

F.73 i) See F.11/15, iii
ii) Dr. 31 and a scrap, CG. Antonine

F.76 i) Dr. 30 or 37 base, CG. Hadrianic or early Antonine
ii) A flake of Dr. 37, with the same column and zig-zag border as F.6, ii, and almost certainly from the same bowl.

F77 i) Dish, SG. First century
ii) –, CG. Hadrianic or early Antonine

F.79 Dish, with the quarter-round moulding of Dr. 15/17, but with a flat base outside the footring, as on Dr. 17. The pale orange, micaceous fabric and dull orange glaze are characteristic of 1st-century Lezoux ware. The form must be Tiberian or early Claudian

F.84 Dr. 31, CG. Mid- to late Antonine

F.85 Dr. 33, EG, from the Argonne or Rheinzabern. Late 2nd or early 3rd century

F.89 Dr. 18/31, slightly burnt, CG. Hadrianic

F.90 i) Dr. 18, SG. Neronian-Flavian
ii) Dr. 30 or 37, 31 (two), 33, 36, 37 (see F.6, ii), 46 and several scraps, CG. All apparently Antonine and some clearly after AD 160

F.94 i) A jar, EG (Rheinzabern). Late 2nd or early 3rd century.
ii) Dr. 37, EG. The ovolo (Ricken and Fischer 1963, E17) and vertical rows of squarish beads (*ibid*, 0256?) are on a stamped bowl of Iulius viii from Rheinzabern (Ricken 1948, Taf. 212, 16). Probably early 3rd century

F.95 Dr. 37, EG. Rheinzabern ware, with a freestyle scene, including a lion (Ricken and Fischer 1963, T8 variant?), boar (*ibid*, T74) and bear (*ibid*, T57?). Not assignable to a particular potter, but probably late 2nd century.

F.100 i) –, CG. Hadrianic or Antonine
ii) Jar, EG (Rheinzabern). Late 2nd or early 3rd century

F.101 i) See F.14
ii) Dr. 30, 33, 37, a fragment of a (gritted?) samian mortarium and – (two), CG, Antonine
iii) Dr. 31, Curle 21 (Rheinzabern) and –, EG. Late 2nd or early 3rd century

F.102 Dish, EG (Rheinzabern). Late 2nd or early 3rd century

F.105 i) Dr. 37, SG. The pale fabric and purple-brown glaze suggest Montans ware. The basal wreath probably consists of rosettes, as on a 2nd-century bowl from Richborough. Trajanic or Hadrianic
ii) Dr. 31 (two), Curle 21 and a jar, CG. Antonine
iii) Dr. 38 (?), CG. Mid- to late Antonine

F.108 i) Dr. 31, 38, Curle 15, a dish and –, CG. Antonine
ii) Dr. 45, CG, *c*. AD 170–200
iii) Dr. 30 or 37 and 45, EG. Late 2nd or early 3rd century

F.110 Dr. 37, CG. The decoration includes a naked warrior with shield, apparently not otherwise recorded, and a coarse wavy line above. Hadrianic-Antonine

L2 i) Dr. 30 rim, SG. Neronian or early-Flavian
ii) Dr. 29 (two), SG, *c*. AD 70–85
iii) Dr. 35, in orange, micaceous fabric, with moderately glossy orange glaze. First-century Lezoux ware, probably Flavian
iv) Dish, in pale buff fabric, with purple-brown glaze. Probably 1st-century Montans ware
v) Dr. 37, SG. The trident-tongued ovolo is on a stamped bowl of Sulpicius from Wilderspool. The decoration includes a panel with a satyr (O. 597) in a thick chevron arcade with a central boss. Cf. Jacobs 1913, no. 8 for the same figure in a different arcade, but with the same batons attached, *c*. AD 80–110
vi) Dr. 30 or 37, SG. Flavian or Flavian-Trajanic. See F.50
vii) Dr. 18/31R, 37, Curle 15 and a 'black samian' jar, with non-metallic coat, CG. Hadrianic or early Antonine
viii) Dr. 30 or 37 (six rims, two burnt), 31 (at least 10), 33 (at least six), 37 (two, one burnt), 38, 44, 72 *etc*, a jar with black coat and appliqué leaves and – (five), CG. Antonine
ix) Dr. 30 or 37, 31R, 37 (two, in the styles of Servus iv (see F.6) and the Paternus v group), 79 (two) and 79 or Ludowici Tg, CG. Mid- to late Antonine
x) A gritted samian mortarium, CG, *c*. AD 170–200
xi) Dr. 37, EG. The ovolo (Ricken-Fischer, E17) and pan-mask (*ibid*, M9) in a chevron arcade (*ibid*, KB126) are all on bowls from Rheinzabern in the style of Florentinus (Ricken 1948, Taf. 113, 16; 114, 9). Late 2nd century
xii) Dr. 31, 33 (Argonne), 37 (five?), 43 (at least two), 45 (at least four, one from Trier, two or more from Rheinzabern and one perhaps from the Argonne), Ludowici Ti', a jar and several scraps, EG. Late 2nd or 3rd century, mostly Rheinzabern ware. Also two colour-coated sherds

L2/L3 Two joining sherds of Ludowici form Ti' variant, larger and shallower than usual. The fabric strongly suggests an origin at Rheinzabern. Late 2nd or early 3rd century.

L3 i) Dr. 27, SG, drilled for riveting. Probably pre-Flavian
ii) Dr. 30, SG. First century
iii) Dr. 18/31R and 33a, CG. Hadrianic
iv) Dr. 31 (five), 33 (four), 37?, Curle 21, Curle 23 and a dish or bowl, CG. Antonine
v) Many CG scraps. Second century
vi) Dr. 37, EG. A double medallion contains a kneeling stag (O. 1705B), as used at Lavoye (Ricken 1934, Taf. XII, 49). Second half of the 2nd century
vii) Dr. 43 (with collar decorated *en barbotine* wine birds and tendrils) and 45 (with grit extending up to the inside of the collar), both from Rheinzabern. Late 2nd or early 3rd century
viii) A jar with 'cut-glass' decoration, probably Trier ware. Late 2nd or 3rd century
ix) A dish and a dish or bowl rim, shaped as a disc with a hole in the middle, EG. Late 2nd or 3rd century

L3 area beneath F.1
i) Dr. 37 or, more probably, 29, SG. The yellowish-cream fabric and purple-brown glaze suggest 1st-century Montans ware. Probably pre-Flavian
ii) Dr. 37, CG. A panel with wavy-line border contains a beaded ring (Rogers C290) and probably has a beaded rosette at the bottom of the border. The next panel contains a satyr with double flute (D. 311 = O. 610). Not assignable to a particular potter, though the maker was clearly a member of the Quintilianus i group, *c*. AD 125–150
iii) Dr. 30 or 37, 31, 33, 37, 38 or 44, a 'black samian' jar and several scraps, CG. Antonine
iv) Dr. 30 or 37 and 32, both from Rheinzabern, and a jar in Trier fabric, EG. Late 2nd or 3rd century

L3 associated with F.20/21
i) Dr. 30 or 37 (burnt), 31 and 38, CG. Antonine
ii) –, CG. Hadrianic or Antonine

L3 F.47 i) Dr. 37, SG. Flavian or Flavian-Trajanic

ii) Dr. 30 or 37 rim, SG. The yellow-cream fabric and brown glaze suggests Montans ware. Probably Trajanic or Hadrianic
iii) A jar and – (two), CG. Hadrianic or Antonine
iv) A jar with 'cut-glass' decoration, CG, *c*. AD 150–200
v) A gritted samian mortarium, very worn inside, CG, *c*. AD 170–200
vi) – (three), EG (Rheinzabern). Late 2nd or early 3rd century
vii) Dr. 36, heavily burnt. Undatable

L3 inside Building 2, cut by kilns
i) –, SG. First century
ii) –, CG. Hadrianic or Antonine
iii) –, burnt. CG. Antonine
iv) Dr. 37, EG. Late 2nd or 3rd century

L4 i) –, SG. Flavian or Flavian-Trajanic
ii) – (three), CG. Hadrianic or Antonine
iii) Dr. 30 or 37 (burnt), 31, 33 and 38, CG. Antonine
iv) Dr. 45, with lion's-head spout (Rheinzabern or Argonne) and – (three, two Rheinzabern, one Argonne), EG. Late 2nd or early 3rd century

L4 east of F.8
Dr. 37, CG. Hadrianic or early Antonine

L4 beneath F.47
i) – (three), CG. Hadrianic or Antonine
ii) Dr. 30 or 37 and a dish or bowl, CG. Antonine
iii) Dr. 79 *etc*, EG. Probably late 2nd century. Also a colour-coated sherd

F.116 i) Dr. Ludowici Ti' variant, EG (Rheinzabern). Late 2nd or early 3rd century
ii) –, EG (Argonne). Second half of the 2nd century

F.123 Dr. 29, SG. The pale fabric and brown glaze suggest an origin at Montans. Both surviving panels in the lower zone have rows of leaf-tips, one with an animal among them. Probably mid-1st century

T2 i) Dr. 37, SG. Flavian-Trajanic
ii) Dr. 30 or 37 (with internal groove below the lip), 37 and –, SG. Probably Montans ware, but not closely dateable
iii) Dr. 18/31 or 31 and 36, CG. Hadrianic or early Antonine
iv) Dr. 31, CG. Early Antonine
v) Dr. 31 (five), 36 and four jars, one with 'cut-glass' decoration, CG. Antonine
vi) Dr. 31 (two), 31R and 79, CG. Mid- to late Antonine
vii) Dr. 45 and a gritted samian mortarium, CG, *c*. AD 170–200
viii) Many CG scraps, mainly Antonine
ix) EG ware of late 2nd- and early 3rd-century date, with forms 31R, 33, 37 (at least four, one heavily burnt), 43 (with barbotine vegetation on the collar), 45, burnt (Trier), Ludowici Tb, two jars, one with moulded gadroons, the other with 'cut-glass' decoration, two gritted samian mortaria (from the Argonne and Rheinzabern) and several scraps.

L4 (small-find 380) A cup (Dr. 33?), stamped] DΛ[. Almost certainly a stamp of Daccius ii of Lavoye, to judge by the orange fabric and glaze. The potter worked in the early to mid-Antonine period, stamping forms such as 18/31 and 80

The Bonded Store

SUMMARY

The catalogue below consists of a maximum of 489 vessels, including unidentified forms. The dominance of central Gaulish products from Lezoux is obvious (Table 10). Vessels represented by more than one sherd are shown as, for example, Dr. 37 (1/2), *i.e.* two sherds from one vessel.

Catalogue

AREA A

A1003 i) –, CG. Hadrianic or Antonine
ii) Walters 79 or Ludowici Tg, CG, with stamp of Cobnertianus. *c*. AD 160–90

A1004 i) Dr. 15/17, SG. Neronian or early Flavian
ii) Dr. 36 (?) (rim), SG. Flavian or Flavian-Trajanic
iii) Curle 15 (rim) and a dish or bowl, CG. Hadrianic or Antonine
iv) Dr. 18/31 (rim) and Curle 11 (rim), CG. Hadrianic or early Antonine
v) Dr. 31 (base and footring), Curle 23 (rim) and 'black samian' jar, CG. Antonine
vi) Dish (?), EG (Rheinzabern). Late 2nd or first half of 3rd century

A1005 Curle 23, SG (Montans). Trajanic-Hadrianic

Table 10 The Bonded Store: summary of samian vessel sources.

Samian source	*No. sherds*
La Graufesenque	29
Montans	36
Banassac	4?
Lezoux	369
Lezoux or EG	1
Argonne	16?
Argonne or Rheinzabern	4
Heiligenberg?	1?
La Madeleine	4?
Rheinzabern	22
Trier	2?
East Gaulish unspecified	1?

Based on a maximum of 489 pots, including unidentified forms.

A1010 i) Curle 23 (rim), CG. Mid to late Antonine
ii) Ludowici Tb variant (with fluted rim), EG (Rheinzabern). Late 2nd or first half of 3rd century

A1204 i) Dr. 18 (?) and 18/31 (base and footring), SG. Flavian or Flavian-Trajanic
ii) Dr. 27 (footring), CG. Hadrianic or early Antonine
iii) Dr. 36? (base and footring), Curle 15 or 23 (base and footring) and – (four), CG. Hadrianic or Antonine
iv) Dr. 37 (two) and Curle 15 or 23, CG. Antonine
v) Walters 79 (rim), burnt, CG. Mid- to late Antonine
vi) Dr. 31 (rim) and 33 (base and footring), EG (Argonne). *c.* AD 150–200
vii) Dr. 37 (two), EG (Rheinzabern). Late 2nd or first half of 3rd century

A2003 i) Dr. 18 (?), SG (Montans?). First century
ii) Dr. 30 or 37 (rim), SG. Flavian or Flavian-Trajanic
iii) Dr. 18/31 or 31 (rim), 37, dish or bowl (slightly burnt), an enclosed vessel, a rim, a footring and – (six), CG. Hadrianic or Antonine
iv) Dr. 27 (?) and Curle 11 (flange), CG. Hadrianic or early Antonine
v) Dr. 31 (two, one rim, one footring), 33 (two, one rim, the other burnt) and a jar, CG. Antonine
vi) Dr. 33, 30 or 37 and Walters 80, CG. Mid- to late Antonine
vii) Dr. 45 collar (small), CG. *c.* AD 170–200
viii) (associated with A2007) Dr. 18/31R (base and footring), slightly burnt, CG. Hadrianic or early Antonine
ix) Walters 80 (complete profile), CG. Mid- to late Antonine

A2004 –, CG. Hadrianic or Antonine

A2007 i) Dr. 46 (rim), CG. Hadrianic or early Antonine
ii) Dr. 30 or 37 (?), CG. Hadrianic or Antonine
iii) Dr. 31 (rim), Curle 15? (rim) and dish or bowl, CG. Antonine
iv) Dr. 31 (two, rims), EG (Rheinzabern). Late 2nd or first half of 3rd century
v) Ludowici RSMa or RSMb (collar), EG (Rheinzabern). First half of 3rd century
vi) Dr. 37, CG. Hadrianic or Antonine

A2015 Dr. 30 or 37 and cup or bowl, CG. Hadrianic or Antonine

A2016 Dr. 33 (rim), EG (Argonne or Rheinzabern). Antonine or first half of 3rd century

AREA B

B U/S i) Dr. 33, CG. Antonine
ii) Dr. 37, CG, style of Rogers's P-16. Early Antonine

B1003 Cup, CG. Hadrianic or early Antonine

B1204 i) –, CG. Hadrianic or Antonine
ii) Dr. 33 (two), CG. Antonine
iii) Curle 21, CG. *c.* AD 150–200
iv) Dr. 31R, CG. Mid- to late Antonine

B2003 i) Walters 79/80 (1/4, one rim, one footring), CG. Mid- or late Antonine
ii) Dr. 31 (footring), CG. Mid- to late Antonine
iii) (under chalk) Dr. 30 or 37 (1?/2, one rim), CG. Mid- to late Antonine

B2026 i) Dish or bowl (two), CG. Hadrianic or Antonine
ii) Dr. 27 (1/2, one rim), CG. Early Antonine
iii) Dr. 37, CG. Late Antonine

B2032 Dr. 27g, SG. Neronian or early Flavian

B2044 i) Dr. 31 (rim) and 33 (rim), CG. Antonine
ii) Dr. 31 (rim), with remains of a rivet, EG (Rheinzabern). Late 2nd or first half of 3rd century

B2045 i) Dr. 36, CG. Hadrianic or Antonine
ii) Dr. 31 (rim), EG (Rheinzabern). Late 2nd or first half of 3rd century

B2048 i) Curle 11 (flange), CG. Hadrianic
ii) Dr. 46 (rim), dish or bowl and – (footring), CG. Hadrianic or Antonine

B2049 Dr. 31 (base and footring), CG. Antonine

B2051 Dr. 38 or 44 (footring), heavily burnt, CG. Antonine

B2054 i) – (two), CG. Hadrianic or Antonine
ii) Dr. 37, CG. Antonine

B2061 i) Dish (footring), CG. Antonine
ii) Dr. 32 *etc.* (base and footring), EG (Rheinzabern). Late 2nd or first half of 3rd century

B3003 i) Dr. 31 (rim) and 33, CG. Antonine
ii) Dr. 15/31 (rim) and 31 (with graffito X on outside, after firing), CG. Mid-Antonine

B3004 i) Dr. 18/31 or 31 (rim) and 30 (rim, joining sherd in B3005), CG. Hadrianic or Antonine
ii) Dr. 31 (rim), 33 and dish or bowl, CG. Antonine
iii) Gritted samian mortarium, CG. *c.* AD 170–200. Grits lightly worn
iv) – (1?/2), EG (Argonne or Rheinzabern). Antonine or first half of 3rd century

B3005 i) Ritterling 8 (rim), SG (Montans). Claudian or early Neronian
ii) Dr. 30 or 37 rim, CG. Hadrianic or Antonine. Joins a sherd in B3004
iii) Dr. 37, CG. Hadrianic or early Antonine
iv) Dr. 36 (?) and 37 (probably shaped as a counter), CG. Mid-Antonine
v) Dr. 37, CG. Mid- to late Antonine

AREA C

C1003 i) Dish, SG (Montans). Claudio-Neronian
ii) Ritterling 8 (footring), SG. Neronian
iii) Dr. 30 or 37 (two, one rim) and dish or bowl, CG. Hadrianic or Antonine

iv) Dr. 30 or 37 rim, Curle 11 (rim) and Curle 15 (rim), CG. Hadrianic or early Antonine
v) Enclosed vessel, with barbotine decoration, and dish, CG. Antonine
vi) Dr. 45 and a gritted samian mortarium, CG. *c*. AD 170–200
vii) Dr. 33 (two, one rim), EG (Argonne). *c*. AD 150–200
viii) Dr. 37, EG (Rheinzabern). Late 2nd or first half of 3rd century

C1003a i) –, burnt, CG. First century
ii) Dr. 36 flange, CG. Trajanic
Iii) –, CG. Trajanic or Hadrianic
iv) Dr. 33 (1/2) and –, CG. Hadrianic or Antonine

C1004 i) Dr. 35, CG. Hadrianic or Antonine
ii) Dr. 18/31R (rim), CG. Hadrianic or early Antonine
iii) Dr. 33 (rim), CG. Antonine

C1005 i) Dr. 15/17, SG (Montans). Pre-Flavian
ii) Dr. 37, SG. *c*. AD 85–110
iii) – (two), CG. Hadrianic or Antonine
iv) Curle 11 (flange), CG. Hadrianic
v) Dr. 18/31 or 31 and 18/31R (rim), CG. Hadrianic or early Antonine
vi) Dr. 31 (rim) and 33 (rim), CG. Antonine
vii) Curle 23 (rim), SG (Montans). Hadrianic or early Antonine

C1006 i) Dr. 15/17 (rim), burnt, SG. Pre-Flavian
ii) Dr. 15/17 or 18, SG. Neronian or early Flavian

C1065 Dr. 31, CG. Antonine

C1068 i) – (two), SG (Montans). Claudian or Neronian
ii) Dr. 18/31R and 37, CG. Hadrianic or early Antonine
iii) Curle 15 or 23, CG. Antonine

C1070 i) Dish or bowl, CG. Hadrianic or Antonine
ii) Dr. 18/31R and Curle 15 or 23, CG. Hadrianic or early Antonine
iii) Dr. 33 (two, rims), CG. Antonine
iv) Dr. 45 (collar), CG. *c*. AD 170–200

C1071 i) Dr. 31R, burnt, CG. Mid- to late Antonine
ii) –, EG (Argonne). *c*. AD 150–200

C1077 Walters 79 or Tg, CG. Mid- or late Antonine

C1079 Dr. 15/17 (rim), SG. Neronian

C1080 Curle 11 (flange), SG (Montans). Early Flavian

C2002 Dr. 33 (1/2, joining), CG. Late Hadrianic or early Antonine

C2003 i) Dr. 29 (?), CG. Neronian
ii) Dr. 36 (flange), CG. Trajanic
iii) Dr. 33, 35 or 36 (flange) and – (two), CG. Hadrianic or Antonine
iv) Dr. 18/31 and 30 or 37 (rim), CG. Hadrianic or early Antonine
v) Dr. 35, without barbotine leaves on the flange, CG. Antonine
vi) Curle 21 (1/2, one rim), CG. *c*. AD 150–200
vii) Dr. 33 (rim), CG. Mid- to late Antonine
viii) Dr. 45 (collar), CG. *c*. AD 170–200
ix) Dr. 33 (rim), EG (Argonne). *c*. AD 150–200
x) Dr. 31R (rim, burnt), Curle 21 and a dish, EG (Rheinzabern). Late 2nd or first half of 3rd century

C2004 i) Dr. 33 (three, one rim) and 35 or 36 (flange), CG. Hadrianic or Antonine (Fig. 65.4)
ii) Dr. 18/31 and 18/31R, CG. Hadrianic or early Antonine
iii) Dr. 46 (1/2, one rim), CG. Antonine
iv) Dr. 31R, CG. Mid- to late Antonine
v) Dr. 37, EG (Lavoye). *c*. AD 150–200
vi) Dr. 36, CG, burnt on flange. Flavian or Flavian-Trajanic
vii) Dr. 37, EG (Lavoye). All internal glaze removed and three indentations made, probably by stirring. Second half of 2nd century

C2005 i) Dr. 27 (rim), SG (Montans). Claudio-Neronian. From same vessel as C2097
ii) Dr. 36 flange, SG. Neronian or early Flavian
iii) Dr. 15/17, SG. Pre-Flavian
iv) Dr. 33 (rim), EG (La Madeleine). Hadrianic-Antonine

C2006 Dr. 27g (footring), SG. Claudio-Neronian

C2080 –, CG. Probably pre-Flavian

C2090 i) Small bowl (footring), SG (Montans), joining a sherd in C2093. Late 1st or early 2nd century
ii) Dish (footring), CG. Hadrianic or Antonine
iii) Flagon neck (burnt), CG. Second century

C2093 i) Small bowl, SG (Montans), joining a sherd in C2090. Late 1st or early 2nd century
ii) Dr. 18/31 or 31 (rim), CG. Hadrianic or early Antonine

C2094 i) Dr. 15/17 (rim), burnt, and 15/17? (rim), SG (Montans). Claudio-Neronian
ii) Dr. 30, SG (Montans). First century
iii) –, SG. Pre-Flavian
iv) Dr. 37, SG (Montans). First half of 2nd century
v) Dr. 37 and flat dish, CG. Hadrianic or early Antonine
vi) Dr. 30 and – (five, one footring), CG. Hadrianic or Antonine
vii) Dr. 37, CG, style of the Cerialis ii–Cinnamus ii group. *c*. AD 135–65
viii) Dr. 30 or 37 (rim), 31, 33 (rim) and 33 (burnt), CG. Antonine
ix) Dr. 31 (rim), CG. Mid-Antonine
x) Curle 21, CG. *c*. AD 150–200
xi) Dr. 31, 31R (three, one rim) and Walters 79/80 (heavily burnt), CG. Mid- to late Antonine
xii) Curle 21 (rim), EG (Argonne). *c*. AD 150–200. Mid- to late Antonine
xiii) Cup or bowl, burnt. Undatable

xiv) Dr. 31R (full profile), CG. Mid- to late Antonine. Footring heavily worn
xv) Dr. 33 (full profile), CG, with stamp of Agileito (Fig. 65.2). Hadrianic-Antonine

C2097 i) Dr. 27 (rim), SG (Montans), Claudio-Neronian. From same vessel as a sherd in C2005
ii) Dr. 37, SG (Montans). Flavian or Flavian-Trajanic (Fig. 65.1)
iii) Dr. 18/31 or 31 (footring), CG. Hadrianic or early Antonine

C3003 Dr. 18/31R (rim) and 33, CG. Hadrianic or early Antonine

C3012 i) Dr. 31 (rim), slightly burnt, SG (Montans). Early Antonine
ii) Dr. 38, CG. Antonine

C3013 i) Dr. 18/31 or 31, CG. Hadrianic or Antonine
ii) Dr. 33 (rim), 38 or 44 and a jar (Déchelette 66?), CG. Antonine

C3014 Dr. 33 (?), CG. Hadrianic or Antonine

C3017 i) –, SG (Montans). Claudio-Neronian
ii) Dr. 36 flange, SG (Montans). First half of 2nd century
iii) Dr. 36 and – (four), CG. Hadrianic or Antonine
iv) Dr. 30 or 37 (rim), 33 (two, one rim) and 38 (flange), CG. Antonine
v) Dr. 32 (rim), EG (probably Heiligenberg). Antonine
vi) Footring, EG (Argonne). *c.* AD 150–200
vii) Dr. 37, CG. Mid- or late Antonine. Shaped as a counter (Fig. 65.3)

C3018 Dr. 33 (rim), CG. Mid- to late Antonine

C3021 Dr. 30 or 37 (rim), CG. Antonine

C3022 i) –, SG (Montans). First century
ii) Dr. 18 (rim), SG. Flavian
iii) Dr. 33 (1/2, joining rims), CG. Hadrianic or early Antonine
iv) Dr. 36 or 38 or 44, EG (La Madeleine). Hadrianic-Antonine. Internal glaze ground away
v) Curle 21, CG. *c.* AD 150–200
vi) Dr. 30 or 37, EG (probably Argonne). *c.* AD 150–200

C3023 i) Jar, CG. Hadrianic or Antonine
ii) Dr. 33 (three, rims), CG. Antonine

C3024 i) Dr. 35 (with or without a pedestal), SG (Montans). First century
ii) Dr. 18/31 or 31, CG. Hadrianic or early Antonine
iii) Dr. 33 (1/2, joining), CG. Antonine

C3026 i) Dr. 15/17 (?), SG (Montans). First century
ii) –, CG. Hadrianic or Antonine
iii) Dr. 38 or 44 (rim) and 38 or 44 (base and footring, with all internal glaze gone), CG. Antonine

C3030 Dr. 33 (base and footring), SG (Montans). Trajanic to early Antonine

C3033 i) Dr. 36 (flange) and –, CG. Hadrianic or Antonine
ii) Cup, CG. Hadrianic or early Antonine

C3034 i) Dish, SG. Flavian or Flavian-Trajanic
ii) –, CG. Hadrianic or Antonine

C3036 i) –, SG. First century
ii) Dr. 30R, CG. Late 1st or early 2nd century. Burnt

C4001 U/S Dish, CG. Hadrianic or Antonine

C4003 i) Dr. 18/31 or 31 (rim) and –, CG. Hadrianic or Antonine
ii) Dr. 31, 37 and dish or bowl, CG. Antonine
iii) Curle 21 (?), CG. Mid- or late Antonine. Some internal glaze removed by stirring
iv) Dr. 45 (collar), CG. *c.* AD 170–200

C4014 i) Dish or bowl, CG. Hadrianic or early Antonine
ii) Dish or bowl and cup, CG. Hadrianic or Antonine
iii) Dr. 38 or 44 (rim) and enclosed vessel, CG. Antonine
iv) Dr. 37, CG. Mid- to late Antonine. All internal glaze removed and two indentations made, probably by stirring

C4015 i) Dr. 31 (rim), CG. Antonine
ii) Curle 21? (footring), CG. *c.* AD 150–200
iii) Dr. 31 (base and footring), EG (Argonne). *c.* AD 150–200. Heavily abraded inside and out

C4022 Dr. 31 (rim), CG. Mid-Antonine

C4035 Dr. 37, SG (Banassac). Trajanic-Hadrianic

C4038 Dr. 30 (rim), 35 (rim, without barbotine) and 35 or 36 (rim), CG. Hadrianic or Antonine

C4102 i) Dish, CG. Late 1st or early 2nd century
ii) –, CG. Hadrianic or Antonine
iii) Dr. 27 rim, CG. Hadrianic or early Antonine
iv) Dr. 31 (footring), CG. Antonine

C4103 Dr. 33 (rim), CG. Hadrianic or early Antonine

C4114 Dr. 37, burnt, EG. Late 2nd century?

C5001 Dr. 31 or 31R, CG. Mid- to late Antonine

AREA D

D U/S Bowl, burnt, CG. Antonine. Glaze ground off inside

D1 U/S i) –, CG. Hadrianic or Antonine
ii) Dr. 30 or 37 (footring) and 46? (base and footring), Antonine

D1002 i) Dr. 27 (rim), CG. Hadrianic or early Antonine
ii) Dr. 37, CG. Hadrianic or early Antonine?
iii) Dr. 33 (rim), CG. Antonine
iv) Dr. 31, CG. Mid- or late Antonine

D1002/1004
Dr. 46 (?), CG. Antonine. Heavily burnt, unstamped or stamp eroded away

D1004 i) Dr. 37 and –, CG. Hadrianic or Antonine
ii) Curle 15 or 23, CG. Antonine
iii) Dr. 31 (1/2, one rim), CG. Mid-Antonine
iv) Curle 21, CG. *c.* AD 150–200
v) Flat dish, EG (Rheinzabern). Mid-Antonine

D1007 i) Dr. 29 (?), SG (Montans). Claudio-Neronian. Joining A2009
ii) Rim, CG. Hadrianic or Antonine

D2002 i) Flange and –, SG (Montans). Pre-Flavian
ii) –, CG. Hadrianic or Antonine

D2005 i) Dr. 18/31 or 31 (rim), 30, 30 or 37 (base and footring), 33 (2, one base and footring), Curle 15 (rim) and – (five), CG. Hadrianic or Antonine
ii) Jar, CG. Antonine
iii) Dr. 45 collar, CG. *c.* AD 170–200
iv) Dr. 37, EG (Argonne), with glaze ground away inside. Second half of 2nd century
v) Dr. 31 (1/4, one rim), EG (Rheinzabern). Late 2nd or first half of 3rd century
vi) Dr. 37, CG, style of Attianus ii. *c.* AD 125–145
vii) Dr. 31, CG (Lezoux), with stamp of Magio i. *c.* AD 160–90
viii) Dr. 37, EG, style of Maiiaaus of Trier. Late 2nd or first half of 3rd century

D2006 Dr. 30 or 37, CG. Hadrianic or Antonine

D2008 Cup (?), CG. Hadrianic or Antonine

D2009 i) Dr. 29 (?), SG (Montans). Claudio-Neronian. Joining A2007
ii) –, SG (Montans). First century
iii) – (1/3), SG. First century
iv) Dr. 35/36 (flange), SG (Montans). First half of 2nd century?
v) Dr. 37, SG (Montans?). First half of 2nd century
vi) Dr. 27 rim, burnt, CG. Hadrianic or early Antonine
vii) Dr. 37, SG (Montans). Flavian or Flavian-Trajanic

D2010 i) Dr. 15/17 or 18, SG. Flavian or Flavian-Trajanic
ii) Dish, CG (Lezoux). Flavian
iii) Curle 21, EG (Argonne or Rheinzabern). All glaze ground or eroded away. *c.* AD 150–250

D3001 i) Dr. 18/31 or 31 rim, CG. Hadrianic or early Antonine
ii) Dish or bowl, CG. Antonine
iii) Dr. 31, EG (Argonne). All glaze ground or eroded away. *c.* AD 150–200

D3003 i) Dr. 37, SG. Flavian or Flavian-Trajanic
ii) Dr. 30 or 37, CG. Hadrianic or Antonine
iii) Dr. 38 rim, heavily burnt, CG. Late Hadrianic or early Antonine
iv) Curle 21, EG (Rheinzabern). Late 2nd or first half of 3rd century
v) Dr. 37, CG. Flavian or Flavian-Trajanic
vi) Dr. 37, EG (Rheinzabern). Late 2nd or first half of 3rd century

D3004 i) –, SG. First century
ii) Cup, CG. Hadrianic or Antonine
iii) Dr. 38 (flange) and a bulbous beaker, CG. Antonine
iv) Dr. 18/31R (rim) and 33 (rim), CG. Hadrianic or early Antonine
v) Dr. 31 (rim), CG. Mid- to late Antonine
vi) Dr. 31R, CG. All internal glaze ground or eroded away. Mid- to late Antonine
vii) Dr. 45 (collar) and gritted samian mortarium (base and footring, all internal glaze ground away), CG. *c.* AD 170–200
viii) Dr. 31R, EG (Rheinzabern). Late 2nd or first half of 3rd century
ix) Dr. 37, SG (Montans). Trajanic to early Antonine

D3005 i) Dr. 42 (rim, with part of a strap-handle), CG. Hadrianic or early Antonine
ii) Dr. 33 (rim), CG. Hadrianic or Antonine

D3007 Dr. 18/31–31 (1/2 joining, one rim), CG. Early Antonine

D3008 Dr. 37, SG (Montans). Trajanic to early Antonine

D3010 Dr. 31R rim, CG. Mid- to late Antonine

D4001 i) Dr. 18/31R (rim) and 42 (rim, with strap-handle), CG. Hadrianic or early Antonine
ii) Dr. 30 or 37 (rim), CG. Antonine
iii) Dr. 18/31–31 (1/2, one base and footring), EG (Argonne). Early Antonine
iv) Footring, EG (Argonne). *c.* AD 150–200
v) Dr. 37, CG, in the style of Doeccus. *c.* AD 165–200

D4002 i) Dr. 30 (rim), CG. Neronian-Flavian
ii) –, SG (Montans). First half of 2nd century
iii) Dr. 18/31 or 31 (rim) and Curle 15 (rim), CG. Hadrianic or early Antonine
iv) Dr. 18/31 or 31 (rim), Déchelette 64 (?) and –, CG. Hadrianic or Antonine
v) Dr. 30 or 37 (rim), 46 and a jar, CG. Antonine
vi) Dr. 15/31, 31R and Curle 21, CG. Mid- to late Antonine
vii) Dr 31 (1/2, joining), EG (Argonne or Rheinzabern). Antonine or first half of 3rd century
viii) Dr. 37, EG (Rheinzabern). Late 2nd or first half of 3rd century. Worn inside

D4003 i) Dr. 27, SG (Montans). First half of 2nd century
ii) Dr. 33 and 37, CG. Hadrianic or early Antonine
iii) –, CG. Hadrianic or Antonine
iv) Cup, CG. Antonine

D4005 Jar, CG. Flavian or Flavian-Trajanic

D4007 –, CG. Hadrianic or Antonine

Samian from other sites in Guernsey and Herm

by Brenda Dickinson

Cross-references are supplied to the Gazetteer in this volume. Excavation finds post-2001 are not included here. Abbreviations as for reports above; GMAG indicates an accessioned item at Guernsey Museum.

La Varde, Vale (Gazetteer A1)

GMAG 3386b Dr. 36 (flange), CG. Hadrianic or Antonine (Burns and Burns 1985, fig. 3.13)

GMAG 3386c Dr. 35/36, CG. Hadrianic or Antonine (Burns and Burns 1985, fig. 3.14)
GMAG 3386d Dr. 37, CG. Hadrianic or Antonine (Burns and Burns 1985, fig. 3.15, wrongly labelled as Herm)
GMAG 3386e Dr. 30, CG. Flavian (Burns and Burns 1985, fig. 3.16, wrongly labelled as St Sampson's Harbour)
GMAG 3386f Dr. 37, CG. Antonine
GMAG 3386g Dr. 33 (rim), CG. Hadrianic to mid Antonine (Burns and Burns 1985, fig. 3.12)
GMAG 3386h Dish or bowl, EG (La Madeleine?). Hadrianic-Antonine
Dr. 15/31 (rim), 33, dish and dish or bowl, CG. Antonine
GMAG 3386i Dr. 37 (rim), CG. Hadrianic or Antonine
GMAG 3386j Dr. 18/31 or 31, CG. Hadrianic or Antonine
Dr. 27 (?), CG. Hadrianic or early Antonine?
Curle 21 (?), CG. *c.* AD 150–200
GMAG 3386k – (1/2), CG. Antonine. Decorated with a barbotine animal
GMAG 3386l –, SG. First century
Cup (?), SG (Banassac?). Trajanic to early Antonine
–, (three), CG. Hadrianic or Antonine
Dr. 31R and dish or bowl, CG. Mid- to late Antonine
Dr. 18/31R, burnt, CG or EG. Second century
–, EG (Argonne or Rheinzabern). Late 2nd or first half of 3rd century
GMAG 3386l? Curle 15 or 23, SG. Flavian or Flavian-Trajanic
Dish, burnt, SG (Banassac?). Trajanic to early Antonine
– (two), CG. Hadrianic or Antonine
Dr. 33, CG. Antonine

NB: the GMAG collection includes several more unclassified scraps of samian from La Varde.

Le Creux ès Faïes, St Peter's (Gazetteer A3)
GMAG 3052 Dr. 30 or 37 (rim), CG. Hadrianic or Antonine. Shaped as a pierced disc, heavily cross–hatched on the back, after shaping

Le Tranquesous, St Saviour (Gazetteer A10)
TRS 76 Dr. 30 or 37 rim, SG. Neronian or early Flavian

The Pollet, St Peter Port (Gazetteer A12)
PO 80 T2 L5 Dr. 37, SG (Montans). First half of 2nd century
Dish or bowl, CG. Hadrianic or Antonine
Dr. 31, EG (Rheinzabern). Late 2nd or first half of 3rd century
PO 80 T3 L5 Dr. 37, CG. Hadrianic or Antonine
Dr. 44, CG. Antonine

Grandes Rocques, Castel (Gazetteer A16)
GR86 S/L1 14 Cup, very heavily burnt. Probably CG and 2nd century, if samian at all

Royal Hotel, St Peter Port (Gazetteer A23)
RHS 99 Curle 15 rim, CG. Hadrianic or early Antonine
RHS 01 T4 L3 Cup, SG (Montans). First century
–, CG. Hadrianic or early Antonine
Dr. 31 (base and footring), CG. Antonine
RHS 01 T4 L4 Enclosed vessel (?), SG. Flavian or Flavian-Trajanic
RHS 01 T4 F80 Dr. 30 or 37 (rim), CG. Hadrianic or early Antonine

Route de Carteret, Castel (Gazetteer A24)
RDC 00 B113 Cup or dish (1/2), CG. Hadrianic or Antonine
RDC 01 B119 Cup (footring), CG. Hadrianic or early Antonine

Herm (Gazetteer B9)
GMAG 3387 Dr. 33 (1/3 rims, two joining), CG. Mid- to late Antonine
Dr. 33 (rim), EG (Rheinzabern?). Late 2nd or first half of 3rd century
Footring, EG (Argonne?). *c.* AD 150–200
–, EG, late 2nd or first half of 3rd century
GMAG 3388a Dr. 37, EG (Rheinzabern). Mid- to late Antonine
GMAG 3388b/c Dr. 31, CG. Mid- to late Antonine

La Salerie, St Peter Port (Gazetteer B20)
Dr. 18/31 (base and footring), SG (Montans). First half of 2nd century (Burns and Burns 1985, fig. 3.10)
Dr. 30 or 37 (rim), EG (La Madeleine). Hadrianic-Antonine (Burns and Burns 1985, fig. 3.11)
Dr. 30 or 37 (rim), CG. Antonine (Burns and Burns 1985, fig. 3.9)

Cow Bay, St Peter Port, 1983 (Gazetteer B21)
GMAG 1984.125
Dr. 31, Curle 15 or 23 (two) and Curle 23 (rim), CG. Antonine
Dr. 37 (rim), SG (Montans). Hadrianic-Antonine (Burns and Burns 1985, fig. 3.1)
Curle 23, CG. Antonine (Burns and Burns 1985, fig. 3.3)
Curle 21, EG (Rheinzabern). Late 2nd or first half of 3rd century
Dr. 31R, CG. Mid- to late Antonine
Curle 23 (base and footring), CG. Mid- to late Antonine (Burns and Burns 1985, fig. 3.8)

Dr. 18/31 (rim), CG. Hadrianic or early Antonine
Dr. 38 or 44 (base and footring), CG. Antonine

Cow Bay, St Peter Port, 1985 (Gazetteer B21)

- Hemispherical bowl, CG, but not necessarily Lezoux ware. Unstamped, but with ring incised in base, and with fluting under the base. Second century

CB974 Dr. 31R (rim), CG. Mid- to late Antonine

CB975 Flat dish (base and footring), CG. Early Antonine. Perhaps an early variant of Walters 79 or Ludowici Tg

Cow Bay, St Peter Port, 1997 (Gazetteer B21)

CB973 Dr. 37 (rim), SG (Banassac?), with blurred decoration. Trajanic to early Antonine

- Dr. 33, CG, with stamp of Macrinus iii of Lezoux. *c*. AD 150–80

- Dr. 38 (?) flange, EG (Trier?). Late 2nd or first half of 3rd century?

Cow Bay, St Peter Port, 2001 (Gazetteer B21)

- Curle 15 (rim), CG. Hadrianic or early Antonine

Dredged off harbour (St Sampson's?), 1860 (Gazetteer B35)

GMAG 3386a Dr. 35 (flange), CG. Hadrianic or Antonine. The barbotine leaves on the flange seem to have been made from a lighter clay than the cup itself. Note: this vessel is definitely samian ware; it was previously published as a probable late Romano-British product of the Oxfordshire kilns (Burns 1986, 659, no. 17)

St Peter Port harbour (Gazetteer C7)

1655 Curle 21, CG. *c*. AD 150–200

2544 Dr. 31 (footring), CG. Antonine

G4803 Déchelette 72 (base and foot ring, slightly burnt), CG. *c*. AD 150–200

unmarked Dr. 31 (footring), CG. Antonine
Dr. 37, CG, style of Albucius ii. *c*. AD 150–180

St Peter Port harbour, sea bed (Gazetteer C7)

G5749–49a Curle 23, CG. Mid- to late Antonine. Unstamped, but small boss in the centre of the base, surrounded by fluting.

CATALOGUE OF DRAWN SAMIAN (FIG. 65)

Bonded Store

1. Dr. 37, SG (Montans), context C2097
2. Dr. 33, CG, with stamp of Agileito, context C2094
3. Dr. 37, CG, sherd showing cherub (?) converted to counter, context C3017
4. Dr. 33, CG, base sherd with stamp SEXTIMA, context C2004

Other sites

5. Dr. 33, base with stamp DIVICA, St Peter Port harbour (Gazetteer C7).

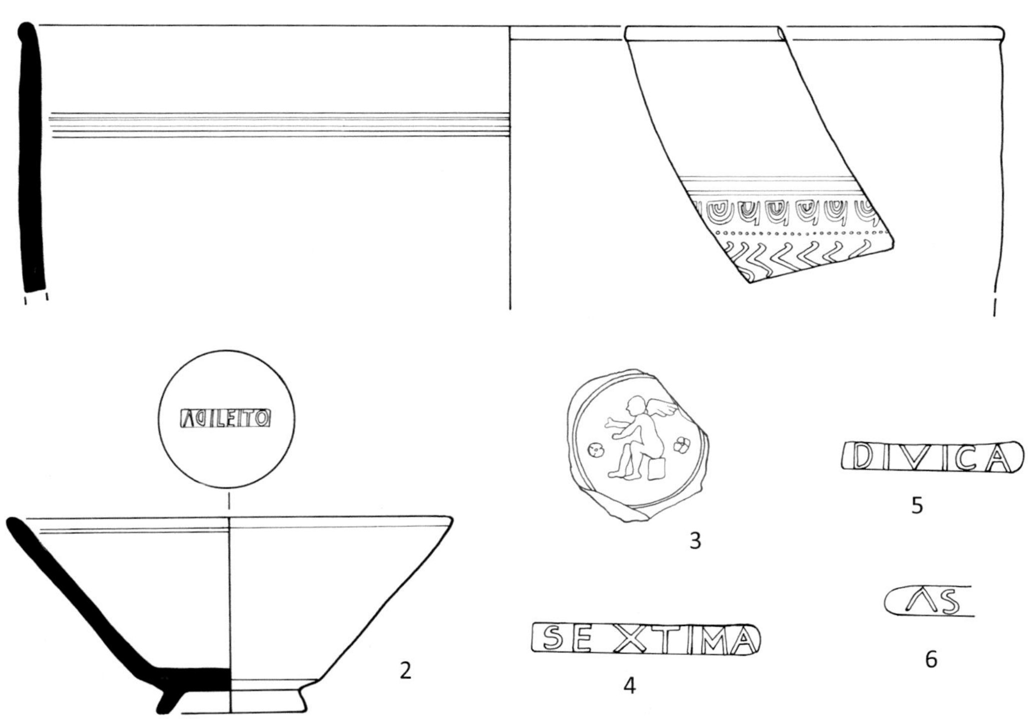

Figure 65 Samian from the Bonded Store and other sites. Scale 1:2 (nos 1–3), 1:1 (nos 4–6).

6. CG, stamp of ASIATICUS, St Peter Port harbour (Gazetteer C7)

Roman pottery from other sites in Guernsey and Herm

by Jason Monaghan

The pottery was viewed by hand on a 'spot dating' basis, which did not involve fabric analysis beyond recognition of broad traded types. The unstratified or residual nature of most of the sherds made more sophisticated analysis redundant for this exercise. Some had previously been examined by Mark Wood and commented on in his work. The material from La Varde, plus some other harbour material, was published by Burns and Burns (1985) and some maritime finds by Monaghan (1988 and 1990).

Most of the harbour or maritime ceramic finds showed some degree of abrasion and many had marine growths upon them. It cannot be ascertained whether the harbour finds came from shipwrecks, were discarded overboard from ships, come from disturbed land sites or were simply dumped in the sea. They represent a random sample of the pottery in use in Guernsey between the 1st and 4th centuries AD. The predominant fabrics are a variety of greywares, probably from northern Gaul. Fittingly for a harbour, there are a significant number of amphora sherds. Harbour finds have tended to include more complete vessels than the land sites. Underwater finds other than the pierheads wreck ('Asterix') have chiefly comprised amphorae, with major concentrations at Little Russel 'site A' (Gazetteer C4) and 'site B' (Gazetteer C2).

Much of the material from terrestrial sites was small and abraded, indicating high residuality (Table 11). Away from the harbour there were far fewer amphorae, and mortarium sherds were very rare. At 9% of terrestrial and littoral finds, samian is by far the most important fineware, although it may have been more easily spotted during the fieldwalk and beachwalk activities. A significant number of sherds in iron-free fabrics appeared to come from flagons, and there were instances of white-slipped oxidised flagons as well. Fabrics are, however, very mixed, showing a diversity of sources beyond the island. Small near-black sherds could not easily be distinguished between true black-burnished ware, its Iron Age predecessor and possibly similar Gaulish pottery.

Cow Bay (Gazetteer B21) yielded a fair cross-section of Guernsey's Roman ceramics, including the noticeable north Gaulish greyware with its light core and sometimes burnished bands. It also yielded examples of the other northern Gaulish grey fabrics which seem to have been a staple of the island. A large piece of terra nigra, and a second found loose in the harbour nearby, represents the early pottery trade.

Both the Savoy (Gazetteer A26) and Royal Hotel (Gazetteer A23) sites yielded similar selections of small sherds of Roman pots, suggesting these may not themselves have been important Roman sites, yet were in the vicinity of such sites which had been extensively disturbed and possibly completely destroyed.

At 209 sherds plus 290 possibly Roman scraps, the Royal Hotel yielded the largest assemblage away from the well-stratified Roman sites. With a high percentage of oxidised sherds, vessels which are apparently flagons, and a high count of 'white' sherds (if they are not post-Roman), there is a suggestion of a highly disturbed cremation cemetery. The presence of micaceous wares and the general absence of BB1 and the Tripod Bowl fabric indicates an early date span, probably 1st to 2nd century. The small amount of tile and the absence of amphorae support this idea. Mortaria are also absent, but are pretty rare in Guernsey overall. Quite a lot of the sherds are rounded, indicating that they have been in the sea or at least on the beach. A large number of very small oxidised scraps were difficult to identify with any certainty, so are excluded from the summary table. Samian is suitably well represented at 10% of sherds, although rather more than this would be expected if it was a classic cemetery with three or four funerary vessels per burial.

Due to the small size and residual nature of most of the sherds at the Royal Hotel, it is possible that a number identified as Roman white ware could be a late/post-medieval white ware such as Beauvais. Likewise small oxidised sherds are often difficult to identify when residual in later contexts. Some of the thinner oxidised sherds are possibly abraded samian.

Graffiti

by R. S. O. Tomlin

Two sherds (nos 1–2, below) found in the same context (C2094) at the Bonded Store bear inscriptions, and there is an inscription on a mortarium from Trench 1, F.69 at La Plaiderie (no. 3). These are likely to represent the earliest personal names recorded from Guernsey.

1. Wall sherd of a flagon in dark fabric with pink oxidised surface, scratched above the shoulder after firing:

   [...]V͡ΛT

Probably *Vat(...)*, an abbreviated personal name.
Although broken to the left, the graffito is probably complete, with V ligatured to 'open' A. The reading [.] MT is just possible, with incomplete M; this would be the name of a Roman citizen reduced to its three initials, but it seems most unlikely. For other examples of the abbreviation VAT, see *RIB* II.7, 2501.573 (London) and II.8, 2503.598 (Old Winteringham). Possible names are all

Table 11 Summary of pottery from small terrestrial sites.

Site	*A*	*M*	*W*	*O*	*G*	*F*	*B*	*N*	*S*	*C*	*X*	*T*	*Q*	*n*
La Varde (A1)	1			1	2				23				1	
Le Déhus (A2)				1										
Le Creux ès Faïes (A3)									2				1	
Lihou (A4)	2											1		a
Castel Church (A6)				2					1			732		b
Cobo (A9)	1											1	2	
Le Tranquesous (A10)	11		20	161	4	2	2	21	1		67		4	c
The Pollet (A12)									5					
King's Road (A13)	19				3		1	3	1		9			
Grandes Rocques (A16)				1					1					
Albecq (A17)					1	1								
Lefebvre Street (A18)	1		1	4	2	1		1	2	2				
Sunrise Cottage (A20)												1		
Fort Grey (A21)								1				2	1097	d
Fisherman's B'h (A22)	1		4	4	4	4	15	2		1	1	3	523	e
Herm (A22?)	1			3	3	1	1		3				10	f
Royal Hotel (A23)			24	90	50	14	2	1	20	6	2	7	15	g
Route de Carteret (A24)				1					3					
Les Canichers (A25)			4	1	7	1			1			1		
Savoy Hotel (A26)	1		8	13	26	8	1		6	3	2			h
St Peter P. School (A27)				2					2			2		
Jethou (A28)							1							
West of airport (A30)	2			11	1	3		2				4		i
Les Vardes quarry (A31)					1			1					3	
St Martin's Ch.(A32)									1					
St Tugual's Ch. (A33)								1						
Le Tertre (A34)				1										
Le Maresquet (A35)												1		
Rue des Prevosts (B10)											1			j
Les Arquets (B11)				1		1								
R. des Saumarez (B12)				2										
La Terre Norgiot (B13)			1	10	1	1	1				3			k
Jerbourg (B14)				1										
Les Prevosts (B15)				1										
Les Paysans (B16)				1										
Fort Le Marchant (B18)			2	1	4	1	3							
Cow B. (B21)/SPPH (C7)	74	7	4	34	85	12	15	14	26	7	12	33	1	l
Jethou (B22)					1									
Bailiff's Cross (B24)			1	7	2							18		m
Herm (B25)							1							
Le Neuf Chemin (B26)					2									
L'Ancresse (B27)	1													
L'Ancresse (B28)	1													

Table 11 Summary of pottery from small terrestrial sites. (Continued)

Site	*A*	*M*	*W*	*O*	*G*	*F*	*B*	*N*	*S*	*C*	*X*	*T*	*Q*	*n*
L'Erée (B30)					1									
Perelle Bay (B31)		1												
Le Crocq (B32)				1										
La Villiaze (B33)				1										
													total (pot)	
terrestrial totals	116	8	69	356	200	50	43	47	98	19	97		1103	
%	10.5	0.7	6.3	32.3	18.1	4.5	3.9	4.3	8.9	1.7	8.8		100	

The table includes only sherds which have been available for examination, and not (for example) those sites with antiquarian records of Roman sherds which cannot now be verified.

Key:

A: amphora; M: mortaria; W: 'white/cream' fabrics; O: oxidised; G: grey coarse; F: fine grey; B: black-burnished, BB1, BB2 and imitations; N: north Gaulish greyware; S: samian; C: colour-coated ware; X: other recognisable; T: tile; Q: briquetage; n: note.

Notes:

a) possibly a few more pieces of tile.

b) totals to 2012 inclusive; additional material has been recovered more recently.

c) all X type pottery is terra nigra.

d) combines Cunliffe excavations of 1999 with antiquarian and recent finds.

e) combines Cunliffe excavations of 1999 with antiquarian and recent finds. X is terra nigra.

f) antiquarian finds probably from the Fisherman's Beach site.

g) X is two mica-dusted sherds; also 290 scraps not identified.

h) X is one shell-tempered greyware sherd, one imitation samian sherd. Also 15 unidentified scraps.

i) also six unidentified scraps.

j) X is terra nigra.

k) X is terra nigra.

l) Combines beach finds from Cow Bay (B21) and harbour finds principally made by diving in the 1980s/90s (C7). Some of the latter (in particular the amphorae sherds) may come from the Little Russel A wreck (Gazetter C4). X includes four *céramique à l'éponge* (probably from A15), two terra nigra, two Argonne, and four MDER.

m) oxidised sherds and tile not all convincingly identified.

rare; in Britain they include *Vatta* (*RIB* 610) and *Vatiaucus* (*RIB* II.3, 2432.4).

2. Wall sherd in pink fabric, scratched after firing:

[...]I VI[...]

The third letter is a downstroke broken at the top, which is therefore incomplete; possibilities such as II = E, M or N, cannot be excluded. Its closeness to V suggests that V was preceded by a space, which would imply that the first I is the end of another name in the genitive case. Since the scratches all seem to be by the same hand, it is possible that the owner had two names, for example [IVL]I VI[IRI], or even that his name was followed by a numeral VI[...], but the latter would be unlikely. But since so little survives, the question remains open.

3. Mortarium, exterior, scratched after firing (Fig. 62.97):

DIV I.S

DIV is likely to be the abbreviated name of the owner, and the likeliest is the Celtic name DIVIXTVS. Any other name in Diu- is very rare indeed. I.S is less certain, but ought to be the numeral '1' followed by s(emis), for 'half', i.e. recording 'one and a half' units. There is no obvious correlation to the size or volume of the vessel, however, and thus the interpretation remains somewhat uncertain.

5

Other finds

Roman brick and tile

by Jason Monaghan

The Bonded Store

Almost 80kg of Roman brick and tile was recovered from the site (Table 12). Much was clearly residual, mixed with some medieval tile and a fair amount of post-medieval (Victorian) brick. The tile was considerably fragmented, with the weight per piece being only 45g compared to 131g at Castel Church (see below). There were 985 fragments with an average weight of 12 grams each that could not be identified as a particular form, and indeed could include some abraded pottery, brick or briquetage. Very few match breaks were observed, suggesting considerable disturbance and redeposition. Flat bricks were indistinguishable from pieces of floor tile so both are combined.

FABRICS

No fabric analysis was performed during the main research, although Phil Mills kindly commented on a number of fabric samples; no sources could be identified and his report is in the archive. The tile was predominantly in a range of terracotta fabrics, but 36 were identified in a variety of off-white iron-free fabrics (Table 13). The most striking feature is the abundance of a strange 'light' fabric making up a quarter of the sherd count and a fifth of the weight. Mills suggested that this was more akin to mudbrick than properly fired ceramic. This lightweight material occurred in both imbrices and tegulae, and was spread across many contexts. Its average sherd weight was 34g compared to 49g for the regular fabrics. The 'mudbrick' tile was virtually inclusion-free and varied in colour from off-white through light grey, light yellow and light terracotta shades. In the hand it feels almost the weight of wood. It is soft, shatters and erodes easily, so the abundance of this tile suggests it came from

Table 12 The Bonded Store: summary of brick and tile.

	No.	*g.*	*% no.*	*% wt*	*wt g/sherd*
flat	10	1767	1.3	2.6	176
imbrex	254	16,767	32.6	24.8	66
tegula	514	49,082	66.1	72.6	95
fragments	985	12,083	excluded	excluded	12
Total	1763	79,699	100	100	45

Table 13 The Bonded Store: summary of tile fabric types.

	No.	*g.*	*wt g/sherd*
'terracotta'			
flat	10	1767	176
imbrex	156	11,956	77
tegula	320	39,112	122
fragments	780	9788	13
subtotal	1266	62,623	49
'iron free'			
imbrex	18	1165	65
tegula	5	255	51
fragments	13	211	16
subtotal	36	1631	45
'light'			
imbrex	80	3646	45
tegula	189	9715	51
fragments	192	2084	11
subtotal	461	15,445	34
Overall total	1763	79,699	45

a building in very close proximity. Its ratio of imbrex to tegula weight is 38%, suggesting that a whole building was tiled in this material. A *tegula* found at the Canichers, St Peter Port, in 2001 was in a similar but not identical light fabric, as were a few pieces from La Plaiderie.

FORM

The ratio of tegulae to imbrices on an intact building is close to 1:1, with perhaps 5–10% more tegulae than imbrices unless imbrices were also used as ridge tiles, which would make the expected numbers even. However, an imbrex will break into fewer pieces than a larger tegula and will be only approximately 40% its weight. The weight of imbrices found at the Bonded Store was 34% of the weight of tegulae, close to the proposed ideal of 40%, indicating that a properly roofed building was in the vicinity.

Of the tegulae, 32 corners were noted in both light and terracotta fabrics (Table 14). There was a marked preference for Warry Type B6 corners for the terracotta tiles (Warry 2006, 44), whereas the light fabric favoured Type C5, although neither was exclusive. One of the light C5 corners could indeed have been modified from a B6. Warry puts C5 as a later type than B6, although they clearly co-existed. Three 'signatures' were observed on tegulae. One tegula had a faint impression which could be a stamp.

None of the tegulae had nail holes, as was also the case at the Castel Church. Warry (2006, 103) noted the frequency of nail holes on tegulae from civilian sites he surveyed (one tile in four) compared with a general absence of nail holes from legionary sites of the 1st and 2nd centuries. The substantial amount of tile found at the assumed late Roman fort at the Nunnery between 2008 and 2012 has likewise yielded no nail-holes. No tile-stamps have been definitely recognised on any Guernsey or Alderney site to date, despite the clear military activity in Alderney.

OTHER TILE AND BUILDING MATERIALS

There were few clearly identifiable flat bricks/floor tiles (pedales/bipedales), no indication of hypocaust pilae, and only suggestions that two fragments may be from box tiles. One fragment may have come from an antefix but could equally be a pottery handle. Other ceramic building material included 33 pieces of daub and one piece of *opus signinum*, totalling 1.7kg.

Table 14 The Bonded Store: summary of tegula corner types.

	left upper	*right upper*	*left lower*	*right lower*	*lower cut–out types (Warry 2006)*
terracotta	2	6	5	8	B6×9; C5×2; D1×1
iron free	–	–	1	–	C5×1
light	1	3	2	4	B6×2; C5×4

A large amount of Victorian and some medieval brick was found, making it difficult to distinguish the pieces of true Roman brick amongst the residual.

WATER-ROLLED OR BURNED TILE

Several contexts featured tile and/or pot which had been rolled in water, including A1203, A2204, C1002, C1004, C1066, C2004, C2092, D2002, D2005, D2009 and D3002. This indicates that this was residual material coming up from the beach – mostly in the post-Roman period. Seven tiles showed signs of burning, but in no significant concentration.

FRAGMENTATION

The fragmentation differs sharply between areas (Table 15). The light 'mudbrick' fabric is distributed across the site, but there is little in Area D, where it all occurs in post-Roman layers. It shows a similar fragmentation to the other fabrics across the areas. In Area B it is mainly in post-Roman contexts except B1204 and B1205, which are at least 3rd century. In Area A, it is all in post-Roman contexts (although A2007 is re-deposited Roman). In Area C, much is again residual, but there is a concentration in Period 2 (C2004) and in the higher Roman contexts in Trench 3 (Table 16). This suggests a late date for the destruction of this building, if not its construction.

Table 15 The Bonded Store: summary of tile fragmentation by area.

	Area A	*Area B*	*Area C*	*Area D*
all fabrics	166	151	1091	346
total weight/g	9963	12,904	50,408	7178
wt g/sherd	60	85	46	21
% all sherds	9.5	8.6	62	20
% weight	12	16	63	9
'light' fabric	69	40	332	18
'light' weight/g	2163	1942	10,837	432
'light' wt g/sherd	31	49	33	24
'light' as % of all weight	22	15	21	6

Table 16 The Bonded Store: summary of tile distribution by phase.

	Phase 1	*Phase 2*	*Phase 3*	*Residual*
all Areas				
sherds	153	1020	135	478
weight/g	6024	42,584	4467	31,363
weight g/sherd	39	42	33	66
Area C only				
sherds	29	765	111	198
weight/g	2267	35,845	3776	12,145
weight g/sherd	78	47	34	61

All the tile is residual in Area A except A1204. In Area C there is none in the lower levels of Trench 1, but a little in the Roman layers above. Area C Trench 3 contained the best stratified tile on the site, down to the hoggin layer C3035 and C3039. The large average sherd size amongst the residual pottery indicates the upper layers were disturbed on a limited number of occasions rather than extensively re-worked.

Castel Church (CCH 99, CCH05 and CCH12)

Some 58kg of Roman tile was derived from a number of shallow trenches excavated beneath the nave of Castel Church in 1999. Additional material was collected in January 2005 from lighting pits and cable trenches dug outside the church around the north of the nave. No material came from pits dug on the south side in 2005. In 2012 a pipe trench was mechanically dug from outside the church, running downhill to the north. Another haul of Roman tiles and *opus signinum* fragments was extracted from the spoil which lay parallel to the trench. No obvious stratigraphy could be seen in the walls of the trench.

It is likely that all this material is residual in medieval or post-medieval levels, although some of the 1999 contexts did not contain any confirmed post-Roman finds. One striking observation is that very little Roman pottery was found, despite the overall quantity of tile being similar to that found at the Bonded Store. Pottery sherds are smaller and more mobile than large pieces of tile and would be expected to be more easily disturbed and moved 'upwards' in the stratigraphic sequence by later activity. It suggests disturbance of destruction deposits rather than of deep Roman stratigraphy. In turn it holds out hope there is a relatively undisturbed site beneath the churchyard.

It is unlikely that the material found beneath the nave in 1999 was an *in situ* Roman deposit, given the loose nature of the ground from which the bulk of the tile came. It is more likely to have been material disturbed via robbing, foundation digging, or pit digging in the post-Roman period.

Some of the tiles are in large pieces, yet there are very few match breaks either within or between contexts. This in itself suggests considerable disturbance from their original deposit, but not the kind of repeat disturbance which would smash up the tiles into small pieces. The fact that many tiles still have quite fragile mortar adhering supports this.

The material recovered from the graveyard in 2005 supports the picture of Roman debris spreading down the hill to the north. Given many centuries of grave-digging, however, this material could have been disturbed from a considerable depth or moved some distance horizontally. Again, no Roman pottery was found.

In 2012, the pipe trench went deeper than the 2005 trench and resulted in another 20kg of tile being brought up, plus 107 *opus signinum* fragments totalling 3.4kg. Some of this was quite broken up by what is presumably repeated disturbance by grave-digging. Some pieces of tile and *opus signinum* were still attached to mortar, suggesting they have not travelled far. The finds tailed-off further down the hill where it is known that the graveyard was 'made up' by several feet in early modern times to accommodate a new tier of burials. This is confirmed by the greater quantity of post-medieval material found to the north (downhill) of the cemetery path. Four Roman pot sherds were found in spoil from this trench.

THE ROMAN BUILDING(S)

The tile is of a fairly homogenous nature, including tegulae and imbrices from the roof and pedales/bipedales from the floor or walls. This homogeneity indicates that the source material was a single building or closely related group of buildings constructed at a similar date. A small amount of daub was recovered, plus grey-white mortar and a pinker mortar which may rank as *opus signinum.* Most of the *opus signinum* came from the 2012 trench. One piece of granite found in 2012 had mortar adhering, with a thin sliver of tile, suggesting that was from a 'bonding' course. Some of the 2012 imbrices have *opus signinum* on top of their curved surfaces, and one has a layer of *opus signinum* below the grey mortar. Some pieces are shaped to suggest tile was once in contact. This opens up questions as to what exact structure this material came from. One, possibly two, pieces of box tile were found. Four tegulae and two imbrices showed signs of burning or overheating, but this is not sufficient to draw any conclusions.

Fragments of plaster were recovered and many tiles had thick mortar on the outer surface. None of this showed any indication of painting or decoration.

The repeat findings of tile on the site, and the quantity of tile found, points to a substantial building once standing on the platform where the church now stands, or very close nearby. It is possible that the building was levelled out, the rubble being quarried for materials, explaining why mainly larger pieces of tile are found in this location, having been robbed out, then subsequently dumped again. There is no evidence to suggest that the site was a kiln site or tile warehouse.

A statue-menhir which stands on the site has been described by Professor Colin Renfrew as possibly the oldest sculpture in the British Isles. Taken with the later choice of the site for a church, this strongly suggests that the Roman building may have been a temple. However, the elevated position and the excellent views to the north also offer the site as being a good position for a small fort or signal station such as is found at the Nunnery, in Alderney (Monaghan 2011–12). Indeed, there is a similarity in the material found on both sites, namely a good deal of residual Roman tile in later layers but not much Roman pottery. John McCormack has also pointed out (pers. comm.) that it is

Table 17 Castel Church: summary of tile.

	No.	*Weight/g*	*% no.*	*% weight*	*Weight g/ sherd*
1999					
flat	79	30,374	18	52	384
imbrex	113	8099	25	14	72
tegula	189	18,970	42	32	100
other	64	1026	14	2	16
Total	445	58,469	99	100	131
2005					
flat	4	2787	13	47	–
imbrex	4	368	13	6	–
tegula	23	2789	74	47	–
other	0	–	–	–	–
Total	31	5944	100	100	–
2012					
flat	80	6559	34	32	82
imbrex	29	3111	12	15	107
tegula	120	9953	52	49	83
other	4	421	1	2	105
scraps	23	834	excluded	excluded	–
Total	256	20,986	99	99	–

the only Guernsey churchyard that was originally square, possibly echoing an original Roman plan. Perhaps the ruin of this Roman building – *castrum* or *castellum*? – lies behind the legendary 'Castel' which gives the church and the parish its name.

QUANTITATIVE ANALYSIS

Some 445 pieces of tile were recovered in 1999, a further 31 in 2005, and 256 in 2012, plus 2kg of small fragments of indeterminate date which were discarded (Table 17). Floor tiles and 'flat bricks' could not be wholly distinguished and a number of smaller fragments classed as tegula could instead have been from floor tiles or bricks.

IMBRICES

In the 1999 dig, the weight of imbrices was *c*.43% the weight of the tegulae. This indicates that a properly roofed building was in the vicinity and there has been no 'sorting' in ancient times to separate tegulae from imbrices. The ratio is 31% in the 2012 trench.

TEGULAE

The tegulae are of standard type, and as at the Bonded Store, none has a nailhole. Five tegulae found in 1999 exhibited 'signatures', plus three more from the 2005 finds. Of the 20 recovered lower corners, 14 had cut-outs of Warry Type B6 and four incomplete pieces could also be Type B. The single type D16 had a flange with an irregular profile, such that a tile maker aiming at a B6 could easily have ended up with a D16 by accident. Warry dates Type B primarily to the 2nd century.

FLAT BRICKS

An interesting proportion of the tiles are flat bricks, smaller ones of 'pedales' size and thick pieces which are assumed to be bipedales. No examples were found of these stacked, as if functioning as hypocaust pilae. Some 42 pieces (half the collection) had mortar or plaster on one or both sides. It is likely therefore that these have been used as bonding courses in a wall. The more intact flat bricks are mostly pedales, roughly 33mm thick and 290mm square (i.e. slightly smaller than a Roman foot). The most complete example came from 1999 (context 022), with a whole edge and two corners preserved. This indicates that an intact tile would weigh approximately 6kg.

Three of the flat bricks were up to 65mm thick and all examples were delaminating. These are probably huge bipedales. The 2012 trench produced fragments of a similar delaminating fabric which included many plate-like shards of fired clay within its fabric. Some of this material was sintered.

FABRICS

The fabric of the majority of the tiles is unremarkable, being various shades of terracotta, with moderate sandy inclusions. The flat bricks are particularly homogenous. A small number of tiles were in aberrant fabrics with higher shell or mica content and some were made in low-iron clay, resulting in pale pink or off-white colouration.

La Plaiderie

Building materials from La Plaiderie were retained selectively on-site, and it is not known to what extent or on what basis they were 'weeded', so a complete record cannot be compiled. Therefore the tile has not been fully quantified for this report, but a review of the boxes of tiles and items on display was undertaken. Some 22 boxes of tile from La Plaiderie remained, of which 20 were exclusively Roman. This compares with 12 boxes from the Bonded Store. Just over 2000 sherds were noted on the record sheets and context T1 F.44 alone yielded 1253 pieces. The original quantity recovered was undoubtedly more than at the Bonded Store.

The material included a small proportion of tiles in the 'light' fabric seen at the Bonded Store. Most tiles fabrics were variations on terracotta, with a coarse sandy fabric being particularly noticeable. The remaining tile examined included:

6 tegulae with 'signatures'
4 tegulae with paw-prints: three dog, one sheep/goat
7 upper right corners of tegulae
14 upper left corners of tegulae
17 lower right corners of tegulae
19 lower left corners of tegulae
2 uncertain lower corners of tegulae
1 nail hole in small sherd of unusual light pink fabric

Tegula cut-out types amounted to 21 of type C5, six of type B6 and ten which were incomplete on the outer edge so could be either C5 or B6. There is clear similarity with both the Bonded Store and Castel Church in the choice of cut-out design and the absence of nail-holes; the only nail-hole in fact coming from a tile of an unusual fabric. As Type C appears to be a later 2nd- and 3rd-century product, a preponderance of Type C at the Plaiderie suggests a later date.

Romano-Celtic Ship PPPH1

The Roman ship from St Peter Port harbour sank *c.*AD 280 (Gazetteer A15). A total of 235 pieces of tile weighing 93.9kg were recovered from the area of the rear hold and the immediate seabed, amounting to:

171 pieces of tegulae, including several with match-breaks
52 pieces of imbrices, with only one match-break
8 box-flue tiles, with one match-break
5 flat brick/floor tiles

Of the 23 tegula lower corners, those available to study amounted to ten of Warry form C5, two were indeterminate B6 or C5, and four were B6 (i.e. both corners of the two reconstructed tiles illustrated in Rule and Monaghan 1993). Two fragments bore dog paw-prints and 13 tegula bottom edges had 'signatures', which were all different. A variety of fabrics was found on the Roman ship, which was clearly not 'local' in terms of its origin. The tile appeared to be part of the ship's structure, rather than cargo.

Briquetage

by Jason Monaghan

The Bonded Store

Briquetage is the name given to low-fired ceramics used in the boiling of salt, generally found in a highly fragmented state. The briquetage was partly sorted by Mark Wood, from fragments found in pottery bags, then partly by Jason Monaghan from pieces extracted from the building materials bags.

FORM AND FABRIC

The briquetage is found in various shades of red/brown through to orange/buff. It is handmade, friable and coarsely tempered with beach sand. A typical range of objects was found including both cylindrical and semi-rectangular boiling vessels, pads, props and shapeless squeezes. Some pieces of hearth or furnace have also become mixed with the briquetage, from which it is barely distinguishable. Likewise some smaller sherds classified as PRE (prehistoric) by Wood are also indistinguishable from those he classed as BQ (briquetage), and have been accounted for here.

DISTRIBUTION ON THE SITE

The briquetage is much less widely spread than the tile, with a greater concentration in Area C (Table 18) (although 61% by count, 62% by weight of tile was also in C). The impression is that salting activity took place on the site from the Iron Age through Phases 1 and 2. However, given the high level of residuality shown on this site it

Table 18 The Bonded Store: summary of briquetage quantity and weight by area and phase.

	Phase							
Area	*Pre-*	*Iron Age*	*1*	*2*	*3*	*Post-Roman*	*Total*	*% by area*
Quantity								
A	–	0	0	0	–	1	1	0.1
B	–	300	34	84	–	33	451	15.7
C	–	113	946	871	147	46	2123	74.1
D	5	18	243	13	0	11	290	10.1
Total	5	431	1223	968	147	91	2865	100
Weight/g								
A	–	0	0	0	–	8	8	<0.1
B	–	1900	221	350	–	236	2707	13
C	–	898	6852	7179	909	336	16,174	77.5
D	30	225	1546	69	0	107	1977	9.5
Total	30	3023	8619	7598	909	687	20,866	100

is useful to compare briquetage finds versus the Iron Age pottery distribution (Table 19). The briquetage is shown, if anything, to have an earlier bias than the IA/LIA pottery and certainly mirrors its residuality in Phases 2 and 3. Salting was therefore most likely an activity of the late Iron Age/Phase 1.

Table 19 The Bonded Store: summary of briquetage and prehistoric pottery sherd count.

			Phase				
	Pre-	*Iron Age*	*1*	*2*	*3*	*Post-Roman*	*Total*
sherd count							
briquetage	5	431	1223	968	147	91	2865
IA pottery	0	26	59	88	10	81	264
% of total							
briquetage	<1	15	43	34	5	3	100
IA pottery	0	10	22	33	14	31	100

A whole group of contexts contain briquetage but no tile, particularly in the stratigraphy from C4118 (Iron Age) to C4043 (Phase 1). There is a match link between C4048 in Phase 1 and C3036/C3034 in Phase 2, suggesting a similar history towards the bottom of the C Trench 3 and Trench 4 contexts. Context C1082, the furnace, also yielded many pieces of briquetage, suggesting that the 'furnace' may have been a salt-boiling area (or that furnace debris is indistinguishable from briquetage in this area). Contexts C3032, C3033, C3034 and C3035 from Roman Phase 2 and C3039 from Phase 1 contain interesting pieces of briquetage including props and parts of straight-sided boiling vessels (Fig. 66).

Catalogue of illustrated briquetage (Fig. 66)

1. Salting vessel, part of base and side (context C3039)
2. Salting vessel, similar form to no. 1 (context C3034)
3. Prop of hand-squeezed clay (context C3039)
4. Prop of hand-squeezed clay (context C3034)
5. Prop of hand-squeezed clay (context C3034)
6. Hand-brick (context C3034)

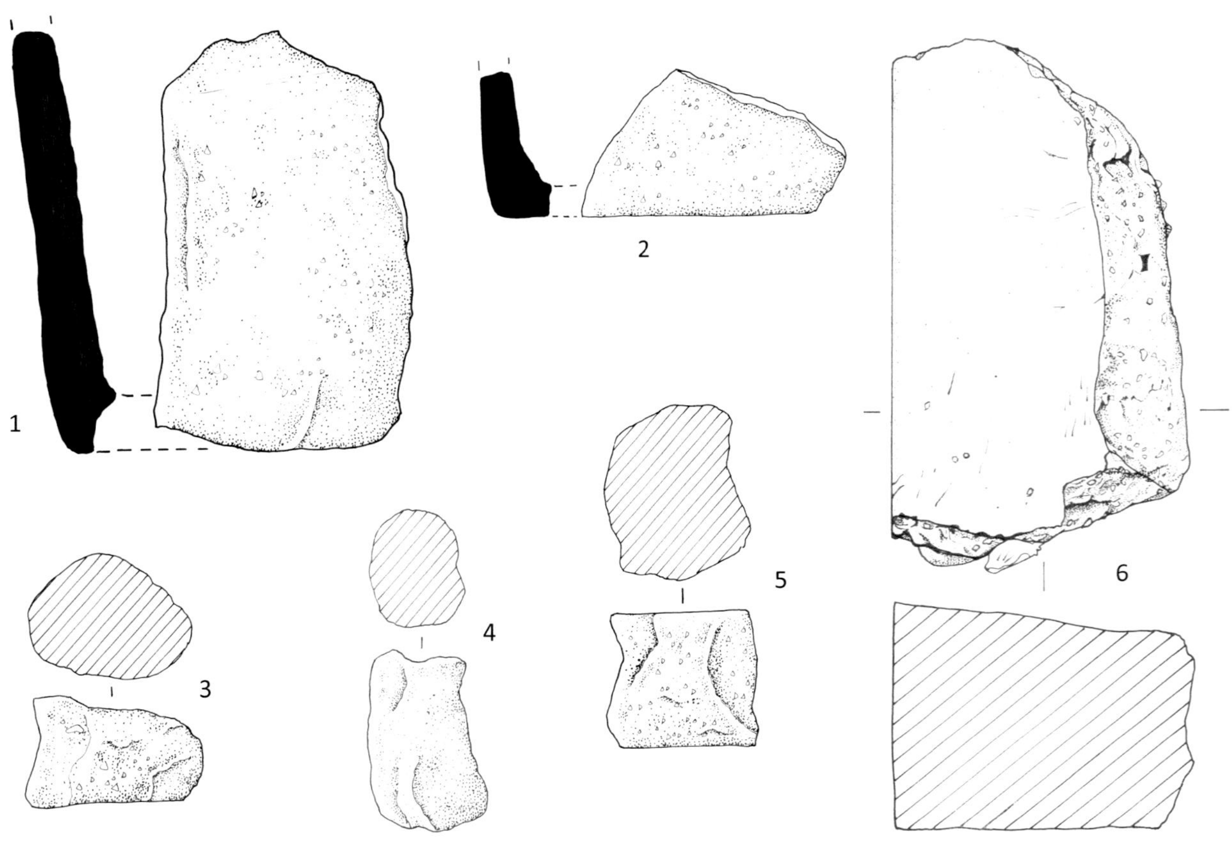

Figure 66 Briquetage from the Bonded Store. Scale 1:2.

Roman coins and coin moulds from La Plaiderie

by Cathy King and George Boon

The Roman coins were identified by Dr Cathy King of the Ashmolean Museum. Comments on the coin moulds were made by the late George Boon in 1984 and 1993. All coins are bronze unless otherwise noted.

Coins

Listed by small-find number:

10. Illegible, sestertius, probably late 2nd/early 3rd century AD (T1/F.20)
21. Silver denarius, Salonina, SALONINA AVG/IVN, AD 253–68 (T1/L2)
22. As or dupondius, early 2nd century AD, perhaps Trajan (T1/F.15)
27. Fragment of probable Roman coin; this coin was later stolen (T1/L2)
71. Illegible, possibly 4th century AD (T1/F.48)
83. Sestertius, Antoninus Pius, rev. Victory inscribing shield, mint of Rome, AD 161–80 (T1/L2)
92. Illegible, probably Roman (T1/L2)
112. Sestertius, Marcus Aurelius, AD 161–80 (T1/F.65)
125. Victorinus, rev. standing female figure, AD 268–70 (T1/F.47)
264. Sestertius, Marcus Aurelius, AD 163–64, *RIC* 861 (T2/F.121)

Coin moulds

Listed by small-find number:

17. One coin mould fragment, 'antoninianus of Gordian III AD 238–44 (obverse) and Philip I AD 244–49 (reverse), with the legend ANNON' (Boon, pers. comm.) (T1/L2)
18. One coin mould fragment, 'obverse of a denarius of Severus Alexander (AD 222–35), and the reverse is almost certainly from another coin of his which can be dated to AD 225' (Boon, pers. comm.) (T1/L2)
386. Four coin mould fragments, including 'part of an obverse impression of a denarius' (Boon, pers. comm.) (T2/F.126)
386a. Five coin mould fragments, including 'two of larger diameter than a denarius, so either an antoninianus or even a small as' (Boon, pers. comm.) (T2/F.126/7)
387. Sixteen coin mould fragments, including 'four... double-sided for denarii; one of these shows part of a seated figure to l. but not enough to make identification possible' (Boon, pers. comm.) (T2/F.127)

Metal small-finds from La Plaiderie and the Bonded Store

by Heather Sebire and Philip de Jersey

The condition of many of the metal small-finds from the Bonded Store was compromised by the underlying granitic geology, creating very acidic conditions in the soil. Metal finds were in many cases very corroded and few recognisable artefacts survived, although there was much detritus from metal-working (see p. 108, below). In contrast to La Plaiderie, no Roman coins were found, which is surprising given the quantity of settlement material that was recovered; this was not considered to be a factor of the difficult lighting conditions on the Bonded Store site, since great care was taken to check spoil during the excavation. One Iron Age coin – a base silver stater of the Baiocasses dating to the mid-1st century BC – was found in a Roman context. The metal finds from La Plaiderie were generally in better condition. A small selection of those from Roman contexts is illustrated below.

Fibulae from the Bonded Store (Fig. 67)

1. Small-find 41 (context A2005). Langton Down type. Corroded copper alloy. Length 59mm, width 25mm, depth 13mm. Eight coils of spring remain inside the head. The bow is decorated with the classic 'light and shade' decorative motif
2. Small-find 298 (context C3033). Coil and shaft fragment of fibula. Copper alloy. Possibly a *Drahtfibel* derivative. Length 47mm, width 11mm, depth 22mm

Catalogue of unillustrated metal small-finds from Roman contexts at the Bonded Store

Listed by small-find number:

31. Copper alloy object, possible fibula pin. Length 41mm, thickness 1.8mm (A1203)
45. Small iron fragment (A1205)
50. Three iron fragments plus 'crumbs', very corroded. (1) Curved flat piece, maximum length 72mm, maximum width 52mm, thickness 1mm plus encrustation. (2) Round with encrustations, diameter 29mm, possibly part of fibula or brooch. (3) Square sectioned 'nail' shaft, length 33mm, width 4–5mm (A1205)
52. Iron object with square section, curved and hollow. Maximum length 16mm, diameter 4mm (B2054)
53. Copper alloy Iron Age coin attributed to the Baiocasses (DT series 344). Thickness post-treatment 3mm, weight post-treatment 3.40g. (B2054)

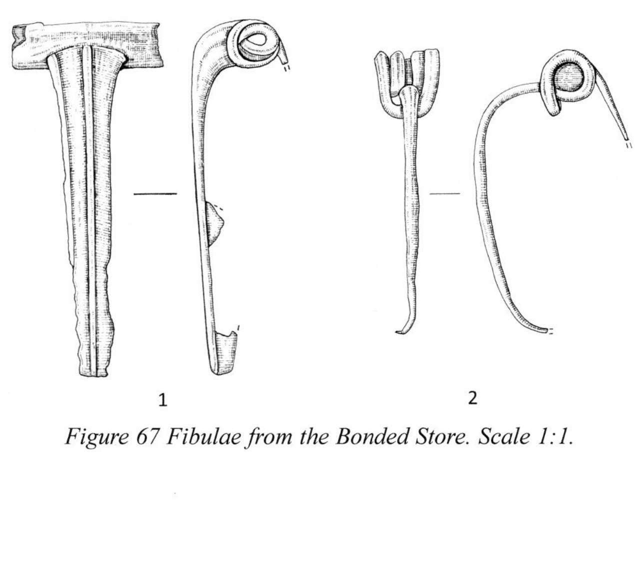

Figure 67 Fibulae from the Bonded Store. Scale 1:1.

57. Small rectangular metal object, maximum width 15mm, maximum length 18mm, thickness 11mm (A1204)
88. Iron nail, corroded. Square in section. Head diameter 13mm, length of whole nail 38mm. (C2093)
89. Iron object, corroded. Maximum length 52mm, minimum width 9mm, maximum width 18mm (C2004)
90. Iron object, possibly a nail. Length 68mm, width 5–9mm (C2093)
92. Three very small, flat metal fragments. (1) length 8mm × width 7mm. (2) length 6mm × width 3mm. (3) length 6mm × width 2mm (C2093)
94. Iron, two flat corroded joining fragments of irregular shape. Overall maximum length 77mm, maximum width 50mm (C2093)
104. Six small fragments of a copper alloy object, possibly a blade. Longest has rounded end. Length 11m × width 7mm (B3102)
105. Copper object, possibly a rivet. Maximum diameter of head 8mm (C2094)
107. Iron object, possibly a blade. Length 24mm, width 21mm, thickness 2mm (C2097N)
115. Iron ring, corroded but with metal residue. Maximum diameter 27mm, hole diameter 7mm, height 10–20mm (C2094)
131. Four fragments of copper alloy; (1) now in two pieces. (1a) maximum length 10mm, maximum width 8.5mm. (1b) maximum length 9mm, maximum width 5mm. (2) maximum length 13mm, maximum width 6mm. (3) maximum length 13mm, maximum width 6mm. (4) maximum length 14mm, maximum width 8mm (C1003)
217. Flat lead strip, folded at one end. Width 15mm, thickness 1mm, length 18mm (D2009)
244. Curved iron fragment, possibly nail, corroded onto pottery rim sherd, now separated. Nail very concreted; shaft tapers but end broken off. Length 58mm, average thickness 19mm. Pot with beaded rim of black-burnished ware, light brown fabric possibly BB2 'cooking pot' (C2094)
249. Iron nail with head, length 33mm (B1203)
254. Iron object, possibly a nail, corroded. A point protrudes through concretion. Length of encrustation 43mm, width 20mm (C2094)
269. Lead sheet folded lengthwise. Length 31mm, maximum width 10mm (D2009)
283. Lead, two fragments with oxidization. Very irregular. (1) Maximum length 19mm, maximum width 19mm. (2) Maximum length 19mm, maximum width 9mm (C3017)
285. Iron object, possibly a nail. Little metal remaining. Maximum length 75mm, maximum width 25mm (C3017)
292. Two iron objects. Encrusted concretions, very little metal remaining. (1) Concretion only with hollow. Maximum length 43mm, maximum width 28mm, maximum height 12mm. (2) Some iron remaining. Maximum length 42mm, maximum width 23mm, maximum height 1mm (C3023)
296. Six fragments of copper alloy, one semi-circular. Possibly part of fibula or brooch (C3022)
317. Many iron fragments and concretion. Largest length 65mm, width 28mm (D4109)

Catalogue of illustrated metal small-finds from probable Roman contexts at La Plaiderie (Fig. 68)

1 Pierced lead counter (T1/F.90, small-find 139)
2 Copper alloy 'foot' (T1/L4, small-find 413)
3 Copper alloy 'foot' (T2/L3, small-find 281)
4 Copper alloy finger ring (T1/F.29, small-find 9)
5 Copper alloy finger ring (T1/F.29, small-find 11)
6 Copper alloy cleaning utensil (T2/L3, small-find 256)
7 Copper alloy cauldron foot (T2/L3, small-find 262)

Miscellaneous small-finds from the Bonded Store and La Plaiderie

by Heather Sebire

In addition to the metal items described above, a number of Roman or probable Roman objects in other materials were recovered from the excavations at La Plaiderie and the Bonded Store. In the catalogue below all objects are from the Bonded Store unless otherwise stated.

Pipeclay figurines (Fig. 69.1–3)

1. Pipeclay Venus figurine, upper section only, 45mm × 36mm × 22mm, La Plaiderie (T1/F.44, small-find 130)
2. Pipeclay figurine. Fragment of a 'Dea Nutrix' figure, consisting of the right hand side of the basket chair in which the suckling matron sat. Dimensions 24mm × 12mm × 7mm (context C3003)
3. Pipeclay Venus figurine representing the lower torso and upper legs, 67mm × 39mm × 13mm (context D1007, small-find 201)

Spindle whorls (Fig. 69.4–9)

4 Ceramic spindle whorl, diameter 36mm, hole diameter 9mm (context C2003, small-find 86)
5 Ceramic spindle whorl, diameter 42mm, hole diameter 9mm (context D4003, small-find 232)
6 Ceramic spindle whorl, diameter 38mm, hole diameter 11mm (context D3012, small-find 233)
7 Ceramic spindle whorl, diameter 36mm, hole diameter 8mm (context C3011, small-find 289)
8 Ceramic spindle whorl, diameter 28mm, hole diameter 4mm (area A trench 2, unstratified, small-find 80)

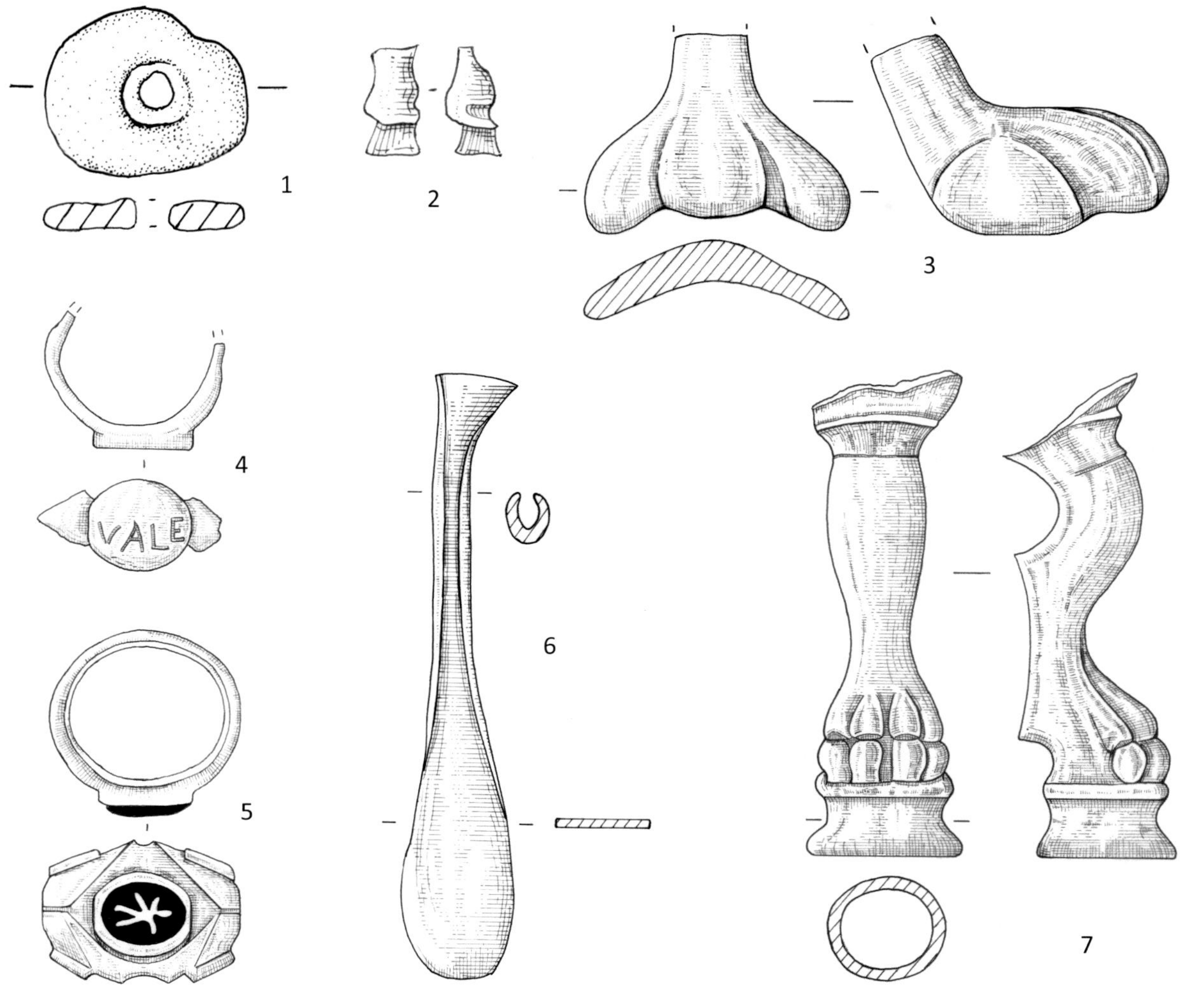

Figure 68 Metal small-finds from La Plaiderie. Scale 1:1 (nos 1–5), 1:2 (nos 6–7).

9 Ceramic spindle whorl, diameter 44m, hole diameter 9mm (context B2025, small-find 124)

Pottery object (Fig. 69.10)

10 Pottery sherd reformed into a gaming piece, 16mm × 14mm (context D4003, small-find 234)

Stone (Fig. 70.1–10)

1. Hone, 94mm × 28mm × 10mm (La Plaiderie, T1/L5, small-find 330)
2. Hone fragment, 26mm × 34mm × 27mm (La Plaiderie, T1/L3, small-find 124)
3. Hone fragment, 40mm × 27mm × 40mm (La Plaiderie, T1/L4, small-find 132)
4. Hone fragment, 24mm × 42mm × 12mm (La Plaiderie, T1/L5, small-find 418)
5. Fragment of stone tool, 56mm × 50mm × 13–32mm, possibly prehistoric but found in a Roman context (La Plaiderie, T1/F.73, small-find 122)
6. Stone rubber, 90mm × 77mm × 45mm (La Plaiderie T1/L4, small-find 419)
7. Quern fragment, 270mm × 204mm × 102mm (La Plaiderie T2/F.123, small-find 287)
8. Hone fragment, 107mm × 53mm × 15mm (context B3004, small-find 103)
9. Broken fragment of smoothed or carved igneous stone with quartz intrusion, 90mm × 50mm × 32mm (context C2094, small-find 239)
10. Stone rubber, 72mm × 65mm × 35mm (context D2009, small-find 270)
11. Lower half of rotary quern, diameter 0.40–0.45m (La Plaiderie, T1/F.90, small-find 214; see Fig. 6)
12. Small fragment of quern in conglomerate, maximum depth 70mm (context D4035, small-find 312; not illustrated)
13. Quern fragment in conglomerate, maximum depth 0.18m, maximum diameter 0.34m (context D4106, small-find 313; not illustrated)
14. Hand-shaped granite sphere, possibly a pestle, diameter approximately 60mm (context C3033, small-find 299; not illustrated)

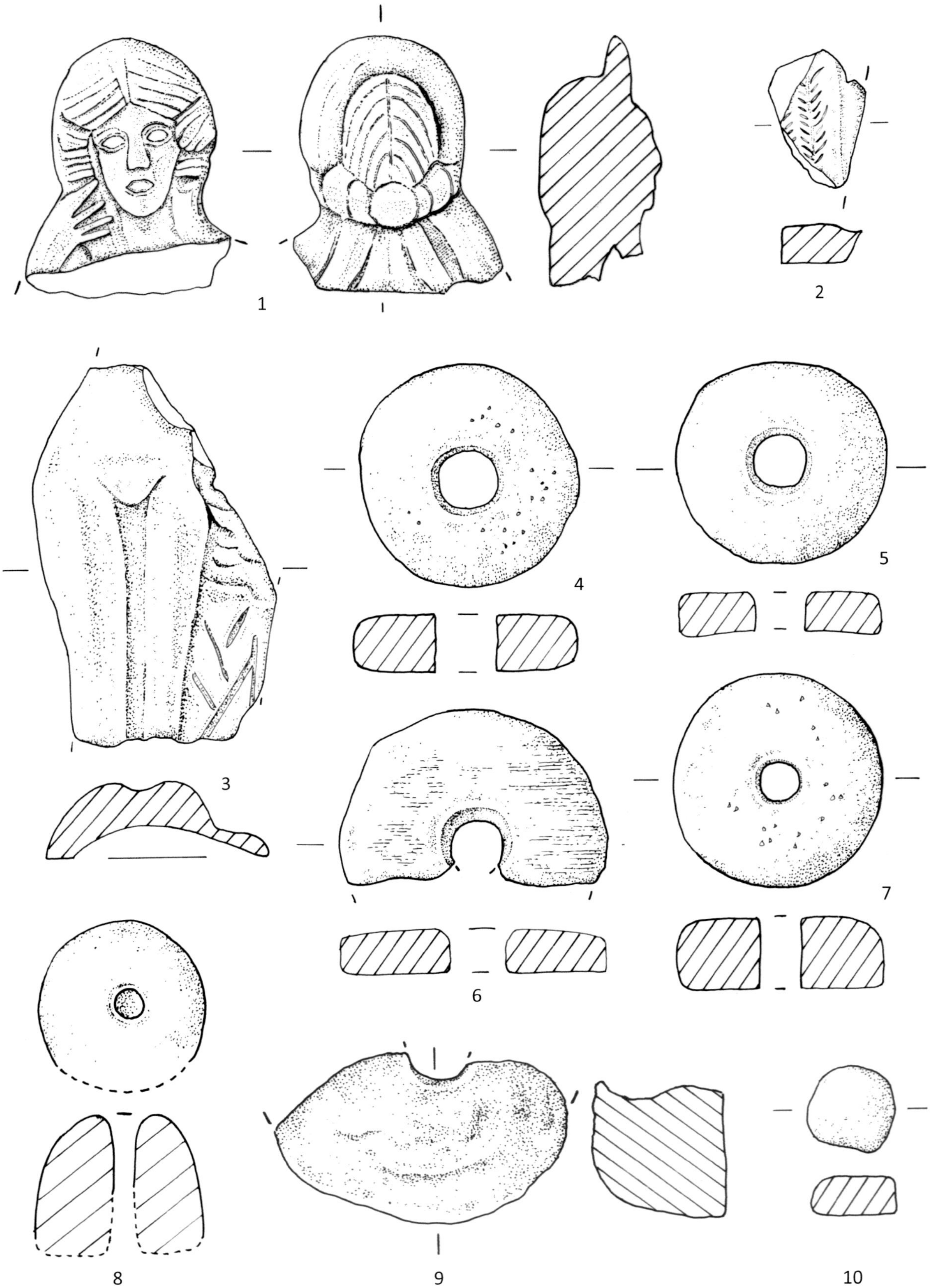

Figure 69 Miscellaneous small-finds from the Bonded Store and La Plaiderie. Scale 1:1.

Figure 70 Stone small-finds from the Bonded Store and La Plaiderie. Scale 1:2 except for no. 7, at 1:4.

15. Fragment of shale, probably from a bracelet, 84mm × 20mm (context C2003, small-find 256; not illustrated)
16. Fragments of shale, possibly from a bracelet (context B2004, small-find 127; not illustrated)

The Bonded Store glass

by Vivien Ferneyhough

The Roman glass assemblage consisted of some 66 pieces including four handle fragments, one window glass fragment and one bead. The majority of the glass is blue-green in colour with a small number of tinted-colourless and colourless fragments, together with one fragment of polychrome glass. All of the Roman glass found during this excavation appears to have been imported, as there has been no evidence to date of glass making or re-working in Guernsey.

From the unstratified glass two fragments are possibly Roman. Both are blue-green in colour with one fragment being water-worn and difficult to identify, while the other is a convex body fragment possibly from a globular unguent bottle. The Bonded Store site yielded a considerable quantity of glass, but mostly of a very small and fragmentary nature; there may therefore be some other fragments in the residual material that are Roman but have not been included in this report.

From Area A, nine fragments were recovered which are broadly dateable to the 1st to 3rd century AD. Of particular note are a fragment of ribbon handle with side ribs, probably from a 'Frontinus' type bottle or a rectangular bottle (Fig. 71.1), a fragment from a tubular base ring with concave kick (Fig. 71.2), and a fire-rounded rim fragment from a cylindrical cup or bowl with fold (Fig. 71.4).

Area B yielded 20 fragments that fall within a date range of the 1st to 3rd century AD. This assemblage contained several fragments from bowls with a horizontal fold (Fig. 71.3). A fire-rounded rim fragment, similar to that from Area A, was found in the same context and may be associated with the bowl fragments. Fragments from a bottle with a tubular folded rim dateable to the 1st or 2nd century AD were also recovered in this area (cf. Price and Cottam 1998, 191–202, fig. 1.4) together with a water-worn tubular rim fragment from a jar, re-worked as a bead (Fig. 71.5). The remaining fragments include a piece of blown window glass and two very small convex fragments, possibly from an unguent bottle. The rest are too small to be truly diagnostic, but may be from bottles or flasks.

Area C yielded 18 fragments ranging in date from the 1st to the early 4th century AD. The most notable is a rib fragment from a polychrome pillar-moulded bowl (Fig. 71.8). This type of cast bowl was being manufactured in the central and west Mediterranean from the late 1st century BC to the end of the 2nd century AD and therefore spans the Augustan, Claudian and Neronian periods (Cool and Price 1994, 14–21; Price and Cottam 1998, 44–6). However, it is well documented that polychrome pillar-moulded bowls were considered to be items of luxury glass and later became regarded as family heirlooms, being passed down through the generations after they were no longer being produced. Therefore it is possible that this fragment entered the archaeological context after the 1st century AD.

The majority of fragments found in Area C are of blue/green glass. Only three very small body fragments of thin colourless glass and one of pale green/colourless were found in this area. One fragment has a horizontal wheel-cut line and is from a cup with a date range of late 1st to 2nd century AD (cf. Price and Cottam 1998, 88–9, 91–7). A ribbed handle fragment (Fig. 71.7), probably from a square bottle, was recovered as well as a base fragment with one circle extant; both fragments are likely to be from mould-blown square bottles (for type see Isings 1971, fig. 20 no. 155). Other fragments worth mentioning are two body fragments from 'Frontinus' type bottles and a fire-rounded rim fragment from a cup or bowl.

Area D produced 21 glass fragments dateable to the late 1st, 2nd and 3rd centuries AD. Again only a small percentage of the glass is colourless and comprises three vertical fire-rounded rim fragments, one of which has a horizontal abraded line below the rim (not from the same vessel) and two body fragments; these fragments are all from cylindrical cups. The majority of fragments recovered in this area are from bottles. Worth noting is a fragment from an angular ribbon handle (Fig. 71.6) with a broad edge rib, and a diagonal folded rim fragment with handle scar; both fragments are from bottles. Among the body fragments, one from a hexagonal bottle and another from a prismatic bottle can be identified (cf. Cool and Price 1994, 179–85).

In summary, although the Bonded Store site is situated close to the historic harbour of St Peter Port, the relatively small assemblage of identifiable Roman glass from this site, and the types represented, seem to suggest that this glass was used in a domestic context rather than being part of a consignment for trade.

The author would like to thank Dr J. Price for her invaluable comments regarding dating and typology.

Catalogue of illustrated glass (Fig. 71)

Abbreviations: BG: blue/green. Br: brown. CL: colourless. G: green. OW: opaque white. PG: pale green. Y: yellow. nos 2, 3, 4 and 6 drawn by Vivien Ferneyhough.

1. BG ribbon handle fragment. Broad folded edge rib. Width incomplete. Probably 'Frontinus' or rectangular bottle (cf. Cool and Price 1994, 204–6; Allen 1998, 31–5). Second or 3rd century AD. A2003, small-find 4

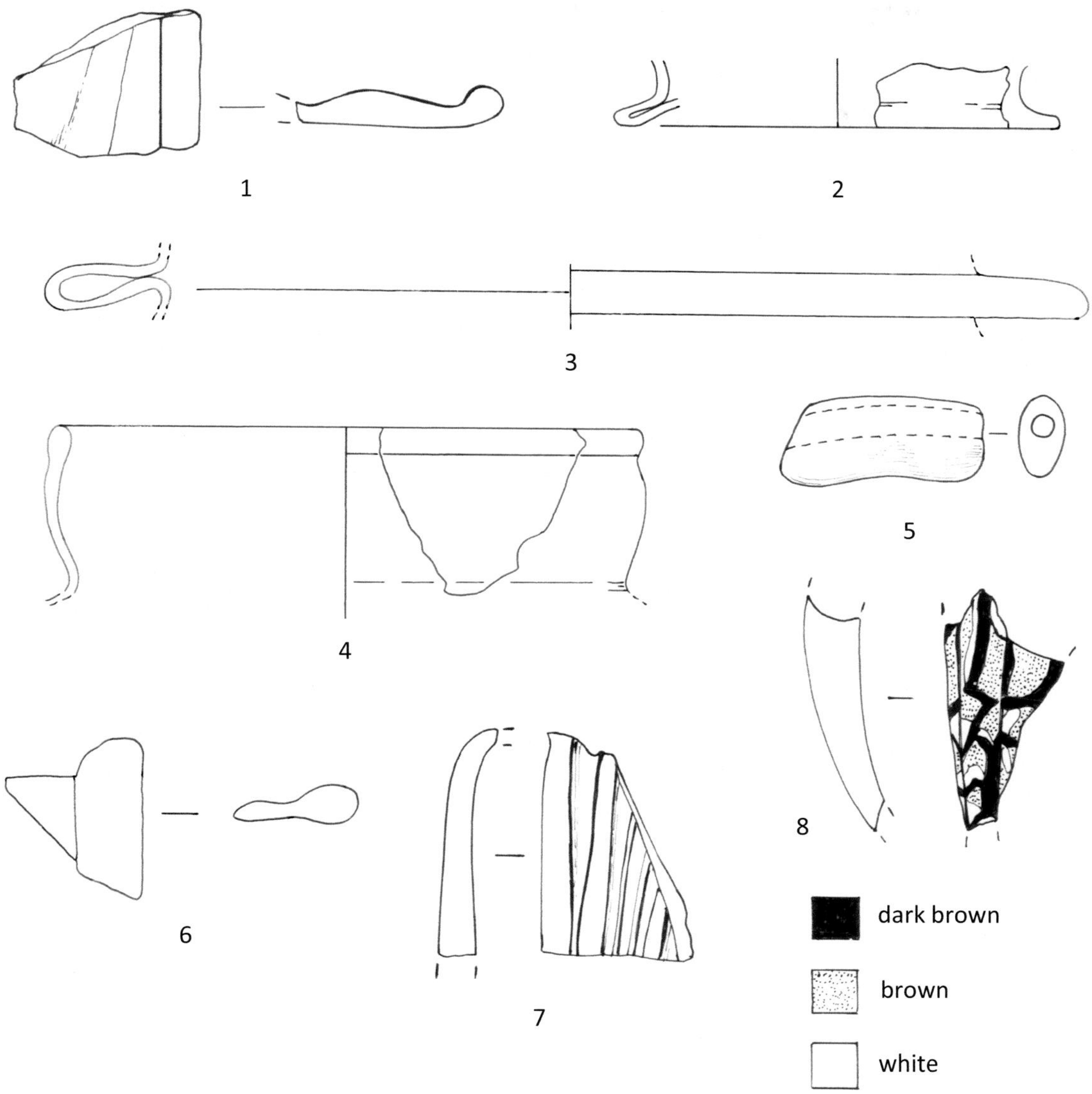

Figure 71 Roman glass from the Bonded Store. Scale 1:1.

2. BG, tubular base ring fragment with concave kick (cf. Price and Cottam 1998, 25–7), probably cup or bowl. Wear on base. Bubbly; slightly abraded. First to 3rd century AD. A2003, small-find 26
3. BG, fragments from bowl with horizontal fold (cf. Cool and Price 1994, 102, fig. 706). Thin-walled glass; small bubbles; slightly abraded. Second or 3rd century AD. B1003, small-find 15
4. BG, fire-rounded rim fragment. Cylindrical cup/bowl with fold (cf. Price and Cottam 1998, 109–10). Small bubbles; slightly abraded. Second or 3rd century AD. A2003, small-find 56.
5. BG, abraded and water-worn. Fragment of tubular rim from jar, re-used as bead. Present length 27mm. Second or 3rd century AD. B3005, small-find 106
6. BG angular ribbon handle fragment from bottle; bubbly, abraded on outer surface of edge rib. Second or 3rd century AD. D2002, small-find 209
7. BG, angular ribbed handle fragment, bottle; bubbly, slightly abraded on edge rib. Second or 3rd century AD. C1068, small-find 71
8. Y/Br glass with opaque white rods. A rib fragment of a polychrome pillar-moulded bowl. First century AD. Cf. Price and Cottam 1998, 44–6. Unstratified, small-find 81

Catalogue of unillustrated glass

Listed by small-find number:

28. BG, two very small fragments, possibly of neck; abraded. Probably Roman. A2003
29. PG/CL body fragment, possibly of unguent bottle; abraded, bubbly. A2003

33. BG convex body fragment, possibly of bottle. Abraded, bubbly, slight weathering. 8–10mm thick. Probably Roman. A2004
48. BG, three joining water-worn and abraded rim fragments. Horizontal tubular folded rim. Bottle. First or 2nd century AD. B2054
54. BG, thin fragment from tubular fold plus small fragment from body of bowl with tubular fold. Fold 1mm thick, body 1.3mm thick. Second or 3rd century AD. B1003
55. BG body fragment, probably of cup/bowl. Slightly abraded; 1.1mm thick. A2003
74. BG body fragment, cylindrical corrugated fragment from 'Frontinus' type bottle, bubbly; vertical mould seam. 1.2mm thick. Second or 3rd century AD. C1071
75. BG, two small convex body fragments. 1mm and 1.5mm thick. C1003
76. BG, small melted body fragment. Probably Roman. C1073
78. BG base fragment of mould-blown square bottle, one part circle extant. Second century AD. C1003A
79. BG, small mould-blown body fragment, possibly of 'Frontinus' type bottle. 0.9mm thick. Second or 3rd century AD. C1004
93. BG, small body fragment, thin-walled vessel, 1mm thick. C2093
99. (one piece)/ 242. (two pieces)
CL, three small body fragments, one from cup with horizontal abraded line, 0.6mm thick. Second century AD. C2094
102. G/CL thick body fragment, probably of bottle; bubbly. 4mm thick. B3004
109. BG, two body fragments, one with raised rib, possibly from bottle. C2094
111. CL small convex body fragment. 1mm thick. Possibly Roman. C2005
113. BG rim/body fragment, fire-rounded edge, cup/bowl, rim 2mm thick, body 1mm thick. Second or 3rd century AD. C2094
117. BG, very small convex fragment; abraded, 0.9mm thick. Identification of type not possible but probably Roman. B3005
130. BG body fragment of bottle or flask; bubbly and abraded. 3mm thick. B3003
202. BG lower body/concave base fragment, probably of flask/small bottle. Wear on base edge. 2mm thick. D1007
215. BG diagonal folded rim fragment with handle scar from bottle/jug. Second or 3rd century AD. D2005
216. BG body fragment of hexagonal bottle, bubbly, 3.5mm thick. Late 1st to late 2nd century AD. D2009
221. G/CL tubular base ring fragment, bubbly. Third century AD. D3003
235. BG, small fragment, possibly of neck. Probably Roman. D3004
236. BG, body fragment of prismatic bottle, abraded. 3.5mm thick. Second or 3rd century AD. D2005
242. *see 99*
259. CL vertical rim fragment of cylindrical cup with fire rounded edge. 2mm thick. Second or 3rd century AD. D1002/1004
260. CL, two joining fragments, vertical rim, fire-rounded edge, cylindrical cup. Second or 3rd century AD. D2001
263. BG body fragment. Abraded. 2mm thick. Probably Roman. A1004
265. BG small body fragment, possibly of small globular bottle. Bubbly and abraded. 1.5mm thick. B1022
266. BG body fragment from cylindrical vessel, abraded, 2mm thick. Probably Roman. D3007
267. BG, thick fragment of water-worn glass, probably Roman. Unstratified
268. BG rim fragment, fire-rounded possibly from bowl; two more small fragments of folded horizontal rim not from same bottle; pale BG bubbly fragment with convex body, straight ribbon handle and lower attachment visible, possibly a jug. Second or 3rd century AD. D4002
271. CL vertical cracked- off rim fragment of cup with cylindrical body and horizontal abraded line. 1.2mm thick. Third century AD. Plus further small body fragment of BG glass. D3003
273. BG, thin convex body fragment, possibly of globular unguent bottle. 1–2mm thick. Unstratified
274. BG body fragment of cylindrical vessel/bottle, plus two very small body fragments; CL fragment of base and base ring plus many de-vitrified fragments. Probably Roman. D2005

La Plaiderie glass

by Vivien Ferneyhough

A small quantity of Roman glass, amounting to some 11 pieces, was recovered from the Plaiderie excavations.

Catalogue of illustrated glass (Fig. 72)

1. BG bubbled glass; flared sheared rim, short neck, upper body expanding out. Unguent bottle, rim diameter 31.4mm, rim thicknesss 1.5mm. F.48, small-find 85
2. BG, slightly bubbled and seeded glass. Broad, straight ribbon handle fragment. With seven promiment ribs visible. Lower attachment of bottle. F.122, small-find 286
3. BG, fragment of base of small 'Frontinus' bottle. Concave base with FRO facing left to right embossed. Cf. Price and Cottam 1998, 209–11; Cool and Price 1994, 206. F.90, small-find 209

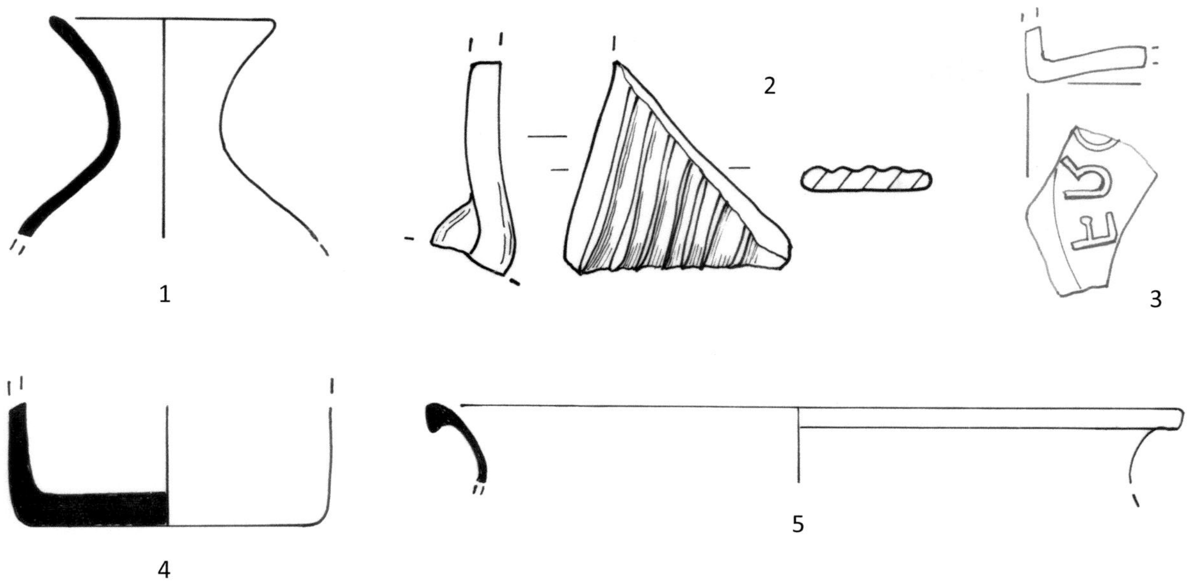

Figure 72 Roman glass from La Plaiderie. Scale 1:1.

4. CL with PG tinge, slightly bubbled glass; base of small cylindrical cup or flask. Slightly concave base with pontil mark. Base diameter 40mm, base thickness 4.5mm. Third century AD. F.44, small-find 127
5. G, fragment of rim, edge rolled out and down. Probably Roman. T2 L3, small-find 363c

Catalogue of unillustrated glass

Listed by small-find number:

121. BG, window pane. Two rounded sides and distorted corner. Possibly Roman. F.72
141. Dark blue bead, hexagonal, with two wider sides. Narrow perforation. Worn at ends. Possibly Roman. F.47
188. BG, slightly bubbled glass. Fragment of neck and shoulder from flask or jug. 2mm thick. F.85
216. G, long ovate bead. Narrow perforation. Possibly Roman. T1 L3
273. BG, fragment of base. Concave with two concentric rings and pontil mark, letter 'F' facing right between the two rings. Probably a cylindrical 'Frontinus' bottle
409. BG, bubbly, fragment of thin (1.5mm) walled vessel. F.102

Intaglios

by Tristan Arnison

1. Bonded Store, context C3017 (small-find 284) (Fig. 73.1) The intaglio is moulded in glass with a flat or slightly convex upper face; it is ovoid, 11.5mm in length and 9.5mm in width. The surface is badly pitted but despite this, the image itself is relatively clear. On the left is a small naked male figure who stands three quarters to the right but with his head in profile and his right arm bent at an angle to his body. On the right, a bearded man is depicted, either crouching or perched on a stool (not visible) in front of the smaller figure. His left leg is extended across the foreground and his right leg is shown behind it. He is somewhat round-shouldered and leans forward, raising his left forearm just above the smaller figure's head. His right arm is, however, angled downwards. There is the faint trace of a vertical undulating line that is most clearly visible in front of the smaller figure's upper thigh.

   This gem appears to belong to the type that has traditionally been interpreted as showing Prometheus creating mankind from clay. It was a device particularly popular on Italic and early Republican gems, although judging by the classicising style employed on this example, it probably only dates to the late 1st century BC. I have argued elsewhere (Arnison 2006, 67–8) that the image may in fact represent a sculptor using a plumb line to take measurements from a clay model.
2. Bonded Store, context D2005 (small-find 212) (Fig. 73.2) This intaglio is engraved on red jasper, measuring 15.5 × 11.35mm, probably dating from the late 2nd or early 3rd century AD. It portrays a *gryllos* consisting of the head of Silenus facing right, conjoined with the head of a boar facing left. Silenus's beard forms the hair of a third head, another bearded male facing downwards. The image is very similar to that on a red jasper intaglio from Silchester (Henig 1978, no. 377). It can be seen simply as an invocation of rural prosperity, although it is also possible to see

1 2

Figure 73 Intaglios from the Bonded Store. Scale 4:1.

it as having a more complex, narrative context (see Arnison 2006, 68–9).

Metal-working debris from the Bonded Store

by Chris Salter

Summary

All the material found was consistent with iron-smithing. The slag types found were typical of small-scale iron-smithing to produce or repair iron artefacts. These mainly came from three contexts, B2004, B2048 and B2054. The size and quantity of material recovered is not compatible with the interpretation of feature B2032 as a smelting furnace. While it was the right size for the base of a truncated iron-smelting furnace, one would expect to see more vitrified hearth-lining and, more importantly, dense furnace slag, usually associated with smelting as well as tap slag.

What can be inferred is that there was an iron-smithing hearth in the near vicinity, and one of its products might well have been the nails found in the hardpan concretion and soil associated with the slag. However, the absence of hammer-scale, which is usually restricted to close to the hearth and anvil, suggests either that it did not withstand the corrosive soil conditions, or that the active hearth and anvil was not in the immediate vicinity.

Smithing hearth bottoms

A number of complete or fragmented smithing hearth bottoms were found in contexts B2004, B2048, B2054 as well as C2094 (see Table 20). This type of slag is formed when the surface layer of the iron is oxidised, when the metal is heated in the hearth and falls off to react with the fuel ash and fused material from the hearth lining. Hearth bottoms often have a distinctive plano-convex cross-section and a D-shape plan, but can be very variable in form. They have to be removed from the hearth at regular intervals to prevent the formation of the slag interfering with the air flow in the hearth. Thus their size and shape gives an indication of the size of the hot zone of the hearth and the scale of the object being worked. In this case, most of the smithing hearth bottoms were relatively small (below 130g) indicating small-scale and/or low-temperature activity. One of the two heavier examples comes from B2048; the heaviest example, from context B2054, consisted of a smithing hearth bottom running into a layer of vitrified hearth lining with some flows, as well as hearth lining in the form of well-fired clay.

Other slag

The remaining material classified varied from material that was close to smithing hearth bottom in form, including fragments of dense irregular slag flow (solidified in furnace), and low-density slag often grading into flows of vitrified hearth-lining flow. All these are normal by-products of iron-smithing. Again these predominantly came from the three contexts B2004, B2048 and B2054.

Hearth lining

Vitrified hearth lining is not necessarily an indication of metal-working as it can be produced in any situation where there is sufficient fuel and air to raise the surface temperature of the walls or floor of the area to the point where the material starts to melt. However, in this case it is reasonable to consider the material to be from the area of the tuyere of the smithing hearth, as the majority of the material is associated with the iron-smithing slags.

Fired clay

Some of this material poses a problem on this site. Much of it consisted of a red sandy-clay mix looking as if it had been heated. A large area of this material formed the bed of what looked like the base of a large furnace. Initially it was thought that this could have been an iron-smelting furnace due to its size, but from the above study of the slag it is clear that this cannot be the case. It may have been the rake-out area of the smithing hearth but unfortunately due

Table 20 The Bonded Store: metalworking residues by context.

Context	Smithing hearth bottom	Slag/SHB	Slag	Low-density slag	Vitrified hearth lining	Fired clay	Fired clay + burnt bone	Iron	Concretion	Natural	Burnt bone	Charcoal	Pitch
B2003				3.3	37.9								
B2004	760.5		182.8		256.5			11.7					
B2048	691.9		91.6		297.8	188.8	19.7	189		15.9	926.2	12.4	
B2054	483.5		511.5		31			34.5		178.1		2	90.9
B3006					93.5								
B2032						323.7				516.2	76.7		
D4003			16	40.4	57.7								
D1002			19.3										
C2100				13.2									
C2104			16.8		8			55.3					
C2108										305			
A1033										2.3			
C1067				37.9									
C1073			31.4					156.4		28.9	14		
C1083									45.4				
C2094	422.5		172	22.7	136.3	50.7		670			5.8		
C1003						236							
C1005		113.6	107.1		115.2			92		138.5			
sf 307					14.7								
Total wt/g	2358.4	113.6	1148.5	117.5	1048.6	799.2	19.7	1208.9	45.4	1184.9	1022.7	14.4	90.9

to truncation of the various features by later buildings and the absence of hammer-scale is it impossible to put this in its true metallurgical context.

Concretion and natural

There was a considerable amount of iron oxide-concreted soil and rock present. Some of this contained corroded iron artefacts. For most the corrosion had gone to the point where there was only a hollow shell of iron oxide around where the original object had been. However, in many instances it was possible to identify the object, with the vast majority being small to medium-sized square nails.

Not all the material from this site was fully sorted due to the fine size of the fragments. Much of the material recorded here as 'natural' was soil and other material concreted together by iron oxides. It is likely that these oxides originated from the corroded iron artefacts from the same context.

Animal bone from the Bonded Store

by Jonathan D. Le Huray

Identification and recording

A total of 2832 animal bone fragments from the Bonded Store were examined, and an archive report compiled (held at Guernsey Museum). Each individual bone fragment was given an identification number in order to aid cross-reference between photos, measurement records, dental-ageing records and the main bone table. Teeth were identified to species, while eruption and wear were recorded following the methods of Grant (1975). All mandibles and loose teeth were recorded. Bone measurements were taken with sliding calipers according to von den Driesch (1976).

Where possible, determination of species and element was accomplished with reference to identification texts including Hillson (1992), Schmid (1972), Wheeler and Jones (1989) and Cohen and Serjeantson (1986).

Burning was observed on a number of bones during excavation and as a result it was deemed worthy to examine this feature in more detail. The presence of cut marks on bone elements was also noted during the analysis and this too was examined in more detail.

Quantification

The high level of bone fragmentation meant that an analysis of bone epiphyses to determine the minimum number of elements (MNE) and the record of skeletal parts present would be extremely biased. As a result a system of zone recording, as developed by Serjeantson (1991), was used to record the distinguishing areas or zones present on each bone fragment (Table 21). This allows the calculation of MNE to be based on the most frequent part of the bone present (Serjeantson 1996, 195).

Table 21 The Bonded Store: zoned and not zoned animal bones.

Zoned bones	*Not zoned bones*
scapula, humerus, ulna, radius, pelvis, femur, tibia, astragalus, calcaneum, metacarpal, metatarsal, phalanx 1, phalanx 2, occiput, horn core	vertebrae, small tarsals, sesamoids, patella, small phalanges, lateral metapodials, disarticulated skull parts, isolated teeth, sternum, hyoid

The minimum number of individuals (MNI) for a particular species is calculated for each bone element by dividing MNE by the number of bone elements present in the skeleton; for example, the MNI for the proximal femur is determined by dividing the MNE for the proximal femur by two. The overall species MNI is based on the highest element MNI observed. MNE for mandibles was based upon those mandibles recorded for tooth wear analysis, since mandibles are not zoned and MNE for all observed mandibles would simply represent the number of identified specimens (NISP). MNE and MNI were not calculated for isolated teeth, ribs or vertebrae.

Where observable, the state of epiphyseal fusion was recorded as fused (F), un-fused (UF), or fusing (FG) for both the proximal and distal epiphyses. This data can be used to examine age profiles of species through the percentage of un-fused early, middle and late fusing bones (e.g. Serjeantson 1996).

Results

IDENTIFICATION

Of the 2832 bone fragments examined, 1746 (61.7%) were unidentified. A further 549 (19.4%) bone fragments could not be identified to species, but could be identified to element. Of these, 132 were classified as cow/horse/deer-size (CSZ), 219 as sheep/pig/dog-size (SSZ), and 198 as ungulate (UNGUL) tooth fragments. The remaining 537 (19.0%) bone fragments were identified to species and element. The majority of these fragments (83.6%) were those species associated with animal husbandry, i.e. cow, sheep/goat and pig (see Table 22). Horse bones comprise of just two loose teeth and as a result this species was not examined in any detail. Rodent and rabbit bones were treated in a similar manner. Bird and fish bones are examined in less detail than those species associated with animal husbandry due to the difficulty in identifying them to species.

QUANTIFICATION – NISP, MNE AND MNI

An analysis of NISP produces the MNE and MNI for each bone element (see Table 23). Maximum NISPs for zones 1–4 are used to obtain proximal long bone MNEs, while maximum NISPs for zones 5–8 are used to obtain distal long bone MNEs. MNIs are calculated for each bone element and the maximum MNI observed provides the species MNI. This

Table 22 The Bonded Store: number of identified specimens (NISP) by species.

	n	*% of identified*
bird	28	5.2
cat	2	0.4
cow	273	50.8
crab	7	1.3
dog	4	0.7
fish	35	6.5
horse	2	0.4
pig	35	6.5
rabbit	1	0.2
rodent	9	1.7
sheep/goat	141	26.3
Total	537	100

Table 23 The Bonded Store: MNE and MNI data for cow, sheep/goat and pig.

	Cow		*Sheep/ goat*		*Pig*	
Element	*MNE*	*MNI*	*MNE*	*MNI*	*MNE*	*MNI*
mandible	1	1	4	2	0	0
horncore	2	1	0	0	–	–
atlas	0	0	0	0	0	0
axis	0	0	0	0	0	0
scapula	1	1	1	1	0	0
proximal humerus	1	1	2	1	0	0
distal humerus	4	2	6	3	0	0
proximal radius	0	0	5	3	2	1
distal radius	1	1	6	3	1	1
proximal ulna	6	3	5	3	0	0
distal ulna	1	1	3	2	0	0
proximal metacarpal	1	1	1	1	1	1
distal metacarpal	1	1	1	1	0	0
pelvis	0	0	4	2	0	0
sacrum	0	0	0	0	0	0
proximal femur	2	1	2	1	0	0
distal femur	2	1	1	1	0	0
proximal tibia	2	1	2	1	0	0
distal tibia	3	2	8	4	1	1
proximal fibula	–	–	–	–	0	0
distal fibula	–	–	–	–	0	0
proximal metatarsal	4	2	5	3	2	1
distal metatarsal	3	2	5	3	2	1
astragalus	8	2	4	1	2	1
calcaneum	2	1	3	1	2	1
phalanx 1	5	1	0	0	0	0
phalanx 2	6	1	1	1	0	0
phalanx 3	6	1	0	0	1	1
max MNI	3		4		1	

produces an overall MNI of three individuals for cattle, four individuals for sheep/goat and one individual for pig. MNI figures for crab and fish bones were not calculated, while an analysis of NISP provides an MNI of one individual for cat, one for dog and three individuals for bird. This is based on the most frequent element observed. No further analysis of bone fusion data, dental recording or bone measurements took place, but raw data is recorded in the archive, held at Guernsey Museum.

BURNED BONES

Of all bone fragments examined, 540 (19.1%) were burned. Of these, 470 (87%) were unidentified, suggesting that the act of burning is related to the resulting fragmentary state of the assemblage. The 70 identified burned bones consisted of 23 cow bones, 10 cow-size bones, 1 fish bone, 5 sheep/goat bones and 31 sheep-size bones.

CUT AND CHOP MARKS

A total of 22 chop marks and 12 cut marks were observed.

GNAW MARKS

Only one case of gnawing was observed in the assemblage, on a cow-size rib.

BIRD BONES

Bird bones recovered most likely represent natural intrusion. This interpretation could be assessed through detailed analysis of the bird bones with a comprehensive reference collection in order to examine specific species.

FISH BONES

A total of 35 fish bones were identified, along with seven fragments of crab shell. Although species identification and calculations of MNI were not attempted for fish bones, an examination of maxillae and dental bones reveals that at least four species of fish are present.

DOG BONES

A total of four dog bones were identified in the assemblage, comprising of one mandible, one humerus, one radius and one tibia.

CAT BONES

Two cat bones were identified in the assemblage, both of which were mandibles. One mandible was recovered from the unstratified layer of trench 3, Area D, while the other was recovered from the same context as the dog mandible

(D4004). These specimens are most likely to represent the use of this species as a household pet.

Conclusions and further study

Burning observed on a high proportion of bone fragments is related to the high level of fragmentation in the assemblage. This burning is most likely the result of cooking for meat, since the majority of burned bone elements represent elements which form the extremities of the skeleton, e.g. foot bones, skull bones and ribs.

Cut and chop marks support the interpretation of burning as the result of food preparation since the majority of bone elements with cut and chop marks are either those elements with high proportions of meat, or those elements directly connected with elements with high proportions of meat: femur, humerus, ulna and tibia; astragalus, metatarsal and pelvis.

The dog bones could represent either dogs used for hunting or simply dogs kept as pets. The association of dog and cat mandibles in the same context suggests that the dog bones represent animals kept as pets during occupation of the later phases of the site. The context in which they were found, D4004, was a disturbed layer.

Environmental finds from the Bonded Store

by James Rackham

Methods

Eight samples were submitted for environmental assessment from the excavations at the Bonded Stores.

Sample volume and weight were measured prior to processing. The samples were washed in a 'Siraf' tank (Williams 1973) using a flotation sieve with a 0.5mm mesh and an internal wet sieve of 1mm mesh for the residue. Both residue and flot were dried, and the residues subsequently refloated, to ensure the efficient recovery of charred material. The dry volume of the flots was measured and the volume and weight of the residue recorded. Two of the samples were wash-over floated in a bowl. One produced no residue at all, while the other produced a residue that was dried and sorted. The waterlogged flots were kept wet.

The residue was sorted by eye, and environmental and archaeological finds picked out, noted on the assessment sheet and bagged separately. A magnet was run through each residue in order to recover material such as hammerscale and prill. The dry flot of each sample was studied using ×10 magnification and the presence of environmental finds (i.e. snails, charcoal, carbonised seeds, bones *etc*) was noted and their abundance and species diversity recorded on the assessment sheet. A sub-sample of the waterlogged flots was scanned and the diversity and abundance of seeds, insects *etc* was noted. These, along with the finds from the sorted residue, constitute the material archive of the samples.

The individual components of the samples were then identified and the results are summarised in Tables 24, 25 and 26, below.

Results

A total of 26.5 litres of soil was processed, which washed down to leave residues of sub-rounded and angular/sub-angular granite gravel, pebbles and coarse sand, with occasional inclusions of charcoal, bone, pottery and root pseudomorphs. Two samples (3 and 5) contained preserved organic material, and one sample (3) washed down to leave a single waterlogged flot and no residue.

The samples produced a limited range of artefacts and ecofacts (Tables 24 and 25). Finds included 59 sherds of pottery, fragments of brick/tile, magnetic material, a single fragment of iron and two small sherds of glass. The majority of the pottery was recovered from the Roman deposits (samples 1 and 4) within the confines of the Roman wall, and from an undated deposit (sample 2, context 3034), although sample 1 (context C3005) contained the greatest number of pot sherds per litre. Magnetic material was recovered in varying densities from all seven residues, consisting of magnetised stone crumb with no hammerscale or prill present. The greatest densities were from a Roman deposit within the area of the Roman wall (context C3035) and from an Iron Age layer sealed by silts (context C3044).

In terms of environmental remains, the materials recovered included bone, snail shell, charcoal, charred and uncharred plant remains, and preserved wood. Most of the bone, the majority of which is burnt, calcined and unidentifiable, is associated with the later phases of activity (Table 24). A sheep/goat innominate bone was present in sample 4, and a few fragments of burnt fish bone were identified in sample 5001 (context 3021). Charcoal is present in all bar one sample (3), but generally in low densities, with only four samples (5001, 2, 4 and 5) containing fragments suitable for further analysis.

Identifiable charred plant remains averaged 2.72 items per litre, ranging from 0.2 items per litre (sample 5) to 10.6 items per litre (sample 4). Cereal grain was present in six of the eight samples and cereal chaff and weed seeds in four of them (Table 25). The cereals present are predominantly barley (*Hordeum* sp.), including hulled (*Hordeum* sp. var. *vulgare*) and six-rowed hulled barley (*H. vulgare* var. *vulgare*) (Table 26), the latter identified on the basis of lateral or 'twisted' grains being present, characteristic of that variety. The presence of wheat is indicated by wheat chaff, some of which can be identified as possible emmer-type wheat (*Triticum* cf. *dicoccum*), but the fragmented state and poor preservation of the remains precluded further identification. Other charred plant remains included a single

Table 24 The Bonded Store: finds from the processed samples in phase order.

Sample no.	*Context*	*Phase*	*Sample vol. (l)*	*Residue vol. (ml)*	*Pot#/g*	*Mag. (g)*	*Fe no.*	*Brick/tile weight (g)*	*Bone (g)*	*Comments*
6	D1008u	prehist.	2	50	–	3	–	–	–	
6	D10081	prehist.	2	50	–	2	–	–	–	
5	C3044	Iron Age	5	1200	9/4	13	1	–	2	
3	C3045	Roman	2	–	–	–	–	–	–	
1	C3005	Roman	1.5	200	9/3	2	–	–	1	
4	C3035	Roman	5	1200	15/25	15	–	162*	8	*may include some pottery
5001	C3021	C2 +	4	450	3/82	2	–	–	10	two chips of glass
2	C3034	Roman	5	1500	23/28	1	–	–	2	

Table 25 The Bonded Store: environmental finds from the processed samples in phase order.

Sample no.	*Context*	*Sample vol. (l)*	*Flot vol. (ml)*	*Charcoal***	*Wood**	*Charred grain**	*Charred chaff**	*Charred seed**	*Waterlogged seed**	*Snail**	*Comments*
6	D1008u	2	1	0/2	–	–	1	–	–	–	indet. cereal chaff
6	D10081	2	2	1/2	–	1	–	–	–	–	indet. cereal fragment (<2mm)
5	C3044	5	34	2/3	1	1	–	–	5	–	barley, nettle, bramble, elder, goosefoot, insects, indet. calcined and unburnt bone
3	C3045	2	300	0/0	5	–	–	–	5	–	nettle, bramble, elder, goosefoot, rose/bramble-type thorns, insects
1	C3005	1.5	3	2/4	–	1	1	1	–	–	?barley, indet. cereal chaff
4	C3035	5	35	3/5	–	2	2	2	–	–	barley, barley and wheat chaff, vetch/vetchling, grasses, sedge, rose/bramble-type thorns, sheep innom., indet. calcined bone fragments
5001	C3021	4	11	4/5	–	1	–	1	–	1	barley, ?pale persicaria, Vallonia costata, much small calcined bone fragments, burnt fish bone
2	C3034	5	15	3/5	–	1	1	1	–	–	?barley, wheat chaff, indet. chaff and seed, indet. calcined and unburnt bone

* abundance: 1 = 1–10, 2 = 11–50, 3 = 51–150, 4 = 151–250, 5 = 250+
** charcoal figures as abundance > 2mm/abundance < 2mm

seed of *Polygonum* cf. *lapathifolium* (pale persicaria), two *Vicia*/*Lathyrus* (vetch/vetchling), one small *Gramineae* (grass) and one *Carex* sp. (sedge) (Table 26).

At the assessment stage only a proportion of the waterlogged flots (samples 3 and 5) were scanned, and were found to be abundant in degraded plant material and weed seeds. Wood was also abundant in sample 3. Charcoal was present in low densities in sample 5 only, which also contained a single barley grain. The suite of wood species is generally consistent in both samples with species identified including *Chenopodium* sp. (goosefoot), *Urtica dioica* (common nettle), *Sambucus* cf. *nigra* (elderberry?), and

Table 26 The Bonded Store: archaeobotanical remains from processed samples.

	Phase	*Prehistoric*		*Iron Age*	*Roman?*	*Roman*		*C2 +*	*unphased*
	context/ sample no.	*D1008/6u*	*D1008/6l*	*C3044/5*	*C3045/3*	*C3005/1*	*C3035/4*	*C3021/ 5001*	*C3034/2*
cereal grain									
Hordeum vulgare var. *vulgare*	six-row hulled barley	–	–	–	–	–	2	–	–
Hordeum sp. var. *vulgare*	hulled barley	–	–	1	–	–	2	1	–
cf. *Hordeum* sp.		–	–	–	–	1	–	–	2
cereal grain frags. (>2mm)		–	–	–	–	2	16	1	1
cereal grain frags. (<2mm)		–	+	–	–	–	+	–	+
cereal chaff									
glume bases *Triticum* cf. *dicoccum* (Schrank.) Schubl.	emmer-type wheat	–	–	–	–	–	4	–	–
glume bases *Triticum* sp.	wheat	–	–	–	–	–	4	–	4
rachis internodes *Hordeum* sp.	barley	–	–	–	–	–	4	–	–
rachis indet.		–	–	–	–	–	5	–	1
indet. chaff		1	–	–	–	1	–	–	1
wild species									
Chenopodium sp.	goosefoot	–	–	*	*	–	–	–	–
Vicia/Lathyrus (3-4mm diameter)	vetch/ vetchling	–	–	–	–	–	2	–	–
Polygonum cf. *lapathifolium* L.	pale persicaria?	–	–	–	–	–	–	1	–
Urtica dioica L.	common nettle	–	–	***	***	–	–	–	–
small indet. *Gramineae*	small grasses	–	–	–	–	–	2	–	–
Carex sp.	sedge	–	–	–	–	–	1	–	–
Sambucus cf. *nigra* L.	elderberry	–	–	**	**	–	–	–	–
Rosaceae thorns	rose/ bramble thorns	–	–	–	***	–	11	–	–
Rubus sp.	blackberry/ raspberry	–	–	**	**	–	–	–	–
indet.		–	–	–	–	–	–	–	1
total identified charred items		1	–	1	–	4	53	3	10
ditto, per litre of sample		0.5	–	0.2	–	2.67	10.6	0.75	2

+ = frequency score between 1 and 10

Abundance scores for waterlogged remains: * = present, ** = frequent, *** = abundant

Rubus sp. (blackberry/raspberry). As only a proportion of the waterlogged flots was assessed, absolute counts were not taken at this stage, but the relative abundance of each species was recorded (Table 26).

Other plant material consisted of leaf fragments and degraded plant matter as well as frequent occurences of *Rosaceae* (rose family) thorns. The survival of the predominantly robust plant components and seeds (i.e. thorns, elder, bramble and nettle seeds) suggests that the material has suffered significant degradation with the probable loss of the more fragile elements and seeds, which undoubtedly biases the assemblages.

Discussion

Neither sample of the material from context D1008, assigned to the prehistoric period, produced much evidence of occupation or activity, and indeed very little overall, with no remains that could constitute domestic debris. No pottery or bone and only very low densities of magnetic material and charcoal, together with single fragments of indeterminate cereal grain and chaff, were present in samples 6 'upper' and 6 'lower'. This lack of evidence might suggest limited domestic activity, but charred plant remains are consistently at low density on most prehistoric sites.

Barley is the only cultigen represented by cereal grain in all of the samples, but wheat outnumbers barley amongst the cereal chaff fragments from the Roman samples. The presence of wheat chaff but no wheat grain is unusual and cannot simply be attributed to preservational bias, as experimental work has demonstrated that chaff, particularly free-threshing rachis internodes (such as those of barley), is more fragile and less likely to survive the charring process than the more substantial and robust cereal grains (Boardman and Jones 1990). The presence of wheat chaff and the absence of wheat grain may therefore be due to differential processing and storage of the barley and wheat crops. It should be noted, however, that the cereal and weed species identified are mostly represented by one or two seeds or chaff components only, and so do not constitute suitable material for making inferences with regard to crop-processing activities, broader inferences about arable husbandry regimes or the local habitat and environment.

The greatest concentration of artefacts and ecofacts is associated with the Roman deposits, with samples 1 and 4 containing, respectively, 2.67 and 10.6 identifiable charred items per litre, and the evidence suggests the activities are possibly domestic in nature. The presence of cereal grain and chaff suggests that crop-processing activities may have taken place on or adjacent to the site. However, the nature and degree of processing cannot be determined due to the low numbers of grain, chaff and weed seeds recovered. The presence of species such as blackberry/raspberry and elder could represent potentially exploited food resources, or more prosaically indicate that brambles, and probably elder, grew in the area, as thorns are frequent and it is very unlikely that they would arrive onto site as a result of collecting the fruit for consumption.

Contrary to expectation, the samples contain no apparent corroborative evidence for metal-working activities being performed on, or within the vicinity, of the site. Slag is not present in any samples, and the magnetic material recovered from the samples contains no hammerscale or prill, which is indicative of iron working. In addition, the density of magnetic material from the deposit opposite the area of the Roman slag furnace is very low.

Note: at a later stage in the excavations Dr Mark Robinson of Oxford University visited the site and took samples of the layer of silt beneath the Roman wall, in the central area of the site (trench CT3, context C3043). The following waterlogged seeds were found, with nettle seeds being the most numerous: *Chenopodium* (goosefoot), *Urtica dioica* (stinging = common? nettle), *Rubus fruticosus* (blackberry), *Verbena officinalis* (vervain), *Mentha aquatica* (water mint), *Sambucus nigra* (elder), and *Juncus* mix (reeds/rushes).

Context C4064, in trench CT4, contained rich charcoal indenting of *Quercus* (oak) and *Corylus avellana* (hazel), but no seeds. The burnt spread C3022, in trench CT3, contained a small amount of *Corylus avellana* (hazel) charcoal and some burnt bone fragments including a fish vertebra.

6

Gazetteer of Roman sites and finds on Guernsey and Herm

by Tanya Walls, Philip de Jersey and Jason Monaghan

The following Gazetteer lists all known sites and finds of Roman material from the islands of Guernsey and Herm, and the waters around them, up to and including 2015 (Fig. 74). The entries are split into three main groups:

A. Roman finds from excavated sites on Guernsey and Herm
B. Roman finds from non-excavated sites, Guernsey and Herm (land and inter-tidal)
C. Roman finds from non-excavated sites, Guernsey and Herm (underwater)

Group A, the excavated sites, are listed by date of first excavation. Groups B and C are arranged by material and then by date of discovery. There is some overlap between these three groups, particularly for sites in the inter-tidal zone (such as Cow Bay, St Peter Port) and for some locations (such as Castel parish church) which have revealed Roman evidence in a number of different forms. These sites are cross-referenced to one another. Every entry has an MGU reference that relates to the Historic Environment Record maintained at Guernsey Museum, and which in most cases will provide additional information. Where a site or find has been published, details of the most useful or significant publication are provided here. A number of briquetage sites have been included although their dating is often uncertain.

A. Roman finds from excavated sites on Guernsey and Herm

1. ***La Varde passage grave, Vale*** (MGU161 and MGU4410) (excavated 1837)
Neolithic passage grave apparently revisited during the Roman period. A number of samian sherds in the Guernsey Museum collection are thought to be from this tomb, along with several other sherds and a briquetage hand-brick. Two Roman coins, of Gallienus and Constantine, were found near La Varde in 1888.
References: Kendrick 1928, 119; Burns and Burns 1985, 656, 662.

2. ***Déhus passage grave, Vale*** (MGU153) (excavated 1837–47, 1932)
Neolithic passage grave apparently revisited during the Roman period. Two bronze rings thought to be La Tène or Gallo-Roman in date were probably found during the 19th-century excavations, as well as a rim sherd from a Roman flagon; several sherds are recorded from Collum's re-excavation of 1932.
References: Kendrick 1928, 154; Collum 1933, 79–86.

3. ***Le Creux ès Faïes passage grave, St Peter in the Wood*** (MGU190) (excavated 1840–43)
Neolithic passage grave apparently revisited during the Roman period. In addition to the prehistoric finds there were two samian sherds, one of which had been perforated and shaped into a spindle whorl or ornament. There was also a briquetage hand-brick.
Reference: Kendrick 1928, 185.

4. ***Lihou Priory, St Peter in the Wood*** (MGU228) (excavated 1841, 1978, 1990–2003)
The most recent series of excavations of the Benedictine Priory of Notre Dame de Lihou revealed two sherds of Roman amphorae, a few pieces of roof tile and an intaglio cut on a cornelian depicting a man and a goat; this is stylistically dateable to the 1st century BC – 1st century AD, although it may have been re-used in a medieval reliquary or similar object.

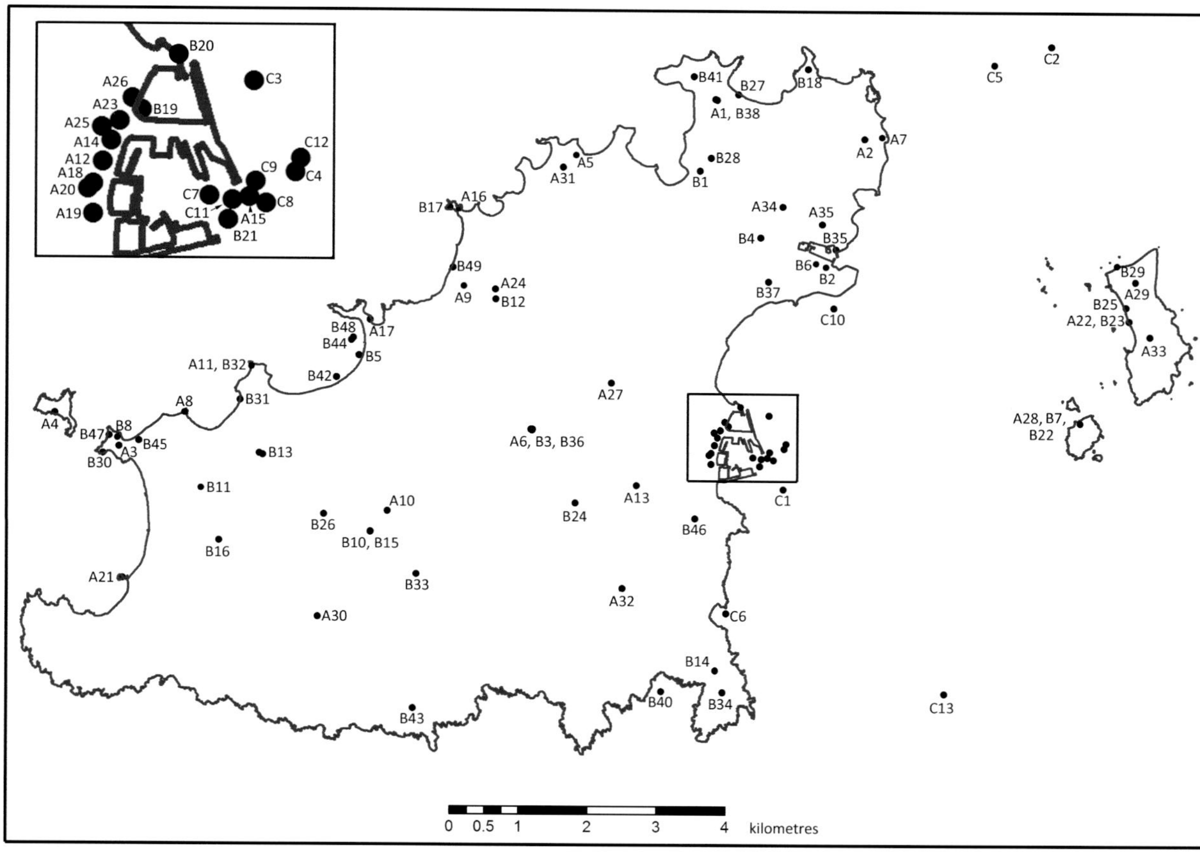

Figure 74 Location of sites listed in the Gazetteer. Sites in and around St Peter Port are shown in the inset, top left.

5. ***Pulias, St Sampson*** (MGU621) (excavated 1852)
Pottery and some briquetage were discovered in a brief examination of this site by F. C. Lukis in 1852.
Reference: Kendrick 1928, 172.

6. ***Castel Parish Church*** (MGU1364 and MGU3549) (excavated 1870s, 2000 and 2005)
This medieval parish church has fragmentary Roman tile built into the north and east walls, along with two Caen stone fragments with Roman-style lettering built into the porch. Excavations beneath the floor of the church and outside the north wall have revealed significant quantities of Roman tile; some 732 pieces have been recovered in the modern excavations and include roof, floor and wall tiles (see p. 95). There was also some unpainted Roman plaster, fragments of *opus signinum* and a few sherds of possible Roman pottery. The position of the church directly adjacent to a megalithic statue-menhir suggests a continuity of religious observance at the site, and therefore a suitable position for a Roman temple. Its commanding position with a view towards Alderney would also make it a prime military site. John McCormack (pers. comm.) has observed that it is the only church in Guernsey which originally had a square churchyard. See also Gazetteer B3.
References: McCormack 1986, 133, 136; Sebire 2005, 166.

7. ***Noirmont, Vale*** (MGU618) (excavated *c*.1912)
A kiln or salt-pan discovered during quarrying, partially excavated before it was destroyed. It consisted of a large rectangular trough with a baked clay floor. Large quantities of briquetage and sherds 'probably of the Gallo-Roman period' were recovered.
Reference: Kendrick 1928, 160–1.

8. ***Le Catioroc, St Saviour*** (MGU4347) (excavated 1958)
Briquetage site with well-preserved kiln bars and hand-bricks. One Iron Age coin was found and the site may be Iron Age or Roman in date.
Reference: Jee 1958.

9. ***Le Feugré, Cobo, Castel*** (MGU1414) (excavated 1967)
The remains of an early medieval long-house, dated by the pottery to *c*.AD 800–1150, were excavated just inland from the coast at Cobo. The finds also included a possible amphora sherd, a fragment of Roman tile and two pieces of briquetage.
Reference: Girard 1981.

10. ***Le Tranquesous, St Saviour*** (MGU254) (excavated 1976, 2014)
Iron Age and early Roman settlement discovered and partly excavated in the 1970s and again in 2014. It was occupied from *c*.80 BC – AD 50 and comprised circular

post-built houses enclosed by palisaded ditches. The site extends over a considerable area.

References: Burns 1977; Walls, de Jersey and Hughes 2014, 625–7.

11. ***Le Crocq, St Saviour*** (MGU2527 and MGU2541) (excavated?1949, 1976 and 1998)
Large quantities of briquetage are present in Guernsey Museum from an otherwise unrecorded investigation at this site in 1949. Decreasing amounts have been recovered in two excavations since then, and much of the site has now been lost to coastal erosion. See also B32.
References: Lihou 1976; Cunliffe and de Jersey 2000, 894–902.

12. ***18–20 The Pollet, St Peter Port*** (MGU543) (excavated 1980–81)
Excavations on this site revealed large quantities of medieval and post-medieval pottery. There were also five sherds of samian pottery.

13. ***King's Road, St Peter Port*** (MGU528) (excavated 1980–83 and 2005–11)
A settlement and cemetery dating from the early Iron Age through to the end of the 1st millennium BC. The presence of Roman material, including a complete samian dish stamped HONORATI, indicates a later occupation of the site.
References: Burns, Cunliffe and Sebire 1996 (1980s excavations); de Jersey 2010.

14. ***La Plaiderie, St Peter Port*** (MGU2216) (excavated 1983–85)
Roman urban settlement (this volume).

15. ***St Peter Port Pierheads*** (MGU2766) (excavated 1984–85)
Romano-Celtic vessel wrecked *c*.AD 280 following a fire on board. At the time of writing this was the most substantial sea-going vessel of the Roman era surviving outside the Mediterranean.
Reference: Rule and Monaghan 1993.

16. ***Grandes Rocques, Castel*** (MGU236) (excavated 1986)
Settlement consisting of two small apsidal-ended houses constructed with large beach pebbles, dated to the first half of the 12th century AD. Finds included a small quantity of Roman material amounting to two sherds of pottery, one of which had been modified to produce a spindle whorl, and two fragments of probable Roman glass, one from a vessel and the other a small disc, perhaps a counter.
Reference: Burns and Batt 1990.

17. ***Albecq, Castel*** (MGU224) (excavated 1995)
The excavated part of this coastal medieval settlement comprised three stone buildings set around a courtyard. There is evidence of further buildings and enclosures on the headland. Two possible Roman sherds were found here.
Reference: de Jersey 2013.

18. ***Le Riches/Lefebvre Street, St Peter Port*** (MGU542) (excavated 1996–97)
Most of the finds from this town site were medieval and post-medieval, but there were also 14 sherds of Roman pottery.

19. ***Bonded Store, St Peter Port*** (MGU541) (excavated 1996–2004)
Roman urban settlement (this volume).

20. ***Sunrise Cottage, Berthelot Street, St Peter Port*** (MGU551) (excavated 1997)
Urban site with mainly medieval and post-medieval finds, but including one Roman brick or tile fragment.

21. ***Fort Grey, St Peter in the Wood*** (MGU2528) (excavated 1999, plus several spot finds)
In addition to briquetage, this Iron Age/Roman salt-working site on the eastern side of the Fort Grey islet has yielded five sherds of possible Roman pottery and two fragments of tile.
Reference: Cunliffe and de Jersey 2000, 903–10.

22. ***Fisherman's Beach, Herm*** (MGU525, MGU2229, MGU2230, MGU3567) (excavated 1999, plus numerous spot finds)
Coastal erosion has exposed Iron Age and Roman material on the west coast of Herm below Fisherman's Cottage. Finds have been recorded since the 19th century and the site was partially excavated in 1999. More than 30 sherds of pottery have been collected and there is also a large quantity of briquetage and a few fragments of Roman tile. The Ashmolean Museum has a fragment of tessellated pavement which is recorded as having come from 'Herm' although the smudged label may in fact have once read 'Herne'. See also B23.
Reference: Cunliffe and de Jersey 2000, 911–32.

23. ***Royal Hotel, St Peter Port*** (MGU2765) (excavated 1999–2001)
Essentially an occupation site of the Early Neolithic and Bronze Age periods, but close to the Roman waterfront, and 231 pieces of Roman pottery and tile (most quite small and some water-rounded) plus 290

small scraps that were possibly Roman were found during excavations.

Reference: Sebire 2011, 245.

24. ***Route de Carteret, Castel*** (MGU518) (excavated 2000–01)
Three sherds of samian pottery were recovered from this Late Neolithic and Bronze Age occupation site, plus a spindle whorl probably fashioned from a Roman flagon base.
Reference: Walkington *et al.* 2001.

25. ***Les Canichers, St Peter Port*** (MGU2696) (excavated 2001–03)
Excavations in a garden at Les Canichers revealed part of a structure tentatively interpreted as a prehistoric cairn. The soil above the cairn contained a significant quantity of fragmentary briquetage. Also in this layer were fourteen sherds of Roman and possibly Roman pottery, and a fragment of tegula.

26. ***Savoy Hotel, St Peter Port*** (MGU3164) (excavated 2002)
Gallo-Roman deposits were identified beneath the demolished Savoy Hotel, including 68 Roman sherds and a small fragment of probable Roman glass.

27. ***St Peter Port School, St Peter Port*** (MGU3407) (excavated 2005)
A structure resembling a prehistoric cist, but associated with medieval pottery and therefore thought to have been disturbed in the Middle Ages. Amongst the finds were two sherds of samian ware and part of a flagon, and two tile fragments.
Reference: de Jersey 2009.

28. ***Jethou*** (MGU6129) (excavated 2007)
One Gallo-Roman rim sherd was found in a re-deposited context in trench A, adjacent to a midden exposure on the north coast of Jethou. See also B22.
Reference: Scarre 2016, 102.

29. ***Herm, various locations*** (excavated 2008–11)
Roman pottery was discovered during excavations undertaken by Chris Scarre at various locations in the northern part of the island. The finds are currently being studied for publication.

30. ***West of Airport, St Saviour/St Peter in the Wood*** (MGU5318) (excavated 2009–12)
Archaeological investigation in advance of the airport runway development found evidence primarily of Neolithic and Bronze Age activity, but among the finds are some 29 Roman and possibly Roman sherds and four fragments of *tegulae*.

31. ***Les Vardes Quarry, St Sampson*** (MGU6752) (excavated 2010)
Extensions to the quarry required an archaeological watching brief and a small excavation. Most of the material collected was prehistoric, but there were also two sherds of Roman greyware and three fragments probably of briquetage.
Reference: Lane and Walls 2010.

32. ***St Martin's Parish Church*** (MGU1362) (excavated 2011)
A small archaeological excavation was carried out adjacent to the west door of the church, revealing three post-medieval burials. A sherd of samian pottery was found.
Reference: de Jersey and Cataroche 2011.

33. ***St Tugual's Chapel, Herm*** (MGU 5705) (excavated 2011)
Pottery finds from excavation of part of the medieval cemetery adjoining St Tugual's Chapel included one definite and two possible Roman sherds.
Reference: de Jersey and Cataroche 2012, 426.

34. ***Le Tertre, Vale*** (MGU3812) (excavated 2014)
One small oxidized body sherd recovered during the excavation of a test-pit in the grounds of Le Tertre.

35. ***Le Maresquet, Vale*** (MGU6796) (excavated 2015)
Fragment of Roman tile found in a test-pit.

B. Roman finds from non-excavated sites (land and inter-tidal)

1. ***Vale Parish Church: brick*** (MGU1371)
Probable Roman brick has been identified within the fabric of the church, in particular inside the building in the south wall near the altar.
Reference: McCormack 2010, 720ff.

2. ***St Sampson Parish Church: brick*** (MGU1372)
John McCormack (pers. comm.) has reported that there are two small pieces of Roman brick in the south and east walls of the church.
Reference: McCormack 2010, 727.

3. ***Castel Parish Church: brick, tile*** (MGU3549) (2012)
A considerable quantity of Roman brick, tile and *opus signinum* was recovered from the spoil of a 44m trench dug for a new water pipe on the north side of the church. See also A6.

4. ***Grosse Hougue, St Sampson: pottery*** (MGU622) (1862)
A single Roman sherd recorded from a destroyed dolmen at Grosse Hougue.
Reference: Kendrick 1928, 172–3.

5. ***Vazon Bay, Castel: pottery*** (MGU2555) (19th century)
Three sherds of coarse pottery, probably Roman, were found in exposed peat deposits.

6. ***Hougue du Moustier, St Sampson: briquetage*** (MGU628) (19th century)
Briquetage hand-bricks were found when this *hougue* was quarried in the 19th century.

7. ***Jethou: briquetage*** (MGU3554) (19th century)
Some reports of two midden sites on the north coast of Jethou note that briquetage was present in these deposits when observed in the 19th century. No briquetage has been identified in more recent examination, although it may have been eroded away.
References: Kendrick 1928, 221; Scarre 2016, 88, 97.

8. ***Fort Saumarez, St Peter in the Wood: briquetage*** (MGU3634) (1928 and 1995)
Four fragments of briquetage have been found, possibly of Iron Age or Gallo-Roman date.

9. ***'Herm': pottery, briquetage, tile*** (MGU4153) (1949 and other unspecified dates)
A number of artefacts in the Guernsey Museum collection are listed as having been found in Herm, but have no precise provenance. This includes a small collection of briquetage (18 fragments) and a fragment of Roman tile which is likely to have come from the Fisherman's Beach site (MGU525, see A22).
Reference: Burns and Burns 1985, 657–9.

10. ***Field off Rue des Prevosts, St Saviour: pottery*** (MGU2252) (1970s)
One Roman sherd recovered from a field-walk.

11. ***Field at Les Arquets, St Peter in the Wood: pottery*** (MGU1939) (1978)
Two Roman sherds recovered from a field-walk.

12. ***Field at Ruette des Saumarez, Castel: pottery*** (MGU1771) (1978)
Two Roman sherds recovered from a field-walk.

13. ***Fields at La Terre Norgiot, St Saviour: pottery*** (MGU2086 and MGU2087) (1979–80)
Seventeen Roman sherds found in field-walking two adjacent fields.

14. ***Field at Jerbourg, St Martin: pottery*** (MGU1946) (1979)
One Roman sherd recovered from a field-walk.

15. ***Field at Les Prevosts, St Saviour: pottery*** (MGU1943) (1979)
One Roman sherd and two possible Roman sherds recovered from a field-walk.

16. ***Field at Les Paysans, St Peter in the Wood: pottery*** (MGU1762) (1981)
One Roman sherd recovered from a field-walk.

17. ***Grandes Rocques, Castel: pottery*** (MGU1417) (1979)
Three sherds of a samian mortarium, probably made in central Gaul in the late 2nd century AD. The soil on parts of the Grandes Rocques headland has been re-deposited and these sherds may have originated elsewhere in the island.
Reference: Sebire 1985.

18. ***Fort Le Marchant, Vale: pottery, figurine*** (MGU2223) (1982)
Eleven sherds of Roman pottery and part of a pipe clay figurine were discovered during the construction of a car park.
Reference: Burns and Burns 1985, 656, 662.

19. ***North Beach, St Peter Port: pottery, tile, coin*** (MGU2220) (1984)
Roman material was found during harbour development works in 1984. The finds comprise 16 sherds of pottery including a stamped amphora handle, three fragments of tile and a coin (*sestertius* of Marcus Aurelius, Varus or Commodus *c.* AD 161–93).
Reference: Burns and Burns 1985, 654, 659–61.

20. ***La Salerie, St Peter Port: pottery*** (MGU2221) (*c.*1985)
Eleven sherds of Roman pottery, including four samian sherds, were found in sand dredged from the main harbour, and thus probably recently re-deposited.
Reference: Burns and Burns 1985, 654–6, 657, 661–2.

21. ***Cow Bay, St Peter Port: pottery, tile*** (MGU2219) (various dates, mostly 1980s–2000s)
A large quantity of Roman pottery and tile has been collected from the beach below Castle Cornet over a period of many years. Finds include 129 sherds of Roman pottery and 19 fragments of Roman tile, including tegula, imbrex and pedalis. The material may originate from rubbish dumped overboard by ships in the harbour, or have been tipped into the sea from the Roman town. See also C7.
Reference: Burns and Burns 1985, 654, 657 – a selection only; Monaghan 1990, 64–5, 68; see also this volume.

22. ***Jethou: pottery*** (MGU6131) (1993)
A single Roman sherd was found during examination of spoil heaps created by the excavation for a swimming pool. The sherd discovered during excavation in 2007 (see A28) may have come from the same area.

23. ***Long Meadow/Fisherman's Field, Herm: briquetage*** (MGU2270) (1998)

A small collection of prehistoric pottery, Iron Age or Gallo-Roman briquetage and a rolled lead sheet were discovered during field-walking at this location, just inland from the excavated Fisherman's Beach site (see A22).

24. ***Field at Bailiff's Cross, St Andrew: pottery, tile, lead sheet*** (MGU2226) (1999)
A concentration of Roman finds collected during a field-walk, including ten Roman (or possibly Roman) sherds, and tile fragments of a variety of types (*tegula*, *imbrex*, *pedalis*, box), suggesting that a Roman building may have been nearby. A folded lead sheet which may be a *defixio* (curse tablet) was also discovered here.

25. ***Herm: pottery*** (MGU5456) (1999)
A rim sherd was found on a path from the beach on the west coast, near the cholera cemetery.

26. ***Le Neuf Chemin, St Saviour: pottery*** (MGU3302) (2001)
Two sherds of Roman pottery found in a garden.

27. ***L'Ancresse, Vale: amphora*** (MGU5453) (2003)
Amphora sherd, possibly Dressel 1A type, found during building works.

28. ***L'Ancresse, Vale: amphora*** (MGU5938) (2005)
One sherd of Roman amphora found during a watching brief on L'Ancresse Common.

29. ***Mouisonnière Beach, Herm*** (MGU3441) (2006)
Coastal erosion on the north coast of Herm exposed a buried land surface containing fired earth, burnt stones and briquetage.

30. ***L'Erée headland, St Peter in the Wood: pottery*** (MGU4363) (2008)
One Roman sherd.

31. ***Perelle Bay, St Saviour: pottery*** (MGU4872) (2008)
A rim sherd from a mortarium was found in exposed soil deposits at the north end of Perelle Bay. There were also fragments of probable briquetage.

32. ***Le Crocq, St Saviour: pottery, briquetage*** (MGU3171) (2009)
Material eroding from the low cliff south of the main site (MGU2527, see A11) includes more briquetage and a possible Gallo-Roman sherd.

33. ***La Villiaze, St Andrew: pottery*** (MGU6679) (2013)
One sherd of possible Roman pottery collected during a field-walk.

34. ***Jerbourg, St Martin: coin hoard*** (MGU2218) (before 1890)
A hoard of 68 Alexandrine tetradrachms of the late 3rd century (AD 295+) were found at an uncertain location on the Jerbourg headland. Current whereabouts unknown.
Reference: Robinson 1937.

35. ***St Sampson's Harbour, St Sampson/Vale: coins, pottery*** (MGU2217 and MGU4573) (*c*.1860)
Nine Roman coins of the 2nd century AD (Trajan, Antoninus Pius, three of Faustina I, two of Marcus Aurelius and two of Commodus) were found during the construction of the north arm of St Sampson's Harbour. Two sherds of Roman pottery were also recovered.
Reference: Burns and Burns 1985, 652, 656, 659.

36. ***Castel Parish Church: coin*** (MGU4575) (19th century)
A Roman coin found near the Castel Church; current whereabouts unknown.

37. ***Delancey, St Sampson: coin*** (MGU4572) (1880)
Coin of Hadrian (AD 117–38); current whereabouts unknown.

38. ***'near La Varde', L'Ancresse, Vale: coins*** (MGU4410) (1888)
Two Roman coins (of Gallienus, AD 253–268, and Constantine, AD 306–37) said to have been found near La Varde. Current whereabouts unknown.

39. ***'Guernsey': coin*** (MGU4576) (early 20th century)
Bronze coin of Aurelian (AD 270–275); current whereabouts unknown.

40. ***Moulin Huet, St Martin: coin*** (MGU4571) (1922)
Coin of Julia Mamea (died AD 235) found by a diver near Cradle Rock.

41. ***Chouet, Vale: coins*** (MGU5341) (1950s)
Silver antoninus of Philip I (AD 244–249) found with a second Roman coin which is now lost.

42. ***Vazon Bay, Castel: coin*** (MGU4204) (1987)
Bronze coin of the house of Valentinian (AD 364–78) found by a metal detectorist.

43. ***Le Gouffre, Forest: coin*** (MGU6683) (*c*.1990)
Chance find of follis of Constantine the Great, AD 307–10.

44. ***Vazon Bay, Castel: coin*** (MGU4414) (2000)
Dupondius of Antoninus Pius (AD 138–61) or Marcus Aurelius (AD 161–80) found by a metal detectorist.

45. ***L'Erée, St Peter in the Wood: coin*** (MGU4570) (2000)
Bronze nummus of Gratian (AD 367–75) found by a metal detectorist.

46. ***George Road, St Peter Port: coins*** (MGU5486) (*c*.2000)
Two small bronze nummi of Honorius (AD 393–423) or Arcadius (AD 383–408) were reportedly found in a garden. They are in good condition and may be more recent losses.

47. ***L'Eree, St Peter in the Wood: coin*** (MGU4196) (2008)
Dupondius of Marcus Aurelius (AD 161–180) found by a metal detectorist.

48. ***Vazon Bay, Castel: coin*** (MGU6113) (2010)
Sestertius of Hadrian, possibly RIC 611b (AD 121–22), found by a metal detectorist.

49. ***Cobo, Castel: coin*** (MGU6767) (2015)
Chance find of nummus of Valentinian I (AD 364–75). Possibly a modern loss.

C. Roman finds from non-excavated sites (underwater)

1. ***Little Russel: amphora*** (MGU5462) (1968)
An amphora spike dredged up in the Little Russel, south-east of St Peter Port.
References: Keen 1986, 139; Monaghan 1990, 65.

2. ***Little Russel 'Site B', Tautenay: amphorae*** (MGU 5403) (1970s onwards)
Fragments of amphorae dredged from the seabed off the north-east coast of Guernsey over a period of many years suggest a scattered wreck site. All but one of the rims of are of Peacock and Williams class 15 (Haltern 70), of the mid-1st century BC to mid-1st century AD, originating from Baetica (north-east Spain). The 266 pieces recovered (Table 27) include 15 basal spikes; neck and rim parts also come from at least 17 individual vessels. Necks, basal spikes and some body sherds retain traces of a pine tar lining. A second wreck clearly exists in the same area as the assemblage also includes a furrowed rim of 'gauloise' type (Peacock and Williams 55) of the 2nd century, plus part of a distinctive base and three body sherds.
References: Keen 1986, 140; Monaghan 1990, 65, 68.

3. ***Boue Penney: anchor, pottery*** (MGU5463) (*c*.1976)
A possible Roman anchor and a mortarium (second half of the 4th century AD) were discovered just to the north-east of St Peter Port harbour; they may have come from a wreck.
References: Keen 1986, 139; Monaghan 1988, 463–5; Monaghan 1990, 65, 68.

4. ***Little Russel 'Site A': amphorae, tile*** (MGU4582) (1977)
An assemblage of near-intact amphorae and more than 50 fragments were discovered some 200m outside the mouth of St Peter Port harbour. All are Peacock and Williams Class 19 (Beltran IIB) of the 1st or 2nd century AD, originating from Cadiz (south-west Spain) and suspected of containing the fish product liquamen. More remain on the seabed and it is possible that part of a wreck survives beneath an 'amphora mound'.
References: Keen 1986, 140; Monaghan 1990, 65.

Table 27 Summary of amphorae sherds from Little Russel B.

Date and/ or GMAG accession	*Body sherd*	*Base spike*	*Shoulder and lug*	*Neck and handle*	*Rim part*	*Rim whole*	*Total PW 15 (Haltern 70)*	*Gauloise type PW 55*	*Total amphorae*
1970s	0	1	0	0	1	2	4	1	5
1980s–90s	27	1	0	1	0	0	29	0	29
2009.23	0	1	0	0	0	0	1	0	1
2010.29	0	0	0	1	1	0	2	0	2
2010.276	4	3	1	0	0	0	8	0	8
2013.54	16	1	2	2	2	1	24	0	24
2015.7	99	6	12	1	4	0	122	4	126
2015.30	14	0	3	2	2	0	21	0	21
2016.122	33	1	1	0	1	0	36	0	36
2017.45	13	1	3	0	2	0	19	0	19
Total	206	15	22	7	13	3	266	5	271

5. ***La Petite Canupe: pottery, quern*** (MGU4411) (*c.*1975 and 2003)
A mortarium of the 2nd or 3rd century AD and the two parts of a rotary quern were recovered from the seabed off the north-east of Guernsey; they probably originated from a wreck although no certain traces have been identified.
References: Burns and Burns 1985, 662–4 (for mortarium, wrongly attributed to north-west coast); Keen 1986, 139; Monaghan 1990, 68.

6. ***Fermain Bay, St Peter Port: submerged wooden structure, pottery*** (MGU2222) (*c.*1980)
A submerged wooden structure which may be the remains of a pier; it is usually obscured by shingle. Gallo-Roman and medieval pottery has been found nearby, including a fragment of Syrian 'carrot' amphora, but the whereabouts of these finds is currently unknown.
References: Burns and Burns 1985, 656, 662; Monaghan 1990, 65.

7. ***St Peter Port Harbour: pottery, tile*** (MGU5449) (mostly 1980s–90s)
Over a number of years a significant quantity of Roman pottery and tile has been recovered from the harbour by divers. Around 200 pottery sherds have been collected, several of which are large pieces, and there are a few complete vessels. Some appear to have come from the Pierheads Roman ship (A15). There are also numerous fragments of tile. See also B21.
Reference: Monaghan 1990, 65, 66.

8. ***Jean Jehan: tile*** (MGU5477) (1982)
A collection of mostly post-medieval material recovered from the seabed near to the mouth of the harbour included a probable piece of imbrex.

9. ***St Peter Port Harbour: quern*** (MGU5452) (*c.*1994)
The upper portion of a Gallo-Roman rotary quern was found by a diver in the St Peter Port harbour entrance.

10. ***Belle Grève Bay: amphora*** (MGU5476) (1999)
One amphora sherd found by a diver.

11. ***St Peter Port Harbour: pottery*** (MGU5457) (2001)
Four sherds of Roman pottery were collected near the medieval wrecks in the St Peter Port harbour entrance.

12. ***St Peter Port Harbour: pottery*** (MGU5482) (2001)
Part of a Roman greyware jar found outside the harbour.

13. ***Lower Heads: pottery*** (MGU5481) (2009–10)
A fragment of *tegula* and a sherd of possible greyware dredged up near Lower Heads, off the east coast of Guernsey.

Bibliography

Abbreviations

AFEAF Association Française pour l'étude de l'Age du Fer
SFECAG Société Française d'étude de la céramique antique en Gaule

Allen, D. (1998) *Roman Glass in Britain*. Aylesbury, Shire.

Arnison, T. (2006) Two intaglios from St Peter Port, Guernsey. In M. Henig (ed.), *Roman Art, religion and society. New studies from the Roman Art Seminar, Oxford, 2005* (Oxford, BAR S1577), 67–9.

Bémont, C. (1977) Moules de gobelets ornés de la Gaule centrale au Musée des Antiquités nationales. Paris, *Gallia* suppl. 33.

Blaszkiewicz, P. (1992) La place de la Normandie dans l'Empire romaine de la fin de l'indépendance jusqu'au Ve siècle de notre ère. In M. Wood and F. Queiroga (eds), *Current Research on the Romanization of the Western Provinces* (Oxford, BAR S575), 35–61.

Blaszkiewicz, P. and Jigan, C. (1994) La céramique du Bas-Empire en Normandie. In M. Tuffreau-Libre and A. Jacques (eds), *La céramique du Bas-Empire en Gaule Belgique et dans les régions voisines. Actes de la table ronde de céramologie gallo-romaine, Arras, 8–10 octobre 1991* (Revue du Nord, Hors-Série, Collection Archéologie 4), 127–39.

Boardman, S. and Jones, G. (1990) Experiments on the effects of charring on cereal plant components. *Journal of Archaeological Science* 17, 1–11.

Bouquillon, A., Querré, G., Leclaire, A., Tuffreau-Libre, M. (1994) La terra nigra tardive à Arras (Pas-de-Calais): etudes en laboratoire. In M. Tuffreau-Libre and A. Jacques (eds), *La céramique du Bas-Empire en Gaule Belgique et dans les régions voisines. Actes de la table ronde de céramologie gallo-romaine, Arras, 8–10 octobre 1991* (Revue du Nord, Hors-Série, Collection Archéologie 4), 213–24.

Brett, C. E. B. (1975) *Buildings in the town and parish of St Peter Port*. Guernsey, National Trust.

Burns, R. B. (1977) The late Iron Age site at the Tranquesous, St Saviour's, Guernsey. *Transactions of La Société Guernesiaise* XX/2, 188–218.

Burns, R. B. (1986) Recent work on the Iron Age and Gallo-Roman period in the Bailiwick of Guernsey. In P. Johnston (ed.), *The archaeology of the Channel Islands* (Chichester, Phillimore), 89–97.

Burns, R. B. (1987) L'époque gallo-romaine. Un nouveau chapitre de l'histoire de Guernesey. In *Actes du Congrès de Caen 1987* (SFECAG), 29–37.

Burns, R. B. The Gallo-Roman site at La Plaiderie. Guernsey Museum, interim excavation report, unpublished MS.

Burns, R. B. and Batt, M. (1990) Un habitat côtier du XIIe siècle: Le Port aux Malades, Guernesey, Iles Anglo-Normandes. *Revue Archéologique de l'Ouest* 7, 111–14.

Burns, R. B., and Burns, A. G. (1985) Gallo-Roman finds from Guernsey and Herm. *Transactions of La Société Guernesiaise* XXI/5, 652–66.

Burns, R. B., Cunliffe, B. W. and Sebire, H. (1996) *Guernsey: an island community of the Atlantic Iron Age*. Oxford, Oxford University Committee for Archaeology.

Coates, D. (1991) *The ancient and modern names of the Channel Islands: a linguistic history*. Stamford, Paul Watkins.

Cohen, A., and Serjeantson, D. (1986, 2nd edn) *A Manual for the Identification of Bird Bones from Archaeological Sites*. London, Archetype Publications.

Collum, V. C. C. (1933). *The re-excavation of the Déhus chambered mound at Paradis, Vale, Guernsey*. Guernsey, La Société Guernesiaise.

Cool, H. E. M., and Price, J. (1994) *Roman vessel glass from excavations in Colchester, 1971–85*. Colchester, Colchester Archaeological Trust.

Cunliffe, B. W. (1971) *Excavations at Fishbourne 1961–1969. Vol. II: The finds*. London, Reports of the Research Committee of the Society of Antiquaries 27.

Cunliffe, B. W. (1986) The Iron Age in the Channel Islands: a review. In P. Johnston (ed.), *The archaeology of the Channel Islands* (Chichester, Phillimore), 56–67.

Cunliffe, B. W. (1987) *Hengistbury Head, Dorset. Vol. 1: The prehistoric and Roman settlement, 3500 BC – AD 500*. Oxford, Oxford University Committee for Archaeology.

Cunliffe, B. W. (1996) Guernsey and the Channel Islands in the first millennium BC. In R. B. Burns, B. W. Cunliffe and H. Sebire, *Guernsey: an island community of the Atlantic Iron Age* (Oxford, Oxford University Committte for Archaeology), 125–7.

Cunliffe, B. W. and de Jersey, P. (2000) Rescue excavations on Guernsey and Herm. *Transactions of La Société Guernesiaise* XXIV/5, 867–943.

de Jersey, P. (2009) Excavation at Les Ozouets, 2005. *Transactions of La Société Guernesiaise* XXVI/4, 551–61.

de Jersey, P. (2010) L'habitat et la nécropole de King's Road, Guernesey, et l'Âge du Fer dans les îles anglo-normandes. In P. Barral, B. Dedet, F. Delrieu, P. Giraud, I. Le Goff, S. Marion and A. Villard-Le Tiec (eds), *Actes du 33e colloque international de l'AFEAF* (Besançon, Presses universitaires de Franche-Comté), 287–300.

de Jersey, P. (2013) Excavation of a medieval settlement at Albecq, 1994–95 (unpublished archive report, available at *http://www.academia.edu/attachments/30648681/download_file*)

de Jersey, P. and Cataroche, J. (2011) Excavation at St Martin's Parish Church, 2011. *Transactions of La Société Guernesiaise* XXVII/1, 148–68.

de Jersey, P. and Cataroche, J. (2012) Excavation at St Tugual's Chapel, Herm, 2011. *Transactions of La Société Guernesiaise* XXVII/2, 381–431.

Dyson, T. (ed.) (1986) *The Roman Quay at St Magnus House, London: excavations at New Fresh Wharf, Lower Thames Street, London, 1974–78.* London, Middlesex Archaeological Society Special Paper 8.

Frere, S. S., Hassall, M. W. C. and Tomlin, R. S. O. (1992) Roman Britain in 1991. *Britannia* 23, 255–323.

Gillam, J. P. (1970, 3rd edn) *Types of Roman coarse pottery vessels in northern Britain.* Newcastle upon Tyne, Oriel Press.

Girard, P. J. (1981) The story of the excavation of the long house at Le Feugré, Cobo. *Transactions of La Société Guernesiaise* XXI/1, 94–8.

Grant, A. (1975) The animal bones. In B. W. Cunliffe (ed.), *Excavations at Porchester Castle, Vol. 1* (London, Society of Antiquaries Research Report 32), 378–406.

Hartley, K. F. (1990) The mortaria. In J. Monaghan, Pottery from marine sites around Guernsey. *Journal of Roman Pottery Studies* 3, 68.

Hartley, K. F. (1993). The mortaria. In M. Rule and J. Monaghan, *A Gallo-Roman trading vessel from Guernsey* (Guernsey, Guernsey Museum Monograph 5), 87.

Hartley, K. F. (1998) The incidence of stamped mortaria in the Roman Empire with special reference to imports to Britain. In J. Bird (ed.), *Form and fabric: studies in Rome's material past in honour of B. R. Hartley* (Oxford, Oxbow), 199–217.

Henig, M. (1978, 2nd edn) *A corpus of Roman engraved gemstones from British sites.* Oxford, BAR 8.

Hillson, S. (1992) *Mammal Bones and Teeth: an introductory guide to methods of identification.* London, Institute of Archaeology.

Holbrook, N. and Bidwell, P. T. (1991) *Roman finds from Exeter* (Exeter Archaeological Reports 4).

Huld-Zetsche, I. (1972) *Trierer Reliefsigillata Werkstatt I. Materialien zur römisch-germanisch Keramik* 9. Bonn, Habelt.

Isings, C. (1971) *Roman Glass in Limburg.* Groningen, Wolters-Noordhoff.

Jacobs, J. (1913) Sigillatafunde aus einem römischen Keller zu Bregenz. *Jahrbuch für Altertumskunde* 6, Vienna.

Jee, N. (1958) Archaeological report. *Transactions of La Société Guernesiaise* XVI/4, 313.

Keen, R. (1986) A review of Roman material from the sea off Guernsey 1860–1980. In P. Johnston (ed.), *The archaeology of the Channel Islands* (Chichester, Phillimore), 138–41.

Kendrick, T. G. (1928) *The Archaeology of the Channel Islands. Vol. I, The Bailiwick of Guernsey.* London, Methuen.

Knorr, R. (1905) *Die verzierten Terra-Sigillata Gefässe von Cannstatt und Köngen-Grinario.* Stuttgart, Kohlhammer.

Lane, D. and Walls, T. (2010) Watching brief and excavation at Les Vardes Quarry, 2010. *Transactions of La Société Guernesiaise* XXVI/5, 755–72.

Lihou, J. L. (1976) Gallo-Roman salt workings in Guernsey. *Transactions of La Société Guernesiaise* XX/1, 22–5.

McCormack, J. (1986) *Channel Island Churches.* Chichester, Phillimore.

McCormack, J. (2010) The Roman church in Guernsey: early Christianity in the Channel Islands. *Transactions of La Société Guernesiaise* XXVI/5, 720–44.

McGrail, S. (1983) Cross Channel seamanship and navigation in the late first millennium BC. *Oxford Journal of Archaeology* 2, 299–339.

Menez, Y. (1985) *Les céramiques fumigées de l'Ouest de la Gaule.* Quimper, Cahiers de Quimper Antique 2.

Monaghan, J. (1987) *Upchurch and Thameside Roman pottery: a ceramic typology for northern Kent, first to third centuries AD.* Oxford, BAR 173.

Monaghan, J. (1988) The Guernsey Maritime Trust Gazetteer 1984–88. *Transactions of La Société Guernesiaise* XXII/3, 453–65.

Monaghan, J. (1990) Pottery from marine sites around Guernsey. *Journal of Roman Pottery Studies* 3, 63–9.

Monaghan, J. (1998) Roman pottery from the Bonded Store, St Peter Port: a preliminary view. In H. Sebire (ed.), *Guernsey connections: archaeological and historical papers in honour of Bob Burns* (Guernsey, La Société Guernesiaise), 68–70.

Monaghan, J. (2011–12) Investigation of the Roman Tower and Gatehouse at the 'Nunnery' 2011. *Alderney Society Bulletin* 46, 85–97.

Monaghan, J. and de Jersey, P. (2014–15) Further evidence for Roman military activity on Longis Common. *Alderney Society Bulletin* 49, 90–6.

Moser, F., and Tilhard, J.-L. (1987) Un nouvel atelier de sigillée en Aquitaine. *Aquitania* 5, 36–121.

Oswald, F. and Pryce, T. D. (1920) *An introduction to the study of terra sigillata, treated from a chronological standpoint.* London, Longmans, Green and Co.

Peacock, D. P. S. and Williams, D. F. (1986) *Amphorae and the Roman economy: an introductory guide.* London, Longman.

Price, J. and Cottam, S. (1998). *Romano-British glass vessels: a handbook.* York, Council for British Archaeology.

Ricken, H. (1934) Die Bilderschüsseln der Kastelle Saalburg und Zugmantel 1. *Saalburg Jahrbuch* 8, 130–82.

Ricken, H. (1948) *Die Bilderschüsseln der römischen Töpfer von Rheinzabern: Tafelband.* Darmstadt, Speyer.

Ricken, H. and Fischer, C. (1963) *Die Bilderschüsseln der römischen Töpfer von Rheinzabern: Textband.* Bonn, Habelt.

Roach, R. A., Topley, C. G., Brown, M., Bland, A. M. and D'Lemos, R. S. (1991) *Outline and guide to the geology of Guernsey.* Guernsey, Guernsey Museum.

Robinson, E. S. G. (1937) A hoard of Alexandrine coins from Guernsey. *Numismatic Chronicle* series 5, vol. 17, 135–8.

Rule, M. and Monaghan, J. (1993) *A Gallo-Roman trading vessel from Guernsey.* Guernsey, Guernsey Museum.

Santrot, M.-H. and Santrot, J. (1979) *Céramiques communes gallo-romaines d'Aquitaine*. Paris, CNRS.

Sauvaget, R. (1970) Le potier Servus II de Lezouz. *Revue Archéologique du Centre* 34, 127–42.

Scarre, C. (2016) Archaeological investigations on Jethou. *Transactions of La Société Guernesiaise* XXVIII/1, 88–145.

Schmid, E. (1972) *Atlas of Animal Bones*. Amsterdam, Elsevier.

Sebire, H. (1985) A Roman samian mortarium from Grandes Rocques. *Transactions of La Société Guernesiaise* XXI/5, 720–2.

Sebire, H. (2005) *The archaeology and early history of the Channel Islands*. Stroud, History Press.

Sebire, H. (2011) Excavations at the Royal Hotel site. *Transactions of La Société Guernesiaise* XXVII/1, 190–257.

Serjeantson, D. (1991) 'Rid grasse of bones': a taphonomic study of the bones from midden deposits at the Neolithic and Bronze Age site of Runneymede, Surrey, England. *International Journal of Osteoarchaeology* 1, 73–89.

Serjeantson, D. (1996) The animal bones. In S. Needham and T. Spence, *Refuse and Disposal at Area 16 east, Runneymede* (London, British Museum Press), 194–223.

Tyers, P. A. (1996) *Roman pottery in Britain.* London, Batsford.

Vermeersch, D. (1993) La céramique à pate claire du vicus routier de Taverny (Val-d'Oise). In *Actes du Congrès de Versailles, 20–23 mai 1993* (SFECAG), 117–36.

von den Driesch, A. (1976) *A guide to the measurement of animal bones from archaeological sites*. Harvard, Peabody Museum Bulletin 1.

Walkington, H., Renouf, J. T., James, H. C. L. and Sebire, H. R. (2001). A raised beach in western Guernsey: its archaeological and geological significance. *Geoscience in south-west England* 10, 149–153.

Walls, T., de Jersey, P. and Hughes, C. (2014) Archaeology Section Report 2014. *Transactions of La Société Guernesiaise* XXVII/4, 623–30.

Warry, P. (2006) *Tegulae: manufacture, typology and use in Roman Britain*. Oxford, BAR 417.

Wheeler, A. C., and Jones, A. K. G. (1989). *Fishes.* Cambridge, Cambridge University Press.

Williams, D. F. (1973) Flotation at Sīrāf. *Antiquity,* 47, 198–202.

Williams, D. F. (1996) Roman amphorae. In R. B. Burns, B. W. Cunliffe and H. Sebire, *Guernsey: an island community of the Atlantic Iron Age* (Oxford, Oxford University Committee for Archaeology), 49–52.

Williams, D. F. and Wood, M. (1995) Autre exemple de la nouvelle forme de céramique 'à l'éponge' et étude pétrographique des tessons de cette céramique provenant de Southampton et des Iles Anglo-Normandes. In *Actes du Congrès de Rouen 1995* (SFECAG), 151–5.

Wood, M. (1989) Romano-British and Roman pottery from Jersey. *Annual Bulletin of La Société Jers*iaise 25, 175–8.

Wood, M. (1990) Céramiques inédites de la Tène finale et de l'époque gallo-romaine trouvées à Alderney et découverte récente d'amphores à Jersey et Herm (Iles Anglo-Normandes). *Bulletin de l'Association Manche Atlantique pour la Recherche Archéologique dans les Iles* 3, 47–60.

Wood, M. (1991) Céramiques romano-britanniques trouvées à Alet jusqu'en 1986 et étude des relations commerciales d'Alet au Bas-Empire. *Dossiers du Centre Régional Archéologique d'Alet* 19, 35–52.

Wood, M. (1993a) A new form of *céramique à l'éponge* from Roman Britain. *Journal of Roman Pottery Studies* 6, 119–22.

Wood, M. (1993b) Roman pottery from Bitterne Manor pipe-trench excavations of 1991. Southampton City Council, unpublished report.

Wood, M. (1994) La céramique du Bas-Empire dans les îles anglo-normandes et dans deux sites côtiers du golfe normand-breton. In M. Tuffreau-Libre and A. Jacques (eds), *La céramique du Bas-Empire en Gaule Belgique et dans les régions voisines. Actes de la table ronde de céramologie gallo-romaine, Arras, 8–10 octobre 1991* (Revue du Nord, Hors-Série, Collection Archéologie 4), 153–66.

Wood, M. (1996) North Gaulish greyware; terra nigra type ware, etc. In R. B. Burns, B. W. Cunliffe and H. Sebire, *Guernsey: an island community of the Atlantic Iron Age* (Oxford, Oxford University Committee for Archaeology), 52–5.

Appendix: pottery codes

Imported fabrics

AH Alice Holt/Farnham Greywares
AMPH Miscellaneous amphorae
BB1 Black-burnished ware 1
BB2 Black-burnished ware 2
BBT Black-burnished ware type, probably part of BB2 industry, including worn/abraded sherds
BBTA Black-burnished ware type A
BBTB Black-burnished ware type B; coarser than the above
CC Miscellaneous colour-coated wares
CCB *Céramique craquelée-bleutée* (eastern Paris basin)
CF *Céramique fumigée* (Menez 1985)
CGCC Central Gaulish colour-coated wares, including 'black samian'
CGFM Central Gaulish fine micaceous ware
CGWW Central Gaulish white ware, including pipe-clay figurines
DUR Durotrigian ware
EGGS Miscellaneous eggshell wares
EIFL *Eifelkeramik*
EPON *Céramique à l'éponge*
EW 'E' ware (Tyers 1996, 145–6)
F55 Oxidised flagons; body sherds indistinguishable from Normandy amphora fabric PW55
FCB Creamy pink/buff ware
FOX Oxidised flagons/pitchers with reduced core; fine, slightly micaceous fabric similar to PW55
FOXO Miscellaneous oxidised flagons
GB Gallo-Belgic wares
GCF Grog-tempered *céramique fumigée*, probably north Gaulish
GG Gritty greyware; jars with grey surfaces, frequent quartz grains in sandy, fine paste
GOW Gritty oxidised ware, fabric identical to medieval Normandy Gritty Ware (Burns 1987, 34 no. 23)
GROG Grog-tempered ware (Romano-British)
KOLN Cologne colour-coated wares
LEST London-Essex stamped wares (Tyers 1996, 169–70)
MARB Marbled ware
MCF Miscellaneous *céramique fumigée*, distinguished from CF/SCFO *etc* by white/off-white fine micaceous fabrics
MDC Mica-decorated thick coat (gold)
MDER Mica-decorated early Roman ware (gold)
MDERC Copy of MDER; a wheel-made 'local' copy of Breto-Norman MDER
MER Coarse Merovingian/Carolingian wares (some with roller-stamp decoration)
MG Miscellaneous greywares
MONF Mortaria: New Forest colour-coated
MONV Mortaria: Nene Valley
MOPIC Mortaria: Picardy
MORH Mortaria: Rhineland
MORHT Mortaria: Rhineland – Taverny
MORT Mortaria (unknown source)
MORTG Mortaria: Gallic, possibly Breton source
MOX Miscellaneous oxidised scraps
MR Miscellaneous reduced scraps
MSW Micaceous sandy ware; may be a medieval fabric
NFCC New Forest colour-coated wares
NFGW New Forest greywares; may be archived as AH/NF due to difficulty in distinguishing between products of the two centres
NGGW North Gaulish greywares (undifferentiated)
NGGW1 North Gaulish greyware (finer fabric), Nord/Pas-de-Calais/Somme valley
NGGW2 North Gaulish greyware; a coarser version of NGGW1
NGGW3 North Gaulish greyware; differentiated on basis of form, including hooked-rim vessels; many Guernsey examples have an oxidised paste
NGGW4 North Gaulish greyware; off-white fabrics with *terra nigra* type finish, in H (hard) or S (soft)
NGLTN North Gaulish late terra nigra; distinctive C3/C4 bowls (Bouquillon *et al*. 1994, 213–24)
NGSG North Gaulish, fairly hard sandy fabric, fine mica and black inclusions, grey surfaces, often with black streaks visible on exterior
NGWO North Gaulish wares (oxidised)
NVCC Nene Valley colour-coated ware
OXRC Oxfordshire red/brown colour-coated wares
PAR Parchment ware (Romano-British)

PRW	Pompeian red ware (unknown source)
PRW2	Pompeian red ware 2 (Tyers 1996, 158, fabric 2)
PRW3	Pompeian red ware 3 (Tyers 1996, 158, fabric 3)
PW3	Dressel 1A Italian amphorae
PW4	Dressel 1B Italian amphorae
PW6A	Dressel 1/Pascual 1, fabric 1, Spanish amphorae
PW6B	Dressel 1/Pascual 1, fabric 2, Spanish amphorae
PW10	Dressel 2–4 amphorae
PW12	Cam. 189 'carrot' amphorae
PW13	Richborough 527 amphorae (one sherd, identification uncertain)
PW15	Haltern 70/Cam. 185A Spanish amphorae
PW16	Dressel 7–11 Spanish amphorae
PW19	Beltran IIB amphorae
PW24	Oberaden 83/Dressel 25 amphorae
PW25	Dressel 20 Spanish amphorae
PW26	Dressel 23 or 49 Spanish amphorae
PW27	Pelichet 47/Gauloise 4 Gallic amphorae
PW30	Gauloise 5 Gallic amphorae
PW31	Dressel 28/Gauloise 1 amphorae
PW33	Africana I/Beltran 57 amphorae
PW38	Dressel 30 Algerian amphorae
PW46	Late Roman Palestinian amphorae
PW47	Kapitan II 'hollow foot' amphorae
PW55	Gauloise 12 'furrowed-rim' amphorae (some sherds indistinguishable from F55 flagon sherds)
QT	Quartz-tempered wares, probably from various production sites in NW/northern France
QTG	Quartz-tempered greywares, probably from various production sites in NW/northern France
QTW	Quartz-tempered white ware; quartz inclusions larger than QTG
RC	Rough Cast wares, most from Argonne/Sinzig, but see also CGCC and KOLN
RHT	Rhenish wares (Trier)
SAM	Terra sigillata (undifferentiated)
SAMCG	Terra sigillata, central Gaul
SAMEG	Terra sigillata, east Gaul
SAMSG	Terra sigillata, south Gaul
SCFO	Smooth *céramique fumigée* (oxidised paste) (Menez 1985), central Gaul, Armorica and many unknown centres
SCFR	Smooth *céramique fumigée* (reduced paste) (Santrot and Santrot 1979), SW France, Armorica and many unknown centres
SGW	Sandy greyware, probably variant of numerous north Gaulish series of fabrics, particularly NGSG
SOM & SOX	Sandy oxidised micaceous ware, similar to MSW but not as hard or as micaceous
STN	Sandy terra nigra; STN & STNR clearly related to north Gaulish fabrics, especially NGGW and GCF
STNR	Sandy terra nigra, red paste, distinguished from STN due to distinctive paste and soapy feel
TN	Terra nigra
TR	Terra rubra
WNMW	Western Normandy micaceous ware (Wood 1994, 160)
WW1	White ware 1, fine, hard cream/off-white paste, pink blotches on external surface, recognised only in ring-neck flagon
WW2/3	White ware 2/3, fine, fairly hard, light grey/off-white paste, some sherds with pale orange/buff surface (central Gaul?)

Local fabrics (certain and probable)

AQG	Coarse quartz/granitic fabrics (local). Prehistoric to late Iron Age; includes local copies of LIA imports where not designated as LIA (Burns *et al.* 1996, 48–9, local fabrics 1, 2, 4, 5 and 6)
AQR	Finer granite and quartz fabric (local and probably local). Some wheel-made, so LIA onwards. Much variation in fabric, some sherds indistinguishable from TBF series
AR	Fine sandy grey/brown fabric (local?). (Burns 1977, 202–3, coarse wheel-made local pottery type IV)
TBF1	Tripod bowl fabric 1 (probably local) (Wood 1994, 161–2). Usually black but wide variation in coarseness as well as colour of TBF series
TBF1 GREY	Tripod bowl fabric 1 grey (probably local) (Wood 1994, 161–2). Grey colour and finer fabric than TBF1
TBF2	Tripod bowl fabric 2 (probably local) (Wood 1994, 161–2). Grey but less proficiently made, colour more uniformly light brown/grey
VES	Vesicular fabric (local?) (Burns *et al.* 1996, 48–9, fabric 3, later Iron Age)

Other coded pottery

ER	Coarse early Roman pottery (various types, basically AQR and AR)
IA	Coarse Iron Age pottery (various, AQG)
LIA	Late Iron Age pottery (various)
MED	Medieval pottery (various)
PH	Prehistoric pottery (various)
PH (PMED)	Post-medieval pottery (various)
BMAT	Building materials
TILE	Tile
BQ	Briquetage